I0047694

SQL Server Analysis Services 2012 Cube Development Cookbook

More than 100 recipes to develop Business Intelligence solutions using Analysis Services

Baya Dewald

Steve Hughes

Paul Turley

[PACKT] enterprise
PUBLISHING
professional expertise distilled
BIRMINGHAM - MUMBAI

SQL Server Analysis Services 2012 Cube Development Cookbook

Copyright © 2013 Packt Publishing

All rights reserved. No part of this book may be reproduced, stored in a retrieval system, or transmitted in any form or by any means, without the prior written permission of the publisher, except in the case of brief quotations embedded in critical articles or reviews.

Every effort has been made in the preparation of this book to ensure the accuracy of the information presented. However, the information contained in this book is sold without warranty, either express or implied. Neither the authors, nor Packt Publishing, and its dealers and distributors will be held liable for any damages caused or alleged to be caused directly or indirectly by this book.

Packt Publishing has endeavored to provide trademark information about all of the companies and products mentioned in this book by the appropriate use of capitals. However, Packt Publishing cannot guarantee the accuracy of this information.

First published: December 2013

Production Reference: 1181213

Published by Packt Publishing Ltd.
Livery Place
35 Livery Street
Birmingham B3 2PB, UK.

ISBN 978-1-84968-980-9

www.packtpub.com

Cover Image by William Kewley (william.kewley@kbbs.ie)

Credits

Authors
Baya Dewald
Paul Turley
Steve Hughes

Reviewers
Dan English
Stevo Smočilac

Acquisition Editors
Edward Gordon
Llewellyn Rozario

Lead Technical Editor
Anila Vincent

Technical Editors
Dipika Gaonkar
Kapil Hemnani
Edwin Moses
Mrunmayee Patil
Siddhi Rane
Tarunveer Shetty

Proofreaders
Cathy Cumberlidge
Bernadette Watkins

Copy Editors
Sarang Chari
Mradula Hegde
Dipti Kapadia
Gladson Monteiro
Karuna Narayanan
Lavina Pereira
Laxmi Subramanian

Project Coordinators
Rahul Dixit
Cheryl Botelho
Mary Alex

Indexer
Rekha Nair

Production Coordinator
Kyle Albuquerque

Cover Work
Kyle Albuquerque

About the Authors

Baya Dewald has been working with Microsoft SQL Server for over 15 years and with Analysis Services since its debut in 1999. He has architected, developed, and administered databases with millions of users and cubes measured in terabytes. Throughout his career, he has held various certifications, including Microsoft Certified Solution Developer, Microsoft Certified Systems Engineer, and Microsoft Certified Database Administrator. He has managed DBA teams and published over 100 technical articles in SQL Server Magazine, SQL Professional, Tech Target, and InformIT. He has also contributed to several technical books as a co-author and technical reviewer. He can be reached at baya.dewald@gmail.com.

First and foremost, I'd like to thank my family for allowing me to dedicate long hours to working on this book. I am also thankful to my friend Scot Reagin for his encouragement and support while writing this book and to my friend and mentor Kevin Kline who helped me find excellent co-authors. Thanks too to all reviewers, particularly to Dan English, for their useful and thought-provoking comments that helped to make this book more useful to the readers.

Paul Turley is a mentor with SolidQ and is a Microsoft SQL Server MVP. He consults, writes, speaks, teaches, and blogs about business intelligence and reporting solutions. He works with companies around the world to visualize and deliver critical information to make informed business decisions. He is the director of the Oregon SQL PASS chapter and user group, and the lead author of *Professional SQL Server 2012 Reporting Services* and 11 other books by *Wrox and Microsoft Press*. Paul blogs at SqlServerBiBlog.com.

Special thanks to my wife and daughters for their support and understanding. Thanks to all the mentors and staff at SolidQ, a truly world-class organization.

Steve Hughes is a Practice Lead at Magenic. In his current role, he develops strategy and helps guide data, business intelligence, collaboration, and data integration development using Microsoft technologies, including SQL Server, SharePoint, and BizTalk. He continues to deliver data and business intelligence solutions using these platforms. He has been working with technology for over 15 years with much of that time spent on creating business intelligence solutions. He is passionate about using data effectively and helping customers understand that data is valuable and profitable. He also has experience working with a large software company as a service vendor and there received awards for customer satisfaction and engineering excellence.

In 2010, he received the *Consultant of the Year* honor at Magenic. He has delivered multiple presentations on SQL server, data architecture, and business intelligence over the years. Steve can often be found at Professional Association for SQL Server (PASS) events where he serves as a regional mentor and is active with the Minnesota SQL Server User Group (MNPASS). He shares his insights from the field on his blog at http://dataonwheels. wordpress.com.

I want to thank my wife, Sheila, and our four children—Kristyna, Alex, Andrew, and Mikayla—for their patience as I worked on this project. Their support has been awesome in this and my other endeavors. I also want to thank the team at Packt Publishing and the reviewers for their guidance throughout the writing of this book as it has allowed us to put together a better product for all of you. Finally, I dedicate all my efforts to my father-in-law, Ed Jankowski, without whom I would have never been involved in software at all. We all miss you, Ed.

About the Reviewers

Dan English is a Microsoft SQL Server MVP and the Business Intelligence Practice Manager at Superior Consulting Services in Minneapolis, MN. He has been developing with Microsoft technologies since 1996 and has focused on data warehousing and business intelligence since 2004. He has presented for the Minnesota SQL Server user group, the Microsoft Minnesota BI user group, and Minnesota TechFuse, along with SQL Server and SharePoint Saturday events. He is also an avid blogger and tweeter.

He holds a Bachelor of Science degree in Business Administration from the Minnesota State University, Mankato. He is an MCITP: Business Intelligence Developer 2005 and 2008 and a Microsoft Certified Technology Specialist (MCTS) for Microsoft SQL Server Business Intelligence—Implementation and Maintenance and also for Microsoft Office SharePoint Server 2007—Configuring.

He and his wife, Molly, live in Minnesota and have two children, Lily and Wyatt.

Stevo Smočilac is an Associate Principal Consultant at Magenic, a Microsoft Gold Certified Partner that specializes in business intelligence solutions.

He has over 12 years' experience working in software development, the last seven of which have focused on designing, implementing, managing, and administrating technical solutions developed using Microsoft SQL Server and the Microsoft Business Intelligence stack. He has been involved in all phases of the BI development lifecycle from envisioning through operational support and is passionate about the field of business intelligence.

He is currently a Virtual Technology Solutions Professional (V-TSP) for business intelligence, a Microsoft Certified IT Professional, and holds a B. Tech degree in Information Technology.

Originally from South Africa, he now resides in the (much colder) northeastern United States with his wife, Talya. When not in front of his computer, he can often be found either playing the guitar or riding his mountain bikes.

www.PacktPub.com

Support files, eBooks, discount offers and more

You might want to visit www.PacktPub.com for support files and downloads related to your book.

Did you know that Packt offers eBook versions of every book published, with PDF and ePub files available? You can upgrade to the eBook version at www.PacktPub.com and as a print book customer, you are entitled to a discount on the eBook copy. Get in touch with us at service@packtpub.com for more details.

At www.PacktPub.com, you can also read a collection of free technical articles, sign up for a range of free newsletters and receive exclusive discounts and offers on Packt books and eBooks.

![PACKTLIB logo]

http://PacktLib.PacktPub.com

Do you need instant solutions to your IT questions? PacktLib is Packt's online digital book library. Here, you can access, read and search across Packt's entire library of books.

Why Subscribe?

- ▶ Fully searchable across every book published by Packt
- ▶ Copy and paste, print and bookmark content
- ▶ On demand and accessible via web browser

Free Access for Packt account holders

If you have an account with Packt at www.PacktPub.com, you can use this to access PacktLib today and view nine entirely free books. Simply use your login credentials for immediate access.

Instant Updates on New Packt Books

Get notified! Find out when new books are published by following @PacktEnterprise on Twitter, or the *Packt Enterprise* Facebook page.

Table of Contents

Preface

SQL Server Analysis Services 2012 Cube Development Cookbook is a friendly companion to individuals implementing and managing business intelligence applications using Microsoft's flagship product, SQL Server Analysis Services. The book provides step-by-step recipes for developing Analysis Services objects. Readers will learn how to develop business intelligence solutions using the Analysis Services multidimensional model as well as the Tabular Model. In addition to development recipes, the book also includes recipes for administering, securing, monitoring, troubleshooting, and scaling Analysis Services solutions. The book discusses methods beyond the initial cube design, exploring cube maintenance with partitions and designing effective aggregations, as well as options for synchronizing analytics solutions. Filled with tips and recommended best practices based on years of experience, the book is designed to quickly get the reader from beginner level to the point of comfortably architecting solutions.

What this book covers

Chapter 1, Introduction to Multidimensional Data Model Design, discusses the value of business intelligence as well as challenges faced when undertaking a business intelligence project and how to overcome them. You will learn high-level differences between Analysis Services tabular and multidimensional models and when each is appropriate. Finally, you will learn the differences between star and snowflake schemas for dimensional modeling.

Chapter 2, Defining Analysis Services Dimensions, starts off by explaining how to define data sources and data source views. You will learn how to extend data source views beyond the model available in the relational database. The chapter's main focus is on teaching you how to build and customize most commonly encountered dimensions within the Analysis Services multidimensional model.

Chapter 3, Creating Analysis Services Cubes, explains how to define measure groups and measures while setting appropriate properties. You will learn how to relate database dimensions to each measure group and implement basic as well as advanced measure aggregation functions, including distinct count and semi-additive measures. The chapter also discusses cube file structures and teaches the most effective strategies for measure group partitioning and building aggregations. Finally, you will learn various methods of deploying your multidimensional projects to your Analysis Services instances.

Chapter 4, Extending and Customizing Cubes, builds on the foundation of cube development laid in *Chapter 3, Creating Analysis Services Cubes*. You will learn how to make your solutions more useful to the business by adding calculated measures, named sets, actions, key performance indicators, perspectives, translations, and measure expressions to your cubes.

Chapter 5, Optimizing Dimension and Cube Processing, teaches basic and advanced options for processing multidimensional objects through XMLA, SQL Server client tools, as well as using SQL Server Integration Services (SSIS). This chapter also demonstrates how you should monitor and tune processing performance.

Chapter 6, MDX, explains how to write the most commonly encountered Multidimensional Expressions (MDX) queries and calculations. You will learn how to return data on query axes, limit and sort query output, define calculations and named sets, and navigate dimension hierarchies. The chapter also explains the basic functions used within MDX scripts and introduces the framework for monitoring and tuning MDX queries.

Chapter 7, Analysis Services Security, teaches how to manage multidimensional model security at the Analysis Services instance, database, cube, dimension, and cell levels. In addition to basic role-based security, the chapter also includes a recipe for implementing dynamic security.

Chapter 8, Administering and Monitoring Analysis Services, starts off by providing an overview of Analysis Services configuration options. Next, you learn how to create and drop databases, monitor and troubleshoot Analysis Services instances, and check the size of each object. Additionally, you will learn various methods for scaling out your multidimensional business intelligence solutions using backup and restore, synchronization, and the detach and attach options.

Chapter 9, Using Tabular Models, teaches you how to define data sources and models and load data into Tabular Models. You will learn how to define hierarchies, define calculated measures, and extend the Tabular model using key performance indicators. The chapter also explains recommended strategies for processing, partitioning, and securing Tabular Models.

Chapter 10, DAX Calculations and Queries, introduces the reader to Data Analysis Expressions (DAX) fundamentals as it applies to defining calculations within the Tabular Model and querying the model. You will learn how to write calculated columns and measures in the Tabular Model designer and DAX queries within SQL Server Management Studio.

Chapter 11, *Performance Tuning and Troubleshooting Tabular Models*, discusses the Analysis Services Tabular Model's usability limits. The reader will learn about diagnosing issues, optimizing performance, and memory use using various tools for troubleshooting suboptimal performance, which include Windows Resource Monitor and SQL Server Profiler.

Appendix, *Miscellaneous Analysis Services Topics*, discusses various Analysis Services topics that don't lend themselves to effective presentation in a recipe format. The chapter teaches you about various dimension properties, as well as outlining considerations for multidimensional design when developers are not permitted to create objects in the relational data sources.

What you need for this book

You will need Microsoft SQL Server 2012 Analysis Services multidimensional as well as tabular instances to which you have administrative access in order to follow along with the examples presented in this book. All examples are based on the Adventure Works sample relational database and Adventure Works Analysis Services database, which can be downloaded from `www.codeplex.com`. Each chapter referencing these samples includes a link to sample downloads.

Who this book is for

The book is for individuals intending to build, maintain, use, and administer business intelligence solutions exploiting Microsoft SQL Server Analysis Services multidimensional as well as tabular databases. The intended audience includes seasoned professionals who have worked with databases and are embarking on more complex business intelligence solutions as well as for people who have built Analysis Services solutions in the past but would like to hone their skills further by administering, tuning, and scaling databases.

Conventions

In this book, you will find a number of styles of text that distinguish between different kinds of information. Here are some examples of these styles, and an explanation of their meaning.

Code words in text, database table names, folder names, filenames, file extensions, pathnames, dummy URLs, user input, and Twitter handles are shown as follows: " Temporary files can be found under the `<TempDir>` folder as specified in the `msmdsrv.ini` configuration file."

A block of code is set as follows:

```
<ErrorConfiguration
    <KeyErrorLimit>-1</KeyErrorLimit>
    <KeyErrorLogFile>C:\key_errors.txt</KeyErrorLogFile>
    <KeyNotFound>ReportAndStop</KeyNotFound>
    <KeyDuplicate>ReportAndContinue</KeyDuplicate>
      <NullKeyConvertedToUnknown>ReportAndContinue
        </NullKeyConvertedToUnknown>
    <NullKeyNotAllowed>ReportAndStop</NullKeyNotAllowed>
  </ErrorConfiguration>
```

New terms and **important words** are shown in bold. Words that you see on the screen, in menus or dialog boxes for example, appear in the text like this: " Now if you query the cube as a role member and choose **All Products** as the product category, you will see a different number than what you would see as the total of **Bikes** and **Accessories**."

> Warnings or important notes appear in a box like this.

> Tips and tricks appear like this.

Reader feedback

Feedback from our readers is always welcome. Let us know what you think about this book—what you liked or may have disliked. Reader feedback is important for us to develop titles that you really get the most out of.

To send us general feedback, simply send an e-mail to feedback@packtpub.com, and mention the book title via the subject of your message.

If there is a topic that you have expertise in and you are interested in either writing or contributing to a book, see our author guide on www.packtpub.com/authors.

Customer support

Now that you are the proud owner of a Packt book, we have a number of things to help you to get the most from your purchase.

Downloading the example code

You can download the example code files for all Packt books you have purchased from your account at `http://www.packtpub.com`. If you purchased this book elsewhere, you can visit `http://www.packtpub.com/support` and register to have the files e-mailed directly to you.

Errata

Although we have taken every care to ensure the accuracy of our content, mistakes do happen. If you find a mistake in one of our books—maybe a mistake in the text or the code—we would be grateful if you would report this to us. By doing so, you can save other readers from frustration and help us improve subsequent versions of this book. If you find any errata, please report them by visiting `http://www.packtpub.com/submit-errata`, selecting your book, clicking on the **errata submission form** link, and entering the details of your errata. Once your errata are verified, your submission will be accepted and the errata will be uploaded on our website, or added to any list of existing errata, under the Errata section of that title. Any existing errata can be viewed by selecting your title from `http://www.packtpub.com/support`.

Piracy

Piracy of copyright material on the Internet is an ongoing problem across all media. At Packt, we take the protection of our copyright and licenses very seriously. If you come across any illegal copies of our works, in any form, on the Internet, please provide us with the location address or website name immediately so that we can pursue a remedy.

Please contact us at `copyright@packtpub.com` with a link to the suspected pirated material.

We appreciate your help in protecting our authors, and our ability to bring you valuable content.

Questions

You can contact us at `questions@packtpub.com` if you are having a problem with any aspect of the book, and we will do our best to address it.

1
Introduction to Multidimensional Data Model Design

In this chapter we will discuss the differences between Multidimensional databases (cubes) and Tabular Models in order to help you decide which is best for meeting your particular needs. More details on how to implement each of these will be covered in the rest of this cookbook. In this chapter we will explore the following concepts:

- ▸ The business value of Business Intelligence
- ▸ The challenges and barriers faced when implementing Business Intelligence
- ▸ Strategies for overcoming these challenges and barriers
- ▸ Choosing multidimensional or Tabular Models
- ▸ Star- and Snowflake-relational schema
- ▸ A sample scenario for choosing the Snowflake schema

Introduction

Business Intelligence (BI) used to be a competitive advantage for businesses that could afford it. Today, BI is increasingly becoming a fundamental and critical function of every business, which means it can no longer operate on an exclusively strategic basis. Also, it must be responsive to changing business needs in a time frame that allows the business to address those needs. The demand for more responsiveness (less time to implement) of BI continues to increase in parallel with the demand for more functionality.

In response to this increasing pressure on BI to perform at "Business speed", a new capability has emerged in the form of Self-service BI. These Self-service tools allow business users to acquire and analyze data from a variety of sources according to their specific needs at that moment. There are challenges and concerns that come with giving this capability to business users. We'll discuss these in detail in this chapter, but Self-Service BI is a good and growing solution to an important business need.

Microsoft's offerings for Self-Service BI include tools such as Power Pivot, Power View, and Tabular Models in Analysis Services. These tools continue to gain acceptance and are an increasingly presumed capability in Microsoft BI environments. It's not always clear, however, what precise mix of these tools, along with multidimensional cubes, relational data marts, and other presentation tools such as Excel and Reporting Services, would be optimal for any given situation.

There are a large number of variables in determining this optimal mix and we won't be discussing all of them in this cookbook. Our focus will be on the choice between and recipes for implementing Multidimensional cubes and Tabular Models.

The business value of Business Intelligence

"Making better decisions faster" is a common phrase used to describe the purpose of BI, but understanding how this purpose translates into value for the business is the key in understanding why and how BI should be implemented.

Making better decisions is valuable for the strategic management of an organization; making those decisions faster is possibly better, but strategic decisions tend to have longer time frames. So, faster is often not always better or even necessary. Making better operational decisions faster, given the much higher frequency and shorter decision time frame, is of great value to the business. For this discussion we'll focus on this less often considered operational value of BI.

Operational decisions are made every day by people at all levels in the organization. The nature of these decisions vary greatly, including things such as troubleshooting and resolving a specific question, finding a more efficient process for performing a task, or determining an appropriate staffing level for the coming week.

Regardless of the specifics, operational decisions are generally concerned with improving efficiency, increasing productivity, improving quality of the product, or lowering cost. BI can provide the information necessary to identify opportunities for improvement in these areas as well as to make informed decisions on how to implement these improvements. But, the greatest value is realized only when that information is of high quality and is available when needed. Poor quality or late information makes for poor quality or late decisions.

Challenges and barriers of effective BI

The need to deliver accurate information quickly is the fundamental challenge for Business Intelligence. The production of high quality information in a useful format takes time—data must be acquired, cleansed, modeled, and stored over continuous update and enhancement cycles. If any of these aspects of properly managing data are given less than appropriate attention, the quality of the information suffers—you take a short cut for speed of delivery and risk a reduction in the quality of the final product.

Even the highest quality information is of little value if it comes too late to be helpful. So the pressure is on meeting the business requests for information now, not in the several days or weeks it might take to define requirements, update the data model, develop ETL processes, test, validate, and finally make the information available in the data warehouse. Businesses often cannot wait and so they develop alternatives for acquiring and "managing" their own data. These alternatives, though they may answer the need for speed, inevitably result in both redundant data and inconsistent information.

Over time, technology and business groups have developed strategies and techniques aimed at coming closer to aligning managed data and the much faster business cycles. Improvements in traditional data storage engines, including the development of multidimensional models and ETL tools have helped. Iterative and agile development methodologies have given BI more of a continuous improvement than waterfall behavior and have made the environment more nimble. Still, there remained a gap where IT could not respond quickly enough to business demands, and businesses did not have the skill and discipline to sufficiently manage high quality data.

Overcoming BI challenges and barriers

Self-Service BI is a good, and still improving answer for bridging the Business Intelligence technology and business gap. More than just tools and technology, Self-Service BI involves a commitment to cooperation and continuous—organic—improvement. With the right tools and cooperation between IT and business, it's now possible to provide long-term and high-quality managed data while also giving businesses the capability to meet their information needs in their needed time frame.

The Self-Service tools, such as Power Pivot, Power View, and the Analysis Services Tabular Model introduced with the SQL Server 2012, allow business resources to acquire, analyze, and share information relatively independent of IT and with a relatively low requirement for technical skill—the emphasis is on "relatively". It is possible for a business person to acquire data from a variety of resources through the use of tools provided by wizards and graphical interfaces. However, there remains the need for a higher than average technical capability—not a developer level but an analyst level resource is the typical profile. Also, though there is no requirement to involve IT or the managed data environment, these resources remain a source of considerable capability and information, and Self-Service users should look to them first to check if their needs may be met.

Traditional managed data and emerging Self-Service BI are, therefore, not competitive nor alternative technologies but rather complimentary technologies that together are a comprehensive, robust, and nimble information environment. Self-Service BI is the *pointed end of the spear* in which analysts self-serving information are in direct contact with the business and are tasked with responding quickly to information requests. As such, these analysts are the first to be aware of emerging and recurring questions and the information needs that answer those questions. By regularly harvesting this knowledge, those in charge of maintaining the managed data environment have a clear direction as to how their environment should evolve. Incorporating the newly identified, and vetted by Self-Service, sources and business rules for analysis into the data warehouse continuously improves the quality and depth of the still very valuable managed data environment.

Choosing multidimensional or Tabular Models

Given the complimentary nature of managed and Self-Service data environments, it's reasonable to assume that in most organizations, at least one data warehouse will exist and will be available as the primary source of information.

Prior to the introduction of Tabular Models, cubes were often implemented as the outermost information interface for reporting and analysis. This configuration provided preaggregated values, ad-hoc analysis functionality, and a central store for business calculations. However, the development and maintenance of the Cube is in the exclusive domain of IT, and the business calculations are written in the **MultiDimensional eXpressions** (**MDX**) language (not the easiest of languages to learn). So, cubes are the logical (multidimensional) extension of the managed data environment. They provide high quality information and are consistent as well as fast to query, but dependent on their defined relational sources and, as a result, often slow to respond to changing needs.

The Tabular Model, like cubes part of the Analysis Services platform and multidimensional in nature offers much greater flexibility for the introduction of new data sources and subsequent definition of new dimensions, attributes, and measures.

No formal ETL or data modeling is required; so, turnaround times for updates are greatly reduced, and no MDX is needed in order to define calculated values, as this is done via the new language, **Data Analysis Expressions** (**DAX**). Though the DAX language is considered by many to be easier to learn and use than MDX, it is not, in its current version, as capable as MDX. So, while certain basic operations are easier to express in DAX compared to MDX, implementing complex calculations is much more difficult using DAX. Although this book isn't dedicated to MDX or DAX, you can learn about the useful constructs of these languages in *Chapter 6, MDX* and *Chapter 10, DAX Calculations and Queries*.

In most environments, both cubes and Tabular Models will be used as each provides a useful and specific set of functionality. Determining which should be used for a given set of requirements will depend on the particulars of those requirements, but the following checklist provides a high-level guideline for selecting the most appropriate tool.

A Cube is best if the following requirements are satisfied (not a comprehensive list, more of a top five):

- **You need Writeback functionality**: Writeback is most commonly used for budgeting and what-if analysis. It's not the most widely used functionality but can be a very important part of some BI environments. This functionality is not currently supported in the Tabular Model.

- **You have complex calculations**: It's difficult in DAX to create complex calculations, which are relatively straightforward in MDX.

- **You plan to have Named sets**: Named sets are very useful and user friendly. However, they are not currently supported in Tabular Models.

- **You have Many-to-Many relationships**: While many-to-many relationships are possible in Tabular Models, they are complicated to set up, whereas in cubes these relationships are native and relatively easy.

- **You will use Role Playing Dimensions**: Like many-to-many relationships, Role Playing Dimensions are possible in Tabular Models, but they are complex to set up and also not very intuitive for users.

A Tabular Model is best if the following requirements are satisfied (again, not a comprehensive list):

- **You need the ability to quickly add additional or external data**: The Tabular Model allows you to connect to a wide variety of sources, while the cube is far more constrained on its source requirements. The Tabular Model also offers greater data compression compared to the multidimensional model. Generally, the cycle for Tabular Model development will be shorter compared to that for multidimensional model development.

- **Your model is relatively simplistic**: As mentioned earlier, complex design scenarios, such as many-to-many relationships as well as parent-child or role playing dimensions can be implemented with the Tabular Model, but it would require much greater effort compared to the effort with the multidimensional model.

- **Fastest possible query performance is required**: The Tabular Model is entirely stored in memory, so it is very fast at query time. Note that cubes are cached as they are queried, so there is a point at which the Cube may match the Tabular Model for a similar query but, in most cases, the Tabular Model will outperform the Cube for sheer query speed.

► **You want to use Power View or intend to run reports at a low granularity of data**: An add-in for SQL Server Reporting Services, Power View is an ad hoc visualization and analysis tool with which users may explore Power Pivot or the Tabular Model data in a familiar Office-like interface. Prior to SQL 2012 SP1, Power View could not use a Cube as a source. This is no longer a limitation with the release of SP1. The Tabular Model is also likely to be more efficient to retrieve data at low granularity, as opposed to retrieving just the summary values.

For additional information on the comparison between tabular and multidimensional models, refer to http://technet.microsoft.com/en-us/library/hh212940.aspx.

Star- or Snowflake-relational schema

There continues to be much discussion, and often debate, over the question of whether a Star or Snowflake schema is preferred and whether cubes or Tabular Models may be required.

> In the Star schema, each fact table is directly related to every dimension table; in the Snowflake schema, some dimension tables may be further normalized and connected to the fact table through other dimensions. You can use Star or Snowflake data models for building multidimensional as well as Tabular Models.

The answer is that either architecture is acceptable, and in most environments, the best choice is not one or the other but rather a mix of both.

Before making a decision on using a Star or Snowflake architecture for your relational scheme, it's important to understand the key characteristics of each. Stars are denormalized models, most typically seen in data marts. Though not optimal for data maintenance activities (as they are heavily data redundant), Stars are very fast to query and due to their far less complex schema, they are easier for business users to navigate. Snowflakes, on the other hand, are normalized models, most typically seen in data warehouses. Since they are normalized, Snowflakes are optimized for data maintenance, but the requirement of joining many tables to retrieve data mean a more complex overall schema and slower queries.

Given that our primary goal in BI is to provide access to data as quickly and intuitively as possible, Stars are generally considered to be the preferred "outer" data layer. Outer in this case implies that we may have (and often we do have) a normalized (Snowflake) data warehouse, which is the primary persistent managed data store. The denormalized (Star) Data Mart is populated from the Data Warehouse as a way of positioning data for optimal user, reporting, and application use. Cubes and Tabular Models, like all analysis tools, benefit greatly from this optimization but can consume the normalized data warehouse as well—usually not as efficiently.

However, this does not mean that my Data Mart must be entirely comprised of denormalized Star structures. You will find that as your environment matures, you will be faced with the fact data of differing grains along shared (conformed) dimensions. In such instances, you should consider normalizing (Snowflaking) those specific dimensions in order to accommodate those different facts. This is a good example of a Data Mart that is still considered a Star architecture but contains a small number of Snowflake dimensions.

A sample scenario for choosing the Snowflake schema

Here's an example of a design decision process that would lead you to a Snowflake dimension. Start by assuming that all the dimensions in the Data Mart (versus the Data Warehouse, where we may have different ideas) will be modeled as Stars.

We start in our first design with a single dimension, Geography, containing the following columns:

- `skGeography` (surrogate key)
- `PostalCode` (business key)
- `CityID`
- `CityName`
- `StateID`
- `StateName`
- `CountryID`
- `CountryName`

We have one fact source table containing, say, population data with the following columns:

- `CensusDate`
- `PostalCode`
- `PopulationCount`

In ETL, we would join this source table to the dimension table on the business key `PostalCode` to retrieve the surrogate key and use this to load the data mart fact table:

- `CensusDate`
- `skGeography`
- `PopulationCount`

Now, let's introduce a second fact source table containing projected population data, but with a different grain. Let's assume this data comes in, not at the Postal Code grain but rather at the State grain. We'd have a source table with columns such as follows:

- ProjectionDate
- StateID
- ProjectedGrowth

We can't join this new source table to our existing Geography dimension because if we do so, we will get back many surrogate keys—each representing one postal code within the specified state. So, we need to Snowflake (partially normalize) the Geography dimension so that it will support the grain of each of our fact source tables, giving us two dimension tables similar to the the the following two bullet lists:

dimGeography:

- skGeography
- PostalCode
- CityID
- CityName
- skGeographyState

and dimGeographyState:

- skGeographyState
- StateID
- StateName
- CountryID
- CountryName

Notice that we did not fully normalize the dimension (postal code and city both exist in the first table, state and country in the second). We just normalized the dimension enough to give us a single relationship between each of our two facts and this dimension.

2

Defining Analysis
Services Dimensions

In this chapter, we will cover the following recipes:

- ▶ Defining data sources
- ▶ Defining data source views
- ▶ Defining entity relationships in DSV
- ▶ Extending data source views
- ▶ Creating named calculations and queries
- ▶ Creating simple dimensions
- ▶ Building dimension hierarchies
- ▶ Setting up dimension properties
- ▶ Setting up the essential attribute properties
- ▶ Browsing dimension data
- ▶ Sorting the attributes
- ▶ Customizing advanced attribute properties
- ▶ Creating parent-child dimensions
- ▶ Creating date and time dimensions

Introduction

This chapter explains how to build and configure most commonly encountered **SQL Server Analysis Services** (**SSAS**) dimensions. Each Analysis Services multidimensional project consists of dimensions and cubes; knowing how to define and customize dimensions is essential for building successful business intelligence solutions. Analysis Services builds data structures based on one or multiple relational data sources. Therefore, before creating dimensions and cubes, you need to define data sources and their corresponding data source views—layers of abstraction between the relational database and Analysis Services objects. After you define data source views, you can create simple dimensions using a dimension wizard and subsequently customize and enhance dimensions as needed using a dimension editor.

SQL Server Data Tools (**SSDT**) is the primary client tool for developing Analysis Services solutions. In prior versions of SQL Server, the same tool was called **Business Intelligence Development Studio** (**BIDS**). To open SSDT navigate to **Start | All Programs | SQLServer 2012 | SQL Server Data Tools**. After you're happy with the objects you created within SSDT, you can deploy object definitions to an Analysis Services instance where you can process the objects (meaning loading data from the relational source into Analysis Services) and browse the data. The primary tool for administering Analysis Services, along with other products included within the SQL Server product suite, is called **SQL Server Management Studio** (**SSMS**).

> Note that throughout this book, we will use a sample SQL Server database, Adventure Works 2012, along with the corresponding sample Analysis Services database. You can download the mentioned samples from `www.codeplex.com` if you'd like to follow along (look for Adventure Works Multidimensional Models SQL Server 2012).

Defining data sources

Each Analysis Services project could use multiple data sources. The traditional approach is to first build a staging relational database where you import data from various data repositories within your enterprise. Subsequently, you would build a dimensional model using a Star or Snowflake schema, as opposed to a normalized model you would typically use for a transactional database, for your data warehouse that has fact and dimension tables. Lastly, you build the Analysis Services solution using the dimensional model within the relational data source. This approach is still recommended, because it allows you to have more control over your data cleansing routines prior to building Analysis Services objects.

On the other hand, SSDT does give you the flexibility to connect to various relational databases and define necessary data structures within data source views, if you don't have the luxury of building the staging area or the star schema database. However, this flexibility comes with a price because your transactional relational databases aren't likely to have data in the format you need for Analysis Services. Transforming data while you build SSAS objects adds an unnecessary overhead. Furthermore, you can accomplish certain data cleansing and transformation operations much more simply and more efficiently while using **SQL Server Integration Services** (**SSIS**) rather than doing so within Analysis Services. Keep this in mind as you learn how to create data sources.

How to do it...

Once you launch SSDT, go to **File** | **New Project** and then select **Analysis Services Multidimensional** and **Data Mining Project**. Provide a descriptive name for the new project, for example, SSAS Cookbook Chapter 2, and save it to the location of your choice. At this point you should see the project with the necessary folders within the SSDT's **Solution Explorer** window. To define a data source perform the following steps:

1. Right-click on the **Data Sources** folder in the **Solution Explorer** window and select **New Data Source**. This activates **Data Source Wizard**, as shown in the following screenshot.

2. Now, click on **New...**.

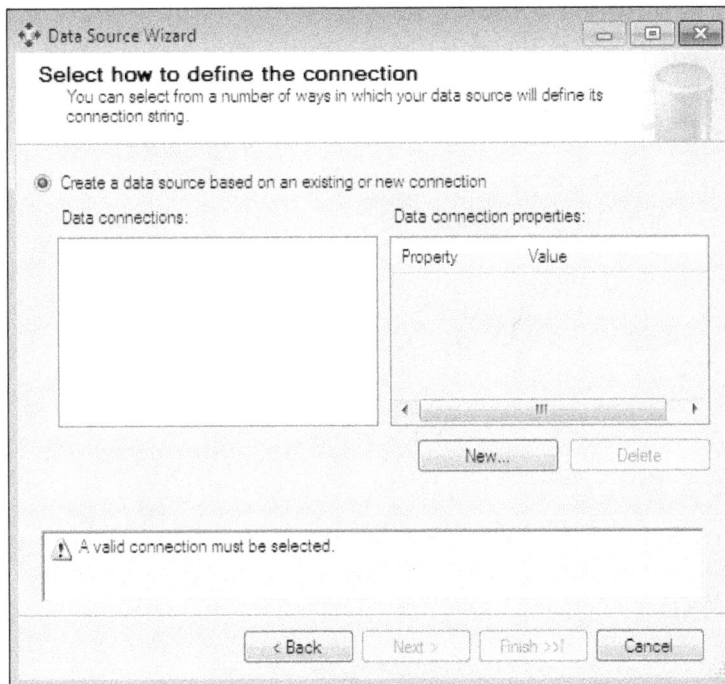

3. The Connection Manager allows us to choose a .NET or OLE DB provider, which we want to use for connecting to the relational data source.

4. Click on the **Provider** dropdown to see the list of available providers. You have a number of choices out of the box; you could source data from the SQL Server, Oracle, Access, or SQL Server Compact databases, among others.

5. The Connection Manager will show more options if you install additional drivers (for example, Sybase or Teradata driver), which aren't included with the default Analysis Services installation. Note that you have several options for connecting to SQL Server data sources, including the SQL Server Native Client or OLE DB provider. For this exercise, let's use the OLE DB provider for the SQL Server.

6. Provide the name of the SQL Server relational instance. For this example, I'll use a `Julia-PC\SQL2012` instance. You may use the SQL Server or Windows Authentication for connecting to the SQL Server relational instance.

> If you're using the default SQL Server instance, you only need to provide the host name. If you're using a named instance, you may provide the host name along with a slash and the instance name or the host name followed by a comma and the port number.

7. Specify the database you wish to connect to—in this case `AdventureWorksDW2012`. You can also click on the **Test Connection** button to verify connectivity to the data source, as shown in the following screenshot:

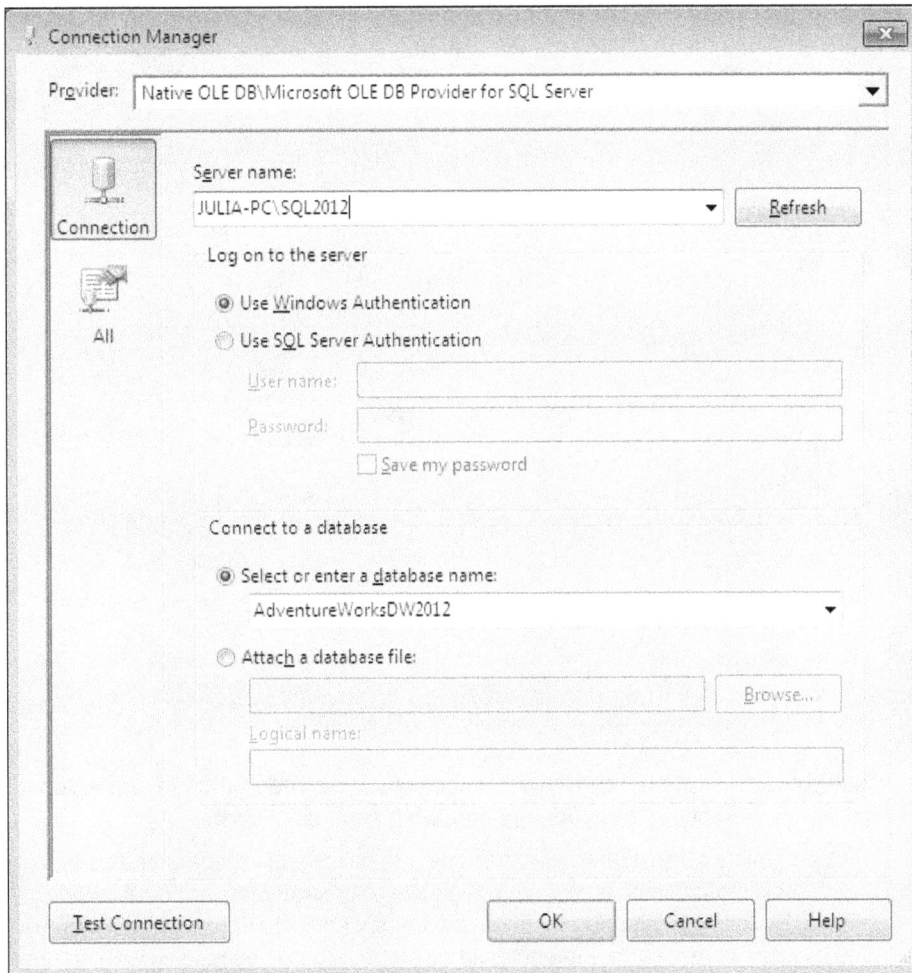

Note the **All** button on the **Connection Manager** dialog's left pane, just under the **Connection** button. Once you click on **All**, you can configure all the properties for the connection on a single tab. This tab is particularly useful if you are working with non-SQL Server data sources that require additional configuration besides simply specifying the server name and connection credentials. The number of properties you can set will vary from one provider to another. In some cases you must specify the majority of the settings as a single long string under "extended properties".

8. Once you're happy with the settings for a relational data source configuration, click on **OK** to return to the **Data Source Wizard**. Now the wizard shows the connection you defined as shown in the following screenshot:

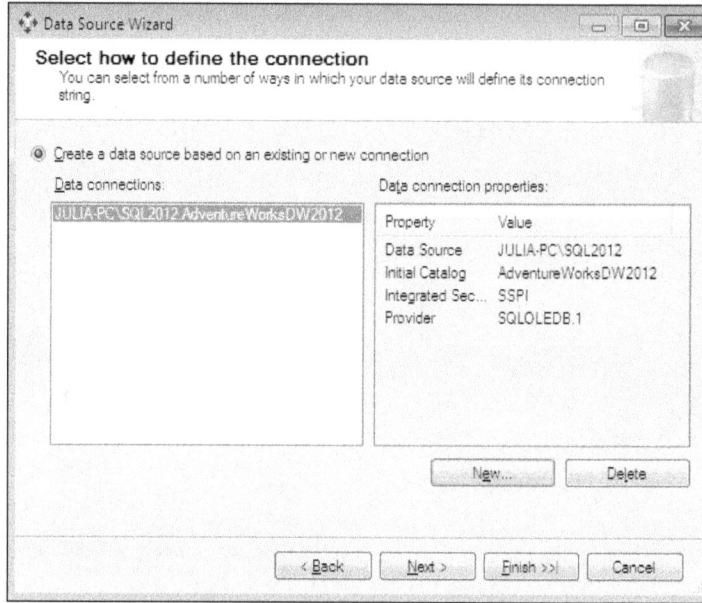

9. Once you click on **Next**, you're ready to configure the information for impersonation. You have several impersonation options, which are as follows:

   □ Use a specific Windows username and password. I recommend using this option since it ensures a high-level of security for your data source. Exploiting this option in an environment where multiple SSAS developers work on the same project could be cumbersome because co-workers aren't supposed to share their passwords. In such a case it is a common practice to use a generic user ID (perhaps with a non-expiring password), which all developers can share. Keep in mind that you will need to keep the account's password up-to-date. If you use an account with a password that will expire, you must update the data source definition each time the password changes. Note that Analysis Services never scripts passwords; although you can script the data source definition using SSMS, it will not display any passwords. If the password is incorrect, Analysis Services will report an error: **Logon failure; unknown user name or bad password**.

- Use the service account. This option uses the credentials of the account running the Analysis Services service. You must be a member of the Analysis Services administrator group (also known as server role) in order to use this impersonation option. We'll discuss the server role in *Chapter 7, Analysis Services Security*. If the service account isn't permitted to log on to the relational data source, Analysis Services will report an error, for example, **Login failed for user ABCDomain\XYZUser**.

- Use the credentials of the current user. This option is normally used for data mining, which is beyond the scope of this book. Do *not* use this option for defining data sources not intended for data mining. If you mistakenly use this option, Analysis Services will report an error: **Data Source XYZ contains an ImpersonationMode that is not supported for processing operations**.

- The **Inherit** option uses the impersonation option defined at the database level. As mentioned earlier, each project could have multiple data sources, and therefore it could be beneficial to re-use the definition for each source based on the database- or project-level setting.

10. Choose the appropriate impersonation level and click on **Next**.

> To see the impersonation information defined at the database level, right-click on the project in the **Solution Explorer** window and select **Edit Database**. This will allow you to edit Analysis Services' database-level properties. You will find the `DataSourceImpersonationInfo` property within the SSDT **Properties** window.

11. Once you click on the ellipsis button, you'll find that it has the same four options as the impersonation tab of each data source (the **Default** option is synonymous with **Inherit**).

> If impersonation is set to **Default** at the database level and **Inherit** at the data source level, the data source will use the Analysis Services service account for connecting to the relational database. For example, if you're using Windows' authentication to connect to a SQL Server relational source, you need to ensure that the account running the Analysis Services service has necessary permissions to read data from SQL Server database objects.

12. The last screen of the wizard asks for a data source name. Be sure to supply a descriptive name before you click on **Finish** so that you can easily differentiate between multiple data sources. The newly defined data source will show up in the `Data Sources` folder within SSDT.

How it works...

If you have worked with various relational database platforms, you would be aware of the similarities; they all consist of tables, rows, and columns. But you might also recall the differences, for example, the flavour of the SQL language used by the SQL Server could be somewhat different from the one utilized by Oracle, Sybase, or Teradata. So you might wonder how SSAS knows which syntax works for each type of data source. If you check the `Cartridges` folder under your Analysis Services installation directory (by default, this folder will be under `c:\Program Files\Microsoft SQL Server\instance name\OLAP\ bin\`), you will find XSL files for each supported data source. These cartridge files control how SSAS interacts with various relational databases.

There's more...

Now that you have created the data source, you can review and edit its properties by right-clicking on it in the **Solution Explorer** window within SSDT and selecting **Open**. This screen reveals a few additional properties, which can be useful for fine tuning your data source configuration; they are given in the following bullet list:

- **Isolation**: This property configures the transaction isolation level for retrieving data from relational tables. The default (and recommended) value is `Read Committed`. You also have an option of using the snapshot isolation level. The discussion of transaction isolation levels is beyond the scope of this book. However, you should be aware that different isolation levels use different types of locking strategies to ensure data consistency.

- **Query timeout**: This property allows you to specify the number of seconds during which SSAS should run the SQL statement used for processing any object within this data source, after which the relational query should timeout. If you have a busy relational database used to populate SSAS objects, the stability of the relational source might be more important than having up-to-date data in Analysis Services. Therefore, you might want to throttle the amount of time a processing query takes to run. The default value is `0`, which means that queries aren't limited at the data source level. Analysis Services has a configuration property that controls how long processing queries should run before the timeout; please refer to *Chapter 8, Administering and Monitoring Analysis Services*, for more information.

- The maximum number of connections property defaults to 10, and controls how many connections SSAS can establish with the data source while processing its corresponding objects.

Defining data source views

Data source view (**DSV**) serves as a layer of abstraction between a relational data source and SSAS objects. You can import existing tables and views from relational sources into a DSV. DSVs also allow defining new columns and views (named calculations and named queries, respectively) based on the existing structures within your data sources. Let's learn how to create and enhance DSVs.

Getting started

A prerequisite to building a DSV is defining at least one data source. Build a data source before working on DSVs by following a previous recipe.

How to do it...

To define a DSV, perform the following steps:

1. Right-click on the **Data Source Views** folder in SSDT's **Solution Explorer** and choose **New Data Source View**. This activates the **Data Source View Wizard**. This wizard allows using the existing data source or defining a new one. If you choose to create a new data source, you will go through the same steps we discussed earlier in this chapter. For this example let's use the existing data source.

2. The following screen allows choosing tables and views we want to include in the DSV. You can add or remove objects using the left and right arrows in between the **Available objects** and **Included objects** panes of this dialog.

   Note the **Filter** textbox; it comes in very handy in large databases with thousands of tables and views. You can enter a string in the **Filter** textbox to limit the list of available objects to those objects whose name contains the mentioned string.

3. The **Add Related Tables** button automatically adds any tables that have foreign key relationships with the tables already in the **Included objects** list.

4. It is not uncommon to see the Analysis Services project built on top of a relational database that includes primary and foreign keys. However, referential integrity adds an overhead while loading data. If you load data from various sources into fact and dimension tables, you might not want to define table relationships in SQL Server but rather specify such relationships in the DSV.

5. For this example, select the **DimDate (dbo)** table from the available objects list, and click on the right arrow button (**>**) to move it to the included objects list.

6. Next click on the **Add Related Tables** button, and you'll see several fact tables added to the list.

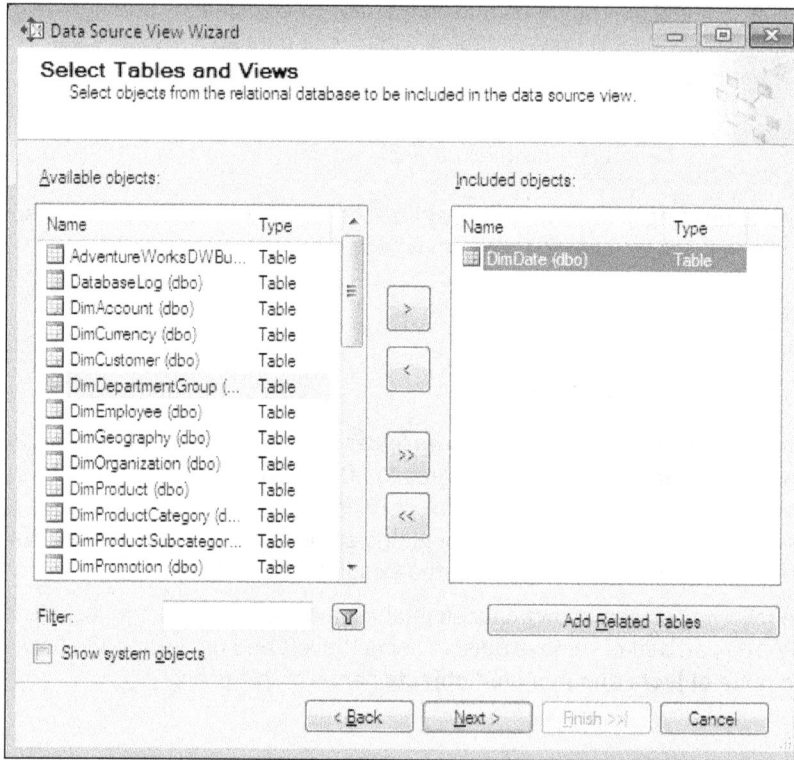

7. Click on the **Next** button to move on to the final screen of the wizard, allowing you to specify a name for the new DSV. Be sure to specify a descriptive name so you can easily differentiate this DSV from others.

8. Click on the **Finish** button after you name the DSV. Adventure Works DW2012 DSV should now include the **DimDate (dbo)** table along with several fact tables.

> You can right-click on any object within the DSV and select the **Explore Data** option to browse the sample data found in this object—doing so runs a query against the relational data source.

Defining entity relationships in DSV

While creating a data source view, you noticed that SSDT automatically detected primary and foreign keys between `DimDate` and `fact` tables and established their respective relationships. If our data source does not have referential integrity constraints, we would have to define the logical primary keys and necessary relationships directly within the DSV.

To set up relationships between two objects within a DSV, dimension objects (tables or views) must have a primary key column and fact tables must reference this column. The column names in fact and dimension tables do not need to match, but they must have compatible data types. For example, you cannot create a relationship between an integer and string columns.

How to do it...

Let's get started; the following are the steps to define the entity relation in DSV:

1. To define a logical primary key on an object that does not already have one, right-click on the column that uniquely identifies each record in the table and select **Set Logical Primary Key**. To check how relationships are defined in the DSV you created, double-click on the line connecting `FactFinance` to `DimDate`. As shown in the following screenshot, the relationship includes the table names of both primary and foreign keys:

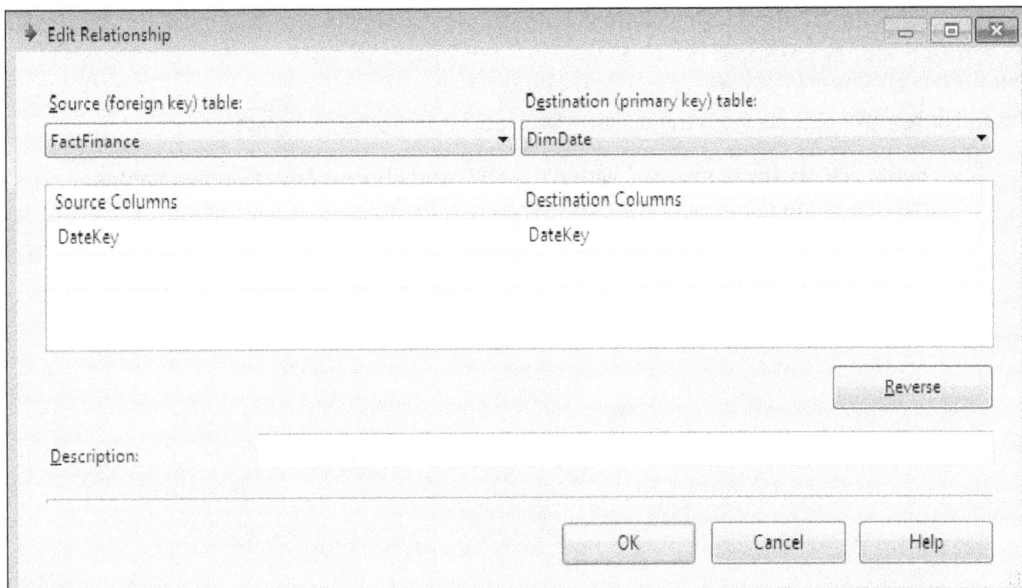

2. To create a new relationship, you must click on the Foreign Key column in the fact table and drag it to the dimension table's Primary Key. Alternatively, you can right-click on the blank area within the DSV and select **New Relationship**; this will bring up the **Edit Relationship** dialog (as shown in the preceding screenshot).

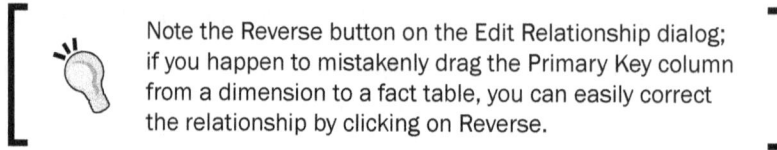

> Note the Reverse button on the Edit Relationship dialog; if you happen to mistakenly drag the Primary Key column from a dimension to a fact table, you can easily correct the relationship by clicking on Reverse.

3. The DSV we created in the previous section has multiple relationships from some fact tables to **DimDate**. For example, the **FactResellerSales** table has **OrderDateKey**, **ShipDateKey**, and **DueDateKey** columns, each referencing the **DateKey** column in the **DimDate** table.

Extending data source views

Now that you know how to create a DSV, you are ready to learn how to extend it. In the previous recipe we imported a few tables from a relational data source, but that might not be sufficient to complete your data model. You may need to import objects from multiple data sources, define calculations, or add new data views.

How to do it...

To add or remove objects from the existing DSV, perform the following steps:

1. Right-click on any blank area within the DSV and choose **Add/Remove Tables**; this opens the corresponding dialog shown in the following screenshot:

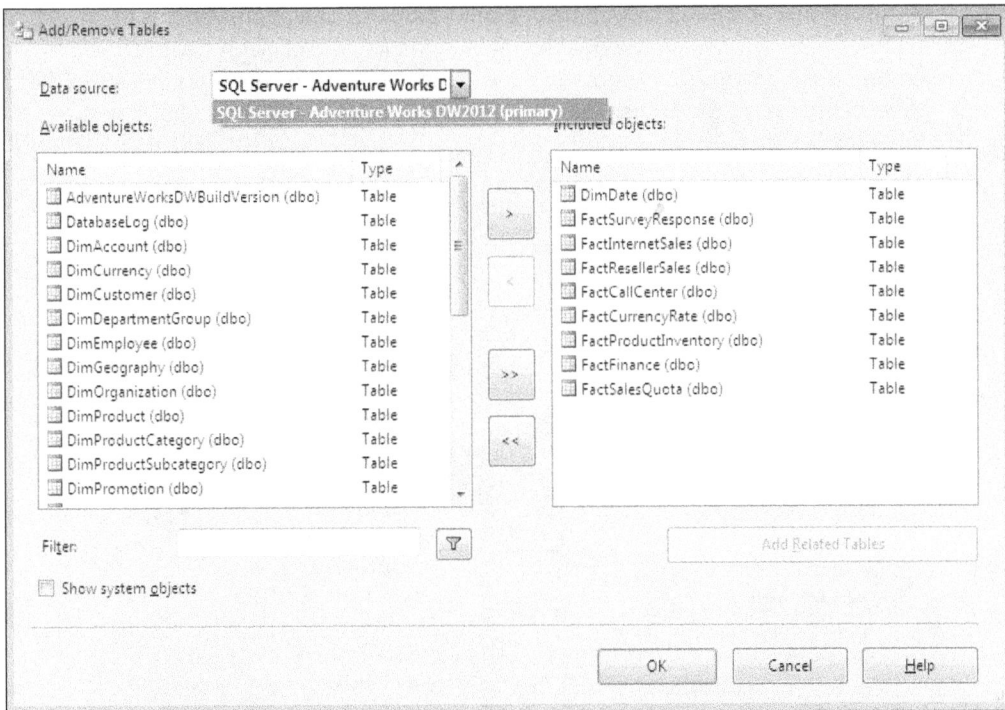

2. This screen should look familiar from the previous section when you first created the DSV. You could easily add or remove objects to the DSV by clicking on appropriate buttons. One notable difference is the **Data source** drop-down box. If we had defined multiple data sources, we could import objects into the same DSV using multiple sources. In order to include objects from multiple data sources into a single DSV, the primary data source must be SQL Server; as you can see from the previous screenshot, the dialog clearly identifies the primary data source.

3. Be aware that generally it is not recommended to use the same DSV to combine data from multiple sources. Importing data from multiple data sources will result in the use of the OPENQUERY syntax for getting data from non-primary data sources, which could be less optimal than having a single data source or a separate DSV for each data source. However, you can only define relationships among objects found in the same DSV; hence, each DSV would have to have separate measure groups. You will learn more about measure groups in _Chapter 3, Creating Analysis Services Cubes_.

4. If you proceed with adding the remaining tables and views found in the Adventure Works DW 2012 sample database, you'll find that the DSV becomes somewhat cluttered and difficult to read. Clearly, a DSV for a real-world application with dozens or even hundreds of tables will be even more complicated to decipher. Fortunately you can right-click on any blank area within a DSV and choose the **Zoom** option to have the DSV fit the available screen space.

5. You also have an option to find a particular table; this option brings up the list of tables. Once you click on the desired table in the list and click on **Ok**, SSDT will focus on that table on the DSV. Alternatively, you can achieve the same by clicking on the table of interest in the **Tables** list on the leftmost pane in SSDT, as shown in the following screenshot:

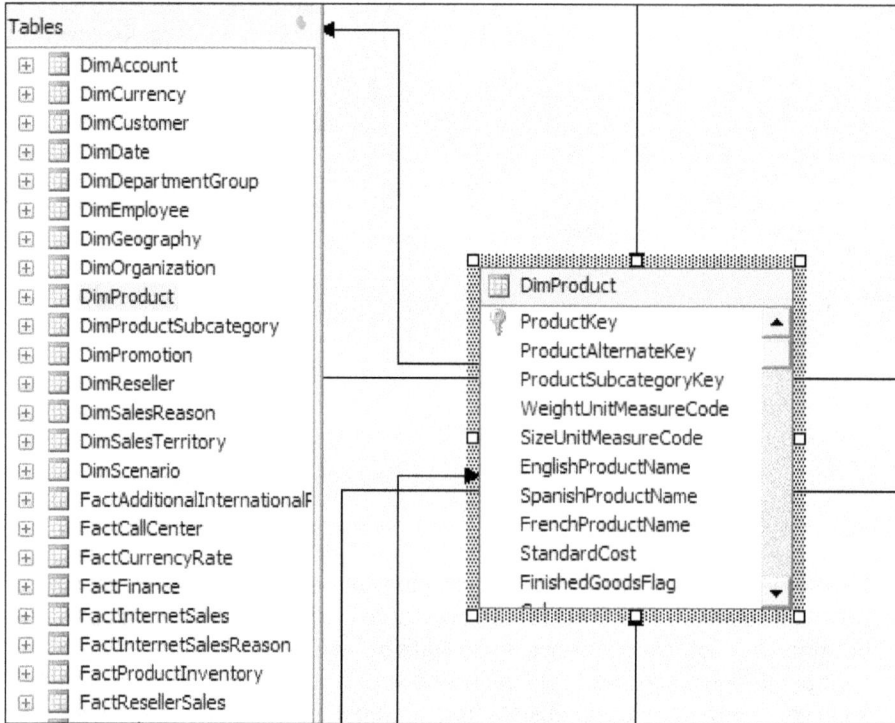

6. Since the list of tables included in an SSDT project can get unwieldy, you can create multiple diagrams based on the same DSV. For example, you could build a separate diagram for each group of fact and dimension tables. To create a new diagram, right-click anywhere within the **Diagram Organizer** window (found in the top-left corner of SSDT when a DSV is open) and choose **New Diagram**. Once the new diagram is created, you can give it a descriptive name and add tables/views by following the same steps as when building the DSV.

Creating named calculations and queries

Named calculations allow extending an existing object to include data structures necessary for defining a dimension. The most common example is of combining the first and last name columns into a single column named as **full_name**. Similarly, we could concatenate the quarter and year columns to define a full description for each calendar quarter, as in `Quarter 2, 2013`. If you have sufficient access to the relational database, you have an option of creating any views you need for building dimensions; this approach is favored by many data warehouse and cube developers. However, it is also plausible that you won't have permission to create or alter relational objects. There is no need to worry though; named calculations are here to help. For example, suppose you have the Employee dimension based on the `DimEmployee` table, which includes the `FirstName` and `LastName` columns. This could be great for relational design, but you'll need to define a named calculation if you want to expose a string concatenating the first and last names as a single dimension attribute.

In addition to named calculations, you can also define named queries. These are most useful when you'd like to present columns from multiple tables together as a single entity. With named queries you can also join tables found in multiple databases on the same SQL Server instance. If you have necessary permissions to create and alter objects in the relational source, it's best to define relational views (the relational database administrator will advise you if you have such permissions); however, if you cannot modify the relational source, you will have to resort to using named queries. You should also consider the advantages/drawbacks of using named queries versus relational views. If the view is beneficial for relational queries in addition to populating an SSAS object, it makes more sense to create the view in the relational database. On the other hand, if the view is specific to your Analysis Services solution, it may make more sense to use a named query as opposed to creating a new relational object.

How to do it...

To create the **full_name** named calculation, perform the following steps:

1. Right-click on `DimEmployee` within the DSV and choose **New Named Calculation**. This opens the **Create Named Calculation** dialog.
2. Enter **FullName** in the column name text box and specify `FirstName + ' ' + LastName` as the expression. Optionally, you could also enter a description for the named calculation.

3. Now, the `DimEmployee` table shows the **FullName** column along with a calculator icon in the DSV. To confirm you get the desired result with your named calculation, you can right-click on `DimEmployee` and choose **Explore Data**.

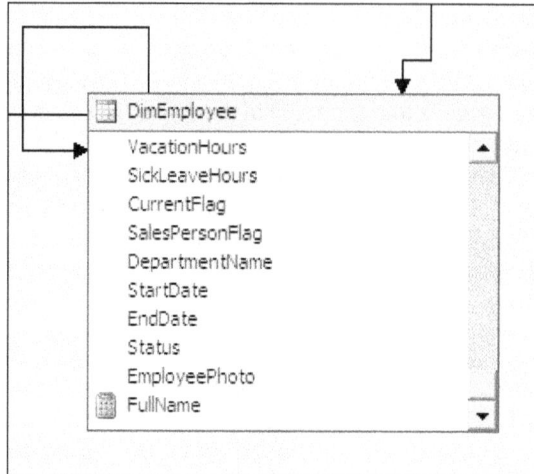

```
DimEmployee
    VacationHours
    SickLeaveHours
    CurrentFlag
    SalesPersonFlag
    DepartmentName
    StartDate
    EndDate
    Status
    EmployeePhoto
    FullName
```

To create a named query, realize that AdventureWorks DW 2012 contains a snowflake schema for product subcategories; however, suppose we want to build the Product dimension based on just one entity, we should include the subcategory data.

4. Right-click on the blank area in the DSV and choose **New Named Query**; this opens the **Create Named Query** dialog. You have an option to either use a generic query builder, which simply accepts SQL statements, or the **Visual Data Tools** (**VDT**) query builder, which allows you to pick and choose columns you wish to include in the query.

5. Switch to the generic query builder, enter the following query, and click on the run button as shown in the next screenshot:

```
SELECT
    DimProduct.ProductKey,DimProduct.ProductAlternateKey,
    DimProduct.ProductSubcategoryKey,DimProduct.
    WeightUnitMeasureCode,
DimProduct.SizeUnitMeasureCode,DimProduct.
    EnglishProductName,
    DimProduct.StandardCost, DimProduct.FinishedGoodsFlag,
    DimProduct.Color,DimProduct.SafetyStockLevel,
    DimProduct.ReorderPoint,DimProduct.ListPrice,DimProduct.[Si
    ze],DimProduct.SizeRange,DimProduct.Weight,DimProduct.
    DaysToManufacture,
    DimProduct.ProductLine,DimProduct.DealerPrice,
    DimProduct.Class,DimProduct.Style,DimProduct.ModelName,
```

```
      DimProduct.EnglishDescription,DimProduct.StartDate,
      DimProduct.EndDate,DimProduct.Status,
      DimProductSubcategory.EnglishProductSubcategoryName
   FROMDimProductINNERJOIN DimProductSubcategoryONDimProduct.
      ProductSubcategoryKey=DimProductSubcategory.
      ProductSubcategoryKey
```

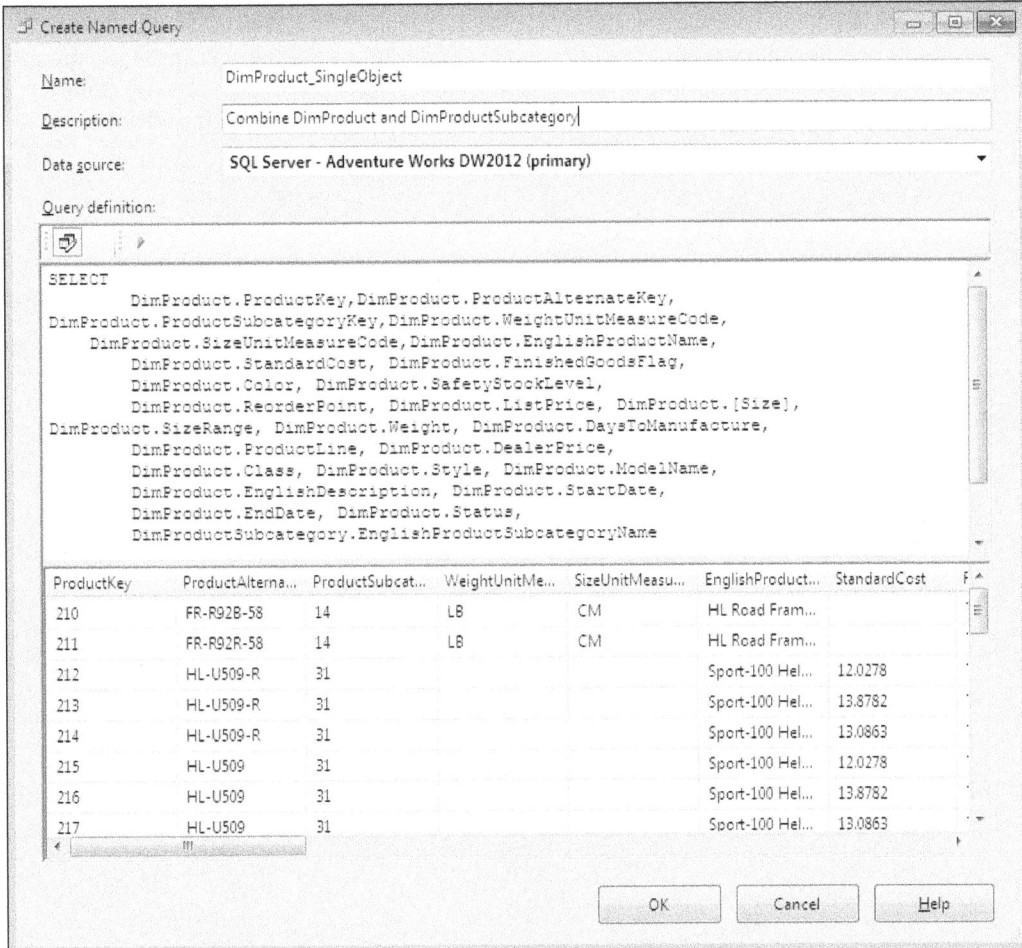

6. This dialog allows you to preview the query you are about to save to DSV. Switching to the VDT query builder will let you review the query design visually.

7. Once you click on **OK**, the named query is saved to your DSV. You can now add the logical primary key and define relationships with the named query as you would with tables and views imported from the relational data source.

Creating simple dimensions

The Analysis Services dimension allows examining data across a specific business vertical. For example, the Product dimension allows managers to see which products generated the most revenue, and the Geography dimension helps determine the most profitable regions. Each dimension is based on a corresponding table or view in the relational data source; dimension table's columns will correspond to SSAS dimension attributes. Analysis Services allows creation of very simple as well as very complex dimension structures. There are many dimension and attribute properties which let us customize each dimension to meet specific business requirements. Let's begin by creating a simple dimension and then working our way through more complex ones.

Getting ready

To complete this recipe, we must have at least one data source view with necessary tables, views, named queries, and named calculations.

How to do it...

To create a dimension perform the following steps:

1. Right-click on the `Dimensions` folder in SSDT's **Solution Explorer** and choose **New Dimension**. This activates the **Dimension Wizard**. The introductory screen provides some choices for building dimensions: we can use an existing table, generate a table, or create a server-level time dimension. A large majority of your dimensions will be based on tables or views that already exist in the relational source. Date- and time-related dimensions occasionally make sense if they are to be created through Analysis Services, as discussed later in this chapter. For this example choose **Use an existing table** and click on **Next**:

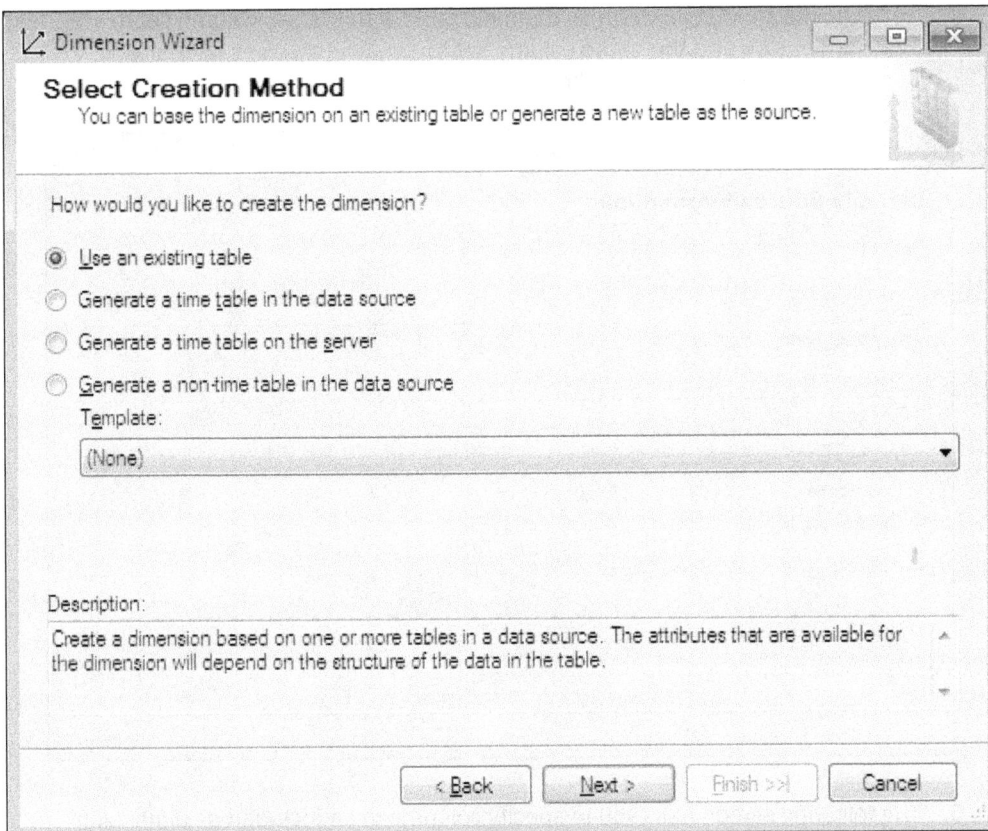

2. The following screen asks you to specify the data source view where the dimension table is found along with the dimension key and its corresponding name.

3. Recall that when creating a data source view, we imported table definitions from a relational source, including any primary and foreign keys used to relate fact tables to dimension tables. Additionally, if the source dimension table did not have a primary key, we defined the logical primary key within the DSV. A dimension's key attribute must uniquely identify each dimension row. The name column is presented to Analysis Services users while browsing the dimension and is optional for the key attribute. This is because you may or may not want to expose the key attribute for querying. Our project currently contains a single DSV, which is automatically detected and selected by the wizard. If we had multiple DSVs, you could pick the one from which you wanted to build the dimension.

4. Let's choose `DimPromotion` as the main table with the key column set to `PromotionKey` and the name column set to `EnglishPromotionName` as shown in the following screenshot:

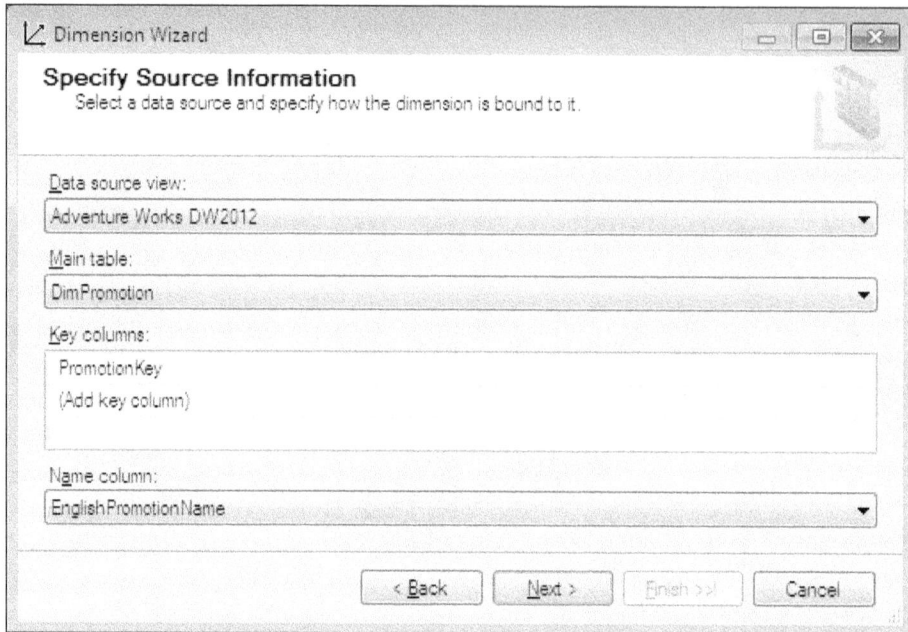

5. The following screen asks you to specify columns to be included as dimension attributes. You can specify attribute names, which do not have to match the dimension table column names.

> The dimension wizard asked us to specify the `main` table; this is because a dimension could be built upon multiple tables. For example, if you use a Snowflake schema, each dimension could consist of multiple related tables.

6. Choose descriptive attribute names that will be meaningful to cube users. Business people often don't care how cube architects name tables and columns, but they do need to know what data each attribute represents. Therefore, it is quite common to have lengthy attribute names, which include spaces—a practice that is generally avoided when naming relational database columns.

7. Although we included `PromotionKey` as the dimension's key attribute, let's name it `Promotion Name`. Additionally, let's include **English Promotion Type**, **English Promotion Category**, **Discount Percent**, **Start Date**, **End Date**, **Minimum Quantity**, and **Maximum Quantity** attributes; it is best to spell out words completely in attribute names rather than cause ambiguity in users' minds.

8. Enabling browsing and attribute type options allows us to set a couple of important properties. You may want to include an attribute in the dimension without enabling cube users to slice data by this attribute. For example, the key attribute could simply be an identity column—a monotonically increasing value that has no business meaning and won't be useful for browsing. On the other hand, columns that aren't available for browsing could be useful for sorting other attributes.

9. Most of the attributes will be classified as regular, but occasionally you will need special attribute types; clicking on the attribute type drop-down box will show you the choices: **Account**, **Currency**, **Date**, **Geography**, and **Other**. Each attribute type has multiple subtypes associated with it.

10. Leave all the attributes of the type **Regular**, and click on next after ensuring your screen looks like the following screenshot:

> Do keep in mind that special attribute types are available and can be set after the dimension has been created.

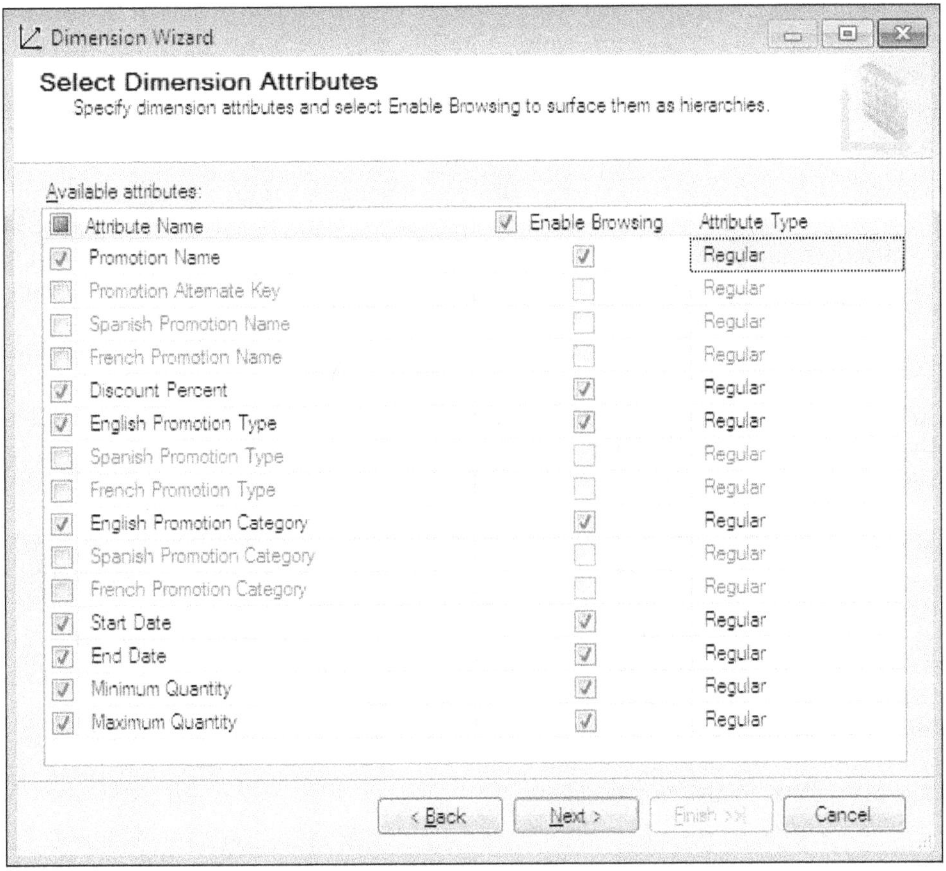

11. The previous screen simply asks you to name the dimension. Again, remember that business users will browse the data using dimension names, and therefore names should be meaningful. Name the dimension as **Promotion** and click on **Finish**. At this point, your SSDT project will show `Promotion.dim` under the `Dimensions` folder; as you might guess, the `.dim` extension stands for dimension, and each dimension object within the project will have this extension.

12. Double-click on `Promotion.dim` to open the dimension editor, and review the dimension structure created by the wizard. The DSV pane shows the only table included in the promotion dimension, and the properties' window shows numerous properties we could set to customize the dimension. Highlighting any attribute in the leftmost pane will allow setting the properties for that attribute.

13. Hover your mouse pointer over the squiggly line under the promotion dimension in the leftmost pane and you'll see the warning: **Create hierarchies in non parent-child dimensions**. This brings us to the next recipe, that is, creating dimension hierarchies.

How it works...

The only language through which you can communicate with the Analysis Services server is **Extensible Markup Language for Analysis** (**XMLA**). Whether applying project changes you develop through the SSDT user interface or processing objects using SSMS (or the .NET code), all actions applicable to Analysis Services are translated into XMLA before being sent to the server.

If you right-click on any object within your SSDT solution (this means the SSDT project, not the live database) and choose **View Code**, SSDT will display the full XMLA for that object. Generally you would not have to edit the XMLA code, but occasionally SSDT might raise errors while you're editing a solution, and it's very difficult to work around these errors. In these rare cases, you might find that changing a few letters in the XMLA code (for example, switching from one data type to another) is easier than troubleshooting a potential bug in the SSDT user interface. Of course, you must know exactly what you're doing before editing the XMLA code directly, and you should make a backup of the solution prior to applying any changes. Reviewing the code that SSDT generates behind the scenes is a great way to become familiar with XMLA for Analysis Services' structures.

Building dimension hierarchies

Analysis Services hierarchies specify the navigation path for browsing dimension data. There are two types of hierarchies: attribute and user-defined hierarchies. For example, in the promotion dimension we just created, we immediately have a hierarchy for each attribute: `Promotion Name`, `Start Date`, `End Date`, `English Promotion Category`, `English Promotion Type`, `Discount Percent`, `Minimum Quantity`, and `Maximum Quantity`. Attribute hierarchies contain two levels.

The top-level is referred to as the **All** level and includes the aggregated value for all the members included in the attribute. For example, the **English Promotion Category** attribute hierarchy's All level will show the aggregate value of sales for all the promotion categories: **Customer**, **No Discount**, and **Reseller**. The other level in the same hierarchy will show individual promotion categories, such as **Customer**.

User hierarchies combine multiple attributes and must be defined explicitly. In this recipe we will create a user hierarchy, which allows displaying the summary data for each promotion category, then drilling down to the promotion type, and finally exposing individual promotion names.

How to do it...

Let's learn how to define multiattribute hierarchies by using the following steps:

1. Right-click on the **English Promotion Category** attribute and choose **Start New Hierarchy**. This adds a new hierarchy object to the **Hierarchies** pane.

2. Drag the **English Promotion Type** attribute and drop it under the **English Promotion Category** attribute in the newly created hierarchy. Repeat the same for the **Promotion Name** attribute, placing it under **English Promotion Type**. The dimension structure should now resemble the following screenshot:

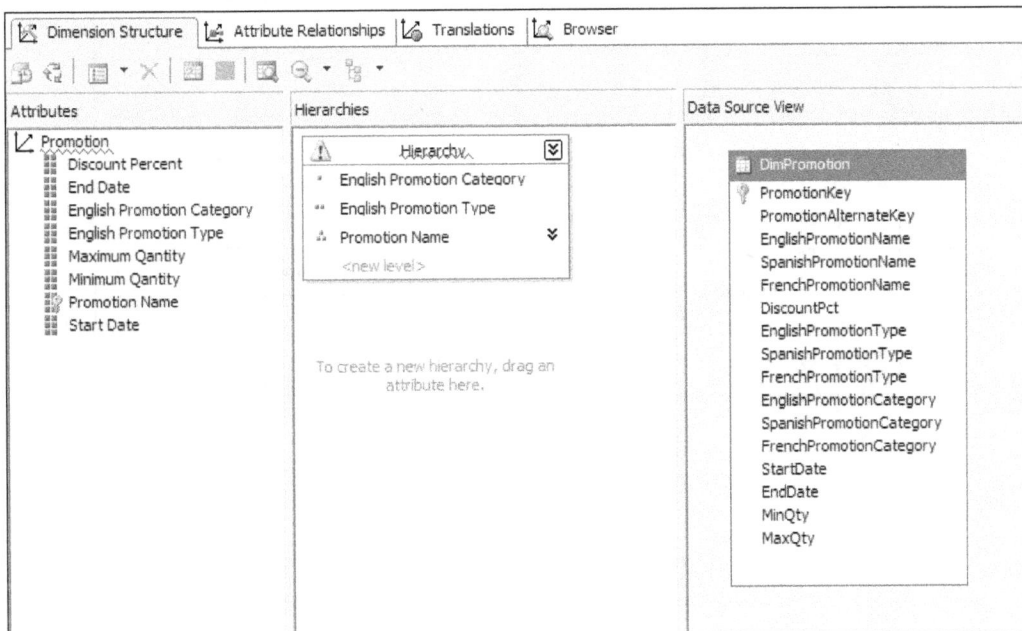

3. Now let's provide a meaningful name to the hierarchy so that our users know what data they're browsing. Right-click on the hierarchy, choose **Rename**, and then enter **Promotion Categories and Types**.

4. Alternatively, you can also edit the hierarchy name property within the **Properties** window. Now, the **Promotion Categories and Types** hierarchy contains three levels: **English Promotion Category**, **English Promotion Type**, and **Promotion Name**. Highlighting any attribute within the hierarchy allows renaming of the level. For example, suppose that the majority of our users are fluent in English and hence we don't need to include the word "English" in level names. Therefore, let's remove this word from the corresponding levels and arrive at the final design of our hierarchy to include **Promotion Category**, **Promotion Type**, and **Promotion Name** levels.

5. Now, you're happy with hierarchy-level names, but SSDT shows another warning; this is because we haven't defined attribute relationships yet. Attribute relationships define how Analysis Services should roll up data from one hierarchy level to the next. In this case we know that each promotion category can have multiple types, and each type can have multiple promotion names. Switch over to the **Attribute Relationships** pane within the promotion dimension editor; currently, you'll see the relationships as shown in the following screenshot:

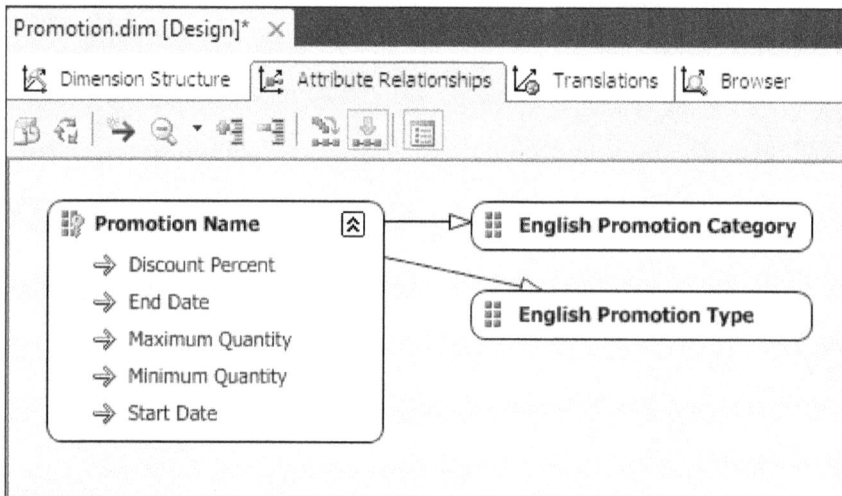

There's more

Analysis Services creates a relationship from the key attribute to each non-key attribute by default because the key attribute must uniquely identify each non-key attribute. But note that **English Promotion Category** and **English Promotion Type** appear to the right of **Promotion Name** (key attribute), whereas all other non-key attributes appear under **Promotion Name**. This is because you included the promotion category and promotion type levels in a user-defined hierarchy. Right-click on the **English Promotion Type** attribute and choose **New Attribute Relationship**. Doing so brings up the **Create Attribute Relationship** dialog. Set the related attribute as **English Promotion Category** and leave the relationship type as **Flexible (may change over time)** as shown in the following screenshot; then click on **OK**. Attribute relationships are always one-to-many; in this example, each category could have many promotion types. A relationship type can be flexible or rigid. Rigid relationships are rare; they indicate that each member of the related attribute will always be associated with the same member of the source attribute. For example, January 21, 2013 will always be associated with the month January 2013; similarly, each calendar month will always be associated with the corresponding year. The classification of each promotion type can change over time; hence, we should leave the relationship type at the default value of **flexible**. Relationship types make an important difference during dimension processing; you will learn more about processing in *Chapter 5, Optimizing Dimension and Cube Processing*.

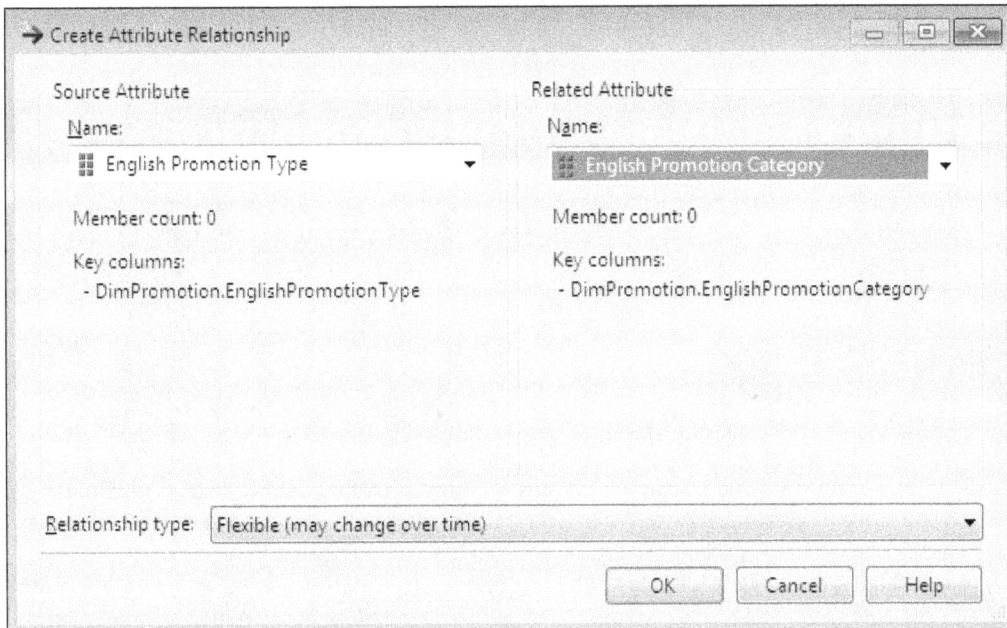

User hierarchies do not always have to include relationships between each combination of levels. For example, users might want to browse data by the promotion start date and the discount percent. However, the same discount percent might be applicable to multiple start and end dates, depending on the quantity of the product a customer decides to purchase. Therefore, we have a many-to-many relationship between the start date and the discount percent, and we cannot define an attribute relationship between these two levels. If a hierarchy contains attribute relationships defined between each combination of levels, it is called a natural hierarchy. Analysis Services builds additional indexes for natural hierarchies, which help optimize the query performance. Therefore, to achieve optimal query performance, always define the necessary attribute relationships when applicable.

All other attributes included in the Promotion dimension (minimum and maximum quantity, start and end dates, discount percent) will be directly related to the promotion key because each may be applicable to multiple promotions. Once you've defined the relationship between the promotion type and category attributes, save your changes and return to the **Dimension Structure** tab; you will find that SSDT no longer displays the squiggly line, which acts as a warning, under the Promotion Categories and Types hierarchy.

Setting dimension properties

You can customize each dimension by setting their respective properties to the desired values through the **Properties** window after you select the dimension on the **Dimension Structure** tab. Please refer to *Appendix A, Miscellaneous Analysis Services Topics* for a table summarizing the most frequently used dimension properties.

Setting essential attribute properties

While running the **Dimension Wizard** to create the Promotion dimension, you learned that each attribute has name and key properties. Choosing appropriate columns for these properties is essential for having the correct attribute design, so we will discuss them in greater detail here.

How to do it...

The steps for setting essential attribute properties are as follows:

1. The key property must uniquely identify the attribute and could consist of multiple columns. For example, if we have a date dimension that includes the quarter number column, with values quarter 1, quarter 2, and so on, this column alone won't be sufficient to uniquely identify each quarter because quarter names would be duplicated for each year. Instead, the key property should be set to a combination of quarter and year columns. If we don't explicitly specify the attribute key, Analysis Services will use the same column as the attribute key and name, but attribute names might not always be unique. If we check the properties of the **Promotion Type** attribute, we find the following settings:

▷ KeyColumns	DimPromotion.EnglishPromotionType (WChar) [...]
NameColumn	(none)

2. However, a quick check of the `DimPromotion` relational table will show duplicate promotion type values. For instance, the Excess Inventory promotion type exists for both **Reseller** and **Customer** promotion categories. If we leave the dimension design at its current state, Analysis Services processing will fail reporting duplicate values. Instead, let's specify a composite key consisting of the promotion type and promotion category columns. Click on the ellipsis button to the right of the **Key Columns** property; this will open the **Key Columns** dialog. Note from the screenshot that you could choose columns from multiple source tables (if we were using a snowflake schema). Add the **EnglishPromotionCategory** column to the **Key Columns** list and click on **OK**:

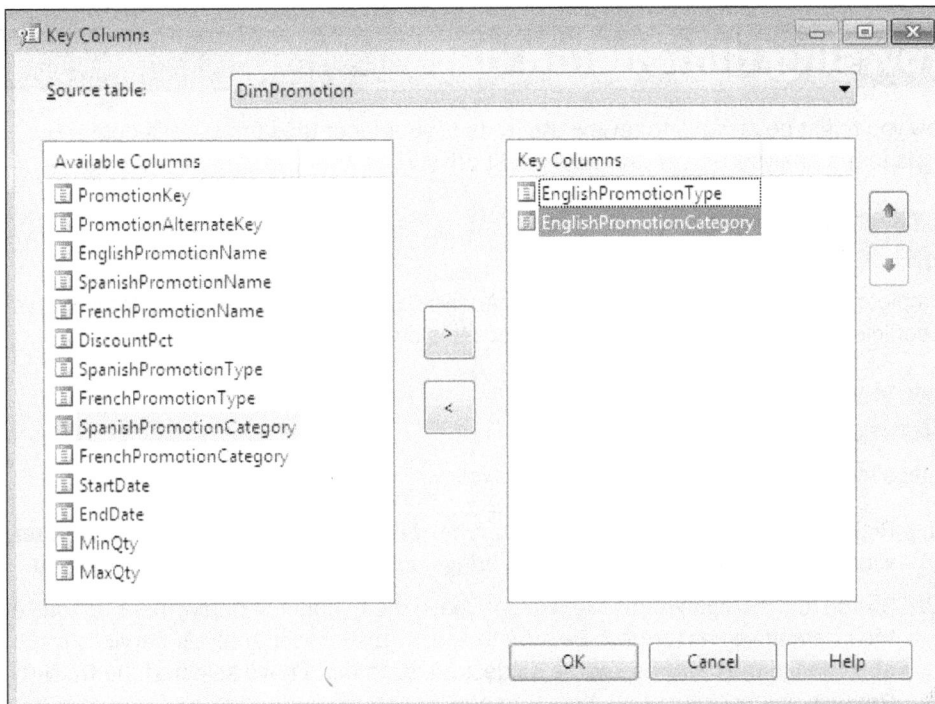

3. Now, SSDT displays a squiggly line under the **EnglishPromotionType** column, and we must specify the name column property for any attribute that has multiple key columns. Right-click on the ellipsis button next to the **NameColumn** property to activate the **NameColumn** dialog. Choose the **EnglishPromotionType** column and click on **OK**. At this point SSDT will remove the missing-name-column warning from the **EnglishPromotionType** attribute.

> In this example, we used a composite key for the promotion type attribute. This practice is acceptable for relatively small dimensions, but if you're working with large dimensions it is best to use narrow keys (meaning a single column, preferably with an integer data type) for each attribute. It is a common and recommended practice to create additional keys in a relational database to assure the uniqueness of each attribute member.

Browsing dimension data

By now you might be anxious to review the fruits of your labor thus far, so let's deploy our changes to the Analysis Server and take a test drive.

Getting ready

To complete this recipe, you need to have an Analysis Services 2012 instance for which you have sufficient permissions to deploy and process a database.

How to do it...

The steps for browsing dimension data are as follows:

1. Right-click on the `SSAS_Cook_book_Chapter2` project in the **Solution Explorer** window and choose **Properties**; this brings up the project property pages dialog.

2. Switch to the **Deployment** tab. We can leave the majority of deployment options at their default values for now. Be sure to specify the correct Analysis Services instance and change the database name as desired. Note that I have selected the **Do Not Process** processing option. I recommend this option during project deployment because it helps separate two operations, deployment and processing, and therefore makes debugging corresponding problems easier.

3. The default value for **Processing Option** is **Default**, which will bring each object included in the deployed database to a fully processed mode. Once you are comfortable with your processing option, Analysis Server name and database name, click on **OK**.

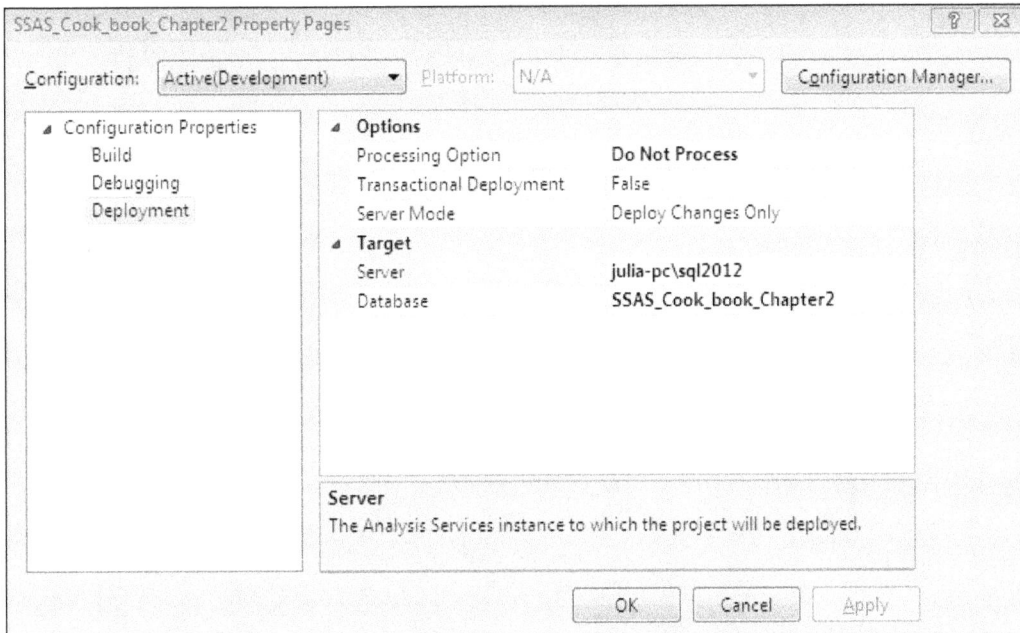

4. Right-click on the project again and choose **Deploy**. If you have followed along each step, your Analysis Services instance should reflect a new database called `SSAS_Cook_book_Chapter2`, which will have the data source, DSV, and the Promotion dimension you created. You can review database objects in SSMS. Right-click on the Promotion dimension and choose **Process** (either from SSDT or SSMS); use the default option to run the **Process Full** option and click on **OK**.

5. After you process the promotion dimension, activate the **Browser** tab in SSDT. Here you'll see each promotion grouped under the respective type and category, per the next screenshot. Note that, by default, the browser shows the user hierarchy, but you could also browse attribute hierarchies by clicking on the **Hierarchy** drop-down box and choosing the hierarchy of interest:

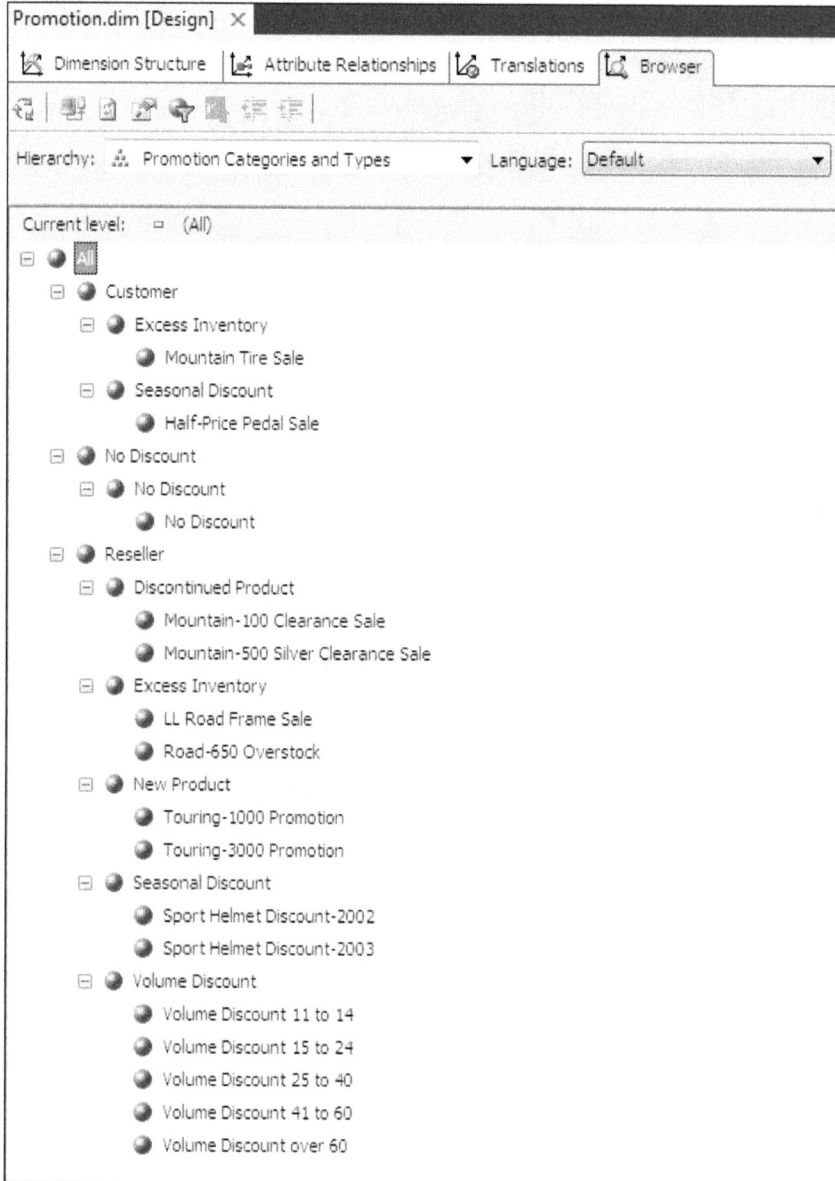

Promotion.dim [Design] ✕

  Dimension Structure | Attribute Relationships | Translations | Browser

Hierarchy: Promotion Categories and Types   ▼   Language: Default   ▼

Current level: ⊡ (All)

- ⊟ ● All
  - ⊟ ● Customer
    - ⊟ ● Excess Inventory
      - ● Mountain Tire Sale
    - ⊟ ● Seasonal Discount
      - ● Half-Price Pedal Sale
  - ⊟ ● No Discount
    - ⊟ ● No Discount
      - ● No Discount
  - ⊟ ● Reseller
    - ⊟ ● Discontinued Product
      - ● Mountain-100 Clearance Sale
      - ● Mountain-500 Silver Clearance Sale
    - ⊟ ● Excess Inventory
      - ● LL Road Frame Sale
      - ● Road-650 Overstock
    - ⊟ ● New Product
      - ● Touring-1000 Promotion
      - ● Touring-3000 Promotion
    - ⊟ ● Seasonal Discount
      - ● Sport Helmet Discount-2002
      - ● Sport Helmet Discount-2003
    - ⊟ ● Volume Discount
      - ● Volume Discount 11 to 14
      - ● Volume Discount 15 to 24
      - ● Volume Discount 25 to 40
      - ● Volume Discount 41 to 60
      - ● Volume Discount over 60

How it works...

As discussed earlier in this chapter, all the commands are sent to the Analysis Services instance using the XMLA language. You can review the statements SSDT creates during project deployment as well as during processing using the **SQL Server Profiler**, which is by far the best tool for learning Analysis Services. The Profiler allows choosing the type of events and columns you wish to capture and monitor. You can invoke the Profiler by navigating to **Start | All Programs | SQL Server 2012 | Performance Tools | SQL Server Profiler**. We will discuss Profiler in greater detail later in this book. For now, feel free to capture deployment and processing statements to learn the basics of Profiler.

Sorting the attributes

By default, each dimension attribute is sorted according to its key column values, but this may or may not fit your requirements. Additional options include sorting the attribute by its name or by another attribute's name or key. For example, ordering a month attribute within the date dimension based on an attribute name will clearly not work; this is because we would see February prior to January since the letter "F" precedes "J" in alphabetical order. More than likely we want to see data sorted based on the occurrence of months in a calendar, rather than alphabetically. We can manage the sorting of an attribute using the OrderBy and OrderByAttribute properties. In this recipe we will sort the **English Promotion Type** attribute based on **English Promotion Category**.

How to do it...

Let's get started with sorting the attributes:

1. Click on the **English Promotion Type** attribute on the **Dimension Structure** tab to list the properties of this attribute.

2. Within the **Properties** window, change the OrderBy property to **AttributeKey** and **OrderByAttribute** to **English Promotion Category**. To sort an attribute by another attribute's key or name, you must first define attribute relationships between the source attribute and the sorting attribute. In this case you have already defined the relationship between **English Promotion Type** and **English Promotion Category**. Therefore, you can pick **English Promotion Category** from the **OrderByAttribute** drop-down list.

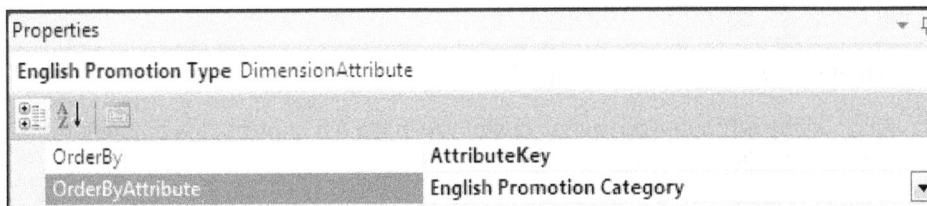

Properties		▾ ₽
English Promotion Type DimensionAttribute		
OrderBy	AttributeKey	
OrderByAttribute	English Promotion Category	▾

3. Save and deploy your changes, reprocess the Promotion dimension, and browse its **English Promotion Type** attribute hierarchy again. This time you'll see that instead of being sorted alphabetically, promotion types appear in the order of their corresponding categories:

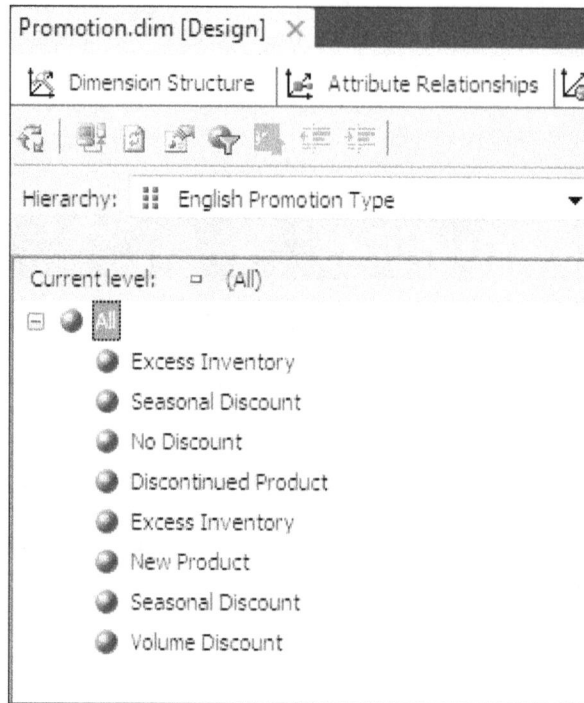

Promotion.dim [Design] ✕

Dimension Structure | Attribute Relationships

Hierarchy: ▦ English Promotion Type ▼

Current level: ▫ (All)

⊟ ● All
- Excess Inventory
- Seasonal Discount
- No Discount
- Discontinued Product
- Excess Inventory
- New Product
- Seasonal Discount
- Volume Discount

Customizing advanced attribute properties

Analysis Services allows customizing a number of attribute properties. Discussing each property with their corresponding screenshots would make this chapter extremely lengthy. Therefore, we will discuss commonly used advanced properties here and mention other relevant properties elsewhere in the book. We will refer to relevant dimensions available within the Adventure Works 2012 sample database so that you can examine existing dimensions instead of having to define each one of them from scratch.

How to do it...

To set a dimension attribute's property, perform the following steps:

1. Click on the attribute you wish to customize in the list of attributes on the leftmost pane of the dimension editor in SSDT.

2. Set focus to the **Properties** window to see a list of all the properties for the selected attribute.

3. Pick the property you want to change and set its value as desired.

4. Note that you cannot modify any property that is grayed within the properties window. For example, the **ProcessingState** and **ID** properties are read-only and cannot be changed.

How it works...

The `AttributeHierarchyEnabled` property controls whether the attribute is enabled for browsing. Recall that the **Dimension Wizard** allowed specifying whether each attribute should be enabled for browsing. The default value is `true`, which means users will be allowed to browse the data. Additionally, if the attribute hierarchy is not enabled (meaning that you set the `AttributeHierarchyEnabled` property to `false`), you will not be able to include it in any of the user-defined hierarchies. However, users can still query such attributes as member properties of other (enabled) attributes. An attribute that has a relationship with another attribute is known as the member property. For example, the `e-mail address` attribute in the `Employee` dimension has `AttributeHierarchyEnabled` set to false, but it is related to the `Employee` attribute and hence can be queried as the member property of the `Employee` attribute. To expose the `e-mail address` member property within Excel pivot table you would right-click on the `Employee` attribute (once it is selected on rows' axis) and navigate to **Show Properties In Report | Email Address**. Keep in mind that Analysis Services will not build indexes on any attributes for which the `AttributeHierarchyEnabled` property is set to "false". This will shorten the dimension's processing time but will also result in slower query performance for disabled attributes.

The `AttributeHierarchyVisible` property controls whether the attribute shows up in the list of attributes through which you can browse the data. The default value is true. Normally, it is recommended to set this property to false for attributes that are included in any user hierarchies. For example, since we included the promotion type and the promotion category in the user hierarchy, we could set the `AttributeHierarchyVisible` property for both of these attributes to false.

`AttributeHierarchyOptimizedState` can be set to **Fully Optimized** or **Not Optimized**. If the attribute is rarely used, we could set it to **Not Optimized** to prevent Analysis Services from building indexes for this attribute—doing so will reduce the total dimension size and shorten the processing time. Always keep this property to **Fully Optimized** (default value) for frequently used attributes to ensure the performance is optimal.

The `DefaultMember` property defines the member of the attribute hierarchy that is queried if the **MultiDimensional eXpressions** (**MDX**) statement does not explicitly reference a member from this hierarchy. You will learn the essentials of the MDX query language in *Chapter 6, MDX*. For now it's important to note that regardless of which hierarchies are explicitly mentioned in the MDX query, all hierarchies are queried. If a hierarchy isn't mentioned in the statement, its default member will be queried. Each hierarchy has a default member implicitly specified; by default, it is the **All** member. For example, if an MDX query doesn't reference any member of the **PromotionType** attribute hierarchy, the query will return values for all the promotion types. You can set the `DefaultMember` attribute by clicking on the ellipsis button next to this property; this activates the **Set Default Member** dialog. You can choose **No custom default**, choose a member from the list or specify an MDX expression to derive the default member. The last option is useful if you want to determine the default member dynamically. For example, in a time dimension, you could specify the MDX to identify the current month and use it as the default member. Alternatively, you could also supply MDX to find the last month for which the sales amount is greater than zero.

The `IsAggregatable` property controls whether the attribute hierarchy has the **All** level. The default value is "true". If you set this attribute's value to false, then the "All" level will not exist. Furthermore, since there is no "All" level, you should define an explicit default member to be used by queries which do not explicitly reference this hierarchy.

The `DiscretizationMethod` property allows grouping attribute members so that you don't have to show the full list but rather a few groups that represent the entire population of members. For example, the customer dimension has the yearly income attribute. As you might guess, each company could have millions of customers with many different income levels, so breaking down sales by each salary value would produce an impractical result set. Instead, we need to come up with a few income brackets to identify product sales' trends for each salary range. Of course, you can define your own way of categorizing income brackets. Alternatively, you could let Analysis Services do it for you—simply choose one of the predefined discretization algorithms: automatic, equal areas or clusters. The `DiscretizationBucketCount` property lets you specify the number of buckets you would like the cube users to see while browsing this attribute.

The `AttributeHierarchyOrdered` property controls whether the hierarchy is ordered. The default value is true. If a particular attribute is not used for querying very often, you can save some processing time by setting this property to false; in this case the `OrderBy` property is ignored and member values aren't sorted.

Creating parent-child dimensions

Business models often include entities that have a large number of levels. If you work for a large corporation, you don't have to think very long to come up with an example of a drawn-out hierarchy, simply refer to your organizational chart. You're likely to have entry-level employees who report to first-level managers, who in turn report to several other levels of managers, followed by directors, senior directors, vice presidents, and so on. The exact titles and number of levels in the food chain might vary, but you get the idea. Such structures are by no means limited to human resources; many organizations could have buildings that roll up to facilities that in turn roll up to networks and so on. The main challenge is that of modeling the large and unpredictable number of levels in a single dimension. If the number of levels in a hierarchy varies, the object is known as a *ragged hierarchy*. For example, in a given enterprise, there might be five levels of managers between John and the **Chief Executive Officer** (**CEO**) but only four levels between Jane and the CEO; even though both Jane and John are entry-level associates. If the number of levels is unknown or if it could change over time, it's best to use the Analysis Services parent-child hierarchy feature.

We build parent-child hierarchies upon self-referencing entities, meaning the dimension table will contain a key column and another column that references the key column. For example, the Adventure Works 2012 sample database has the `DimEmployee` table, which contains `EmployeeKey` and `ParentEmployeeKey` columns. The `ParentEmployeeKey` column refers to the `EmployeeKey` column because the parent employee (manager) is also employed by the same company and unless she is a CEO, she's also likely to have a manager. When we add this table to the DSV, Analysis Services automatically detects that the entity is self-referencing—the `ParentEmployeeKey` column refers to `EmployeeKey`.

How to do it...

Let's learn how to create a parent-child dimension using the following steps:

1. Invoke the **Dimension Wizard** as you would with a regular dimension. Select the **Use Existing Table** option.

2. Specify `DimEmployee` as the source table, `EmployeeKey` as the key column, and `FullName` as the name column. Refer to the *Creating named calculations and queries* recipe for defining `FullName`. Ignore any related tables the wizard might detect; they're irrelevant for this example.

3. Choose `Employee Key, Parent Employee Key, Title, Hire Date,` and `Department Name` as regular attributes.

4. Name the dimension as `Employee`. The wizard automatically detects self-reference and creates a parent-child hierarchy.

5. Once the dimension is created, rename the `Parent Employee Key` attribute to `Employees`, set the attribute `Type` property to `Person`, and the `Usage` property to `Parent`. The `Type` property assigns commonly used attribute types, such as person, account, currency, date, and so on to the attribute. Also rename the `Employee Key` attribute to `Employee`.

6. Set the `NamingTemplate` property to `Employee Level *;`. This property assigns the name to each level in a parent-child hierarchy. Since we cannot reasonably predict the number of levels (and we don't know the job titles at each level), we'll simply call each level Employee Level N, where *N* is the integer starting at Employee Level 02 (the top level is All).

7. Set the `MembersWithData` property to `NonLeafDataHidden`.

8. Save and process the dimension.

How it works...

If you have created a parent-child dimension as shown in the preceding section, the dimension browser will show the employees arranged in accordance to the organizational chart. Had we left the naming template property at its default (blank) value, the levels would simply be called level 02, level 03, and so on. Checking the **Hierarchy** dropdown confirms that the **Employee** dimension includes other, non-parent-child hierarchies as well: hire date, department name, and title. Refer to the following screenshot:

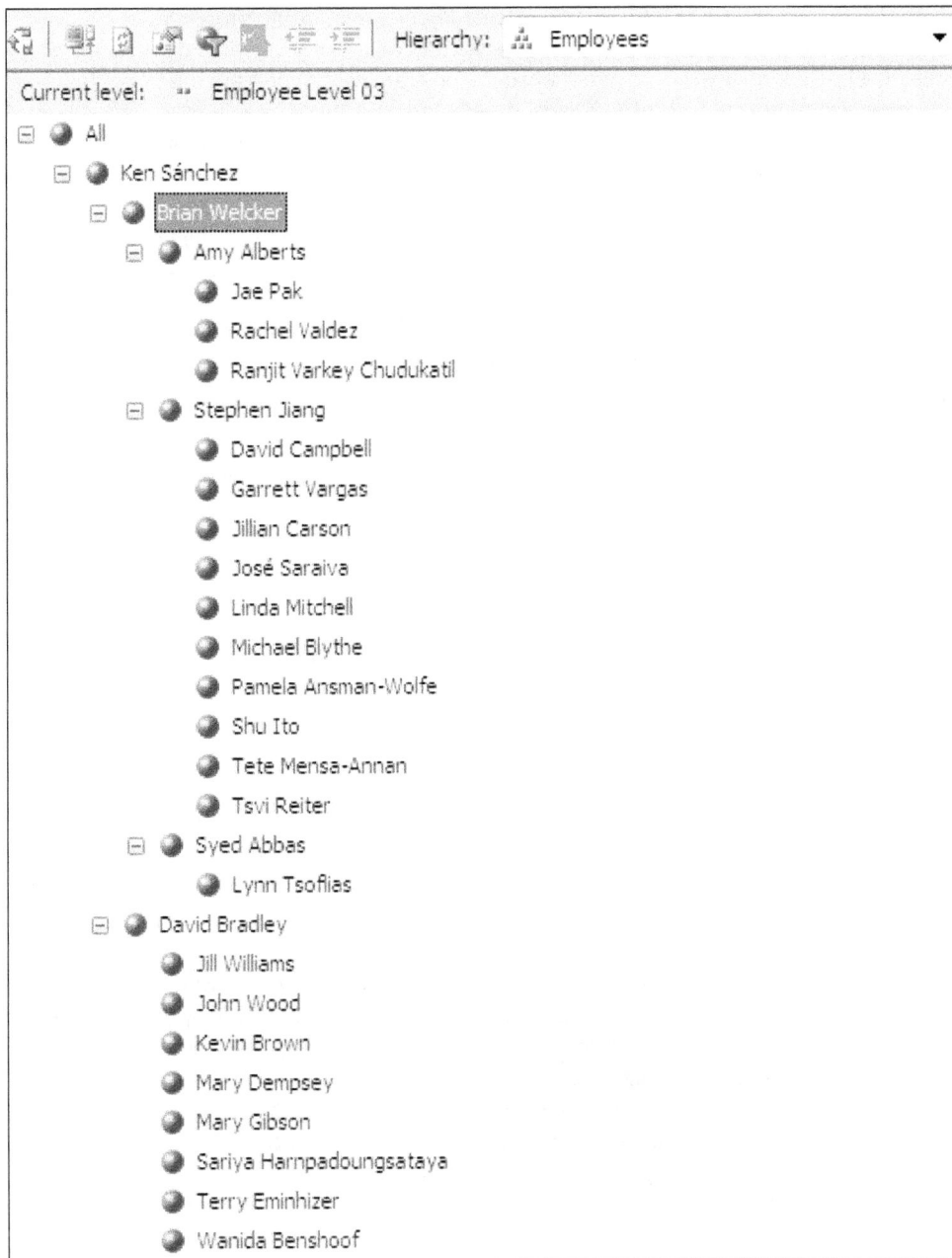

```
⟨⟩ │ ⊞ ⊡ ⊡ ⊕ ▣ ≡ ≡ │ Hierarchy:  ⚊ Employees                                    ▼
```

Current level: ᵃᵃ Employee Level 03

⊟ ● All
   ⊟ ● Ken Sánchez
      ⊟ ● Brian Welcker
         ⊟ ● Amy Alberts
            ● Jae Pak
            ● Rachel Valdez
            ● Ranjit Varkey Chudukatil
         ⊟ ● Stephen Jiang
            ● David Campbell
            ● Garrett Vargas
            ● Jillian Carson
            ● José Saraiva
            ● Linda Mitchell
            ● Michael Blythe
            ● Pamela Ansman-Wolfe
            ● Shu Ito
            ● Tete Mensa-Annan
            ● Tsvi Reiter
      ⊟ ● Syed Abbas
         ● Lynn Tsoflias
   ⊟ ● David Bradley
      ● Jill Williams
      ● John Wood
      ● Kevin Brown
      ● Mary Dempsey
      ● Mary Gibson
      ● Sariya Harnpadoungsataya
      ● Terry Eminhizer
      ● Wanida Benshoof

In the preceding example, you learned yet another important attribute property: `MembersWithData`. This property advises Analysis Services how to handle data values at non-leaf levels. Generally in a regular dimension, non-leaf levels aggregate data from leaf levels; for example, we'll sum up January, February, and March sales in order to find the value for the first quarter. In a parent-child scenario, the story is somewhat different because each manager could have her own sales in addition to the sales reported for salespeople whom she manages. Analysis Services creates "data members" for such managers; each data member reflects the data found in the underlying relational source, rather than the aggregation of subordinate salespeople's sales. You set the `MembersWithData` property for the **Employees** hierarchy to `NonLeafDataHidden` so that managers' data members don't show up. The default value for the `MembersWithData` property is `NonLeafDataVisible`; if you keep the default value, a manager's sales figure will show up as though she was reporting to herself. For example, notice that the list of Amy Albert's direct reports includes Amy Alberts after I switch the property to `NonLeafDataVisible`:

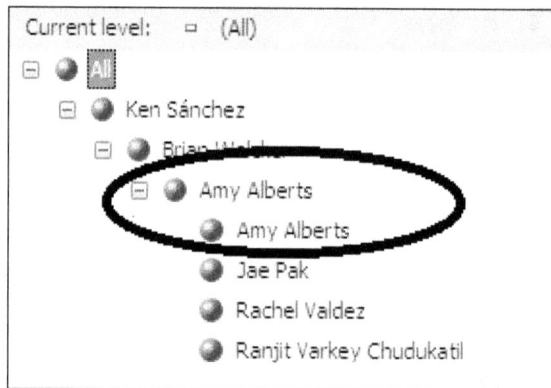

There's more...

Unfortunately, the flexibility that parent-child dimensions offer does come with a price of performance penalty. In general you should try to use flattened dimensions with a finite number of levels in lieu of parent-child dimensions when possible. For example, we could model the sample Employees hierarchy to include six levels (Employee Level 1 through Employee Level 6) since this is a sample database and number of levels will not change. In real-world applications you may or may not have such luxury; if your company decides to add a new layer of employees, you would have to modify your dimension structure and reprocess the measure groups referencing this dimension. If you can't completely avoid parent-child structures, try to limit each cube to only one parent-child dimension.

Creating the date and time dimensions

The date and time dimensions (sometimes also referred to as periodicity dimensions) are essential for the majority of data warehousing and business intelligence solutions. Analysis Services offers a couple of different options for creating time dimensions; you can create a corresponding table that contains the necessary columns in the relational database, or use a time dimension defined on the Analysis Services server. Creating the time dimension using a table in the underlying data source isn't very different from creating other dimensions; the primary difference is that you advise Analysis Services that the dimension you're creating should be of the time dimension type. This enables you to use certain MDX functions that are specific to time dimensions. The server-side time dimension does not have a corresponding relational table; this option is useful when you do not have necessary permissions to create or alter relational objects. Additionally, you don't have to maintain data or use storage space for a server-level time dimension. However, a server-level time dimension does have some limitations and might not fit every requirement.

How to do it...

To create a server-level time dimension perform the following steps:

1. Invoke the **Dimension Wizard** as you would with a regular dimension.

2. The **Select Creation Method** dialog allows you to pick the type of dimension you're about to create. As you saw earlier in this chapter (the *Creating simple dimension* recipe), you can define a dimension based on an existing table. Additionally, you could also have Analysis Services generate a time table within your relational data source as long as you have sufficient permissions to do so. The other option is to define the time dimension on the server without creating the dimension table in the data source. For this example, select the **Generate a time table on the server** option and click on **Next**.

3. The following screen allows choosing time periods you wish to include in your server-level time dimension. As shown in the screenshot, you can choose the first and last calendar dates included in the dimension, the first day of the week, time periods (day, month, quarter, year, and so on), as well as the language for time members. Unfortunately, the server-level time dimension does not support time periods under date; for example, you don't have the option to include hour, minute, or second levels, which could be quite useful for some scenarios (for example, we might want to examine stock prices by hour). Having a relational table for your time dimension, of course, allows the flexibility of including finer attributes. Ensure that the **Define Time Periods** screen looks similar to the following screenshot before you click on **Next**.

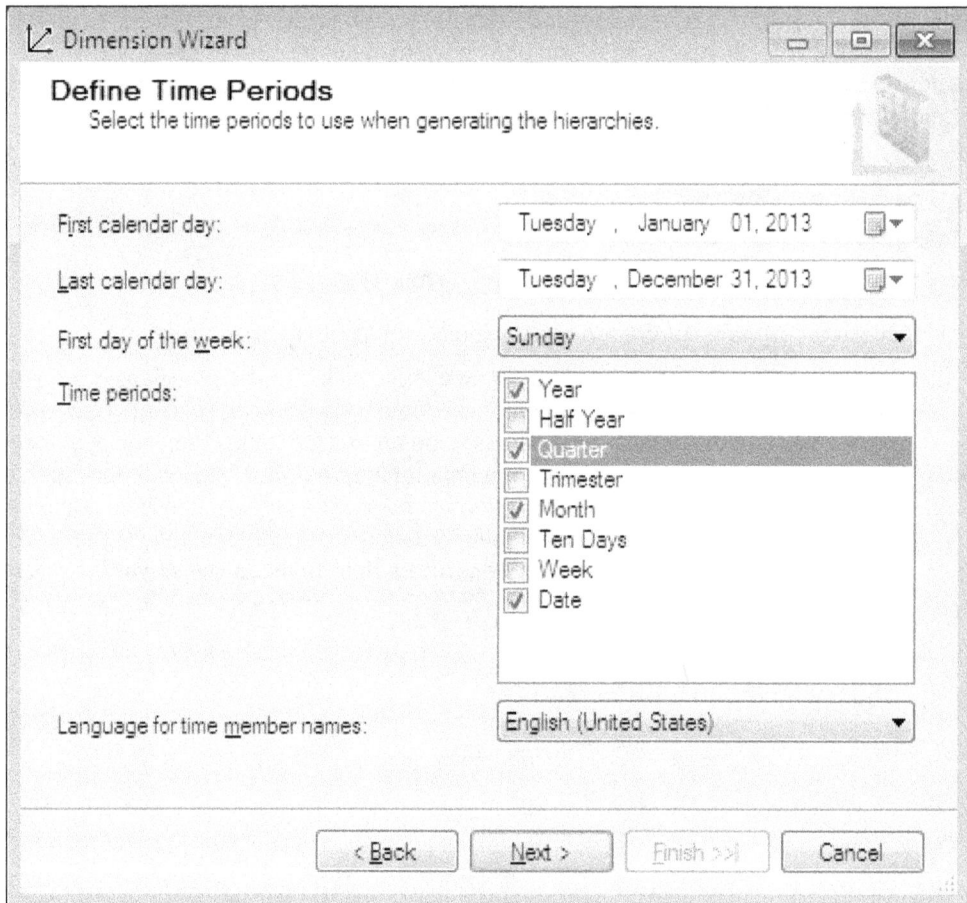

Dimension Wizard

Define Time Periods
Select the time periods to use when generating the hierarchies.

First calendar day: Tuesday , January 01, 2013

Last calendar day: Tuesday , December 31, 2013

First day of the week: Sunday

Time periods:
- ☑ Year
- ☐ Half Year
- ☑ Quarter
- ☐ Trimester
- ☑ Month
- ☐ Ten Days
- ☐ Week
- ☑ Date

Language for time member names: English (United States)

< Back   Next >   Finish >>| Cancel

---

4. The next screen lets you choose the type of calendars to be included in the time dimension. By default, the dimension will only include a regular calendar, but you can also include fiscal or manufacturing calendars. Should you choose any non-standard calendars, the dimension will have several additional attributes; you can review the list of all the attributes on the final screen, which also allows you to specify the dimension name.

5. Once you deploy and process your server-level time dimension, you can browse its data.

To create a time dimension based on an existing relational table, complete the following steps:

1. Invoke the **Dimension Wizard** and select the **Use an existing table** option. Choose appropriate columns for time dimension key and name.

2. On the **Select Dimension Attributes** screen, choose the attributes you wish to include in your time dimension. Additionally, change the **Attribute Type** option by clicking on the drop-down menu and choosing the respective attribute type. For example, for **English Month Name** you would select **Date→Calendar→Month**.

3. Once you provide a descriptive name for the dimension, click on **Finish**. If you check the dimension's **Type** property, it will be set to **Time**, and the **English Month Name** attribute's type property will be set to **Months**. If you forget to set some attribute properties while working through the wizard, you can correct the property value within the dimension designer.

There's more...

This chapter taught you how to define and configure data sources, create and extend DSVs, and design the most commonly encountered dimensions. There are other types of dimensions, which are seldom used in real-world applications. With the knowledge you acquired in this chapter, you are ready to build typical dimensions. You should refer to product documentation for any intricate scenarios requiring more specialized dimension types.

A common requirement for enterprise-level cubes is to handle transactions that occur in multiple timezones. The simplest approach is to convert all time-related values into a common timezone within the relational database. Although you could implement support for various time zones in the Analysis Services solution, doing so will require significant effort and could impose significant overhead for your queries. Please refer to http://cwebbbi.wordpress.com/2005/11/01/handling-time-zones/ for further information.

3
Creating Analysis Services Cubes

In this chapter, we will cover the following recipes:

- ▸ Defining measure groups and measures
- ▸ Setting measure properties
- ▸ Browsing the cube data
- ▸ Dimension usage with measure group
- ▸ Examining cube file structures
- ▸ Partitioning strategies
- ▸ Defining partition slice
- ▸ Merging partitions
- ▸ Defining aggregation designs
- ▸ Distinct count measure groups
- ▸ Enabling write-back feature
- ▸ Deployment options

Introduction

This chapter contains recipes for building **SQL Server Analysis Services** (**SSAS**) cubes. Much like we did in *Chapter 2, Defining Analysis Services Dimensions*, let's start with building straightforward cubes and then work our way up to more complex requirements.

Before you delve into building cubes, you need to become familiar with terms describing the architecture of an Analysis Services cube. Each Analysis Services database may contain one or more cubes. You can build each cube based on one or multiple fact tables found in the relational data warehouse. Each measure group represents a collection of numeric metrics (or *measures*) found in a single fact table. However, depending on the requirements, you may have to build several measure groups based on a single fact table. Each measure group within a cube may use multiple dimensions available within the database. Not all database dimensions need to be exposed with each measure group. Each measure group can be split up into multiple *partitions* to speed up processing as well as querying operations.

Defining measure groups and measures

The first cube recipe will create a simplistic cube based on the `FactResellerSales` fact table and will include only two dimensions: promotion and date.

To create a cube and its related entities, you must first define the data sources from where we'll import data and **Data Source Views** (**DSVs**), which define necessary relationships between dimension and fact tables, as well as dimensions you intend to include in your cube. Please refer to *Chapter 2, Defining Analysis Services Dimensions*, for recipes on defining data sources, DSVs, and creating dimensions

Getting ready

Create a new SSDT project called `SSAS_Cookbook_Chapter3` and save it to any location of your choice. Create a data source view with all the tables via the `AdventureWorksDW2012` database. Add the promotion dimension as discussed in *Chapter 2, Defining Analysis Services Dimensions*. Also add the date dimension based on the `DimDate` table and include the year, month, and date attributes. The date attribute should be based on the `DateKey` column, and use `FullDateAlternateKey` as the name column. The date attribute should also be the key attribute of the dimension. The month attribute must use the `MonthNumberOfYear` and `CalendarYear` columns as keys and the `EnglishMonthName` as the name column. Be sure to create attribute relationships between the month and year attributes.

How to do it...

Let's build your first cube by performing the following steps:

1. Right-click on the `Cubes` folder in the **Solution Explorer** window and choose **New Cube**. This activates the cube wizard.

2. Much like the dimension wizard, the cube wizard also allows you to build a cube-based on existing tables.

3. Other alternatives include creating an empty cube or generating tables in the relational data source. Creating an empty cube will allow you to add necessary measure groups and dimensions manually. You will be able to add/remove dimensions and measure groups even if you create a cube-based on existing tables, so the empty cube option isn't particularly useful. Generating tables in the data source option allows you to use one of the built-in templates to create the sample Adventure Works SQL Server database tables.

4. For this exercise let's choose **Use existing tables** and click on **Next**, as shown in the following screenshot:

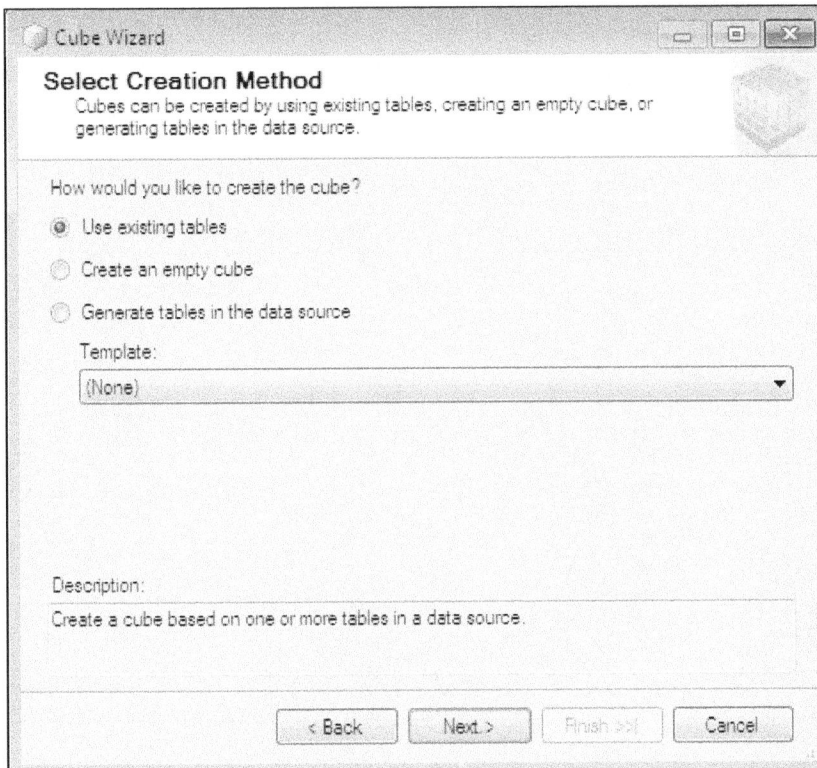

5. The following screen allows you to choose the data source and the fact table(s) to be included in the cube. Since the project only contains one data source view, the wizard automatically uses it by default. Notice the **Suggest** button: if you click on this button, SSDT will recommend tables that could be used as measure group sources. Since measures are normally numeric, SSDT will suggest using tables that contain numeric columns. If you choose multiple fact tables, the cube will include a separate measure group for each of them. Let's only check `FactResellerSales` and click on **Next**:

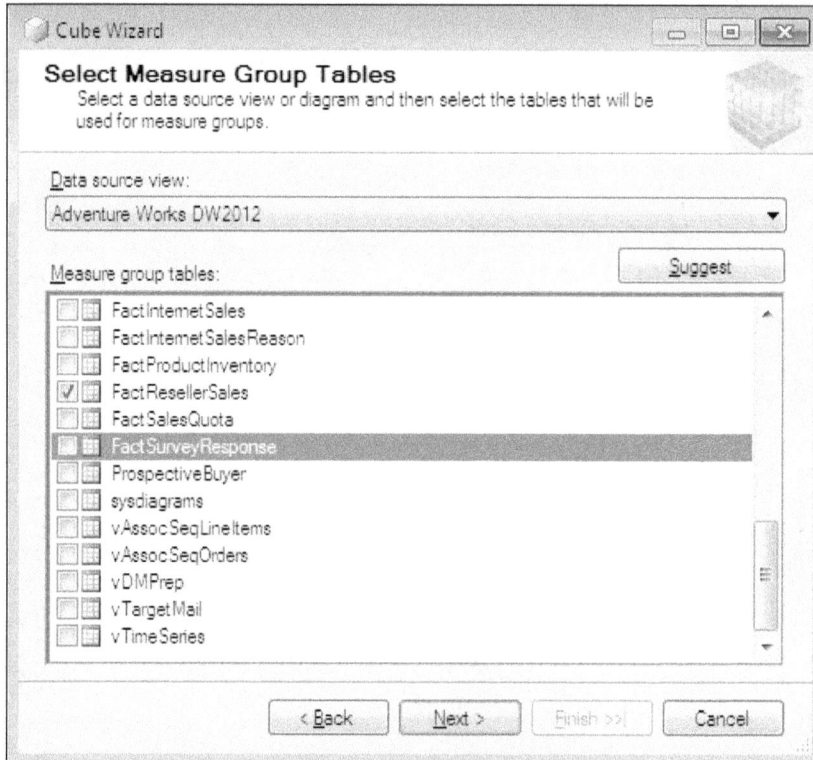

6. You can choose the measures you wish to include in the cube on the following screen. The wizard automatically preselects all the numeric columns, but this may or may not be the desired outcome. For example, although **Revision Number** is indeed a numeric column, exposing it as a measure would not add any value to reseller sales analysis, so let's uncheck it. The revision number is not additive; also, we cannot add revision numbers across orders to obtain any meaningful value. However, metadata items such as revision number (or invoice number) can indeed be useful for reporting and could be included in fact dimensions, as you will learn later in this chapter.

7. The wizard includes a count of rows for each fact table, in this case, **Fact Reseller Sales Count**. We can rename measures within the Cube Editor, so let's leave measure names as found on the screen and click on **Next**, as shown in the following screenshot:

Note that if you set focus on any measure and right-click on it, you can rename the measure. For example, the screenshot shows the Unit Price Discount Pct measure selected so that we can spell out the word "percent" to avoid any confusion. As with dimension attributes, it is essential to provide meaningful names for your measures.

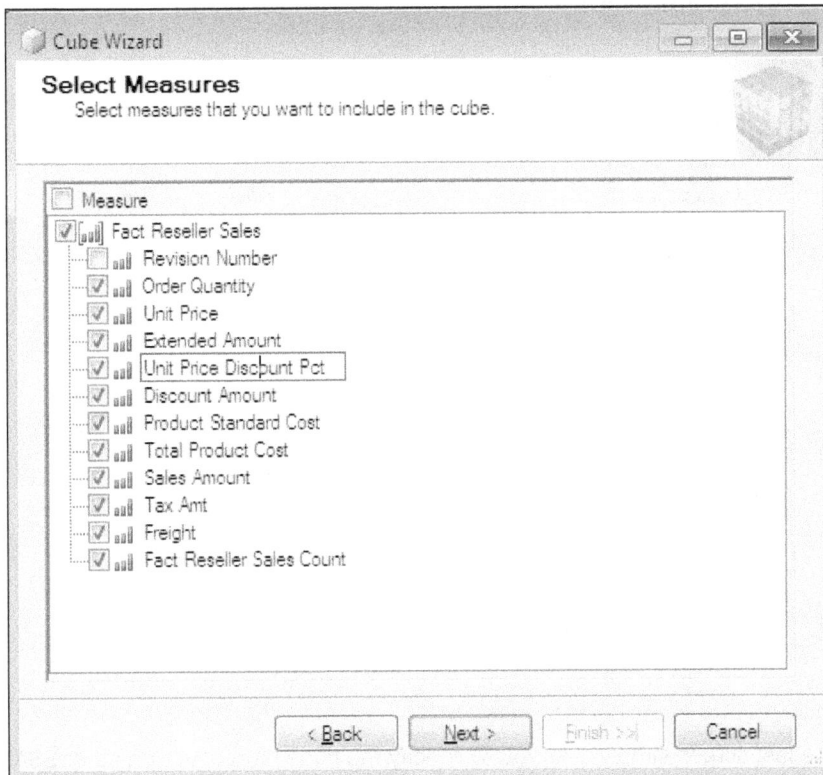

8. The next screen asks for dimensions you would like to include with the cube. Since you only have two dimensions (promotion and date), include both and click on **Next**.

9. The wizard detects relationships with other tables and suggests creating additional dimensions via the following screen. As shown in the screenshot, you have an option to create **Sales Territory**, **Currency**, **Product**, **Fact Reseller Sales**, and **Employee** dimensions based on existing tables. Additionally, the wizard suggests creating a dimension based on the fact table: FactResellerSales.

10. Although you should never expose fact level dimensions for ad hoc querying/browsing data, such dimensions could be very useful for reporting. For example, we could include the invoice numbers and order revision numbers on a report, and neither of these attributes could be conveniently exposed through other dimensions. Though this might sound like a nice shortcut for creating dimensions, the cube wizard doesn't provide any facilities to customize dimension or attribute properties. Therefore, I do not recommend this method of building dimensions. Instead, uncheck the box next to **Dimension** and click on **Next** as shown in the following screenshot:

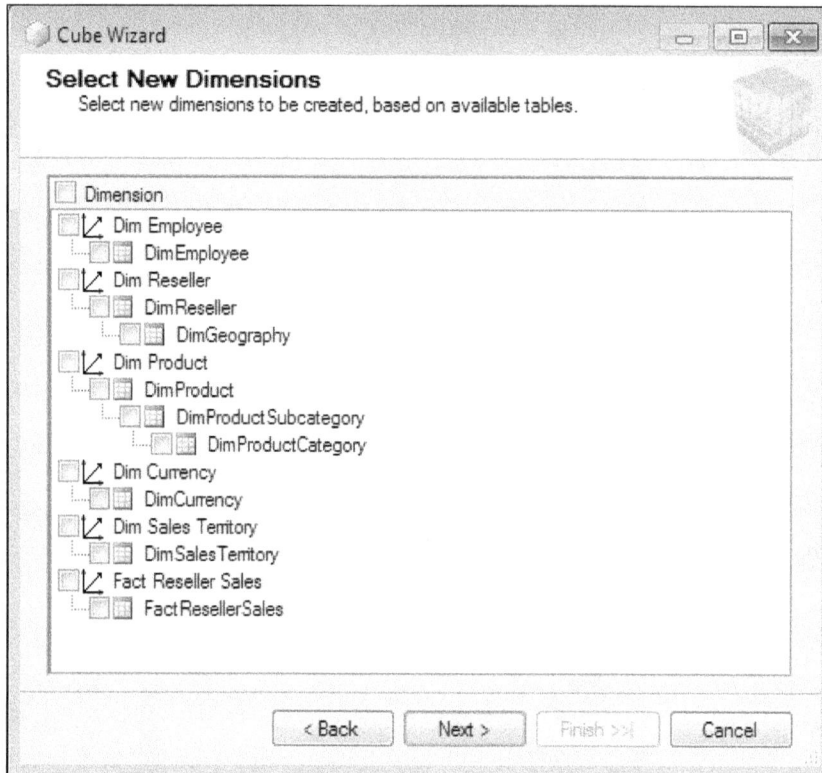

11. The last screen simply asks you to specify the cube name. As with other SSAS objects, you should choose descriptive, meaningful names for your cubes.

Note that every object (cube, dimension, attribute, measure, and so on) within
the Analysis Services project has an ID (identifier) and name. The object ID
defaults to its name at the time of object creation. You *cannot* change the
object's identifier without dropping and recreating the object. This might not
sound like a big deal, but keep in mind that all the XMLA commands refer to
the object's identifier. For example, if you have a dimension that you happen to
initially name "my snazzy dimension," then this would be the string you will see
anytime you process the dimension, even if you later rename the dimension
to "employees". Having non-descriptive identifiers makes debugging difficult,
so get in the habit of naming objects appropriately when creating them.

12. After you complete the cube wizard, the SSDT cube design window should resemble
the following screenshot. As you can see, the cube designer has multiple tabs on the
top ribbon; each of these has a specific purpose you will learn about. The data source
view window includes the tables you used to create the cube. The **Measures** and
Dimensions windows include the listing of measures and dimensions respectively.

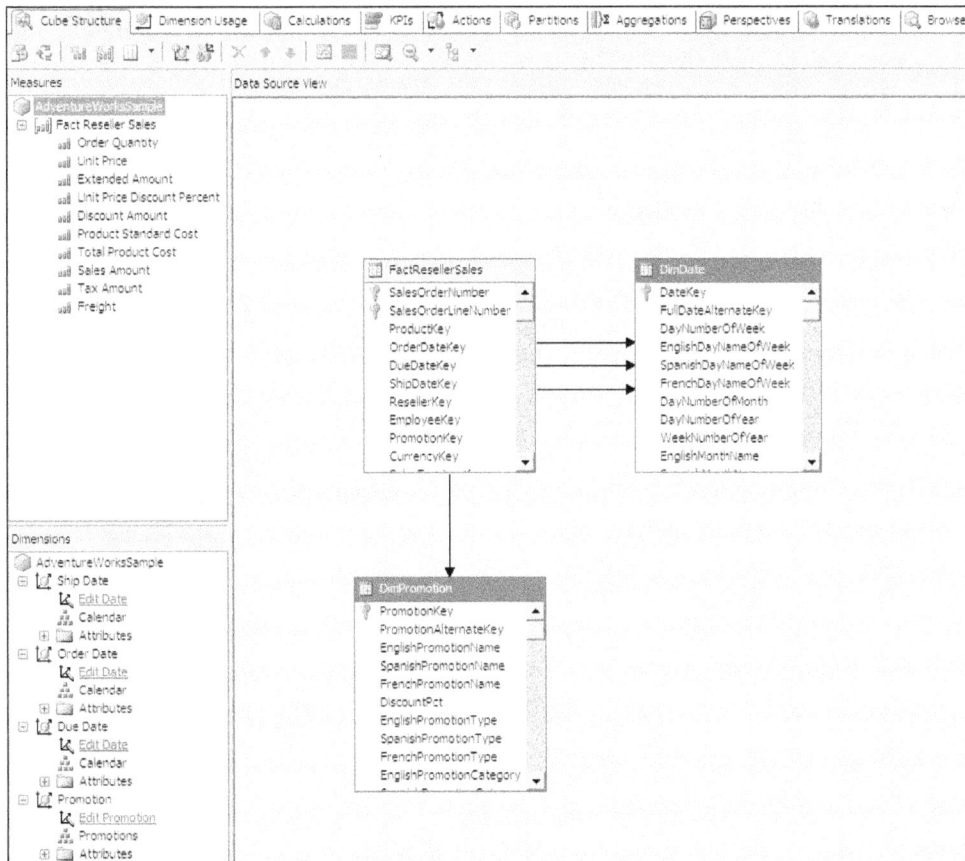

13. You should notice on the **Dimensions** pane that the cube has four dimensions even though we had advised the **Cube Wizard** to only include date and promotion dimensions.

14. Recall from *Chapter 2, Defining Analysis Services Dimensions*, that each dimension table could have one or multiple relationships with the fact table. The `FactResellerSales` references date dimension's `DateKey` column three times: `OrderDateKey`, `DueDateKey`, and `ShipDateKey`.

15. The **Cube Wizard** recognizes this and creates three separate cube dimensions based on a single date dimension available in the database. Such dimensions are called *role playing* dimensions. They can be very helpful—instead of storing data in three separate tables, corresponding to three SSAS objects, you only have to store and process date-related data once.

> The role playing dimension is a great feature but sadly does *not* provide the option of renaming attributes. When you expose role playing dimensions for browsing, it would be very helpful if we could show "ship date month" under the Ship Date dimension and "due date month" under the Due Date dimension. Unfortunately we are limited to having just one attribute name, "month". If you require the additional flexibility of having different attribute names, you must create separate physical dimensions for ship and due dates—you can't use role playing. One way to work around this limitation is by creating single-level, user-defined hierarchies within each role-playing dimension. For example, you could build a ship date month hierarchy within the ship date, a due date month within the due date, and so on.

16. If you click on the plus sign (**+**) next to each dimension within dimensions' window, you will see the attributes and hierarchies available within the database dimension. Using the **Properties** window you can set various properties for each dimension and attribute within the scope of the current cube. The dimensions included in the cube are referred to as *cube dimensions*; as discussed before, each measure group (or even each cube) may or may not include all database dimensions.

17. The **Visible** property advises SSAS whether a particular attribute or user hierarchy should be available for browsing within the cube. The **Aggregation** wizard uses the **Aggregation Usage** property to determine whether a particular attribute should be included in aggregations—precalculated summary tables. You will learn how to build aggregations later in this chapter.

18. Clicking on the **Edit** option for each dimension simply opens a dimension editor. Keep in mind that cube dimension properties do not have to match database dimension properties; for example, the date attribute could be visible in a database dimension but hidden in a particular cube, where exposing such a level of detail is not desired.

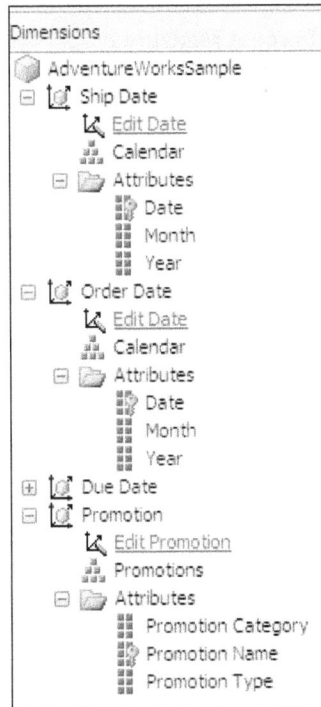

Setting measure properties

Now let's focus our attention on the measures window; this allows configuring various properties for the measure group and for each measure.

How to do it...

To set the properties perform the following steps:

1. Highlight the measure (or measure group) of interest and edit its properties in the **Properties** window.

2. Set the **FormatString** property to **Currency** for the **Unit Price, Extended Amount, Discount Amount, Product Standard Cost, Total Product Cost, Sales Amount, Tax Amount** (spell out the amount in the measure name field), and **Freight** measures. Set the **FormatString** property to **Percent** for the **Unit Price Discount Percent** measure.

3. Set the **Display** Folder property to **PRICE** for the **Unit Price, Extended Amount, Sales Amount, Tax Amount**, and **Freight** measures. Set the **Display Folder** property to **COST** for the **Product Standard Cost** and **Total Product Cost** measures.

4. Save your project; set deployment properties as shown in *Chapter 2, Defining Analysis Services Dimensions*, and deploy and process your database.

   The **Unit Price Discount Percent Measure** properties are shown in the following screenshot for your reference:

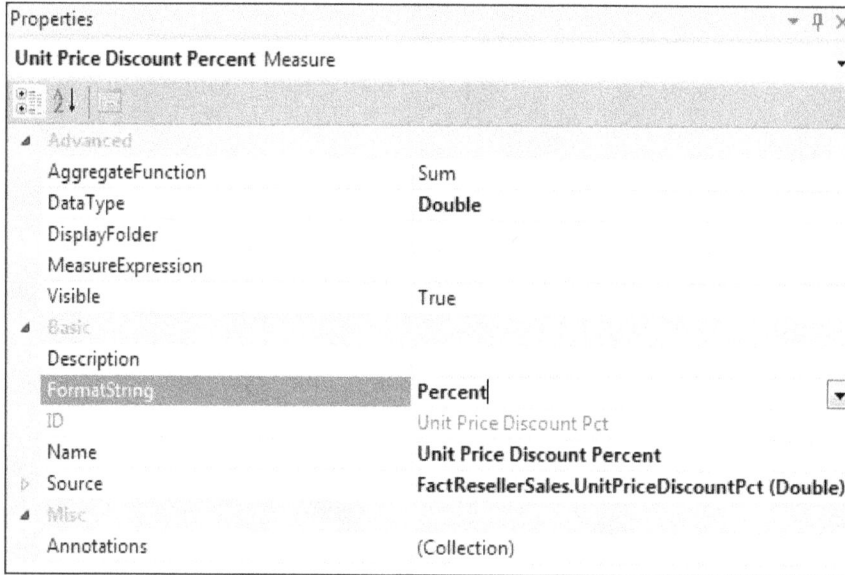

Properties	▾ ↕ ×
Unit Price Discount Percent Measure	▾

⊿ Advanced	
AggregateFunction	Sum
DataType	**Double**
DisplayFolder	
MeasureExpression	
Visible	True
⊿ Basic	
Description	
FormatString	Percent
ID	Unit Price Discount Pct
Name	**Unit Price Discount Percent**
▷ Source	**FactResellerSales.UnitPriceDiscountPct (Double)**
⊿ Misc	
Annotations	(Collection)

There's more...

The following table lists the most commonly used measure properties:

Measure property	Explanation
Aggregation Function	This function determines how measure values are supposed to be aggregated from the bottom-level (also known as *leaf level*) to the top-level of each hierarchy. SSAS supports *additive*, *semi-additive*, and *non-additive* aggregate functions. The semi-additive functions require a time dimension (the dimension's type property must be set to "time"). Such measures can only be aggregated across the time dimension. The non-additive measures cannot be aggregated across any dimension and are reported only at the leaf level.
	Analysis Services supports the following measure aggregation functions:
	▸ **SUM**: This is the sum of values;
	▸ **COUNT**: This is the count of values;
	▸ **MIN**: This reports the smallest value;
	▸ **MAX**: This reports the largest value;
	▸ **DISTINCT COUNT**: This is the count of unique values;
	▸ **NONE**: This reports a non-additive value only at the leaf level;
	▸ **ByAccount**: This aggregates non-additive values depending on the account; this function is specifically for financial reporting / accounting applications. The `ByAccount` measure requires a dimension, which has the type property set to account;
	▸ **AverageOfChildren**: This reports the semi-additive average value determined by summing the values found at a lower-level and dividing them by the count of values;

Measure property	Explanation
	▸ **FirstChild**: This reports the first semi-additive value, for example, the value of January 01 if you browse January's data;
	▸ **LastChild**: This reports the last semi-additive value, for example, the value of January 31st if you browse January's data;
	▸ **FirstNonEmpty**: This reports the first semi-additive, non-null (non-empty) value. For example, if the first date in January with a non-null value is January 10th, you will see the data of January 10th when browsing the data for January;
	▸ **LastNonEmpty**: This reports the last semi-additive non-null (non-empty) value.
DataType	By default, SSAS measures inherit the data type from the underlying data source. However, the list of supported data types varies from one relational platform to the next, so you need to ensure that the relational type can be mapped to the SSAS type.
DisplayFolder	By default, all the measures show up under the Measures folder in the client application. If you have multiple measure groups within a single cube, measures would be listed under the corresponding measure groups. If you have many measures within a measure group, it makes sense to organize related measures into folders, for example, cost-related measures could be included in the COST folder and price-related measures under PRICE. The DisplayFolder property allows you to type in the folder name. If you have used a folder name once, you can choose the same name for another measure from a drop-down box instead of having to retype it.
MeasureExpression	This function allows specifying the MDX formula for deriving a measure's value based on another measure. Measure expressions are useful for many-to-many relationships discussed later in this chapter. You will learn more about measure expressions in *Chapter 4, Extending and Customizing Cubes*.
FormatString	This is a very useful property for customizing how the measure is presented to cube users. For example, we could specify that the measure should be formatted in currency or percent. You can also specify the number of digits to the right of a decimal point.

Measure property	Explanation
Visible	The supported values of this property are true (default) and false. You might want to create a measure that is used for further calculations but should not be exposed to the user. In such a case you'd set the measure's visible property to false.
Source	This function defines various properties of the relational column used as the source of the measure. You can set the data type and size (for seldom-used textual measures). The additional useful properties in this group include: ▸ NullProcessing: This property advises SSAS whether null values should result in an error or be quietly translated to zero. In terms of Analysis Services, zero is the same as NULL. ▸ InvalidXMLCharacters: This property advises SSAS how to treat invalid XML characters at query time. You might need to tweak this property for dimension attributes more frequently than measures, since measures are normally numeric whereas dimension attributes could include special characters such as &, <, and >, which have special meanings in XML. Data with such characters is generally processed fine but could return errors during querying (the error will simply state "invalid character," and will not provide any specifics). You have an option to *remove* invalid characters or *replace* them with a question mark (?).

Browsing the cube data

Now that you have created, deployed, and processed a cube, you're ready (and probably anxious) to review the result. You can browse cube data using SSDT, an SSMS cube browser, or a client tool of your choice. Prior versions of SSMS and SSDT (formerly known as Business Intelligence Development Studio or BIDS) used Office Web Components (OWC), which is a deprecated technology and is no longer available with Analysis Services 2012. Although OWC had its share of issues, with the SSMS 2008R2 (and earlier) cube browser, we could navigate through user hierarchies one level at a time. Unfortunately SSMS and SSDT 2012 no longer offer this functionality, which is very limiting, as you will see shortly. With SSMS 2012, Microsoft included a shortcut to launch Excel, which provides a much richer user interface for browsing cube data. Of course, this design presumes that each developer would have Microsoft Office (or at least Excel version 2007 or later) installed on the same machine where you have SSMS, which may or may not be true. Hopefully, the following release of SQL Server will include a better cube browser. The good news is that if you still have SSMS 2008R2, you can use it to browse SSAS 2012 cubes.

How to do it...

To browse a cube perform the following steps:

1. Connect to the Analysis Services instance where you deployed and processed your solution.

2. Navigate to the database you created, expand the `Cubes` folder, right-click on the cube, and select **Browse**. Within SSDT you can simply click on the **Browser** tab of the cube editor.

3. You see that measures are listed under the **Fact Reseller Sales** measure group and some of them are organized further into `COST` and `PRICE` folders. Expand the `COST` folder and drag the `Total Product Cost` measure into the grid area. Alternatively, you can right-click on the measure and select **Add to Query**. Do the same with the **Unit Price** measure found in the `PRICE` folder.

4. Next expand the `Due Date` dimension and add the `Due Date.Calendar` hierarchy to the query.

5. Notice that SSMS/SSDT browsers immediately flatten out the hierarchy and list every single member found in the hierarchy. This might not cause a huge concern for a sample database with a few hundred members in the calendar hierarchy, but real-world applications are likely to have much larger dimensions.

6. Flattening the result set does not allow you to have the same experience offered by Excel and other cube-browsing tools. Note that the SSMS cube browser ignored the formatting choices we applied to the **Unit Price** and **Total Product Cost** measures.

7. The new cube browser does offer a nice improvement in being able to review and edit the MDX generated by SSMS. If you click on the **Design Mode** button found at the right-most corner of the top ribbon, you will see the following MDX statement:

```
SELECT
NON EMPTY { [Measures].[Unit Price], [Measures].[Total
   Product Cost] } ON COLUMNS,
NON EMPTY { ([Due Date].[Calendar].[Date].ALLMEMBERS ) }
  DIMENSION PROPERTIES MEMBER_CAPTION, MEMBER_UNIQUE_NAME ON
  ROWS
  FROM [AdventureWorksSample]
CELL PROPERTIES VALUE, BACK_COLOR, FORE_COLOR,
   FORMATTED_VALUE, FORMAT_STRING, FONT_NAME, FONT_SIZE,
   FONT_FLAGS
```

Downloading the example code

You can download the example code files for all Packt books you have purchased from your account at http://www.packtpub.com. If you purchased this book elsewhere, you can visit http://www.packtpub.com/support and register to have the files e-mailed directly to you.

8. Do note that although you can edit the MDX, you cannot include functions that are not supported by the cube browser. For example, the browser does not support sorting data, so neither can we include the *order* function to sort data nor can we include any dimension, except for measures on columns (yet another limitation of the 2012 cube browser).

9. The cube browser does allow us to filter data. Click on the **Select dimension** drop-down box above the result set and select the Promotion dimension. Next, select the **Promotions** hierarchy, and set the filter to **Volume Discount 41 to 60** (filter expression dropdown allows you to pick an option from the list of available promotion categories, types, and names). Switch to the design view again to see the updated MDX. Notice that this time the query used a subselect (subquery) to limit the output. Also have a look at the following code:

```
SELECT
NON EMPTY { [Measures].[Unit Price], [Measures].[Total
  Product Cost] } ON COLUMNS,
NON EMPTY { ([Due Date].[Calendar].[Date].ALLMEMBERS ) }
DIMENSION PROPERTIES MEMBER_CAPTION, MEMBER_UNIQUE_NAME ON
  ROWS
```

```
FROM
( SELECT
( { [Promotion].[Promotions].[Promotion Name].&[5] } ) ON
  COLUMNS
   FROM [AdventureWorksSample])
WHERE ( [Promotion].[Promotions].[Promotion Name].&[5] )
CELL PROPERTIES VALUE, BACK_COLOR, FORE_COLOR,
   FORMATTED_VALUE, FORMAT_STRING, FONT_NAME, FONT_SIZE,
   FONT_FLAGS
```

With the updated MDX, the result set is much smaller, as shown in the following screenshot:

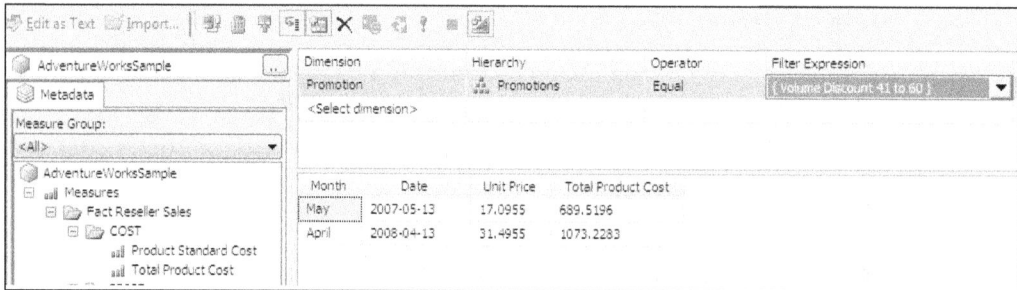

10. Click on the Excel icon found next to the **Language** dropdown on top of the screen—the icon's tool tip states **Analyze in Excel**. Again, the prerequisite for analyzing in Excel is that you have Excel installed on your computer. Excel isn't part of the SQL Server product suite and isn't installed as part of the Analysis Services installation.

11. This opens an Excel worksheet with a Pivot Table. Select the **Unit Price** and **Total Product Cost** measures, then drag the `Promotions` hierarchy onto rows and `Due Date.Calendar` hierarchy on filters. Now your Pivot Table should resemble the next screenshot, and you can browse the data as in any other Pivot Table—choose various years within the due date dimension's calendar hierarchy and expand and collapse the **Promotions** hierarchy to review different promotion categories, types, and names. We could also include ship date or order date hierarchies on rows, columns, or filters as shown in the following screenshot. Note that Excel recognizes the formatting we applied to measures.

	A	B	C
1	Due Date.Calendar	All	
2			
3	Row Labels	Unit Price	Total Product Cost
4	⊞No Discount	$26,190,467.25	$72,731,911.96
5	⊞Reseller	$855,388.50	$7,248,202.42
6	Grand Total	$27,045,855.75	$79,980,114.38

PivotTable Fields

Choose fields to add to report:

- Due Date
  - ✓ Due Date.Calendar
  - More Fields
- Order Date
  - Order Date.Calendar
  - More Fields
- Promotion
  - ✓ Promotions

Drag fields between areas below:

FILTERS
Due Date.Calen... ▼

COLUMNS
Σ Values ▼

ROWS
Promotions ▼

Σ VALUES
Unit Price ▼
Total Product Cost ▼

Now that we're in the most ubiquitous cube browsing tool Excel we can easily create useful reports. For example, the following report analyzes 2007 and 2008 reseller sales based on promotions:

Due Date.Calendar	(Multiple Items)					
	Column Labels					
	Unit Price		Total Product Cost		Total Unit Price	Total Total Product Cost
Row Labels	2007	2008	2007	2008		
⊟No Discount	$9,783,838.34	$5,582,712.99	$28,278,262.38	$15,124,875.10	$15,366,551.33	$43,403,137.48
⊟No Discount	$9,783,838.34	$5,582,712.99	$28,278,262.38	$15,124,875.10	$15,366,551.33	$43,403,137.48
No Discount	$9,783,838.34	$5,582,712.99	$28,278,262.38	$15,124,875.10	$15,366,551.33	$43,403,137.48
⊟Reseller	$546,424.34	$83,072.78	$4,092,964.77	$926,476.02	$629,497.12	$5,019,440.80
⊟Discontinued Product		$19,096.66		$117,739.24	$19,096.66	$117,739.24
Mountain-500 Silver Clearance Sale		$19,096.66		$117,739.24	$19,096.66	$117,739.24
⊟New Product	$388,653.05		$1,849,552.01		$388,653.05	$1,849,552.01
Touring-1000 Promotion	$220,288.07		$1,129,236.68		$220,288.07	$1,129,236.68
Touring-3000 Promotion	$168,364.98		$720,315.33		$168,364.98	$720,315.33
⊟Seasonal Discount	$1,322.62		$8,898.68		$1,322.62	$8,898.68
Sport Helmet Discount-2003	$1,322.62		$8,898.68		$1,322.62	$8,898.68
⊟Volume Discount	$156,448.67	$63,976.12	$2,234,514.08	$808,736.79	$220,424.79	$3,043,250.86
Volume Discount 11 to 14	$111,686.74	$52,326.20	$1,381,049.70	$596,687.88	$164,012.94	$1,977,737.57
Volume Discount 15 to 24	$41,268.50	$10,553.47	$750,165.81	$179,159.40	$51,821.97	$929,325.22
Volume Discount 25 to 40	$3,476.34	$1,064.96	$102,609.05	$31,816.28	$4,541.30	$134,425.33
Volume Discount 41 to 60	$17.10	$31.50	$689.52	$1,073.23	$48.59	$1,762.75
Grand Total	$10,330,262.69	$5,665,785.77	$32,371,227.16	$16,051,351.12	$15,996,048.46	$48,422,578.28

Dimension usage with measure group

Earlier in this chapter, you built your first cube and experienced how quickly you can build business applications using Analysis Services and Excel. The sample cube was very simplistic in a sense that it only exposed two dimensions, each of which had a direct relationship with the fact table. The Cube Wizard automatically detected such relationships and required minimal developer interaction. There are many real-world applications that have a model very similar to your sample cube. However, other requirements necessitate the usage of more complex fact-to-dimension relationships, which you will learn next.

To define how dimensions relate to various measure groups in your cube, switch over to the tab called Dimension Usage. Instead of creating all the dimensions from scratch, you will use the Adventure Works 2012 sample database. Keep in mind that the sample database exposes every possible dimension relationship type because the database is a learning tool, not necessarily a recommended design.

How to do it...

Let's get started. Perform the following steps to learn about dimension usage using a measure group:

1. Open the Adventure Works 2012 sample database project in SSDT, and double click on the Adventure Works cube. On the cube structure tab, notice that the cube contains multiple measure groups.

2. Switch over to the **Dimension Usage** tab and notice that each measure group is associated with some, but not all, cube dimensions. If you click on the intersection of any dimension with a measure group, SSDT will enable an ellipsis button next to the intersection, as shown in the following screenshot:

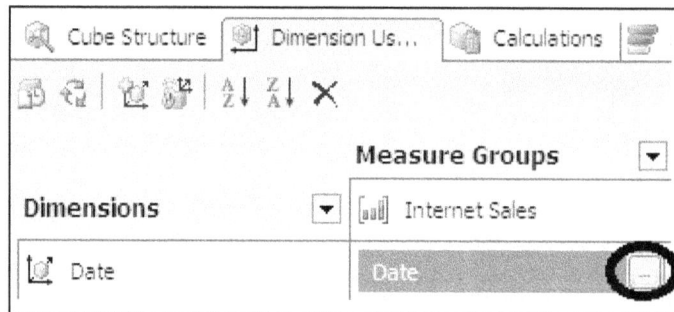

Clicking on the ellipsis button opens the **Define Relationship** dialog where you specify a dimension's relationship with the measure group. The following table summarizes the types of relationships you can define:

Relationship Type	Explanation and examples

No relationship	This relationship type indicates that the dimension is not related to the measure group. For example, the Employee dimension is not related to the Internet sales measure group because customers do not interact with salespeople while shopping online. If you do attempt querying Internet sales measures based on the Employee dimension, you can expect one of two outcomes:
	
	   1. Analysis Services will return the same measure values for each members of the Employee dimension;
	
	   2. Analysis Services will return null values for each employee.
	
	Ignore Unrelated Dimensions measure group property controls the way SSAS treats dimensions with no relationship to the current measure group. The default value of this property is `TRUE`, which produces results outlined with the outcome 1. The other value is `FALSE`, which results in the outcome of 2.

Regular	This relationship type implies that the dimension is directly related to the measure group through one of its attributes, normally the key attribute. Once you specify the relationship type, you must specify the dimension column and the corresponding measure group column (the names of these two columns do not have to match). You must also specify the granularity. In most cases you use dimension's key attribute to relate it to the measure group. For example, the Promotion dimension is directly related to Internet sales through the Promotion Key. It is possible to relate a dimension through a non-key attribute; if you do so, you *must* ensure that attribute relationships are defined from the relating attribute to all the other attributes within the dimension. Recall that all non-key dimension attributes are directly related to the key attribute, and that is how SSAS ensures that data is aggregated correctly. For example, budgeting measure groups could be related to the date dimension on month, quarter, or year attributes instead of the key attribute, which is normally set to individual dates.

Relationship Type	Explanation and examples
Fact	Fact dimensions are built upon the fact table and therefore have a one-to-one relationship with fact records. Fact tables often contain millions or billions of records, therefore, fact-level dimensions should *not* be exposed for ad hoc queries. Instead, they can be used for reporting such attributes as an invoice number or an order revision number. Some literature refers to fact-level dimensions as degenerate dimensions. For example, the Internet sales order details dimension has a fact relationship with the Internet sales measure group. This dimension is exposed using Internet details drillthrough action. You will learn about actions in *Chapter 4, Extending and Customizing Cubes*.
Referenced	This relationship type indicates that a dimension is related to the measure group through another dimension. The referenced dimension and the intermediate dimension must have a common key, which you specify while defining such a relationship. For example, the `FactResellerSales` table does not have a `GeographyKey` column, so we cannot use a direct relationship for a geography dimension. Instead, we use the Reseller dimension as the intermediary between `FactResellerSales` and `DimGeography` and specify `GeographyKey` as the reference dimension attribute and the intermediate dimension attribute. Note that you have an option to `materialize` the referenced relationship. It is recommended to `materialize` referenced dimensions so that Analysis Services builds necessary indexes during the processing time instead of resolving the relationship at query time.
Data mining	This relationship type is used for data mining, which is beyond the scope of this book.

Relationship Type	Explanation and examples
Many-to-many	This relationship type requires an intermediary measure group to resolve many-to-many relationship between a dimension and a measure group. For example, each Internet sale could be associated with multiple sales reasons: television advertisement, manufacturer, review, or promotion. Similarly, each of these reasons for sales is associated with multiple sales orders. Therefore, you cannot build a direct relationship between the Internet sales measure group and the Sales Reason dimension. Instead, you can build an intermediate fact table called `FactInternetSalesReason` and include only three columns: `Sales Order Number`, `Sales Order Line Number`, and `Sales Reason Key`. Next, you can relate the `FactInternetSales` table to `FactInternetSalesReason` using the `Sales Order Number` and `Sales Order Line Number` columns. Next, relate the `FactInternetSalesReason` key to the `DimSalesReason` table using `SalesReasonKey`. You can review the relationship between tables using a *sales order reasons* diagram within the data source view. On the dimension usage tab, you must relate the Sales Reason dimension with the Sales Reasons measure group using a regular relationship. Next, relate the sales reason dimension to the Internet sales measure group using a many-to-many relationship, specifying the reasons for sales as the intermediate measure group.
	Although the many-to-many relationship offers great flexibility and is essential for some modeling scenarios, it should be used *only* when necessary and handled with care. Keep in mind that many-to-many relationships are not materialized; instead, Analysis Services runs a query against the relational data source to derive the MDX query results during the execution when using ROLAP. Even if you use the MOLAP storage, Analysis Services has to perform the in-memory join operation of the data, which has already been imported as part of processing. *Chapter 4, Extending and Customizing Cubes*, provides additional information about many-to-many relationships.

Examining cube file structures

It's time to take a break from SSDT and check what's happening under the hood. Unlike other database platforms, each SSAS database consists of many files. Analysis Services does not expose its transaction log, nor does it have system databases as `master` or `tempdb`. Instead, all of the metadata for the entire server resides in the `master.vmp` file, which you cannot read or modify. You don't have to know what's within each database file, but knowing Analysis Services' database file structures can be very helpful during troubleshooting.

How to do it...

Let's get started; perform the following steps to examine the cube file structure:

1. Each of the Analysis Services instances is associated with a data folder, which stores files for all the databases found on this instance.

2. All of the SSAS instance configuration properties are stored in the `msmdsrv.ini` file found in the `CONFIG` folder under your Analysis Services installation directory. `DataDir` is the property that controls the location of the database folders. Each database has its own separate data folder.

3. I will be using the `ssas_cookbook_chapter3` database folder as an example to demonstrate SSAS file structures. If you have followed along with the recipes of this chapter, this database should now have several folders and over 100 files.

4. As seen in the next screenshot, the database folder has separate subfolders for each dimension, data source, and cube. Additionally, it contains metadata XML files for dimensions, cube, data source, and data source view.

Name	Date modified	Type	Size
Adventure Works DW2012.0.ds	2/4/2013 11:22 AM	File folder	
AdventureWorksSample.0.cub	2/5/2013 10:00 AM	File folder	
Date.0.dim	2/5/2013 10:00 AM	File folder	
Promotion.0.dim	2/5/2013 10:00 AM	File folder	
0.CryptKey.bin	2/4/2013 11:22 AM	BIN File	1 KB
Adventure Works DW2012.0.ds.xml	2/4/2013 11:22 AM	XML Document	2 KB
Adventure Works DW2012.1.dsv.xml	2/5/2013 9:22 AM	XML Document	292 KB
AdventureWorksSample.4.cub.xml	2/5/2013 10:00 AM	XML Document	21 KB
Date.3.dim.xml	2/5/2013 10:00 AM	XML Document	18 KB
Promotion.2.dim.xml	2/5/2013 10:00 AM	XML Document	20 KB

5. If you open each dimension folder, you'll find a number of files with different extensions, each of them serving a specific purpose: storing keys, strings, indexes, and so on.

   Under the folder with the `.cub` extension (in the preceding screenshot, the folder name is `AdventureWorksSample.0.cub`), you will find separate folders for each measure group with the extension `.det`, and each partition folder will have the `.prt` extension.

6. Each partition folder contains partition data files, which are usually the largest files, along with header and aggregation files. So remember that each Analysis Services database is a complex structure consisting of cubes, measure groups, partitions, and many files making up each object.

7. If you have been browsing through files by now, you must have probably noticed the file version numbers. Analysis Services updates the file version numbers when the file changes. For example, when you process the promotion dimension, SSAS will increment the file version numbers upon completion of processing.

8. Similarly, if a database exists on the given SSAS instance, and you synchronize it from another instance, the target database version number will be incremented. `Master.vmp` stores all the version numbers.

9. If you happen to delete some files or modify version numbers manually while the server was stopped, the version numbers will not match those found in `master.vmp`, and your object will be corrupted. Therefore, if you want to keep your databases healthy, be very careful about having any extraneous activity within the Analysis Services data folder.

There's more...

Any time you process an object (dimension, partition, cube, and so on), Analysis Services creates a new "shadow" copy of the object and replaces the old object with it upon completion of processing. This allows the database and all the underlying objects to remain available for queries during processing. Likewise, Analysis Services creates shadow folders while restoring and synchronizing databases, so you'll have to account for storage requirements necessary to perform such actions. For example, if you have a 100 GB database and you want to restore it from a backup—while the existing copy remains online—you need to have at least 200 GB of total storage available on the drive, where you store the SSAS data.

Partitioning strategies

Each Analysis Services measure group consists of one or more partitions. When you first create a measure group, it has a single partition; however, for large scale implementations, creating additional partitions is essential. Having multiple partitions benefits both processing as well as querying performance. Partitions can improve query performance because Analysis Services can examine multiple partitions in parallel and therefore return the requested results quicker than if it had to scan a single, very large partition. Additionally, Analysis Services can exclude the partitions which do not contain the relevant data for a particular query request, thereby shortening the total query execution time. Analysis Services can also process multiple partitions in parallel to minimize the total processing time of the measure group. The mentioned benefits can only be achieved with necessary prerequisites in place, and we will discuss those prerequisites in this section. Partitions also ease cube maintenance; most of the cubes retain relevant data for a limited time span, perhaps for a week, a month, or even for a few years. Once data for a specific day, month, or year is no longer needed, you can simply delete the obsolete partitions.

In general you should limit each partition to less than 20 million fact table records. It is also beneficial to split a partition if the corresponding datafile size exceeds 2 GB. These are merely best practice recommendations based on experience; your mileage may vary and you should monitor querying as well as processing performance to determine the most appropriate partition size and row count for each project.

You have multiple options for creating partitions; given in the following bullet list:

1. Use the Partition wizard within the **Partitions** tab of SSDT or SSMS.

2. Use the XMLA command; you can submit the command to the server through the SSMS or the `ascmd.exe` command-line utility. Note that if you're not familiar with `ascmd.exe`, it is an extremely valuable tool for executing XMLA, MDX, and DMX commands from the Windows command prompt (download it from `www.codeplex.com`).

3. Use the **Analysis Management Objects** (**AMO**) interface to create partitions programmatically using .NET or a scripting language of your choice.

How to do it...

Creating a partition through XMLA is straightforward, regardless of the method you choose to use. The statement for creating a partition will be sent to the SSAS server in XMLA language, so it makes sense to first take a look at the XMLA used to define a partition:

1. Connect to an SSAS instance using SSMS, expand the database of your choice, and navigate to **cube | measure groups | partition**. If you have been following along the recipes included in this chapter, you will see a measure group with a single partition in the database you created earlier.

2. Right-click on the **partition**, navigate to **Script partition as | Create to | New Query Editor Window**, and you will see XMLA similar to following:

```
<Createxmlns="http://schemas.microsoft.com/analysisservices
  /2003/engine">
<ParentObject>
<DatabaseID>ssas_cookbook_chapter3</DatabaseID>
<CubeID>AdventureWorksSample</CubeID>
<MeasureGroupID>Fact Reseller Sales</MeasureGroupID>
</ParentObject>
<ObjectDefinition>
<Partitionxmlns:xsd="http://www.w3.org/2001/XMLSchema"xmlns
  :xsi="http://www.w3.org/2001/XMLSchema-
  instance"xmlns:ddl2="http://schemas.microsoft.com/
  analysisservices/2003/engine/2"xmlns:ddl2_2=http://
  schemas.microsoft.com/analysisservices/2003/engine/2/2
  xmlns:ddl100_100="http://schemas.microsoft.com/
  analysisservices/2008/engine/100/100"xmlns:
  ddl200="http://schemas.microsoft.com/analysisservices
  /2010/engine/200"xmlns:ddl200_200="http://
  schemas.microsoft.com/analysisservices/2010/
  engine/200/200"xmlns:ddl300="http://schemas.microsoft.com
  /analysisservices/2011/engine/300"xmlns:ddl300_300=
  "http://schemas.microsoft.com/analysisservices/2011/
  engine/300/300">
<ID>Fact Reseller Sales</ID>
<Name>Fact Reseller Sales</Name>
<Sourcexsi:type="DsvTableBinding">
<DataSourceViewID>Adventure Works DW2012</DataSourceViewID>
<TableID>dbo_FactResellerSales</TableID>
</Source>
<StorageMode>Molap</StorageMode>
<ProcessingMode>Regular</ProcessingMode>
<ProactiveCaching>
<SilenceInterval>-PT1S</SilenceInterval>
<Latency>-PT1S</Latency>
<SilenceOverrideInterval>-PT1S</SilenceOverrideInterval>
<ForceRebuildInterval>-PT1S</ForceRebuildInterval>
<Sourcexsi:type="ProactiveCachingInheritedBinding" />
</ProactiveCaching>
</Partition>
</ObjectDefinition>
</Create>
```

Notice that XMLA contains references to a partition's parent objects: database, cube, and measure group, specifies the partition identifier as well as its name, storage mode, and processing mode. The partition is based on the `FactResellerSales` table, meaning that it will include all the records from this table. You could also bind a partition to a view or a query. Whether you bind each SSAS partition to a table or view is a matter of preference and performance. The **Partition** wizard has the necessary intelligence to warn you that a given fact table is already referenced by an existing partition, and you cannot use it for additional partitions within the same group; otherwise, you would include duplicate records, and your solution would report incorrect results. Binding a partition to a query offers additional flexibility in a sense that you can change the SSAS partition without having to make any changes to the relational objects. Using query binding also allows you to quickly create an empty partition (by adding a condition, which will never be met, such as `SELECT column_1, column_2 FROM fact_table WHERE 1 = 2`), which can later be used as the target for merging multiple existing partitions.

Creating partitions through the wizard

Now that you've seen the XMLA statement for creating a partition, let's see how it is done using the **Partition** wizard within SSDT. Before we create additional partitions, let's limit the original partition to the subset of fact data. Open the solution using SSDT and click on the **Partitions** tab. Next, click on the ellipsis button in the partition source box shown in the following screenshot:

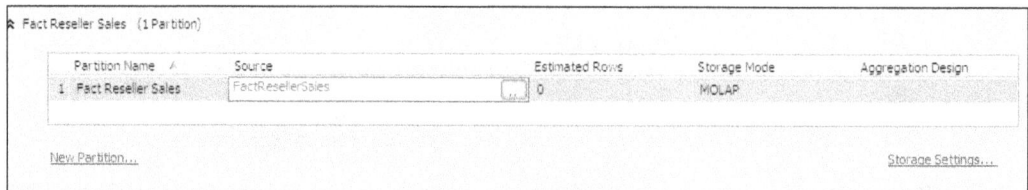

Switch to the Query Binding option in the **Binding Type** drop-down box. In the partition source dialog, you will see that SSDT scripts the SQL statement for you and advises that you should limit the query to those rows that are not included in other partitions of the same measure group. Replace the `WHERE` keyword with the `WHERE DueDateKey< 20051231` clause in the query to limit the partition to Reseller Sales records with a due date prior to December 31, 2005, and click on **OK**. You will see the **Check** button to check the syntax of the query; the **Check** button does not check the validity of the query—it is up to you to ensure that the query returns only the necessary data. Once you save and deploy the changes, the partition will be bound to the query instead of the table; you can then verify this by scripting the partition to a query window within SSMS. This time XMLA will contain `<QueryDefinition></QueryDefinition>` tags instead of specifying the table identifier as shown in the following screenshot:

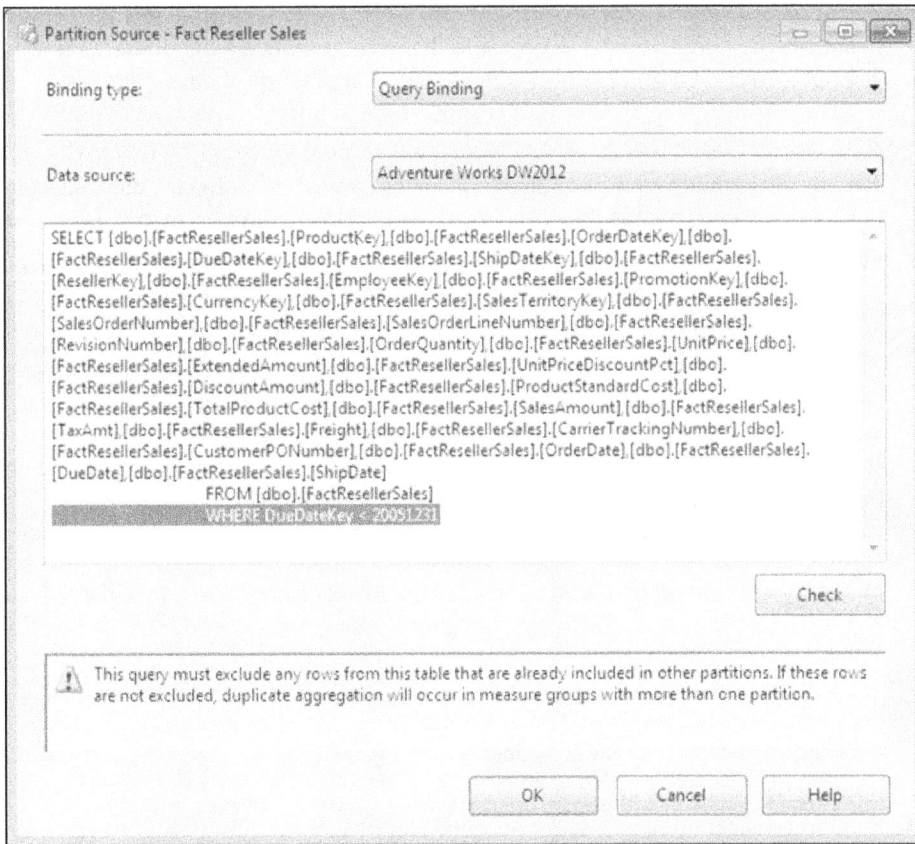

Perform the following steps for creating partitions through wizards:

1. To activate the **Partition** wizard in SSDT, you can click on the **New Partition** link under any measure group on the partitions tab. To activate the same wizard in SSMS, right-click on the `Partitions` folder of a measure group and select **New Partition**. The wizard works the same way using either of the tools; since we already have SSDT open, let's continue working within SSDT.

2. After the welcome screen, the wizard asks you to choose the fact table to be used as the partition source. Note that you can choose the data source which contains the table. Had we not bound the original partition to a query and left it bound to the fact table, we could not have created additional partitions through the wizard.

3. Select `FactResellerSales` and click on **Next**. The following screen allows you to specify the query, which will populate the partition. Once again the wizard warns you not to include duplicate rows already found in other partitions. This time replace the `WHERE` keyword with this code; `WHERE DueDateKey BETWEEN 20051231 AND 20061231`.

4. The following screen allows you to specify processing and storage locations for the partition. You can process the partition on the current instance or on a remote instance.

5. Although processing on a remote instance is possible and could reduce the resource usage on the current instance, this feature is used very seldom and isn't trivial to implement. Keep the default option of processing on the current instance.

6. The choice of storage location is useful in case your database grows so large that you cannot fit all the partitions on the same drive/data volume. By default, a partition is saved in the current instance's data folder as specified in the `msmdsrv.ini` configuration file. I recommend using the default option unless storing the new partition in the current data folder is impossible due to storage limitations. Choosing a non-default location will require additional work should you need to synchronize or restore the database from a backup. Simply click on **Next** to move on to the screen, allowing you to name the partition. In addition, to choosing a descriptive name for the partition, it is very useful to use the same naming convention for all the partitions within a given measure group. For large implementations with dozens or hundreds of partitions, a common naming scheme will save you many maintenance headaches. Let's name the new partition "Reseller Sales 2006" since the sample database is small and yearly partitions will suffice.

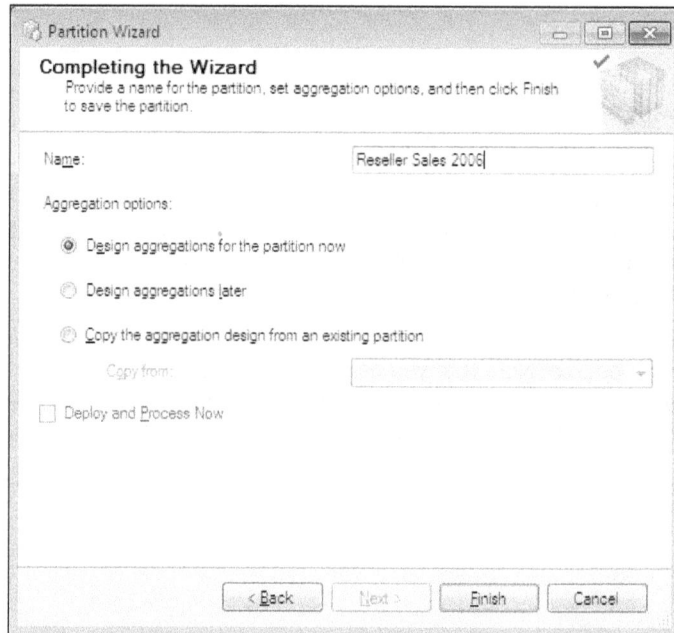

7. As the screenshot shows, the final wizard screen allows building aggregations immediately, copying aggregation designs from an existing partition or designing aggregations later. You will learn about aggregations later in this chapter; for now choose the **design aggregations later** option. Designing aggregations later also allows us to check the **Deploy and Process Now** box. Once you click on **Finish**, SSDT will proceed with deploying changes, and you'll have the option to process the newly created partition.

Creating partitions through AMO

If you have a relatively small database with a handful of partitions, using XMLA statements through SSMS or running through a wizard several times a year will suffice. In an enterprise environment, partition management must be automated because running the wizard 24 times per day (for hourly partitions) is too labor intensive. Furthermore, creating partitions might only be a small portion of the scheduled job streams. The sequence of scheduled jobs could collect data from various source systems, populate a relational warehouse, and manage Analysis Services objects as new data becomes available. Even if you're not a programmer, don't despair, as you can automate the creation of partitions with relatively easy commands using the PowerShell scripting language. Of course Powershell is not the only language you can use to create partitions; feel free to experiment with a language of your choice. Here are sample Powershell commands for creating a new partition based on an existing model partition. You can customize the script for your environment:

```
# Script to create a new partition based on existing partition
#load the Analysis Services assembly first so you can instantiate
  Analysis Services server object (# MicrosoftAnalysisServices.dll
  #will be found under your Analysis Services installation #folder:
[Reflection.Assembly]::LoadFrom("E:\Program Files\Microsoft SQL
  Server\110\SDK\Assemblies\Microsoft.AnalysisServices.dll")|out-
  null
$instance="Julia-PC\SQL2012"
$amoServer= new-object Microsoft.AnalysisServices.Server
#connect to the instance:
$amoServer.Connect($instance)
#connect to the database, cube and measure group of interest:
$db=$amoServer.databases.GetByName("ssas_cookbook_chapter3")
$cube = $db.cubes.GetByName("AdventureWorksSample")
$mg=$cube.MeasureGroups.GetByName("Fact Reseller Sales")
#clone the existing partition:
$new_partition = $mg.partitions.GetByName("Reseller Sales
  2006").clone()
```

```
# set id, name and query definition properties for the new
  partition:
$new_partition.id = "Reseller Sales 2008"

$new_partition.name = "Reseller Sales 2008"

$new_partition.Source.QueryDefinition = "SELECT * FROM
  FactResellerSales WHERE DueDateKey BETWEEN 20080101 AND 20081231"

# store new partition's identifier in a variable for the next
  step:
$partition_id = $amoServer.Databases[$db].Cubes[$cube].
MeasureGroups[0].partitions
  .Add($new_partition)

# send the new partition definition to the server:
$amoServer.Databases[$db].cubes[$cube].MeasureGroups[0].Partitions
  [$partition_id].Update()

$amoServer.databases[$db].update()

#disconnect from the server
$amoServer.disconnect()
```

Once you run the script and refresh the partition list in SSMS, you will see the newly created "Reseller Sales 2008" partition. You can examine its properties by scripting it into a new query window to confirm that the ID, name, and query definition are set correctly.

Partition storage mode options

Each partition can use one of the three storage options summarized in the following table:

Storage Option	Explanation	Advantages	Drawbacks
Multi-Dimensional OLAP (MOLAP)	This storage option stores data in Microsoft's proprietary, highly compressed format.	It offers superior performance. MOLAP storage is used by the majority of successful SSAS implementations.	Data must be read from the relational database and written to MOLAP structures. Hence data is duplicated and users must wait until processing is complete and it is available for querying.

Storage Option	Explanation	Advantages	Drawbacks
Relational OLAP (ROLAP)	This storage option retains data in the relational database. If defined, aggregations are created as additional tables in the relational database, thereby increasing its size.	Data is not duplicated and processing simply validates SSAS metadata. Therefore, data is available for querying very soon after it arrives in the relational database. Use ROLAP only if data latency issues cannot be overcome with the implementation of MOLAP storage.	Any MDX queries submitted to MSAS will be translated into relational SQL queries. ROLAP performance is generally worse than that offered by MOLAP. If you need many aggregations, the relational database size could grow exponentially.
Hybrid OLAP (HOLAP)	This storage option keeps data in the relational database but creates aggregations in the MOLAP format. If the data requested by a query is not found by scanning aggregations, the relational database is queried.	It does not create a copy of relational data. If the requested data is found in aggregations, the response time is as fast as it is with MOLAP.	HOLAP is very seldom used because it requires much tuning to offer the benefits of either ROLAP or MOLAP. Aggregations are only built when using the `ProcessFull` option, not with `ProcessIndexes`. So, each time we run `ProcessUpdate` on dimensions (effectively dropping aggregations), we must also perform the full process of all the partitions to rebuild indexes and aggregations.

Since we can specify the storage mode at the partition level, each measure group could contain both ROLAP and MOLAP partitions. For example, if 90 percent of your queries check the current data and only 10 percent of them reference the historical data, you could use MOLAP for the most frequently queried partitions and ROLAP for historical ones.

Defining partition slice

As mentioned earlier, Analysis Services can intelligently decide which partitions to check for each query. For example, if we submit a query requesting reseller sales data for year 2005, SSAS should only have to check the Reseller Sales 2005 partition and not spend any time examining datafiles for 2006 or any other partitions. To exclude irrelevant partitions, Analysis Services checks the index files found within each partition folder; these files contain the range of internally assigned key values. You have already seen that we can partition measure groups by date; indeed, the majority of SSAS projects are partitioned by one of the levels found in the date dimension: day, month, quarter, or year. However, sometimes partitioning only at the date level is insufficient—you may have large volumes of intraday data that represents only a small portion of the total daily volume. In such case you can create partitions based on multiple attributes, for example, we could partition reseller sales data by date and product category. According to SSAS documentation, when using MOLAP storage, SSAS should always exclude irrelevant partitions, even when data is partitioned by multiple attributes. If you use ROLAP, on the other hand, data remains in the relational tables; to help SSAS query only the relevant partitions, we must define the partition slice property. Through practical implementation of SSAS projects on various versions of the product, I also recommend setting the slice property on MOLAP partitions because it is essentially a query hint for the SSAS engine. Additionally, the algorithm for detecting the correct partitions is particularly susceptible to errors when you partition data by multiple attributes. Another advantage of setting partition slice is that it prevents loading incorrect data into the partition—if you attempt to process a partition with an incorrect query definition, processing will fail with an error stating that the criteria specified by the partition slice have been violated.

How to do it...

You can set the partition slice through SSMS or SSDT. Keep in mind that you must process the partitions after setting its slice. Even if you have previously processed a partition and later need to update the slice, you will have to re-process it after the slice property is set.

Refer to the following steps to set the partition slice:

1. Right-click on the partition and choose **properties**.

2. Click on the ellipsis button next to the slice property to open the **Partition Slice** dialog. You can specify the MDX within the dialog by picking the appropriate attribute member. For example, the slice for Reseller Sales 2006 partition would be `[Due Date]`, `[Year]`, and `[2006]`. Had we partitioned data by year and promotion category, the slice definition would be: `[Due Date].[Year].&[2006] [Promotion].[Promotions].[Promotion Category].&[Customer]`.

3. You will learn more about MDX in *Chapter 6, MDX*. It is important to note that the partition slice can reference each hierarchy *only* once.

Merging partitions

Merging multiple partitions is common as the partitions age (become less frequently queried) or when you need to reduce the total number of database files. For example, in the year 2013, we might not be particularly interested in data from the 1990s but could expect historical data to be queried occasionally. If so, we could keep monthly partitions for the current year but merge partitions for each previous year into yearly partitions and perhaps even merge all of the 1990s data into a decade-level partition. If you work in an environment where data must be aggregated many times each day, you might create multiple partitions throughout the day and later merge all intraday partitions into a single daily partition. As you will learn in *Chapter 8, Administering and Monitoring Analysis Services*, synchronization speed is largely dependent on the number of files that must be transferred. Therefore, merging partitions could also optimize synchronization speed.

How to do it...

To merge partitions you must identify the `source` and `target` partitions. You can use an empty target partition or an existing partition that already has data. In either case both source and target partitions must be fully processed before you can merge them. Suppose we would like to merge 2007 and 2006 partitions into the main partition called **Fact Reseller Sales**, which will act as the target; for reference, perform the following steps:

1. Right-click on the **Partitions** folder within SSMS, and select **Merge Partitions** to open the **Merge Partition** dialog:

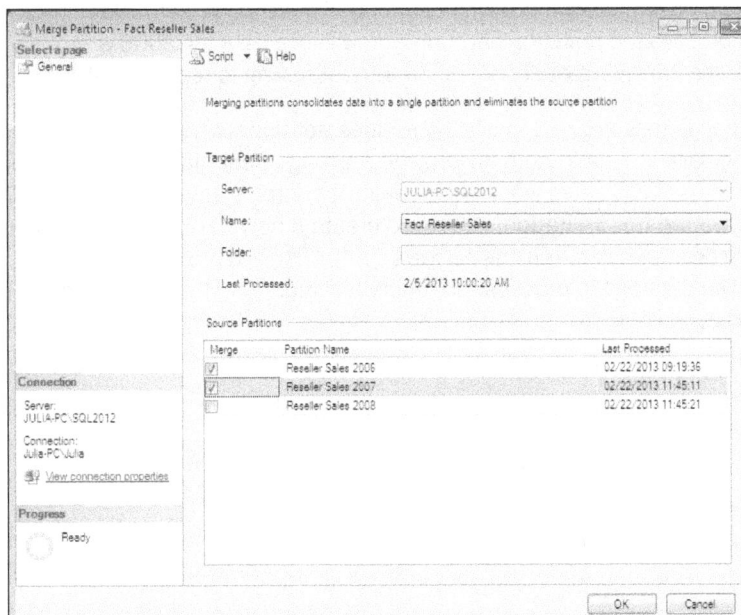

2. Choose **Fact Reseller Sales** as the target, **Reseller Sales 2006** and **Reseller Sales 2007** as sources, and click on **OK**. Alternatively, you could also script the XMLA command, which would be similar to the following:

```
<MergePartitionsx mlns="http://schemas.microsoft.com/
analysisservices/2003/engine">
<Sources>
<Source>
<DatabaseID>ssas_cookbook_chapter3</DatabaseID>
<CubeID>AdventureWorksSample</CubeID>
<MeasureGroupID>Fact Reseller Sales</MeasureGroupID>
<PartitionID>Reseller Sales 2008</PartitionID>
</Source>
</Sources>
<Target>
<DatabaseID>ssas_cookbook_chapter3</DatabaseID>
<CubeID>AdventureWorksSample</CubeID>
<MeasureGroupID>Fact Reseller Sales</MeasureGroupID>
<PartitionID>Fact Reseller Sales</PartitionID>
</Target>
</MergePartitions>
```

Unfortunately merging partitions does have its share of limitations. For example, the query definition of the resulting partition will be the same as the query definition of the target partition. Let's suppose we had set the target partition's query to only include 2005 sales. Once we merge 2006 and 2007 into the target, the resulting partition will contain data for all three years. However, the query definition will remain set to only include 2005 data. Now, if you intentionally or accidentally process the resulting partition, you will lose data for 2006 and 2007. Fortunately, you can update the partition's query definition without having to reprocess it.

Another limitation is that `MergePartitions` does not update the target partition's slice. So the resulting partition could actually provide a wrong query hint to the server, indicating that it only contains 2005 sales whereas in reality it contains sales for 2005, 2006, and 2007. To work around this limitation, you could create a new partition with the correct slice, include a query definition that returns no rows ("`SELECT column1, column2 … FROM fact_table WHERE 1=2`"), process the empty partition, and then use it as the merge operation's target.

Defining aggregation designs

Aggregations are precalculated summary tables that provide query results much faster than if you were to query the full fact table. For example, the sample `FactResellerSales` table contains over 60000 rows. Instead of reading through 60000 rows to find the sum of total product cost, SSAS can read a single row in the aggregation table. In real-world applications with billion-row fact tables, the difference is much more pronounced, especially when summarized values are grouped by dozens of attributes. Unfortunately aggregations don't come free of charge; they are calculated as part of partition processing and therefore increase the total processing duration. Aggregations could also use significant amount of disk space. Therefore, designing aggregations is an art of balancing performance improvement with the overhead of processing time and additional storage.

SSDT and SSMS offer two wizards for designing aggregations: Aggregation Design Wizard and Usage Based Optimization Wizard. To activate either of these wizards from SSMS, right-click on any partition (or the **Partitions** folder) and select either the **Design Aggregations** or **Usage Based Optimization** option, respectively. Both wizards are aptly covered in product documentation, so we will not include any screenshots here.

The aggregation design wizard allows you to specify the relative significance of each dimension attribute you wish to include in aggregations. It can also count the number of rows in the fact table and compare it to the count of rows found in each attribute to determine approximate performance improvement offered by each potential aggregation. If the wizard determines that the aggregation file size will be at least one third (1/3) of the full data file size, the aggregation will not be considered. This is limiting because you may well have the most important query that is executed hundreds of times per day that would benefit from a very large aggregation. Another limitation is that counting rows in a fact table with billions of rows or in very large dimensions could take unacceptably long and hence isn't always a practical option. Nevertheless, many developers use the aggregation design wizard as the starting place when they don't have a lot of time to dedicate to performance tuning and the initial data set is relatively small.

Usage-based Optimization (**UBO**) wizard allows building aggregations depending on query history. To use this wizard you must first enable query logging by editing Analysis Services configuration properties (you can right-click on the SSAS instance and select properties to view and modify configuration options). The relevant properties are as follows:

1. `Log\QueryLog\CreateQueryLogTable`: Set this property to `True` unless you intend to create the relational database table manually. The default value is `False`.

2. `Log\QueryLog\QueryLogConnectionString`: This property sets connection properties for the SQL Server relational database where you intend to store query logs. By default, logs are not collected and therefore the default value is blank.

3. `Log\QueryLog\QueryLogTableName`: This is the name of the relational table where the query log will be stored. The default value is `OLAPQueryLog`.

4. `Log\QueryLog\QueryLogSampling`: To capture every query request set this property to `1`. The default value is `10`, which means only one out of every 10 query requests will be logged. Keep in mind that capturing every query on a very busy SSAS server will result in a large amount of data and could cause performance overhead.

The term "Query Log" is a bit of a misnomer because if you examine the table, the most relevant column, called dataset, contains a collection of ones and zeros separated by occasional commas and not the actual MDX query. The content of the dataset column is called a subcube and is expressed as a vector of dimension attributes. For example, 000,000,001,000 indicates that my query requested a subcube, which included an explicit reference to only one attribute from the third dimension. The other three dimensions are represented with three zeroes each because the query did not explicitly reference any of the three attributes included in those dimensions. Perhaps a more accurate name would be a subcube log, because each MDX query can request multiple subcubes and the entire cube space can be defined as the collection of subcubes. Apart from the naming convention, the query log is very useful; as you will see shortly, subcubes determine the essence of aggregation design.

Usage-based Optimization wizard reads the query log table, reporting the total number of queries, distinct queries, and users, as well as the average response time. If you log every subcube request on a busy SSAS server, you could soon have a huge query log table. So the wizard allows filtering subcubes based on the execution date and the number of users who requested a particular subcube. Next, the wizard translates the subcube vectors into attributes and allows you to count the rows in the fact/dimension tables. You can also override the estimated counts to increase the likelihood of UBO aggregating data for a specific attribute. Though useful, the UBO wizard suffers from similar limitations as the aggregation design wizard—it won't consider aggregations over a certain size and counting rows might not work in every situation. Note that both the wizards allow creating a new aggregation design, merging new aggregations with the existing aggregation design, and applying designs to partitions. You also have an option to process the affected partitions immediately.

If you click through the wizard and save the aggregation design, you'll be able to see this design in SSMS under the `aggregation design` folder. Right-click on the aggregation design and select the **script to new query window** option to understand the difference between aggregation files and aggregation design. For example, the following is an aggregation design created using the UBO wizard (list of all dimension attributes is omitted to save space):

```
<Create xmlns="http://schemas.microsoft.com/analysisservices/2003/
    engine">
<ParentObject>
<DatabaseID>ssas_cookbook_chapter3</DatabaseID>
<CubeID>AdventureWorksSample</CubeID>
```

```
<MeasureGroupID>Fact Reseller Sales</MeasureGroupID>
</ParentObject>
<ObjectDefinition>
<AggregationDesignxmlns:xsd="http://www.w3.org/2001/XMLSchema
  "xmlns:xsi="http://www.w3.org/2001/XMLSchema-
instance"xmlns:ddl2="http://schemas.microsoft.com/analysisservices
  /2003/engine/2"xmlns:ddl2_2="http://schemas.microsoft.com/
  analysisservices/2003/engine/2/2"xmlns:ddl100_100=
  "http://schemas.microsoft.com/analysisservices/2008/engine
  /100/100"xmlns:ddl200="http://schemas.microsoft.com/
  analysisservices/2010/engine/200"xmlns:ddl200_200=
  "http://schemas.microsoft.com/analysisservices/2010/
  engine/200/200"xmlns:ddl300="http://schemas.microsoft.com/
  analysisservices/2011/engine/300"xmlns:ddl300_300=
  "http://schemas.microsoft.com/analysisservices/2011/engine
  /300/300">
<ID>UBO AggregationDesign</ID>
<Name>UBO AggregationDesign</Name>
<EstimatedRows>47572</EstimatedRows>
<Dimensions>
<Dimension>
<CubeDimensionID>Ship Date</CubeDimensionID>
<Attributes>
<Attribute>
<AttributeID>Date</AttributeID>
<EstimatedCount>2191</EstimatedCount>
</Attribute>
<Attribute>
<AttributeID>Month</AttributeID>
<EstimatedCount>72</EstimatedCount>
</Attribute>
<Attribute>
<AttributeID>Calendar Year</AttributeID>
<EstimatedCount>6</EstimatedCount>
</Attribute>
</Attributes>
</Dimension>
</Dimensions>
<Aggregations>
<Aggregation>
<ID>Aggregation 0</ID>
<Name>Aggregation 0</Name>
<Dimensions>
<Dimension>
```

```
<CubeDimensionID>Ship Date</CubeDimensionID>
</Dimension>
<Dimension>
<CubeDimensionID>Order Date</CubeDimensionID>
</Dimension>
<Dimension>
<CubeDimensionID>Due Date</CubeDimensionID>
<Attributes>
<Attribute>
<AttributeID>Calendar Year</AttributeID>
</Attribute>
</Attributes>
</Dimension>
<Dimension>
<CubeDimensionID>Promotion</CubeDimensionID>
</Dimension>
</Dimensions>
</Aggregation>
</Aggregations>
</AggregationDesign>
</ObjectDefinition>
</Create>
```

As you can see, the aggregation design contains only one aggregation, `Aggregation 0`, which aggregates the Calendar Year attribute. We can easily extend this aggregation design XMLA to include additional aggregations and additional attributes. When you assign the aggregation design to a given partition, you're simply changing the partition's metadata so that Analysis Services knows which attributes to aggregate when you process the partition. To create the actual aggregation files, we must use the `ProcessIndexes` option, which rebuilds both index and aggregation files. Note that the partition must already contain data before you can use the `ProcessIndexes` option to add indexes and aggregations.

Using BIDS Helper for customizing aggregations

The Analysis Services user community has published a number of very useful *free* tools through `www.codeplex.com`. One of these tools is BIDS Helper. The tool is distributed with an installation wizard and takes only a few clicks to integrate it with SSDT. BIDS Helper offers much useful functionality, and I recommend that you become familiar with the tool. BIDS Helper allows you to customize aggregations using Aggregation Manager.

How to do it...

To design aggregations using BIDS Helper, perform the following steps:

1. Click on a cube within SSDT and select **Edit Aggregations** to activate **Aggregation Manager**.

2. As shown in the next screenshot, **Aggregation Manager** displays and allows the editing of existing aggregation designs. You can also create new aggregation designs. For reference, have a look at the following screenshot:

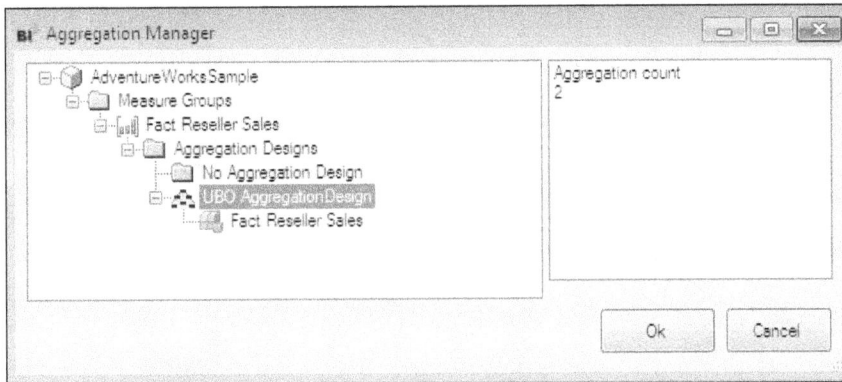

3. Right-click on the existing design and select **Edit**. Within the dialog you will see that you can check those attributes you wish to aggregate.

4. Alternatively, you could also copy a particular dataset from the query log table and paste it into the **Aggregation Definition** column.

5. The tool also allows you to add aggregation definitions directly from the Query Log. For example, you could specify the SQL statement to find only those subcubes that took excessively long to retrieve, or those that were executed by a user who complained about slow queries.

6. You can also use **Aggregation Manager** to provide more descriptive names for your aggregations instead of using the generic **Aggregation 0**.

7. Once you're happy with your aggregation design, you can apply it to the necessary partitions, save your changes, and review the results in SSMS.

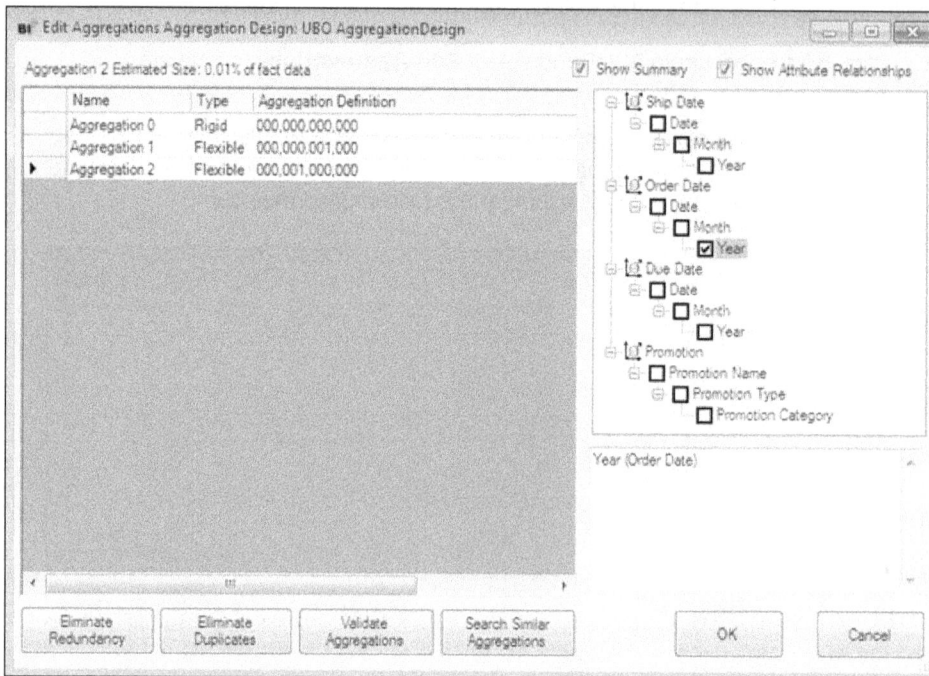

Unlike UBO and **Aggregation Design** wizards, **Aggregation Manager** does not limit the size of aggregations, nor do you have to provide row counts for each attribute. Clearly, you should be careful not to design too many aggregations,so that you don't run out of disk space or tremendously increase the processing time. However, I recommend becoming familiar with **Aggregation Manager** in case you need greater control over aggregation designs than that offered by SSDT/SSMS wizards.

There's more...

As mentioned earlier in this chapter, you can use the `ProcessIndexes` processing option to build indexes and aggregations on a given partition for which data has already been loaded (The `ProcessFull` option includes `ProcessIndexes`). In some environments it might be beneficial to make data available to users even before indexes and aggregations are built. MOLAP storage often outperforms relational queries by an order of magnitude, even if you don't build any aggregations and indexes, thus business users can query data faster even before we add the speed-boost with indexes and aggregations. In this case you can allow Analysis Services to build aggregations "lazily" using a background thread. The term "lazy" indicates that the thread uses minimal resources and works only when sufficient system resources are available.

Therefore, building aggregations lazily could take considerably longer than through `ProcessIndexes`. The configuration property that controls whether the lazy thread is activated is `OLAP\LazyProcessing\Enabled`—the default value is `1`, which means the lazy thread is active. If you prefer not to have the lazy thread building missing aggregations or indexes, set the property to `0`. You must also set the `ProcessingMode` property on the cube, measure group, or partition level to customize data availability.

Distinct count measure groups

As you learned earlier in this chapter, the `DISTINCT COUNT` aggregation function supplies the count of unique values within a fact table. Analysis Services handles `DISTINCT COUNT` measure groups somewhat differently than measure groups that include measures with other aggregation functions.

How to do it...

To implement a distinct count measure, perform the following steps:

1. Right-click on an existing measure group and select **New Measure**.
2. Change the **Usage** to **Distinct count** and choose the column **Analysis Services**, which should be used for counting distinct values.
3. SSDT will create a separate measure group for the distinct count measure.
4. Give the new measure a descriptive name and set the necessary properties.

There's more...

The SQL query for processing a partition using a `DISTINCT COUNT` measure group includes an `ORDER BY` clause to ensure that the data is sorted based on the column identifying the `DISTINCT COUNT` measure. Therefore, the data in each `DISTINCT COUNT` measure group is sorted based on the `DISTINCT COUNT` measure column. Although this may not sound like a huge limitation, it does affect how SSAS resolves `DISTINCT COUNT` MDX queries. If you partition the `DISTINCT COUNT` measure group by the date dimension attribute (which is the most commonly used approach for normal measure groups), Analysis Services will have to check every partition for every query because distinct count data values could be spread across all partitions. This also means that SSAS cannot eliminate any partitions during queries; if your measure group has 100 partitions, querying each partition for every query can severely lengthen the query execution time. An alternative approach is to partition `DISTINCT COUNT` measure groups based on the `DISTINCT COUNT` column value. Doing so effectively serves as a query hint because SSAS only has to check for specific partition(s) and not others.

For example, the Adventure Works 2012 sample database contains the Internet orders measure group, which is partitioned by year so that the SQL query defining each partition limits the rows by `OrderDateKey`. A more effective way of partitioning this measure group would be to specify the range of `SalesOrderNumbers` (`SalesOrderNumber` is the `DISTINCT COUNT` column) to be included in each partition. The following queries could be used to define four partitions based on the `SalesOrderNumber` column:

```
SELECT * FROM FactInternetSales
WHERE SalesOrderNumberBETWEEN'SO43697'AND'SO55999'

SELECT * FROM FactInternetSales
WHERE SalesOrderNumber BETWEEN'SO57000'AND'SO63999'

SELECT * FROM FactInternetSales
WHERE SalesOrderNumber BETWEEN'SO64000'AND'SO69999'

SELECT * FROMFactInternetSales
WHERE SalesOrderNumber>'SO70000'
```

If we expect the majority of our queries to check the number of orders by a calendar year, a more effective strategy would be to partition the measure group by the sales order number as well as the order date.

Enabling write-back feature

The write-back feature allows data analysts to perform what-if analysis and is typically used for budgeting applications. For example, an operations manager might want to see what the profit margins would look like if her team were to achieve a cost reduction of 10 percent. Although not frequently used, write-back is a useful feature.

Analysis Services does not overwrite any values in the existing fact tables from which it sources data. Rather, it creates a new partition for storing the write-back data. The new partition is based on a table that could be stored in the same database as the primary fact table or in a different relational database. SSAS derives requested values at the query execution time by aggregating write-back and regular partition values. Note that the write-back feature works *only* on measure groups that have measures using the `SUM` aggregation function. If you have followed along with the examples in this chapter, you must remove the `Fact Reseller Sales Count` measure before enabling write-back.

How to do it...

To enable write-back on a measure group, perform the following steps:

1. Right-click on the measure group's **Writeback** folder in SSMS, and select **Enable Writeback** to activate the dialog shown in the next screenshot.

2. Specify the data source where you want to store the write-back data; you may use the existing data source or define a new one. Also specify the table name; by default, the table will have the `WriteTable_` prefix.

3. Specify the storage mode for the write-back partition, either MOLAP or ROLAP. Once you click on **OK**, Analysis Services will create the write-back partition. You need to process the write-back partition before SSAS creates the relational table.

4. Any queries against the write-enabled measure group will query both regular and write-back partitions; the SQL Profiler will display the following messages:

Messages	Description of the action
Progress Report Begin	Started reading data from the "**Fact Reseller Sales**" partition.
Progress Report Begin	Started reading data from the "**WriteTable_Fact Reseller Sales**" partition.
Progress Report End	Finished reading data from the "**Fact Reseller Sales**" partition.
Progress Report End	Finished reading data from the "**WriteTable_ Fact Reseller Sales**" partition.

Note that in order to actually write the data back into the cube, you must have a client application that supports write-back. The discussion of client application implementation details is beyond the scope of this book.

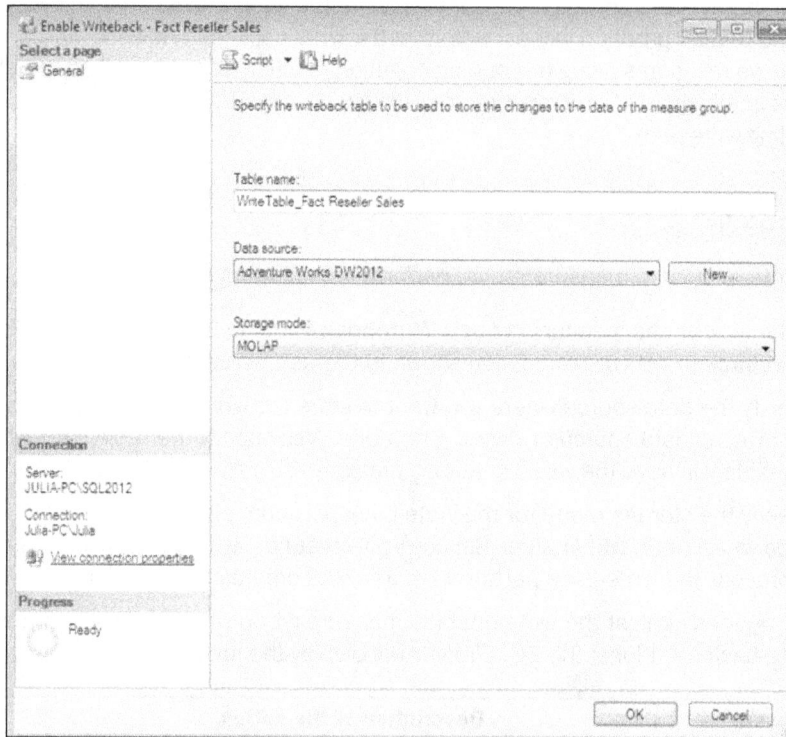

If your users are happy with their changes to the cube data values, SSAS provides an option to convert write-back partition into a regular partition. Simply right-click on the `Writeback` folder again and select **Convert to Partition**. The ensuing dialog box will allow you to specify the partition name and whether you wish to copy aggregation design from any existing partition.

If you no longer wish to support write-back capability, click on the `Writeback` folder and select **disable Writeback**. You will need to drop the relational table manually.

Deployment options

You have already learned that you can deploy an SSDT project to an SSAS instance. For enterprise-level applications, it is imperative to maintain source control—SSDT projects can be checked in and out of version control software. Since the entire Analysis Services database can be scripted using SSMS in XMLA language, you can also save copies of database definition in that format. Scripting is also helpful when moving databases from test to quality assurance and subsequently to production environments. However, scripting a complex database with hundreds of partitions can take prohibitively long. In some cases, even deployment through SSDT can hang and might never complete. Fortunately, there is an additional option for deploying SSAS database projects: the Deployment Wizard.

How to do it...

Let's learn how to use the **Deployment Wizard** by performing the following steps:

1. To activate the wizard navigate to **Start | All Programs | Microsoft SQL Server 2012 | Analysis Services | Deployment Wizard**.

2. After the welcome screen, the wizard lets you specify the location of the file with an `.asdatabase` extension—this file is created in the bin subfolder when you build a project with SSDT.

3. After you specify the target server and database name, the wizard displays options shown in the following screenshot:

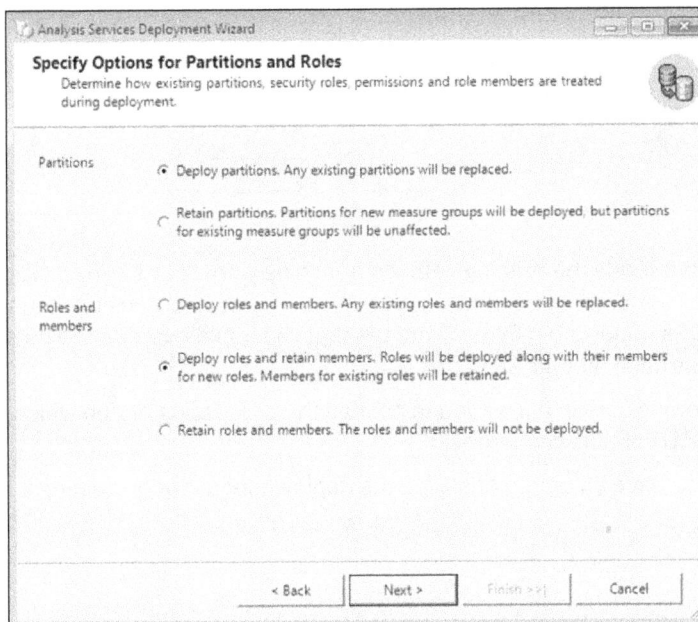

4. Unlike deployment from SSDT, which completely wipes out the existing database and replaces it with the new project, the **Deployment Wizard** allows you to retain partitions for existing measure groups and only deploy partitions of the new measure groups. Similarly, you have a choice of retaining existing security role members.

5. The next screen allows you to change the data source connection strings so that the test SSAS database can source data from the test relational database, while the production instance sources data from the corresponding production SQL Server instance.

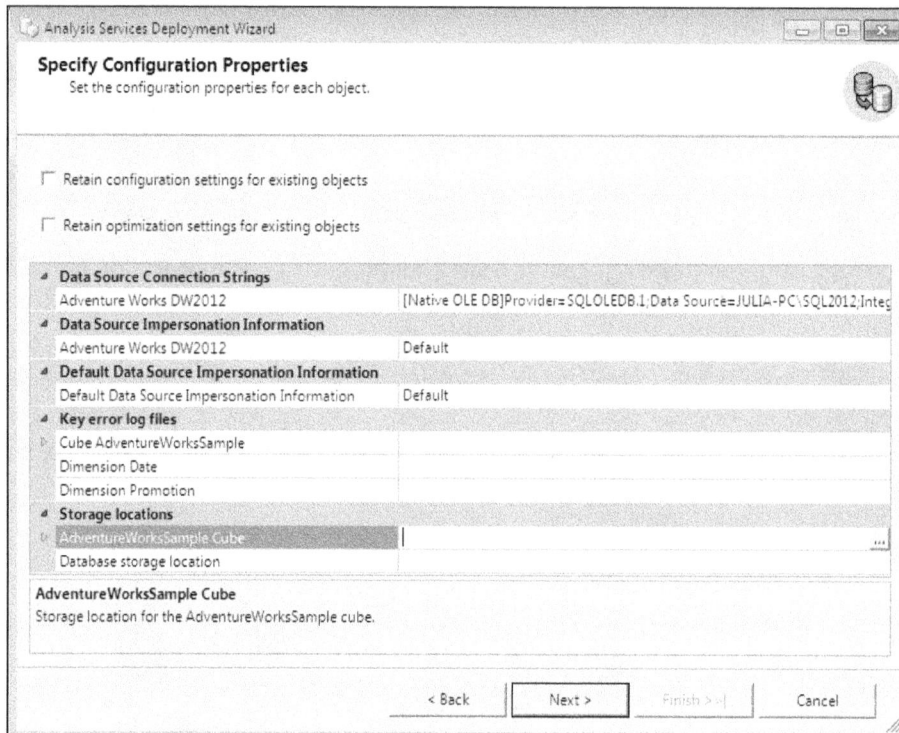

6. The wizard reads the existing settings from files with .configsettings, .deploymentoptions, and .deploymenttargets extensions found in the SSDT solution's bin folder. Note too that you could override the database as well as cube storage locations.

7. The following screen allows you to change the processing option which you had set within SSDT project properties.

8. Lastly you have an option of saving the deployment script or running it immediately.

4
Extending and Customizing Cubes

In this chapter, we will cover:

- ▸ Defining calculated measures
- ▸ Defining named sets
- ▸ Defining drillthrough actions
- ▸ Defining URL actions
- ▸ Defining reporting actions
- ▸ Defining key performance indicators
- ▸ Defining perspectives
- ▸ Defining translations
- ▸ Defining measure expressions

Introduction

This chapter contains recipes for extending **Analysis Services** cubes with calculations, actions, and key performance indicators (KPIs). Additionally, you will learn how to customize cubes using **translations**, **perspectives**, and **measure expressions**.

As you learned in the previous chapters, Analysis Services cubes expose data found in relational data sources. The primary advantage of polling SSAS cubes in lieu of relational tables is the swift execution of queries achieved by the efficient data storage in the MOLAP format and precalculated summary values called aggregations. However, relational data sources might not contain all numbers helpful for business analysis. For example, you could have sales data for each broker, but the application might also need to compare the average sale amount per broker in the northern states with the respective performance of brokers in the south, east and west regions. You might also need to calculate each product's contribution to total sales per region. Although you could include calculation definitions in each user query, it's preferable to define them at the cube level for two reasons: to provide consistent dataset for all users and to benefit from the SSAS global calculation cache for better query performance.

Actions extend the cube's functionality to the next step that the user might want to take based on data analysis. For example, actions can display additional details for a given dataset, launch a website, and generate a report. The actions are (usually) seamlessly integrated with cube functionality. The recipes in this chapter will teach you about the most commonly utilized action types: drillthrough, URL, and reporting. Actions are defined within the SSDT cube designer's **Actions** tab. You must set certain properties for each action. If you would like to expose additional data, an action's target can be measure-group members. And, if you'd like to expose more data about dimension attributes, dimension-level, hierarchy-level, or attribute-level members could be the target of the action.

Key performance indicators (KPIs) enhance the application by displaying the state of your business using various visual indicators, such as gauges, smiley faces, and speedometers. KPIs are calculations which business users would like to see on their dashboard to get a very high-level overview of the data before they dive into more detailed analysis.

Although seldom used, translations offer the useful functionality of displaying cube data in different languages depending on the user's selection.

Perspectives are similar to relational database views in the sense that they expose a subset of the entire database. Enterprise-level solutions can have multiple cubes, many measure groups, and measures. Being exposed to dozens of dimensions and measures could overwhelm the users; hence, you can create multiple perspectives, tailoring each one to the needs of a particular group of users.

Measure expressions allow for either multiplying or dividing two measures from two separate measure groups, which normally have many-to-many relationships you learned about in *Chapter 3, Creating Analysis Services Cubes*.

As in the previous chapters, all examples in this chapter will reference `Adventure Works DW` sample database.

Defining calculated measures

You can add calculations to the cube at any time by simply typing calculation definitions on the **Calculations** tab and saving the database. Cube-level calculations are stored in the MDX script, which you can review on the cube designer's **Calculations** tab. This tab has two views: **Form View** and **Script View**. The **Form View** is helpful in developing individual calculated members, calculated measures, and named sets. The **Script View** contains all calculations as a single script, which is essentially a collection of MDX statements separated by semicolons. Regardless of whether you use **Form View** or **Script View**, the **Calculations** tab includes the metadata—dimensions and measures as well as a list of all supported MDX functions along with the syntax reference. Additionally, SSDT also includes templates for the most common types of calculations.

Calculated measures are measures derived by performing operations on other, previously defined measures. Calculated members are very similar but reference a dimension other than the special, measures dimension.

Calculations do not change the cube structure, and therefore, do not require reprocessing of dimensions or partitions. However, calculations do increase the cube space by adding new cells—this is accomplished by executing the MDX script. You can monitor what happens under the hood using **SQL Server Profiler**.

Getting ready

Launch SSDT and connect to the existing `Adventure Works` sample database, which has been previously deployed and processed on your instance of Analysis Services. Right-click on the `Adventure Works` cube, choose **Open**, and then navigate to the **Calculations** tab. Also launch SQL Server Profiler, connect to the same SSAS instance, and start a trace using the default trace template. Finally, launch SSMS, navigate to **File | New | Analysis Services MDX Query**, and connect to the same SSAS instance.

How to do it...

First hover your mouse pointer over each icon found on the top ribbon of the **Calculations** tab to become familiar with the environment. Notice the new calculated member button, which looks like a calculator, and the new named set button, which has a couple of dots enclosed in curly braces. Also ensure that you are using **Form View**—you'll switch to **Script View** shortly. Also note the **Calculation Tools** pane in the bottom left-hand corner.

Create a reseller sales moving-average calculation using the following steps:

1. Click on the **Templates** tab within **Calculation Tools**, right-click on **Moving Average**, and choose **Add Template**. This creates a new calculated member and provides the syntax for deriving the moving average.

2. Change the name of the calculation to `Reseller Sales Moving Average`.

3. Edit the expression supplied by the template to the following:

   ```
   Avg ([Date].[Calendar].CurrentMember.Lag(6):[Date].
     [Calendar].CurrentMember, [Measures].[Reseller Sales
   Amount])
   ```

4. Change the measure's **Format String** property to `Currency`, Associated Measure Group to `Reseller Sales`, and Nonempty Behavior to `Reseller Sales Amount`.

5. Click on the **save** button to save the calculation to the server. Quickly switch to SQL Server Profiler to see what takes place behind the scenes—if you examine the Command End event, you will see that SSDT sends an `ALTER` command to the server to change the cube's definition.

6. Next, switch to SSMS, and execute the following query:

   ```
   SELECT {measures.[reseller sales amount],
     measures.[Reseller Sales Moving Average]}  ON 0,
   NONEMPTY([Date].[Calendar].[Month].members) ON 1
   FROM
   [Adventure Works]
   ```

   Here is a partial result of this query:

	Reseller Sales Amount	Reseller Sales Moving Average
[July 2006]	$729,200.55	$729,200.55
[August 2006]	$668,122.85	$698,661.70
[September 2006]	$637,697.79	$678,340.40
[October 2006]	$449,344.69	$621,091.47
[November 2006]	$698,449.60	$636,563.10

Notice that the moving average for July 2006 is the same as the reseller sales amount. This is because the calculation tells SSAS to go back six months and get the average for the last six months. We didn't have any sales prior to July 2006; hence, the average is the same as sales. The moving average for August 2006 is the average of July and August sales, the moving average for September 2006 is the average of July, August, and September, and so on.

Now let's build a calculation to show each reseller type's contribution to the total reseller sales as follows:

1. Right-click on the **Percentage of Total** template, and choose **Add Template** to create a blueprint for the next calculation.

2. Edit the calculation definition as shown in the following code snippet. We check the reseller sales amount to ensure it's not null, if so we compare sales for a given reseller type to total reseller sales (you will learn more about MDX functions in *Chapter 6, MDX*):

```
Case
When IsEmpty
      (
          [Measures].[Reseller Sales Amount]
      )
Then Null
Else ( [Reseller].[Reseller Type].CurrentMember,
          [Measures].[Reseller Sales Amount] )
      /
      (
   Root
          (
              [Reseller]
          ),
          [Measures].[Reseller Sales Amount]
      )
   End
```

3. Set the measure's Format String property to `Percent`, Associated Measure Group to `Reseller Sales`, and NonEmpty Behavior to `Reseller Sales Amount`. Save the database.

4. Next, to check the newly added calculation, launch Excel and create a pivot table against the `Adventure Works` database. Choose the **Reseller Sales Amount** and **Reseller Type Percentage of Total** measures as values and the **Reseller Type** hierarchy on rows to see the following result:

Row Labels	Reseller Sales Amount	Reseller Type Percentage of Total
Specialty Bike Shop	$1,173,474.01	7.30%
Value Added Reseller	$5,628,923.80	35.05%
Warehouse	$9,258,257.62	57.65%
Grand Total	**$16,060,655.43**	**100.00%**

Defining named sets

Named sets group either one or multiple dimension members based on certain criteria. Named sets could be either dynamic or static. Static sets are evaluated once you define the set, whereas dynamic sets are evaluated at the time of query execution. In this section, we will first build a static named set of the top three resellers and validate it with queries, and then make the set dynamic to note the difference.

How to do it...

Let's get started. To build a named set of the top three resellers in terms of sales amount:

1. Right-click on the **Top N Count** template, and choose **Add Template**.

2. Call the named set `Leading Resellers`, and edit the calculation as follows:
   ```
   TOPCOUNT
   ([Reseller].[Reseller].[all resellers].children, 3,
      measures.[reseller sales amount])
   ```

3. Change the **Type** property to **Static**, and save the changes.

4. To verify the named set, switch to SSMS, and execute the following query (the results are shown immediately after the query):
   ```
   SELECT  measures.[reseller sales amount] ON 0,
   [leading resellers] ON 1
   FROM [Adventure Works]
   ```

	Reseller Sales Amount
Metropolitan Equipment	$644,059.49
Corner Bicycle Supply	$616,663.89
Retail Mall	$611,102.67

5. So far so good. Now let's limit the query to calendar year 2007 and check the results again:
   ```
   SELECT  measures.[reseller sales amount] ON 0,
   [leading resellers] ON 1
   FROM [Adventure Works]
   WHERE [Date].[Calendar].[Calendar Year].&[2007]
   ```

	Reseller Sales Amount
Metropolitan Equipment	$307,274.84
Corner Bicycle Supply	$315,833.45
Retail Mall	$291,364.58

6. So, we got the same three resellers. They must have had the highest reseller sales amounts for 2007 as well, right? Wrong. We can easily double-check our result by writing a query that does not reference the named set as shown next. Note that the `Retail Mall` reseller actually shows up in the sixth spot, it's not one of the top three resellers. Our set should have included `Top Sports Supply` instead:

```
SELECT  measures.[reseller sales amount] ON 0,
NONEMPTY(ORDER(reseller.reseller.[all resellers].children,
measures.[reseller sales amount], DESC)) ON 1
FROM [Adventure Works]
WHERE [Date].[Calendar].[Calendar Year].&[2007]
```

	Reseller Sales Amount
Corner Bicycle Supply	$315,833.45
Top Sports Supply	$308,875.49
Metropolitan Equipment	$307,274.84
Registered Cycle Store	$296,124.95
Health Spa, Limited	$294,128.38
Retail Mall	$291,364.58

7. The reason for the inaccurate result is that the static named sets are not evaluated at query time. Instead SSAS derives the top three resellers when you save the calculation. Hence, the same three resellers will be shown regardless of query context. To work around this limitation, go back to SSDT and change the [leading resellers] named set's **Type** to **Dynamic**, and save the changes.

8. Execute the query shown in step 5 again to confirm that the named set works as expected, displaying the top three resellers within 2007; here are the results:

	Reseller Sales Amount
Corner Bicycle Supply	$315,833.45
Top Sports Supply	$308,875.49
Metropolitan Equipment	$307,274.84

Defining drillthrough actions

Drillthrough is a very frequently used functionality that allows the examination of detailed level data values. Earlier versions of Analysis Services allowed for executing queries against the relational data source, thereby enabling leaf-level data to remain in the relational format. Unfortunately, this often led to poor performance, which could not be controlled from SSAS. Starting with SSAS 2005, drillthrough only works within the cube space and requires any detailed data to be imported into the MOLAP storage. Clearly the major drawback of this approach is that we might have to build huge dimensions in order to expose data at the transaction level. An alternative approach is to implement an Excel macro to run a query against the relational data source if the user needs to see such data.

How to do it...

Let us define a drillthrough action as follows:

1. Choose **New Drillthrough Action** after right-clicking on the SSDT **Action Organizer** within the **Actions** tab. Supply a descriptive name for the action.

2. Specify the measure group for which you plan to supply detailed data. Normally drillthrough actions expose data from fact-level (degenerate) dimensions. For example, the sample `Adventure Works` database has the `Reseller Details` action to expose `Reseller Sales Order Details` dimension attributes: carrier tracking number, customer PO number, sales order number, and sales order line.

3. Specify each attribute you'd like to include with the action. You can include attributes from any dimension and measure.

4. Specify additional action properties in the **Properties** window:

    □   `Default`: You can only have one default action per measure group. The default action is invoked by simply double-clicking on the cell of interest. The supported values are `True` or `False`. Note that actions can only be invoked from client tools that support actions.

    □   `Maximum rows`: It advises SSAS to limit the output of the action to a specified number of rows. This property serves two purposes. Firstly, returning too many rows could confuse the user—most users can only decipher several hundred to several thousand rows of data in a reasonable amount of time. Secondly, returning too many rows using the `DRILLTHROUGH` command can impose a severe burden on the SSAS instance. This is especially true when using 32-bit hosts or hosts with a limited amount of memory.

    □   `Invocation`: Its supported values are interactive, on open, or batch. Generally you should use the **interactive** option—you should not present thousands of rows to the user unless this amount of data is necessary.

- ❑ `Application`: It specifies the name of the application that executes the action.

- ❑ `Description`: It supplies additional metadata about the action.

- ❑ `Caption`: This is the string that users will click on to execute the action. Be sure to supply the value that clearly conveys the purpose of the action.

- ❑ `Caption is MDX`: It advises SSAS whether the caption is defined as an MDX expression. Generally this is `FALSE` for drillthrough actions.

5. Save the action by clicking on the SSDT **Save** button.

6. To test the action, create a pivot table in Excel, expose the `Reseller Sales Amount` measure, and display resellers on rows. Right-click on a cell showing `Reseller Sales Amount` for a single reseller, and then navigate to **Additional Actions | Drillthrough....** This opens a new tab within the Excel worksheet and displays all attributes and measures included in the `Reseller Details` action. Clearly the action's caption within the sample database doesn't include much detail about the action—you should not follow this poor practice in the actions you create.

How it works...

Drillthrough actions are implemented using the `DRILLTHROUGH MDX` command. As usual, you can use SQL Server Profiler to see the statement executed behind the scenes. For example, the following MDX command is executed when invoking the `Reseller Details` action for the `Community Department Stores` reseller:

```
DRILLTHROUGH  Select  ([Measures].[Reseller Sales Amount],[Reseller].
[Reseller].&[571])  on 0
From [Adventure Works]
RETURN [Reseller Sales].[Reseller Sales Amount],[Reseller Sales].
[Reseller Order Quantity],[Reseller Sales].[Reseller Extended
Amount],[Reseller Sales].[Reseller Tax Amount],[Reseller Sales].
[Reseller Freight Cost],[Reseller Sales].[Discount Amount],[Reseller
Sales].[Reseller Unit Price],[Reseller Sales].[Unit Price
Discount Percent],[Reseller Sales].[Reseller Total Product
Cost],[Reseller Sales].[Reseller Standard Product Cost],[$Reseller].
[Reseller],[$Promotion].[Promotion],[$Employee].[Employee],[$Delivery
Date].[Date],[$Sales Territory].[Sales Territory Region],[$Reseller
Sales Order Details].[Carrier Tracking Number],[$Reseller
Sales Order Details].[Customer PO Number],[$Reseller Sales
Order Details].[Sales Order Number],[$Reseller Sales Order
Details].[Sales Order Line],[$Product].[Product],[$Ship Date].
[Date],[$Source Currency].[Source Currency Code],[$Date].
[Date],[$Geography].[City],[$Geography].[State-Province],[$Geography].
[Country],[$Destination Currency].[Destination Currency Code]
```

The DRILLTHROUGH command displays details of each sale making up the total Reseller Sales Amount measure for Community Department Stores, showing the order date, ship date, delivery date, customer name, purchased product name, and other attributes. Please reference the online documentation for more information about the DRILLTHROUGH command. Note that if you do not limit the number of rows returned by the drillthrough action, the upper limit is controlled by the server-wide configuration option DefaultDrillthroughMaxRows in the msmdsrv.ini file or through the instance configuration properties in SSMS.

Defining URL actions

URL actions invoke a link with a parameter set to the current dimension member. This functionality is helpful in obtaining additional information about a particular attribute. For example, a URL action in a movie database could look up a particular actor's biography; a URL action in a real estate application could allow navigating to the property's listing, and so on.

How to do it...

To set up a URL action that gets state information from maps.google.com:

1. Right-click on **Action Organizer** and choose **New Action**. Set the **action type** to **URL**, and name the action State Information.

2. Set **target type** to Level Members and **target object** to Geography.Geography. State-Province.

3. Set the action expression to the following:

   ```
   "http://maps.google.com/maps/place?ftid=0x54936e7c9b9f6a55:0x7d4c6
   5db7a0bb876&q=" +
   [Geography].[State-Province].CurrentMember.Name +
   "&hl=en&ved=0CBIQ3g0&sa=X&ei=Li5WUZCeLofFtwflo4H4BA"
   ```

4. Set the invocation property to interactive, the caption to State Information Link. The Caption is MDX property should be set to False.

5. Save the action by clicking on the SSDT **Save** button.

6. To test the action, create a pivot table in Excel with the Geography hierarchy on rows, Reseller Sales Amount measure on columns, and the Geography dimension's country attribute filtered to United States.

7. Expand the Geography hierarchy so that it shows states, then right-click on **Wyoming**, and navigate to **Additional Actions | State Information Link.**

8. Your browser will open the link showing information about Wyoming.

Now let's modify the action slightly to use MDX for deriving the caption:

1. To use an MDX caption, simply set the `Caption Is MDX` property to `True`, and modify the caption to:

   ```
   "View information for " +
   [Geography].[State-Province].CurrentMember.Member_Caption
   ```

2. Once you save the application and refresh the pivot table, the action's caption for `Wyoming` will be `View Information for Wyoming`.

Defining reporting actions

Reporting actions can launch a **SQL Server Reporting Services** (SSRS) report passing the currently selected dimension member as a parameter. Reporting actions are conceptually similar to drillthrough actions in the sense that both types of actions typically display additional detail about the data cell exposed by the cube. The difference is that drillthrough is not as feature-rich as an SSRS report could be, and an SSRS report could retrieve data from the relational source, whereas drillthrough must retrieve detailed data directly from the cube. An SSRS report could contain links to additional resources, whereas enhancing drillthrough data set to include links is difficult at best. Discussion of SSRS report development is beyond the scope of this book, but you will review the reporting action defined within the sample database.

How to do it...

To learn how to define a reporting action, review the `Sales Reasons Comparison` action. The procedure will be as follows:

1. Right-click on **Action Organizer**, and choose **New Reporting Action**. Provide a descriptive name for the action.

2. Set the action's **target type** to `Level Members` and **target object** to `Product.[Product Categories].[Category]`.

3. Provide the SSRS settings: **Server Name** and **Report Path**. **Server Name** is the host/computer on which SSRS is running; **Report Path** should include the report server URL and the **path to the actual report** you wish to display.

4. Provide the parameter name to be passed to the SSRS report. In this case, the parameter name is `ProductCategory` and set the parameter value to the current member's unique name, as in `[Product].[Category].CurrentMember.UniqueName`.

5. Set the `Invocation` property to `interactive`, the `Caption is MDX` property to `True`, and `Caption` to the following:

```
"Sales Reason Comparisons for " +
[Product].[Category].CurrentMember.Member_Caption
```

6. Click on the **Save** button to save the action.

7. To test the action, create a pivot table in Excel with product categories and sales reasons hierarchies on rows and the `Internet Sales Amount` measure on columns. Note that you will only be able to test this action if you have an instance of SSRS set up and available. Additionally, the report must be deployed as well. Right-click on the **Accessories** product category, then navigate to **Additional Actions | Sales Reasons Comparison for Accessories**. This will launch an SSRS report similar to the following screenshot:

Product Category Bikes

|4 4 1   of 1 ▷ ▷| 100% ▾   Find | Next

Adventure Works Cycles

Sales Reason	Europe			North America			Pacific		
	Internet Orders	Internet Sales Amount	Internet Total Product Cost	Internet Orders	Internet Sales Amount	Internet Total Product Cost	Internet Orders	Internet Sales Amount	Internet Total Product Cost
Manufacturer	$352	$1,206,594	$733,050	$803	$2,765,552	$1,680,985	$591	$2,021,543	$1,229,036
On Promotion	$1,118	$2,009,804	$1,182,740	$1,298	$2,217,191	$1,292,029	$1,099	$2,048,147	$1,210,564
Other	$111	$65,666	$39,932	$109	$62,743	$38,311	$84	$49,012	$29,994
Price	$2,275	$3,586,028	$2,120,140	$2,630	$4,158,322	$2,425,635	$1,446	$2,369,977	$1,424,779
Quality	$316	$1,130,733	$686,129	$718	$2,569,198	$1,558,989	$517	$1,849,966	$1,122,559
Review	$226	$436,477	$250,168	$319	$578,245	$328,277	$329	$635,195	$356,565

Defining key performance indicators

You can define a KPI within the SSDT tab called KPIs by specifying the value, goal, status, and trend expressions along with optional properties. A KPI's value is a measure, its goal is the ideal value of the calculation, the status shows the relative condition of the measure compared to the goal, and the trend indicates whether the business is moving closer to the target. For example, the `Adventure Works` sample database has a KPI called `Growth in Customer Base`. This KPI is built upon the `[measures].[growth in customer base]` measure which compares the current time span's customer count with that of the previous time span: the current year is compared to last year, the current quarter is compared to last quarter, and so on. The goal is arbitrarily set to 30 percent increase for each fiscal year, 15 percent for semesters, 7.5 percent for quarters, and 2.5 percent for months. The KPI's status is shown as a green check mark if the goal is met or with a red X sign if we're below target. Lastly, the trend displays an upward arrow if the value is increasing, a downward arrow if decreasing, and a horizontal arrow if the number remains flat.

In this recipe you will create internet order sales growth KPI to monitor Adventure Works internet order traffic health. Let's set modest goals of 20 percent growth per calendar year, 10 percent per calendar semester, 5 percent per quarter, and 2.5 percent per month. We'll consider values within 80 percent as a decent progress.

How to do it...

To define internet order sales growth KPI:

1. Open the Adventure Works cube within the sample database (existing on your SSAS instance) in SSDT and navigate to the **Calculations** tab.

2. Create a new calculated member by entering the following expression on the **Script View**, and save the solution. The expression simply compares the order count for the current time span with the previous time span, reports N/A if we're at the top level (all calendar time) and returns null if the previous time span had no orders:

```
CREATE MEMBER CURRENTCUBE.[Measures].[Internet Order Count Growth]
  AS CASE
WHEN [Date].[Calendar].CurrentMember.Level.Ordinal = 0 THEN "N/A"
WHEN ISEMPTY(([Date].[Calendar].CurrentMember.PrevMember,
     measures.[Internet Order Count])) THEN NULL
ELSE
(([Date].[Calendar].CurrentMember, measures.[Internet Order
Count]) -
([Date].[Calendar].CurrentMember.PrevMember,
measures.[Internet Order Count]) )/
([Date].[Calendar].CurrentMember.PrevMember, measures.[Internet
Order Count])
END,
FORMAT_STRING = "Percent",
VISIBLE = 1 ,  ASSOCIATED_MEASURE_GROUP =
  'Internet Orders'  ;
```

3. Navigate to the **KPIs** tab, right-click on the **KPI Organizer** tab (found in upper left-hand corner), and choose **New KPI**. Rename the KPI to Internet Order Growth, and set **Associated measure group** to Internet Orders.

4. Enter the newly created measure [measures].[internet order count growth] as the **Value Expression**.

5. Define the `Goal Expression` for each level within the `Calendar` hierarchy using the following MDX query:

```
Case
    When [Date].[Calendar].CurrentMember.Level Is [Date].
[Calendar].[Calendar Year]
    Then .20
    When [Date].[Calendar].CurrentMember.Level Is [Date].
[Calendar].[Calendar Semester]
    Then .10
    When [Date].[Calendar].CurrentMember.Level Is [Date].
[Calendar].[Calendar Quarter]
    Then .05
    When [Date].[Calendar].CurrentMember.Level Is [Date].
[Calendar].[Month]
    Then .025
    Else "N/A"
End
```

6. Next choose the thermometer as the **Status Indicator**, icon and define the status expression as follows:

```
Case
    When KpiValue( "Internet Order Growth" ) >=
        KpiGoal ( "Internet Order Growth" )
    Then 1
    When KpiValue( "Internet Order Growth" ) >=
        KpiGoal ( "Internet Order Growth" ) * .80
        And
        KpiValue( "Internet Order Growth" ) <
        KpiGoal ( "Internet Order Growth" )
    Then 0
    Else -1
End
```

7. Lastly choose standard arrow as the **Trend Indicator**, and enter the following MDX query for trend expression:

```
Case
    When IsEmpty(
    ParallelPeriod
        ([Date].[Calendar].[Calendar Year], 1, [Date].[Calendar].
CurrentMember))
    Then 0
    When VBA!Abs
        ((KpiValue( "Internet Order Growth" )
            -
```

```
            (KpiValue( "Internet Order Growth" ),
        ParallelPeriod
         ([Date].[Calendar].[Calendar Year], 1,[Date].[Calendar].
CurrentMember))
              )
              /
              (
                KpiValue( "Internet Order Growth" ),
        ParallelPeriod
          ([Date].[Calendar].[Calendar Year],1,[Date].[Calendar].
CurrentMember))
              ) <=.02
     Then 0
     When (KpiValue( "Internet Order Growth" )
              -
          (KpiValue( "Internet Order Growth" ),
        ParallelPeriod
          ([Date].[Calendar].[Calendar Year],1,[Date].[Calendar].
CurrentMember))
              )
              /
          (KpiValue( "Internet Order Growth" ),
        ParallelPeriod([Date].[Calendar].[Calendar Year],1,[Date].
[Calendar].CurrentMember)
              ) >.02
     Then 1
     Else -1
End
```

Note that we only have three values for status and trend: 1, -1, and 0 because we can only display upward/downward movement or no change in our calculation.

8. Save your solution. Since KPIs are calculations, you do not have to reprocess any object.

9. To test the newly defined KPI, create a pivot table in Excel using the Adventure Works cube. Navigate to the KPI's folder and check the value, goal, status, and trend boxes next to the Internet Order Count Growth KPI. Show the Date.Calendar hierarchy on rows, and you should see a screen similar to the following:

Row Labels	Internet Order Count Growth	Internet Order Growth Goal	Internet Order Growth Status	Internet Order Growth Trend
CY 2005		0.2 ◇		⇨
CY 2006	164.26%	0.2 ◉		⇧
H1 CY 2006	17.77%	0.1 ◉		⇧
Q1 CY 2006	-1.24%	0.05 ◇		⇩
Q2 CY 2006	13.80%	0.05 ◉		⇧
April 2006	4.02%	0.025 ◉		⇧
May 2006	3.38%	0.025 ◉		⇧
June 2006	0.00%	0.025 ◇		⇨
H2 CY 2006	24.39%	0.1 ◉		⇧
Q3 CY 2006	15.28%	0.05 ◉		⇧
July 2006	18.22%	0.025 ◉		⇧
August 2006	11.07%	0.025 ◉		⇧
September 2006	-29.54%	0.025 ◉		⇧
Q4 CY 2006	2.73%	0.05 ◇		⇩
CY 2007	270.53%	0.2 ◉		⇧
H1 CY 2007	17.12%	0.1 ◉		⇩
Q1 CY 2007	4.79%	0.05 △		⇩
Q2 CY 2007	20.56%	0.05 ◉		⇧
H2 CY 2007	370.71%	0.1 ◉		⇧
CY 2008	31.56%	0.2 ◉		⇩
CY 2009	-100.00%	0.2 ◇		⇩
CY 2010		0.2 ◇		⇩
Grand Total	N/A	N/A	◉	⇨

Defining perspectives

As mentioned earlier in this chapter, Analysis Services perspectives are similar to views defined in the relational database. Each multidimensional SSAS project could contain multiple cubes, several measure groups, hundreds of measures, many hierarchies, and thousands of attributes. Many cube users might only need a subset of these attributes to get their job done. Including unnecessary options in the reports and analytical views could simply confuse data consumers; instead, you should try to expose only the essential attributes to each user group by defining perspectives. Unlike relational views, perspectives should not be used for implementing security; they are simply intended to conceal the complexity of your solution.

The Adventure Works sample multidimensional database contains several perspectives, for example, the Direct Sales perspective exposes Internet Sales, Internet Orders, Internet Customers, and Exchange Rates measure groups, whereas the Finance perspective includes measures only from the Financial Reporting and Exchange Rates measure groups. The two perspectives also expose different sets of KPIs, actions and calculations because the groups of employees using the two perspectives are likely to be interested in different datasets.

How to do it...

To define a perspective, the following steps need to be followed:

1. Connect to the `Adventure Works` cube using SSDT and navigate to the **Perspectives** tab. Right-click anywhere within this tab, and choose **New Perspective**. Alternatively, you could click on the New Perspective icon found in the upper left-hand corner of the **Perspectives** tab.

2. Give the perspective a descriptive name to ensure that your users can quickly identify its purpose.

3. Define the **Default Measure** for the perspective by picking one of the measures from the drop-down list. The default measure is returned in a query that does not explicitly specify requested measures or uses the `measures.defaultmember` syntax to reference the desired measure.

4. Uncheck the measures, hierarchies, attributes, KPIs, actions, and calculations that should *not* be available within the current perspective. By default, each new perspective includes all attributes, so every single one of them is checked.

5. Once you are happy with your selections, save the solution.

6. To confirm the perspective works as expected, create a pivot table in Excel using the newly defined perspective. Within Excel's data tab choose **From Other Sources | From Analysis Services**, then enter the name of your Analysis Services instance. Choose your database name from the drop-down list, then ensure the **Connect to specific cube or table** box is checked, and you will see the list of available cubes/perspectives as shown in the following screenshot:

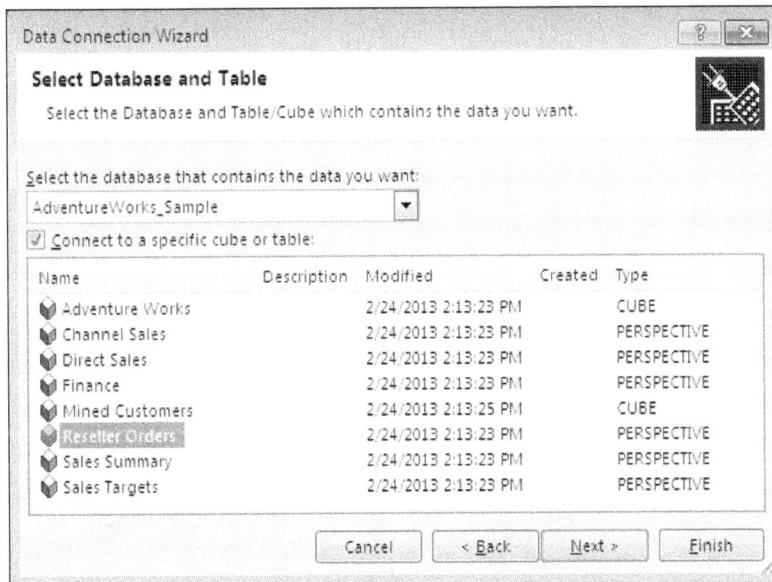

Defining translations

Analysis Services does not translate attributes or measure names for you, but it allows you to specify your own translations in case your application will serve a multilingual audience. You can define translations for dimension attributes as well as cube metadata. The `Adventure Works` sample multidimensional database supplies French and Spanish translations. You can use either SSMS/SSDT or a cube browsing tool of your choice to test translations.

How to do it...

To define translations for dimension attributes, the following steps need to be followed:

1. Right-click on any database dimension within the **SSDT** project, and choose **open.** Navigate to the **Translations** tab within the dimension designer.

2. Right-click anywhere within the **Translations** tab, and choose **New Translation**; doing so will open a dialog box that allows you to choose the language you will be using.

3. The **Translations** tab lists all the dimension attributes. Once you choose the language, you will see a separate column where you can specify the values for each attribute's translation.

4. When you click on each **attribute,** you will see a button on the right-hand side of the cell. Click on the button to activate the **Attribute Data Translation** dialog shown in the following screenshot. In this example, the translation is specified for the day and name of the week in French by choosing the corresponding column from the relational dimension table. Note that you could specify a translated caption in addition to supplying the value from the relational column.

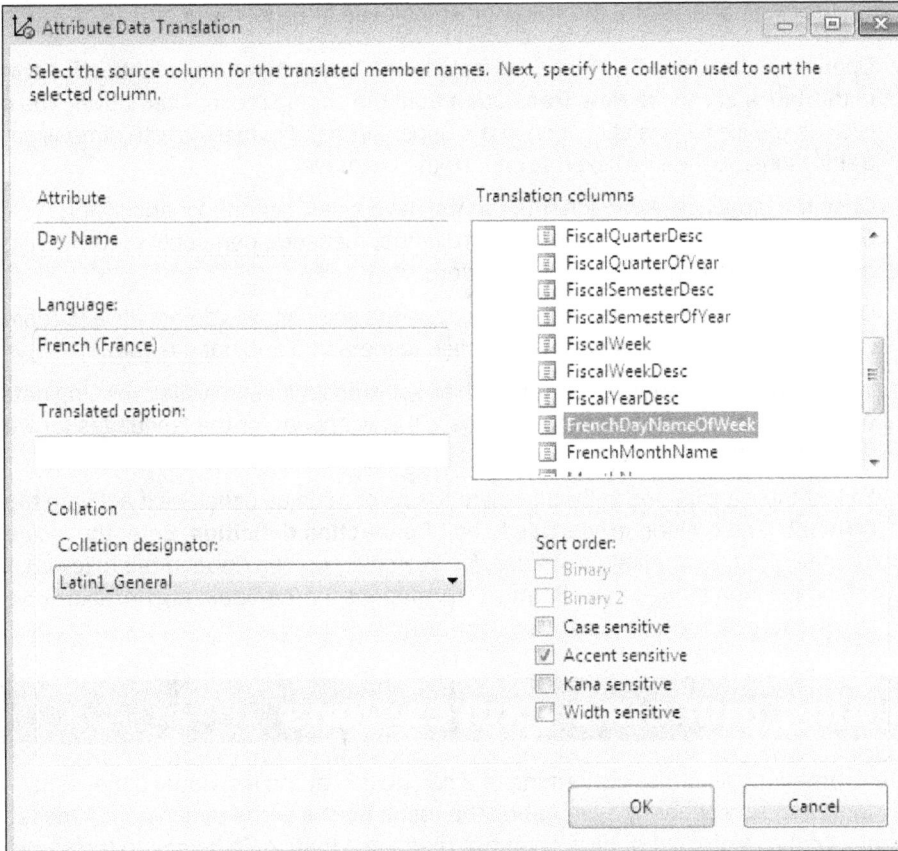

5. In addition to applying translations to each attribute based on a relational column, you could also define translations for metadata items, such as the dimension name and the default member.

6. Save and process your dimension. Processing is necessary because you'll be reading translated values such as **FrenchDayNameOfWeek** name from the relational table.

To define cube-level translations, the following steps need to be followed:

1. Open the cube within SSDT, and navigate to the **Translations** tab. Right-click anywhere in this tab, and choose **New Translation** from the pop-up menu. Alternatively you could click on the New Translation icon in the upper left-hand corner. As with dimension-level translations, you will be asked to choose the language.

2. Once the language is chosen, the tab will have a new column for specifying the translated values for each measure group, measure, perspective, KPI, dimension name, action, and calculation.

3. Once you specify the necessary values, save the solution. You do not have to reprocess the cube because translations are applied to metadata and not the data.

4. You can choose the language you wish to see translations in while browsing data using SSDT or SSMS. Translated values will only appear for the languages for which you defined translations.

5. To test the translations in Excel, define the pivot table as usual, next activate the **Data** tab, and click on **properties** to edit **Connection definition**. Enter the locale identifier for the language of choice, for example, you can append the following to the connection string to see Spanish translations for the Spain region: `Extended Properties="LocaleIdentifier=3082"`.

Defining measure expressions

Measure expressions allow the performing of a calculation at the individual dimension member-level and subsequently aggregating the result for the entire dimension. A measure expression is either a product or division of two measures that could belong to the same or different measure groups. For example, the sample `Adventure Works` multidimensional database contains `Reseller Sales` and `Exchange Rates` measure groups. Since the fictitious bike company operates globally, we might want to express the `[reseller sales amount]` measure in multiple currencies. As you know, the currency rates vary from time to time, and hence, we maintain the `Exchange Rates` measure group that tracks how various currencies perform in comparison to the base currency of the USD. Both `Reseller Sales` and `Exchange Rates` measure groups have direct relationships with the date dimension. However, `Exchange Rates` is also directly related to the destination currency measure group, whereas `Reseller Sales` is not. To relate the `Reseller Sales` measure to the `Destination Currency` dimension, we need a many-to-many relationship with the `Exchange Rates` measure group. This makes sense if you examine `Reseller Sales Amount` values reported in just two currencies: USD and EURO. For simplicity's sake, let's just have a look at the second half of 2006:

Row Labels	Average Rate		Reseller Sales Amount	
	EURO	US Dollar	EURO	US Dollar
CY 2006	**.90**	**1.00**	**€ 4,134,145.70**	**$3,713,626.10**
H2 CY 2006	**.90**	**1.00**	**€ 4,134,145.70**	**$3,713,626.10**
Q3 CY 2006	.91	1.00	€ 2,268,813.51	$2,035,021.19
July 2006	.86	1.00	€ 848,351.92	$729,200.55
August 2006	.93	1.00	€ 750,368.76	$668,122.85
September 2006	.93	1.00	€ 670,092.84	$637,697.79
Q4 CY 2006	.90	1.00	€ 1,865,332.19	$1,678,604.91
October 2006	.92	1.00	€ 487,943.39	$449,344.69
November 2006	.89	1.00	€ 779,749.13	$698,449.60
December 2006	.89	1.00	€ 597,639.67	$530,810.61
Grand Total	**.90**	**1.00**	**€ 4,134,145.70**	**$3,713,626.10**

Note how the average EURO rate has varied from month to month; this is why we need to take the currency rate into consideration for accurately reporting reseller sales amounts during each time period. Measure expressions are intended precisely for this purpose. Also note that the grand total for the second half of 2006 is the sum of the Reseller Sales Amount in EURO for July 2006 through December 2006 and *not* the grand total divided by the average rate for this time span (which would have been 3713626.10/.90 = 4126251.22).

How to do it...

To define a measure expression for the Reseller Sales Amount measure, the following steps need to be followed:

1. Open the Adventure Works **cube**, then expand the Reseller Sales **measure group** under **Measures** pane within the **Cube Structure** tab.

2. Select the Reseller Sales Amount measures, and activate the **Properties** window.

3. Edit the measure expression property to state [Reseller Sales Amount] / [Average Rate]. As mentioned earlier, the measures included in the measure expression could be from the same or different measure groups.

4. Save the solution, and reprocess the Reseller Sales measure group.

5. Since this measure expression is included with the sample database you could remove it first and check the cube values without it to understand the effect of the calculation.

5
Optimizing Dimension and Cube Processing

In this chapter, we will cover:

- ▶ Understanding dimension processing options
- ▶ Learning about basic dimension processing
- ▶ Learning advanced dimension processing options
- ▶ Using out-of-line bindings for dimension processing
- ▶ Dealing with partition processing options
- ▶ Using SQL Server Integration Services to process Analysis Services objects
- ▶ Monitoring and tuning processing performance

Introduction

This chapter discusses various processing options available with dimensions and cubes. As discussed in the previous chapters, all commands sent to Analysis Services use XMLA language—the same holds true for processing commands. You will start by learning the basic processing commands and work your way up to more complex options.

If you use ROLAP storage for any of your SSAS objects, processing simply defines metadata; ROLAP does not copy relational data into multidimensional format. You can reference *Chapter 3, Creating Analysis Services Cubes*, for more information about various storage options. For the remainder of this chapter, we will discuss processing for MOLAP objects.

Processing loads the data from the relational database tables into the Analysis Services objects. The easiest option allows the processing of the entire Analysis Services database, including all dimensions and all partitions. This option is suitable for tiny sample databases or for a proof of concept type implementation that has a few megabytes of data. However, for real-world applications, you must approach processing carefully, as loading many gigabytes or even terabytes of data into the cube daily is not a viable option.

The most common approach is to fully process the database periodically—when it is first deployed and after applying any structural changes. At other times, you should process dimensions incrementally, and process only those partitions whose data has changed or has not yet been loaded into Analysis Services.

Understanding dimension processing options

We must ensure that each dimension referenced, by a particular measure group, has an up-to-date dataset prior to processing any partitions in that measure group. If we attempt to process a measure group before dimensions have up-to-date data, we will encounter missing key errors and the measure group / partition processing will fail.

How it works...

The following table summarizes dimension processing options:

Processing option	Description	Used for
ProcessFull	This option loads a full dimension dataset and rebuilds all indexes. This option invalidates all partitions referencing the current dimension; every partition will have to be fully reprocessed.	Each dimension must first be processed using ProcessFull. From time to time, you should reprocess these dimensions to remove fragmentation introduced by ProcessAdd or ProcessUpdate.
ProcessClear	This option empties a dimension object's contents to "unprocess" the dimension.	This option is sometimes necessary if you reach a 4 GB string store limit (applicable to SSAS versions prior to 2012), and the ProcessUpdate option fails to complete. In this case, use ProcessClear followed by ProcessFull, after ensuring that you use the smallest data type possible for each attribute and that you only load the data values necessary for analytics.

Processing option	Description	Used for
ProcessData	This option loads a full dataset into a previously unprocessed dimension without building indexes.	This option is sometimes useful for 32-bit systems that are short on memory, to ensure the processing of a very large dimension completely, without exhausting all memory.
ProcessIndexes	This option rebuilds indexes on a dimension after it has been populated with a full dataset.	This option is used for same scenarios as the ProcessData option.
ProcessAdd	This option loads only newly added records to the dimension from the most recent time it was fully processed.	This option is the less intrusive of the two incremental processing options for dimensions. Since it does not account for updated or deleted records, ProcessAdd does not invalidate existing partition indexes or aggregations. ProcessAdd is also used for incremental processing with out-of-line bindings, discussed later in this chapter.
ProcessUpdate	This option incrementally refreshes the dimension accounting for all data changes: inserts, updates, and deletes.	This option drops existing partition indexes and aggregations that are invalidated due to dimension data changes. SSAS 2012 has an intelligent engine, capable of keeping the indexes and aggregations that are still valid, instead of wiping out all existing structures. However, ProcessUpdate still has to check every partition referenced by the updated dimension to determine which of these indexes need to be dropped. You must use the ProcessIndexes partition processing option (after running ProcessUpdate on dimensions) to re-create missing indexes and aggregations.
ProcessDefault	This option brings a dimension from its current state to a fully-processed state.	This option is viable if your dataset is small, and finer control over dimension processing isn't a concern.

Learning about basic dimension processing

You can process dimensions using SSMS processing dialog or XMLA script. Alternatively, you could use the `ascmd.exe` command line utility to schedule a dimension processing. While developing the solution, you could also process dimensions using SSDT.

Getting ready

Launch SSMS and connect to the existing `AdventureWorks_Sample` database, which has been previously deployed on your instance of Analysis Services. Expand the `Dimensions` folder within the current database.

How to do it...

To process a dimension, perform the following steps:

1. Right-click on any dimension and choose **Process**; doing so opens the **Process Dimension** dialog.

2. Choose any of the dimension processing options except `ProcessAdd`. This option is not available in the dialog.

3. Click on the **Script** button in the top-left corner of the dialog and choose **Script Action to New Query Editor Window**. The sample XMLA command for processing the **Geography** dimension is as follows:

```
<Batch xmlns = "http://
  schemas.microsoft.com/analysisservices/2003/engine">
  <Parallel>
    <Process xmlns:xsd = "http://www.w3.org/2001/XMLSchema"
             xmlns:xsi = "http://www.w3.org/2001/
                 XMLSchema-instance"
             xmlns:ddl2 = "http://schemas.microsoft.com/
                 analysisservices/2003/engine/2"
             xmlns:ddl2_2 = "http://schemas.microsoft.com/
                 analysisservices/2003/engine/2/2"
             xmlns:ddl100_100 = "http://
                 schemas.microsoft.com/analysisservices/
                     2008/engine/100/100"
             xmlns:ddl200 = "http://schemas.microsoft.com/
                 analysisservices/2010/engine/200"
             xmlns:ddl200_200 = "http://
                 schemas.microsoft.com/analysisservices/
                     2010/engine/200/200"
             xmlns:ddl300 = "http://schemas.microsoft.com/
                 analysisservices/2011/engine/300"
             xmlns:ddl300_300 = "http://
                 schemas.microsoft.com/analysisservices/
```

```
                  2011/engine/300/300">
    <Object>
      <DatabaseID>AdventureWorks_Sample</DatabaseID>
      <DimensionID>Dim Geography</DimensionID>
    </Object>
    <Type>ProcessUpdate</Type>
    <WriteBackTableCreation>UseExisting
      </WriteBackTableCreation>
    </Process>
  </Parallel>
</Batch>
```

4. To change the processing option, simply edit the `<Type>` tag. For example, to use the incremental processing option, `ProcessAdd`, change the line to say:

```
<Type>ProcessAdd</Type>
```

5. Switch back to the **Process Dimension** dialog, and click on the **Change Settings** button. The resulting dialog has two tabs: **Processing options** and **Dimension key errors**.

6. The first processing option allows you to process objects in parallel or sequence. Since you're currently processing a single dimension, this option doesn't make a difference to our processing. However, if you were processing multiple dimensions, you could specify how many of them should be processed in parallel. If you change the degree of parallelism to 3, the XMLA statement will include the following tag after the `<Batch>` command:

```
<Parallel MaxParallel="3">
```

7. Should you choose the **Sequential** button, you will see the multiple options to process all the objects in a single transaction, or to create a separate transaction for each object. Choosing separate transactions adds the following string to the `<Batch>` command:

```
Transaction="false"
```

8. Unfortunately, **SSMS Object Explorer** does not provide a graphical option for processing multiple dimensions at the same time. However, now that you've seen the `<Batch>` command processing a single dimension, it won't be difficult to extend it to include three dimensions, as shown in the following code snippet. Though this might seem like a lot of code, it simply repeats the `<Process>` command while substituting the identifier for the **Promotion**, **Account**, and **Geography** dimensions:

```
<Batch xmlns = "http://schemas.microsoft.com/
  analysisservices/2003/engine">
  <Parallel MaxParallel="3">
    <Process>
      <Object>
        <DatabaseID>AdventureWorks_Sample</DatabaseID>
```

```
        <DimensionID>Dim Geography</DimensionID>
      </Object>
      <Type>ProcessUpdate</Type>
<WriteBackTableCreation>UseExisting
  </WriteBackTableCreation>
      </Process>
      <Process>
        <Object>
          <DatabaseID>AdventureWorks_Sample</DatabaseID>
          <DimensionID>Dim Account</DimensionID>
        </Object>
        <Type>ProcessUpdate</Type>
<WriteBackTableCreation>UseExisting
  </WriteBackTableCreation>
      </Process>
      <Process>
        <Object>
          <DatabaseID>AdventureWorks_Sample</DatabaseID>
          <DimensionID>Dim Promotion</DimensionID>
        </Object>
        <Type>ProcessUpdate</Type>
<WriteBackTableCreation>UseExisting
  </WriteBackTableCreation>
      </Process>
    </Parallel>
</Batch>
```

> If you would like to process multiple dimensions in parallel using SSMS, open the **Object Explorer Details** window by pressing the *F7* button on your keyboard or by navigating to **View** | **Object Explorer Details**. This window allows you to hold down the *Shift* key and select multiple dimensions at the same time. Once you choose multiple dimensions, you can either process or delete them using a single command.

9. SSDT allows processing multiple dimensions using a single batch. Simply click on multiple dimensions while holding down the *Shift* key and choose **Process**. Doing so opens the **Process Dimension** dialog, identical to that available with SSMS, except the dialog lists all the chosen dimensions.

10. Execute the XMLA statement by pressing *F5* and monitor what happens behind the scenes using **SQL Server Profiler** (you can use the default Analysis Services template within **SQL Server Profiler**).

How it works...

SQL Server Profiler will report the following event subclasses during dimension processing:

- Build processing schedule
- Execute SQL
- Read data
- Write data
- Build decode
- Build index
- Object created
- Commit

So running the process update on a dimension involves allocating Analysis Services threads, executing queries against the relational data store, reading data, and subsequently, writing to MOLAP storage, and building indexes prior to committing the transaction.

If you look closely, SSAS also has an event subclass, `object created`, which should more appropriately be named `object updated`. This is because we must update each partition's indexes and aggregations to reflect changes in the dimension data. You can scroll over to the **ObjectName** column within **SQL Server Profiler** to see the list of affected partitions.

If you check the `SELECT` statements submitted to the relational database engine, you will find that they're not exactly identical to the dimension table / view definition. Analysis Services writes a separate query for each attribute and retrieves distinct values. If you find that such queries take too long to complete or if SSAS runs out of memory during dimension processing, you could alter the **ProcessingGroup** dimension property. The default value for this property is **ByAttribute**. Changing the property to the **ByTable** value will advise SSAS to run a single `SELECT` statement for the entire dimension, instead of running separate queries for each attribute. Furthermore, the query will no longer include the `DISTINCT` keyword.

Learning advanced dimension processing options

In the previous recipe, you processed a few dimensions after altering the degree of parallelism. You can specify additional options to handle any errors you might encounter during processing from the same dialog using the **Dimension key errors** tab. You should handle a majority of the data quality issues in the **Extraction, Transformation, and Loading (ETL)** layer of your application. However, in some cases it's acceptable to ignore processing errors, particularly during the development stage when your ETL routines might be half-baked. The following table lists the remaining dimension processing options you can specify:

Processing option	Description
Key error action	The default action in case of an error is to convert the attribute key to the `unknown` member. The other alternative is to discard the record. Though this is a viable alternative during the development phase, you should be careful with discarding dimension records in production since this will also cause Analysis Services to exclude partition data for any ignored dimension records, and by doing so would lead to inaccurate reports.
Processing error limit	The `Ignore errors count` value ignores all errors. The other value is `Stop on Error`. This value allows you to specify the number of errors to ignore before you stop processing or stop logging errors.
Specific error conditions	Conditions include `KeyNotFound`, `KeyDuplicate`, `NullKeyConvertedToUnknown`, and `NullKeyNotAllowed`. In each case, `key` refers to an attribute key column. Each condition allows three ways of dealing with the problem:
	`IgnoreError`: Error is not logged or reported.
	`ReportAndContinue`: Error is reported in the processing dialog, but processing continues.
	`ReportAndStop`: Error is reported and processing stops.
`Error log path`	This allows specifying the name and full path to the file which contains any dimension key related errors encountered during processing.

How to do it...

To customize error handling for a processing command, perform the following steps:

1. Navigate to the **Dimension key errors** tab within SSMS or SSDT and make the desired selections.

2. If you prefer to use XMLA, the command will include the string similar to the following code, immediately after the `<Batch>` tag:

```
<ErrorConfiguration
    <KeyErrorLimit>-1</KeyErrorLimit>
    <KeyErrorLogFile>C:\key_errors.txt</KeyErrorLogFile>
    <KeyNotFound>ReportAndStop</KeyNotFound>
    <KeyDuplicate>ReportAndContinue</KeyDuplicate>
        <NullKeyConvertedToUnknown>ReportAndContinue
            </NullKeyConvertedToUnknown>
    <NullKeyNotAllowed>ReportAndStop</NullKeyNotAllowed>
    </ErrorConfiguration>
```

Using out-of-line bindings for dimension processing

You could use out-of-line bindings for incrementally processing very large dimensions without having to read the full dataset. In this context, the term *binding* applies to the dimension table or view. The sample database only has a handful of records for each dimension table, but in a realistic scenario you could have a client, customer, or even product dimension with millions of members. On a normal day, you could expect only a small number (compared to the total number) of dimension members to be added. Keep in mind that the `ProcessAdd` option reads the entire dataset in order to determine which rows must be added to the SSAS dimension. Running a query against a multimillion row dimension table could add an undue burden to the relational database engine and cause processing to be unnecessarily lengthy. Fortunately, there is a better option: out-of-line bindings.

How to do it...

Let's pretend for a few minutes that Adventure Works has grown by leaps and bounds to become a multibillion dollar enterprise, which sells products to millions of customers. We try to process data many times per day, but can't afford to query the gigantic customer dimension each time. Instead you have built a SQL Server view named `NewCustomers`, which dynamically determines only those records which haven't been added to the Analysis Services dimension (perhaps by checking the `Create Date` column, and comparing it to the last time the dimension was successfully processed). You will use this view to add new customers throughout the week by performing the following steps. Over the weekend, you can run `ProcessUpdate` against the full customer dataset to prune any obsolete records as well as refresh/update existing records that might have changed.

1. Connect to the SSAS instance with `Adventure Works DW` sample database using SSMS, expand the `Dimensions` folder, right-click on the **Customer** dimension, and chose **Process**.

2. Change the processing option to **Process Update**, choose the option to ignore duplicate key errors (as shown earlier in this chapter), and select **Script Action to New Query Window**. Once the statement is scripted, click on **Cancel** on the **Processing** dialog, and edit the `<Type>` tag of the XMLA command to `ProcessAdd`.

3. Switch to SSDT and open the sample database solution (not the live database, but rather the project that defines it). Open the `Adventure Works DW.dsv` data source view.

4. Remove all tables except `Customer` and `Geography` from the data source view. Do not save changes. (In this case, we need the `Geography` table because some `Customer` attributes use columns in the `Geography` table. If your dimension only references a single table, you could remove all objects except the entity referenced by the `Dimension` attributes.)

5. Right-click on the `Customer` table and choose **Replace Table with New Named Query**. Replace **FROM DimCustomer** with **FROM NewCustomers** within the **Edit Named Query** dialog. Leave all column selections and everything else intact.

6. Right-click on the `Adventure Works DW.dsv` data source view and choose **View Code**. Copy the full contents of the resulting XMLA, and paste it into the SSMS window where you have the `ProcessAdd` command for the **Customer** dimension. Be sure the entire statement is within the `<Process>` tag.

7. Remove all content between the `<Annotations>` and `</Annotations>` tags. Also remove the `<CreatedTimestamp>` and `<LastSchemaUpdate>` sections from the XMLA processing command.

8. Save the XMLA command to a file, and execute the processing command in SSMS. If you monitor the processing using **SQL Server Profiler**, you will see a command similar to the following code, confirming that we are using the `NewCustomers` view and not the `DimCustomer` table to refresh the dimension:

```
SELECT
    DISTINCT
  [dbo_DimCustomer].[CustomerKey] AS
  [dbo_DimCustomerCustomerKey0_0],[dbo_DimCustomer].
  [FullName] AS [dbo_DimCustomerFullName0_1],
    FROM
      (

SELECT          CustomerKey, GeographyKey,
   CustomerAlternateKey,
FROM              newCustomers
      )
    AS [dbo_DimCustomer],[dbo].[DimGeography] AS
    [dbo_DimGeography]
    WHERE
    (

    (

    [dbo_DimCustomer].[GeographyKey] =
    [dbo_DimGeography].[GeographyKey]
    ))
```

Dealing with partition processing options

Once you are happy with the dimensions' processed state, it's time to process partitions, measure groups, and cubes.

Although you can process an entire measure group or even an entire cube, those options are rarely used. Instead you're likely to process only the most recent (perhaps daily) partition in each measure group. If you use the `ProcessUpdate` incremental dimension processing option, you will also need to rebuild indexes on some or all partitions in the affected measure groups.

The following table summarizes partition processing options:

Processing option	Description	Used for
ProcessClear	This option empties out the partition's contents to "unprocess" it.	This option could be useful if you're running out of disk space on the data drive and need to quickly free up some space by unprocessing a historically obsolete partition. You can also use this option if you find, and subsequently fix, discrepancies in fact data.
		The same option applies to measure groups, cubes, and databases. If a database is particularly large, deleting it could take an exceedingly long time, unless you first "unprocess" it.
ProcessFull	This option loads a full dataset into a partition, and builds the necessary indexes and aggregations.	Each partition must be fully processed to provide optimal querying performance.
ProcessAdd	This option incrementally updates an existing partition by defining the query which returns only those rows not already found in the SSAS partition. The query could include the condition such as record_create_date > 'last processed date' to limit the dataset.	Though rarely used, this incremental processing option is useful when your relational source has an incomplete dataset during the previous execution of ProcessFull. In the background, SSAS creates a temporary partition, processes it, and subsequently merges it with the existing partition.
ProcessData	This option loads the full dataset, but does not build the aggregations and indexes.	This option is useful on 32-bit implementations that cannot use more than 2 GB of memory. Separating data and aggregation processing could prevent SSAS from running out of memory.
ProcessIndexes	This option creates indexes and aggregations on a partition that already has the full dataset.	This option is necessary after running ProcessUpdate on dimensions. This option could also be required in the case of sparse memory resources.

Processing option	Description	Used for
ProcessClearIndexes	This option drops existing indexes and aggregations without deleting data.	This option is useful after you change the aggregation design and would like to use a new set of aggregations. This option must follow up with ProcessIndexes to build the new aggregations.
ProcessDefault	This option brings the partition from its current state into a fully-processed state.	This option is used only if finer control on the partition processing isn't required.

How to do it...

To process a partition, perform the following steps:

1. Select an existing partition by expanding cubes, measure groups, and partitions' folders within SSMS. Right-click and choose **Process**. You can process multiple partitions by opening **Object Explorer Details**, by pressing *F7* within SSMS, then selecting desired partitions, right-clicking and choosing **Process**.

2. Much like what you saw with dimensions, SSDT allows choosing multiple partitions if you wish to process them in the same batch. To use SSDT for partition processing, navigate to the **Partitions** tab within the cube designer, expand the measure group you're interested in, and click on the partitions you want to process while holding down the *Shift* key.

3. Both SSDT and SSMS allow for setting the same options as with dimension processing. The options you could specify are the degree of parallelism, dimension key errors, and whether the entire batch should be processed in a single transaction.

   Dimension errors could occur during the partition processing if the partition query (or table) references a dimension key that does not exist in the SSAS dimension. This is the reason why you should process dimensions prior to processing any partitions.

   Exercise special care when processing many partitions in parallel. SSAS sometimes attempts to bite off more than it can handle unless you explicitly specify the number of partitions to be processed in parallel. Furthermore, the relational source could also get overburdened if you attempt processing too many partitions in parallel, because processing each one requires sending a hefty query to the relational database.

4. Sadly, SSDT does not provide an option to script the processing command. Not to worry, you can get the XMLA command from **SQL Server Profiler**. For example, the following command processes three partitions in parallel:

```
<Batch xmlns = "http://schemas.microsoft.com/
  analysisservices/2003/engine">
  <Parallel MaxParallel="3">
    <Process>
    <Object>
    <DatabaseID>AdventureWorks_Sample</DatabaseID>
    <CubeID>Adventure Works</CubeID>
    <MeasureGroupID>Fact Internet Sales 1</MeasureGroupID>
    <PartitionID>Internet_Sales_2005</PartitionID>
    </Object>
    <Type>ProcessFull</Type>
    <WriteBackTableCreation>UseExisting
      </WriteBackTableCreation>
    </Process>
    <Process>
    <Object>
    <DatabaseID>AdventureWorks_Sample</DatabaseID>
    <CubeID>Adventure Works</CubeID>
    <MeasureGroupID>Fact Internet Sales 1</MeasureGroupID>
    <PartitionID>Internet_Sales_2006</PartitionID>
    </Object>
    <Type>ProcessFull</Type>
    <WriteBackTableCreation>UseExisting
      </WriteBackTableCreation>
    </Process>
    <Process>
    <Object>
    <DatabaseID>AdventureWorks_Sample</DatabaseID>
    <CubeID>Adventure Works</CubeID>
    <MeasureGroupID>Fact Internet Sales 1</MeasureGroupID>
    <PartitionID>Internet_Sales_2007</PartitionID>
    </Object>
    <Type>ProcessFull</Type>
    <WriteBackTableCreation>UseExisting
      </WriteBackTableCreation>
    </Process>
  </Parallel>
</Batch>
```

How it works...

SQL Server Profiler reports the following event subclasses:

- ▶ Build processing schedule
- ▶ Execute SQL
- ▶ Read data
- ▶ Write data
- ▶ Build aggregations and indexes
- ▶ Aggregate
- ▶ Merge aggregations on disk
- ▶ Object created
- ▶ Commit

Much like with dimension processing, partition processing also involves building processing schedules, allocating SSAS threads, running SQL statements against the relational source, and reading data and writing it into MOLAP storage. Additionally, we build indexes and aggregations (if aggregations are defined and assigned to the partition).

Using SQL Server Integration Services to process Analysis Services objects

SQL Server Integration Services (**SSIS**) is an enterprise-level data ETL tool, which can be used for a multitude of purposes, including the processing of Analysis Services objects. SSIS is a huge product in its own right and even the discussion of its capabilities is well beyond the scope of this book. In this section, you will learn how to create a simple SSIS package that processes various SSAS objects. You could extend the SSIS solution to include a variety of tasks, such as extraction of data from source systems, populating a staging area, populating a Star schema data warehouse, and so on.

How to do it...

To create a SSIS package for processing SSAS objects, perform the following steps:

1. Open SSDT and navigate to **File | New Project**. Choose **Integration Services Project** from the business intelligence templates and provide a descriptive name for the project.

2. Drag **Analysis Services Processing Task** from the SSIS toolbox to the package's **Control Flow** tab. Give the task a descriptive name, for example, `Process Objects in Sample Database`.

3. Double-click on the task to open the **Analysis Services Processing Task** editor. Next navigate to the **Processing Settings** tab to choose objects to be processed.

4. Once you configure a connection to your Analysis Services instance and specify the database, you can choose multiple cubes, measure groups, partitions, and dimensions you wish to process.

5. When you click on the **Impact Analysis** button, SSIS provides you with the list of objects which will be impacted by processing options you chose. For example, fully-processing dimensions will cause partitions to become unprocessed. You also have an option to check the impacted object in order to add it to the list of objects, which will be processed by this task, as shown in the following screenshot:

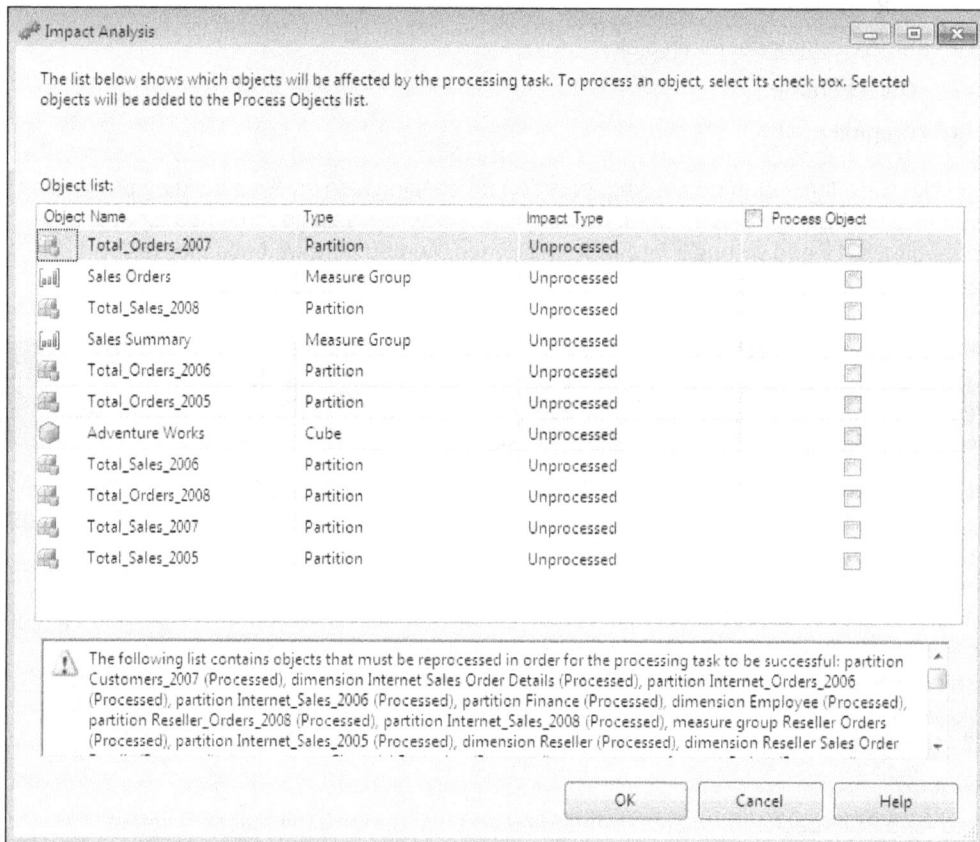

The Impact Analysis window shows:

> The list below shows which objects will be affected by the processing task. To process an object, select its check box. Selected objects will be added to the Process Objects list.

Object list:

Object Name	Type	Impact Type	Process Object
Total_Orders_2007	Partition	Unprocessed	
Sales Orders	Measure Group	Unprocessed	
Total_Sales_2008	Partition	Unprocessed	
Sales Summary	Measure Group	Unprocessed	
Total_Orders_2006	Partition	Unprocessed	
Total_Orders_2005	Partition	Unprocessed	
Adventure Works	Cube	Unprocessed	
Total_Sales_2006	Partition	Unprocessed	
Total_Orders_2008	Partition	Unprocessed	
Total_Sales_2007	Partition	Unprocessed	
Total_Sales_2005	Partition	Unprocessed	

> The following list contains objects that must be reprocessed in order for the processing task to be successful: partition Customers_2007 (Processed), dimension Internet Sales Order Details (Processed), partition Internet_Orders_2006 (Processed), partition Internet_Sales_2006 (Processed), partition Finance (Processed), dimension Employee (Processed), partition Reseller_Orders_2008 (Processed), partition Internet_Sales_2008 (Processed), measure group Reseller Orders (Processed), partition Internet_Sales_2005 (Processed), dimension Reseller (Processed), dimension Reseller Sales Order

6. You can change additional processing settings as you could with SSMS and SSDT: specify the number of objects to be processed in parallel, whether they should be processed in a single transaction or not, as well as custom configuration for dimension key errors. Click on **OK** once you're happy with your selection of the processing settings.

7. To test the task you have just defined, you can right-click on it and choose **Execute Task**.

Another option for executing processing XMLA commands is to use **Analysis Services Execute DDL Task** available under the **Other Tasks** group within the SSIS toolbox. To process objects using this option, first use SSMS to script the processing XMLA command you wish to use and save it to a file. To execute this file using SSIS package, perform the following steps:

1. Drag **Analysis Services Execute DDL Task**, found under the **Other Tasks** group, to the package's **Control Flow** tab. Provide a descriptive name for the task, for example, ProcessDailyPartition..

2. Double-click on the task to launch **Analysis Services Execute DDL Task Editor**. Navigate to the **DDL** tab, and set **Connection** to the instance of Analysis Services where you want to process objects.

3. You have multiple options for the **Source Type** property as follows:

   ❑ **Direct Input**: This option means that you will specify the XMLA command directly in the SSIS package. This only works if you're confident that your XMLA will rarely change. If you choose **Direct Input** source type, SSIS will allow you to specify the XMLA command in the **Source Direct** property.

   ❑ **File Connection**: This option means that you will specify the file containing the XMLA command. This option is more flexible than the **Direct Input** option, because you can change the XMLA file as needed without having to edit the SSIS package.

   ❑ **Variable**: This option is used to specify a variable containing the processing XMLA. This is the most flexible option that allows setting a variable value dynamically, perhaps based on values found in a relational database table.

4. For this example, choose the **File Connection** option for **Source Type** and specify the full path to the file containing the processing command.

5. To test the task, right-click on it and choose **Execute Task**.

6. The **Execute DDL** task could be used to execute any XMLA, not just for processing. For example, you could use the same SSIS task type to create new partitions or synchronize a database from one SSAS instance to another.

Once you're happy with your SSIS package, you could schedule its execution using the SQL Server Agent job, as follows:

1. Create a new job in SSMS, add a new step, and provide a descriptive name, such as `process SSAS objects`.

> Please reference `http://technet.microsoft.com/en-us/library/ms190268.aspx#SSMSProcedure` for more information on how to create a **SQL Server Agent** job.

2. The package can be stored on a filesystem, SQL Server, SSIS package store, or SSIS catalog. For this example, you can keep the package on the filesystem and provide the full path to the package within the **New Job Step** configuration, as shown in the following screenshot:

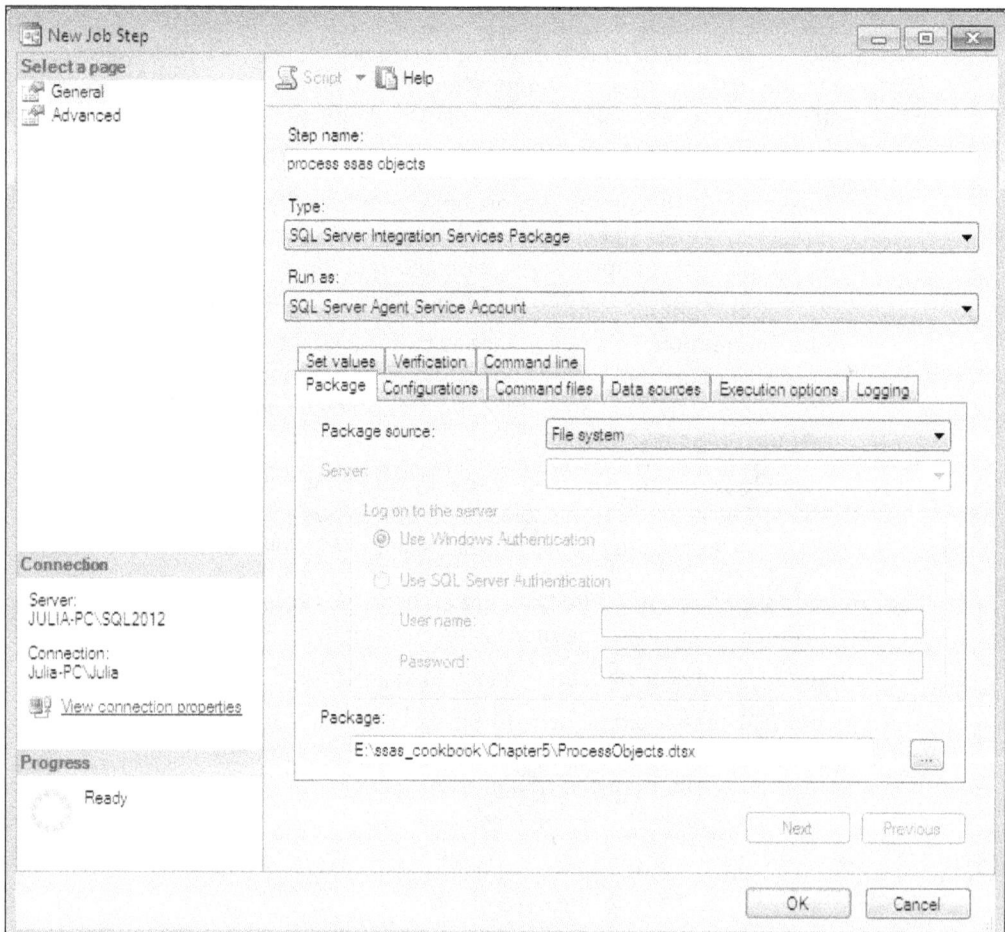

3. As you can see in the preceding screenshot, you have a number of options you can specify for executing the package. Perhaps the most important of these is the **Data Sources** tab, which allows you to specify the SSAS instance on which you wish to process objects. This allows you to easily move your SSIS package from development to QA, and subsequently to production environment without having to edit it directly.

4. Specify any additional job steps, execution schedule, and alerts/notifications as needed before saving the job.

Monitoring and tuning processing performance

The performance of Analysis Services is mainly measured in terms of how quickly you can execute MDX queries. However, if cube data becomes stale it may no longer be helpful to the decision makers. Optimal processing performance ensures timely availability of up-to-date data in a user-friendly, highly efficient format. You can monitor SSAS processing using Performance Monitor (**PerfMon**) as well as **SQL Server Profiler**. Processing performance is heavily dependent on how quickly you can query the relational data source objects, but SSAS hardware and other operations running concurrently could also introduce a bottleneck. There are some Analysis Services configuration options you could tweak to try to improve the processing performance. In this section, you will learn about **PerfMon** counters and **SQL Server Profiler** events useful for monitoring processing, as well as useful configuration options for troubleshooting processing issues.

You can launch **PerfMon** by executing `perfmon.exe` using Run from the Start menu (depending on your operating system the steps might vary, but you can find the executable under the `\Windows\System32` folder). There are a number of **PerfMon** counters you could collect, but choosing too many counters can quickly make the output overwhelmingly difficult to decipher. Instead you should try to focus on specific counters that are particularly useful for detecting the problem you are troubleshooting. The following table summarizes the most useful counters for troubleshooting processing performance:

Counter group: counter	Explanation
Processing: rows read / second	Number of rows read per second while processing dimension or partition data. It would be unfair to specify a range of values that indicates excellent performance, because the rate of reading data will depend on the relational source, hardware, network connectivity, and OLEDB / .NET provider efficiency. Generally OLEDB providers are more efficient than .NET providers.
	When processing many partitions in parallel, it's not uncommon to see SSAS read hundreds of thousands of rows per second on highly tuned systems. If this counter is in hundreds or low thousands, you should check your relational database for tuning opportunities.

Counter group: counter	Explanation
Processing: total rows / read	Total number of rows read since the SSAS instance was started. This counter isn't particularly useful for monitoring current performance, but rather for gauging the level of processing activity since the last restart.
Processing: rows converted / second	Number of rows converted from relational source into a multidimensional format.
Processing: total rows converted	Total number of rows converted from relational source into a multidimensional format.
Processing: rows written / sec	Number of rows written to the disk in a multidimensional format. Again, it is unfair to stipulate the number that constitutes excellent performance, but if this number is much lower than number of rows read per second you need to check the logical / physical disk counters.
Processing: total rows written	Total number of rows written to the disk as part of processing since the instance was last started.
Threads: Processing Pool Job Queue Length	A nonzero value indicates that some processing threads had to be queued up; this is because not enough worker threads were made available for all active processing requests. Keep in mind that processing threads are used for processing as well as querying. Check CPU utilization on the server. If CPU is already busy (>=80 percent), additional worker threads will not help. If the CPU usage is below 80 percent, you could increase the number of available processing threads to improve the processing performance.
Proc Indexes: Current Partitions	Number of partitions for which SSAS is currently building indexes.
Proc Indexes: Total Partitions	Total number of partitions for which SSAS has built indexes since the instance was last started.
Proc Indexes: rows / sec	Number of rows already converted into a multidimensional format, which SSAS reads to build indexes. If this number is low, your SSAS could be short on memory resource.
Proc Indexes: total rows	Total number of rows SSAS has read to build indexes since the instance was last restarted.
Proc Aggregations: Current Partitions	Number of partitions for which SSAS is currently building aggregations.
Proc Aggregations: Total Partitions	Total number of partitions for which SSAS has built aggregations since the instance was last restarted.
Proc Aggregations: Temp file rows written / sec	If SSAS does not have sufficient space to create the aggregations in memory, some of the rows will be written to temporary files on the disk. A nonzero value for this counter indicates that SSAS could use additional memory.

Counter group: counter	Explanation
Proc Aggregations: Temp file bytes written / sec	Number of temporary file bytes written on disk per second. Much like the previous counter, a nonzero value indicates memory shortage.
Processor: % processor time	CPU utilization on the host. This counter isn't specific to SSAS, but rather indicates the total CPU usage. If the counter is at or above 80 percent, you may have a CPU bottleneck. Try to isolate SSAS to its own host if possible.
Physical Disk: Current Disk Queue Length AND / OR Logical Disk: Current Disk Queue Length	A nonzero value of this counter indicates that you could have a disk bottleneck; some disk requests cannot be served right away and have to wait in a queue. If you have a single local disk on your server, the logical and physical disk are the same. Many production implementations use high performance **Storage Area Network (SAN)** or **Solid State Disk (SSD)** data volumes. You could be using SAN with RAID features, when a single volume consists of multiple striped or mirrored disks. In this case, it might be beneficial to monitor each physical disk to determine which one is busy causing SSAS requests to queue up.
Memory: Memory Usage KB	The total amount of memory in KB used by SSAS instance. You will learn more about SSAS memory management in *Chapter 8, Administering and Monitoring Analysis Services*. On older operating systems it might be beneficial to reserve some memory at SSAS instance start-up.

How to do it...

To collect **PerfMon** counters, perform the following steps:

1. Launch **PerfMon** prior to kicking off the processing jobs, expand the `Data Collector Sets` folder, and choose **User Defined**.

2. In the right-hand pane, navigate to **New | Data Collector Set**.

3. Name the collector set `SSAS Processing`, and choose the **Create Manually (Advanced)** option.

4. On the next screen, choose **Create Data Logs** and check the **Performance Counter** checkbox.

5. The screen that follows lets you click on the **Add** button and then pick the counters of interest. If you check the **Show description** box, **PerfMon** will also display a brief description of the highlighted counter.

6. Be sure to define the sample interval. Depending on how busy your server is and how long SSAS processing takes, you could choose to collect counters every five seconds or every minute.

7. The next screen allows you to specify the directory where the log will be stored. By default, **Perfmon** creates the `Perflogs` directory on the system root drive and stores files in that folder. Feel free to override as desired.

8. The final screen allows you to specify the Windows account used to run the data collection. The user must have administrative permissions to the host.

9. Select your **Data Collection Set** and click on the **Start** button to kick it off. Once your processing is done, stop your collection set and review the results.

You can launch **SQL Server Profiler** by navigating to **Start | Microsoft SQL Server 2012 | Performance Tools | SQL Server Profiler**. Although you can collect a large number of **SQL Server Profiler** events and columns, you should exercise care to keep the trace to a reasonable size, while containing the necessary troubleshooting data. Bear in mind that **SQL Server Profiler** does add some overheads to Analysis Server; the more events you collect the larger the overhead.

The following is the list of events I find particularly helpful for troubleshooting processing performance:

Event class and event	Description
Command events: `Command Begin` and `Command End`	Record the start and completion of processing (and any other) commands. Pay attention to other commands taking place on the same instance too, as these could conflict with your processing. For example, a job creating new partitions or deleting historical partitions could block your processing because both operations update metadata.
Errors and warnings: `Error`	Useful for detecting and resolving any errors encountered during processing. For example, missing attribute keys will fail partition processing unless you explicitly specify the option to ignore missing key errors.
Locks: `Deadlock, Lock Acquired, Lock Released, Lock Timeout, Lock Waiting`	Analysis Services' processing job can be blocked if there is a conflicting processing command. Additionally, long running queries may prevent SSAS from updating metadata. You could also experience delays if the processing job runs while the database is being synchronized.

Event class and event	Description
Progress reports: `Progress Report Begin`, `Progress Report End`, `Progress Report Current`, and `Progress Report Error`	Progress reports are particularly useful for monitoring processing in-flight. For example, `Progress Report Current` shows the number of rows read for a partition or dimension being processed, whereas `Progress Report Error` displays the error encountered during a specific object's processing. These events also show the SQL statements executed against the relational database.
Notification events: `Notification`	This event is helpful in detecting when SSAS has completed the creation of new files for the object, and enters the commit phase. During the commit phase, SSAS acquires necessary locks to delete the existing object and replace it with the new set of files. Depending on other activities taking place on the server, the commit phase could be lengthy.

1. Open **SQL Server Profiler**, navigate to **File | New Trace**, and connect to the desired Analysis Services instance.

2. To choose the desired events, switch to the **Events Selection** tab and ensure **Show all events** and **Show all columns** boxes are checked. **SQL Server Profiler** displays a short description of each event and event category.

3. Click on **Run** when you're happy with your selections to collect the trace.

4. Navigate to **File | Stop Trace** when you have collected the desired diagnostics.

5. Navigate to **File | Save As** to save the trace output as a SQL Server table or trace file, if you wish to refer to trace contents later.

> There are a couple of SSAS trace templates included with the **SQL Server Profiler** installation: **Standard (default)** and **Replay**. The default template is fine for most troubleshooting. If you find yourself re-using the same set of counters repeatedly, you can also create your own template. To create a new template navigate to **File | New Template**, and then choose the desired events and columns.

So you collected the troubleshooting artifacts, including the **SQL Server Profiler** and **PerfMon** output. Now what? Since processing performance depends on a number of factors, there are no hard and fast rules for tuning. However, I can provide the list of items that commonly cause poor performance and can be remediated as follows:

- Ensure you have appropriate indexes in the relational database. If you encounter slow performance during the partition processing, be sure to check the query executed by Analysis Services against the relational source. Cut the SQL query captured by **SQL Server Profiler** and paste it into SSMS (presuming that your relational source is SQL Server). Examine the query execution plan and ensure necessary indexes exist.

- Ensure Analysis Services has plenty of memory available to it. If you have multiple SSAS instances running on the same host, or if the host is shared with the SQL Server relational database engine you can use the preallocate configuration option to reserve some memory when the instance starts. Be sure to review SSAS memory configuration properties found in `msmdsrv.ini` as well. Reference *Chapter 8, Administering and Monitoring Analysis Services*, for additional information about configuration options.

- If you see any temporary files created during the aggregation processing, your server does not have sufficient memory. Consider adding memory or separating querying and processing activity onto dedicated SSAS instances. Temporary files can be found under the `<TempDir>` folder, as specified in the `msmdsrv.ini` configuration file.

- Experiment with various degrees of parallelism to see which one works best in your environment. If you have dozens (or even hundreds) of partitions processing, all of them in parallel might not work well, because the relational source might not be able to handle this volume of queries in parallel.

- Watch out for conflicting jobs, for example, processing and synchronization stepping on each other.

- Remember that you have multiple options for dimension processing. Consider using `ProcessAdd` in lieu of `ProcessUpdate` if your dimension tables only have new rows added (no updates or deletes). `ProcessUpdate` needs to check each partition to ensure that none of the indexes have been invalidated. It is not uncommon to see `ProcessUpdate` read dimension data very quickly, but then spend more time refreshing indexes.

- If processing a particular dimension uses an excessive amount of memory and heavily taxes the relational source, consider switching to the **ByTable** processing group option instead of the default value of **ByAttribute**.

- Use out-of-line bindings if you have gigantic dimensions with millions of members.

- If your host does not have much memory it could be helpful to separate the processing partition data from index processing.

▶ If reading data from the relational source is quick but writing takes a long time, be sure to check the disk counters. Remember that each SSAS database could consist of a huge number of files. Suboptimal disk subsystem could hurt both processing and querying performance.

▶ If you have a large database which includes rarely-queried historical partitions, consider using ROLAP storage mode for such partitions, while using MOLAP for frequently-queried partitions.

▶ In rare scenarios, it might be beneficial to experiment with HOLAP. Remember that HOLAP leaves data in the relational format, but builds aggregations on the Analysis Services host. If the relational data source does not support indexed views (that is how ROLAP aggregations are implemented), the only choice is to build aggregations in a multidimensional format. Keep in mind, however, that the Analysis Services engine must scan fact tables (or views) to build aggregations. Reading millions of data rows will be time-consuming, even for building aggregations, hence your processing will be slow. You can't simply run `ProcessIndexes` on partitions after running `ProcessUpdate` on dimensions while using ROLAP; you must fully reprocess partitions, which in this case will mean scanning fact tables specifically to build the aggregations.

▶ If you're processing multiple objects in parallel and see a smaller number of SQL statements sent to the relational source than you expect, based on degree of parallelism, experiment with **BufferMemoryLimit** and **BufferRecordLimit** options. SSAS could overestimate the amount of memory needed for processing each object and, therefore, throttle the number of objects processed. Lowering the value of the mentioned settings can help improve the processing performance by working on more objects in parallel. Also, examine the **Maximum Number of Connections** data source property. Ensure you allow enough connections to your relational data source, but not too many. For example, if you're processing 64 partitions in parallel, but you only allow 10 connections to the data source, you will see that only up to 10 queries will run in parallel and the rest of them will queue up. If your relational database can indeed handle 64 parallel queries, bump up the **Data Source** property to, maximum of 64 connections.

6
MDX

In this chapter, we will cover:

- ▸ Returning data on the query axes
- ▸ Limiting the query output
- ▸ Sorting the query output
- ▸ Defining query-level calculations and named sets
- ▸ Navigating dimension hierarchies
- ▸ Working with the Time dimension
- ▸ MDX script's functionality
- ▸ Monitoring and tuning MDX queries

Introduction

This chapter explains how to write the most commonly encountered **MultiDimensional eXpression (MDX)** queries. You use MDX to model calculations in the MDX script within the cube designer as well as to query the cubes. Although most MDX concepts, functions, and keywords will apply to queries as well as the MDX script, the framework for developing MDX will be distinctly different in each environment.

The basic MDX query construct resembles **Structured Query Language (SQL)** in a sense that both languages include the SELECT, FROM, and WHERE clauses. However, beyond these clauses, the two languages are very different. SQL operates on rows and columns, whereas MDX works on cube cells, tuples, and sets—concepts you must learn to get your mind around the syntax of MDX. Any errors that you encounter when authoring MDX will also refer to the same terms.

Each cube consists of a multitude of cells, with each cell identifying a single member found in each dimension. Although each cube could contain many dimensions, let's consider a cube with only three dimensions:

- **Time**: This dimension contains only one attribute: Year
- **Product**: This dimension contains two attributes: Product Name and Product Color
- **Country of sale**: This dimension contains only one attribute: Country

Let's also suppose that we only have one measure called Sales Amount. The cube consisting of these dimensions will have one cell for each combination of Year, Name, Color, and Country. To further simplify the example, we presume that the cube only contains sales figures for two products, a green sweater and a pair of blue jeans, in the United States and England for the years 2011 and 2012. The following table should help us visualize the cube space:

Year	Product Name	Product Color	Country	Sales Amount
2011	Sweater	Green	USA	200000.00
2011	Sweater	Green	England	NULL
2011	Jeans	Blue	USA	957000.00
2011	Jeans	Blue	England	150000.00
2012	Sweater	Green	USA	250000.00
2012	Sweater	Green	England	350245.00
2012	Jeans	Blue	USA	304892.00
2012	Jeans	Blue	England	384204.00
2011	Sweater	Blue	USA	NULL
2011	Sweater	Blue	England	NULL
2012	Sweater	Blue	USA	NULL
2012	Sweater	Blue	England	NULL
2011	Jeans	Green	USA	NULL
2011	Jeans	Green	England	NULL
2012	Jeans	Green	USA	NULL
2012	Jeans	Green	England	NULL

Notice that the cube space includes many empty cells. For example, the sales amount for green jeans and blue sweaters in both 2011 and 2012 is NULL (or empty) because we did not sell any such products. Also note the large number of cells in an extremely simplistic cube. As we add dimensions, attributes, and measures, the cube space grows exponentially.

To refer to an attribute within MDX, you should specify the dimension, hierarchy, and member names. For example, `[time].[year].[2011]` is an attribute and so is `[product].[product name].[sweater]`. The square brackets around each word are only necessary if the word only consists of digits, if it is an MDX keyword, or if it contains a space.

> You could also identify each dimension member by its key, for example, the following notation identifies a calendar year by its key: `[Date].[Calendar Year].&[2008]`. Note that the ampersand (`&`) sign is followed by the key value of `2008`. As you learned in *Chapter 2, Defining Analysis Services Dimensions*, the attribute key doesn't have to be a numeric value. For example, the following notation identifies the calendar semester of a year by its key CY H1: `[date].[Calendar Semester of Year].&[CY H1]`.

A **tuple** identifies a single cell or multiple cells using a combination of dimensions. Each tuple must be enclosed in parenthesis. For example, `([time].[year].[2011], [product].[product color].[green])` is a tuple defining the cube space consisting of all the green products and the year 2011. Note that this tuple could contain empty cells, meaning the green products that had no sales in 2011 as well. A tuple does not have to include a reference to each attribute from every dimension. In fact, a tuple could only refer to one attribute: `([country].[country].[England])`, which is a valid tuple.

A **set** consists of zero or more tuples. Each set should be enclosed in curly braces. For example:

```
{
([time].[year].[2011], [product].[product name].[sweater]),
([time].[year].[2012], [product].[product name].[jeans])
}
```

The preceding example is a set consisting of two tuples. Note that the tuples you use to construct a set must refer to the same dimensions. We cannot construct a set by combining a tuple referencing only the Country dimension with another tuple referencing time and product dimensions. The majority of MDX functions operate on sets and returns sets.

All of the examples in this chapter will use the sample `Adventure Works 2012` database. To save space we will not list the query results unless necessary. I will refer to the most commonly used MDX functions, but since this is not a book on MDX, I won't discuss the full syntax of each function. You can refer to the SSAS online documentation for the full syntax of each function.

Returning data on the query axes

Each MDX query refers to one or more axes on which data should be returned. You can refer to an axis by its name (columns, rows, pages, and so on) or by its ordinal number, starting at zero. You cannot skip an axis, so each query must include columns (ordinal 0), but could also include rows (ordinal 1), pages (ordinal 2), and so on. The majority of frontend tools can only work with two axes, columns and rows, so don't let this scare you. The SELECT clause of the query must include the definition of all the axes, and the FROM clause defines a single cube (or **perspective**) from which you extract the data. The WHERE clause contains a *slicer* limiting the data set specified in the query's SELECT clause.

Getting ready

To follow the examples in this chapter, please connect to the Analysis Services 2012 instance using the **SQL Server Management Studio** (**SSMS**), right-click on the **Adventure Works 2012** sample database, and go to **New Query | MDX**. This will open a new query window. After typing the query text, you can execute queries by pressing the *F5* key or by clicking on the execute button that includes an exclamation mark (**!**).

How to do it...

Let's get started and look into the steps for returning data on the query axis.

1. Execute the following query to retrieve the total amount of Reseller Sales Amount across all the dimensions:

   ```
   SELECT [Measures].[Reseller Sales Amount] ON 0
   FROM [Adventure Works]
   ```

   Since the query only refers to the Measures dimension, Analysis Services will return data for the default member of each dimension hierarchy. Unless you explicitly define the default member for each attribute while designing a dimension, the default member is ALL.

2. Next, modify the query slightly to include the breakdown of reseller sales by a calendar year:

   ```
   SELECT [Measures].[Reseller Sales Amount] ON 0,
   [Date].[Calendar].[Calendar Year].members ON 1
   FROM [Adventure Works]
   ```

Notice that I have used the `members` function to retrieve a set consisting of every member of the `[Calendar Year]` hierarchy within the date dimension. The `members` function *does not* include any calculated members; you will learn more about calculated members later in this chapter. To include calculated members in the output, use the `allmembers` function instead of `members`.

3. MDX also allows returning sets of multiple hierarchies on each axis using the `CROSSJOIN` function. `CROSSJOIN` accepts two sets as parameters and returns their cross product. For example, the following query will return a cross product of each promotion category with each calendar year on rows and the reseller sales amount measure on columns:

```
SELECT {[Measures].[Reseller Sales Amount]} ON 0,
CROSSJOIN ({[Promotion].[Promotions].[Category].members},
{[Date].[Calendar].[Calendar Year].members}) ON 1
FROM [Adventure Works]
```

You could nest multiple `CROSSJOIN` functions to create a more complex set consisting of multiple dimensions. You could also include cross-joined sets of multiple dimensions on columns. When using a `CROSSJOIN` in MDX, it is important to group all hierarchies from the same dimension together instead of spreading them apart. This will allow the engine to select a more efficient algorithm for the join and should result in improved performance and reduced memory consumption.

4. An alternate syntax for writing `CROSSJOIN` is a single multiplication (`*`) character between each combination of sets. For example, you could rewrite the last query as follows:

```
SELECT [Measures].[Reseller Sales Amount] ON 0,
[Promotion].[Promotions].[Category].members *
[Date].[Calendar].[Calendar Year].members ON 1
FROM [Adventure Works]
```

> Though it is often considered to be the culmination of MDX's power, `CROSSJOIN` of large sets is a rather expensive operation. You can expect query performance to progressively worsen as you add multiple nested `CROSSJOIN` functions. Although the result set could be very useful for reporting purposes, the performance of such queries rarely lives up to the definition of **Online Analytical Processing** (**OLAP**) that expects queries to be completed within a few seconds.

Limiting the query output

MDX supports multiple ways of limiting query results. You could use the `WHERE` clause, often referred to as *slicer*, since it limits the result set by specifying a data slice. You could also use the `FILTER` function to specify the criteria for members included on each axis and thereby derive a more focused result set.

While reviewing the results of queries, as shown in the previous section, you probably noticed that the result sets included some empty cells. As you might imagine, large cubes could include many empty cells, and such data may or may not be desirable in the query's output. You have a couple of options for limiting the output to only non-null (non-empty) values.

How to do it...

Let's get started with limiting the query output.

1. Execute the following queries to limit the output to only the components product category. As mentioned earlier, we can refer to a hierarchy member by its name or by its key, so either of the following statements will return the same output:

   ```
   --Reference "components" category by member name:
   SELECT [Measures].[Reseller Sales Amount] ON 0,
   [Date].[Calendar].[Calendar Year].members ON 1
   FROM [Adventure Works]
   WHERE [Product].[Product Categories].[Category].[components]
   ```

   ```
   --Reference "components" category by member key:
   SELECT [Measures].[Reseller Sales Amount] ON 0,
   [Date].[Calendar].[Calendar Year].members ON 1
   FROM [Adventure Works]
   WHERE [Product].[Product Categories].[Category].&[2]
   ```

2. To reduce the result set based on a specific condition, you can employ the `FILTER` function that accepts a set and a condition as parameters. For example, the following query returns only those members of the city hierarchy where sales have exceeded $200,000:

   ```
   SELECT FILTER([Geography].[City].members, [Measures].[Reseller
   Sales Amount] > 200000) ON 0,
   [Measures].[Reseller Sales Amount] ON 1
   FROM [Adventure Works]
   WHERE [Product].[Product Categories].[Category].[Components]
   ```

3. Previous query's result set includes the `All Geographies` member, which you might not want to list along with individual cities. Fortunately, we could use an additional filter criteria exploiting the `CurrentMember` function to eliminate the `All Geographies` member as follows:

```
SELECT FILTER([Geography].[City].members, [Measures].[Reseller
Sales Amount] > 200000
AND [Geography].[City].CurrentMember.Name<> 'All Geographies') ON
0,
[Measures].[Reseller Sales Amount] ON 1
FROM [Adventure Works]
WHERE [Product].[Product Categories].[Category].[Components]
```

> The `CurrentMember` function must follow a hierarchy and is essential for navigating SSAS hierarchies.

4. Use the `NON EMPTY` keywords or the `NONEMPTY` function to remove empty cells from the results, as the following two queries demonstrate:

```
SELECT [Measures].[Reseller Sales Amount] ON 0,
NONEMPTY ([Date].[Calendar].[Calendar Year].members) ON 1
FROM [Adventure Works]
```

```
SELECT [Measures].[Reseller Sales Amount] ON 0,
NON EMPTY [Date].[Calendar].[Calendar Year].members ON 1
FROM [Adventure Works]
```

> I recommend using the `NONEMPTY` function because it outperforms the `NON EMPTY` keywords. The `NONEMPTY` function can take either one or two sets as the input, and you can nest multiple occurrences of this function if necessary.

5. As mentioned earlier you could nest the `CROSSJOIN` functions to generate a more complex set. You can still use the `NONEMPTY` function to remove unnecessary content from the result set. The only difference is that in this case, you'll be removing empty tuples rather than empty cells, as shown by the next query:

```
SELECT NONEMPTY(CROSSJOIN(CROSSJOIN([Promotion].[Promotions].
[Category].members,
[Reseller].[Reseller].[all resellers].children), product.[product
categories].category.members)) ON 1,
measures.[reseller sales amount] ON 0
FROM   [Adventure Works]
WHERE [Date].[Calendar].[Month].&[2008]&[5]
```

> MDX is not case sensitive. There is no performance advantage for using one format over another, but I generally prefer to type all the functions in uppercase.

6. As you learned, using the NONEMPTY function generally yields results faster than the NON EMPTY keywords. Yet another alternative for removing empty tuples is the NONEMPTYCROSSJOIN function. This function has limitations when working with calculated members and is deprecated. However, you might see references to it in the legacy code. Consider the following query:

```
SELECT NONEMPTYCROSSJOIN([Promotion].[Promotions].[Category].
members,
[Reseller].[Reseller].[all resellers].children, product.[product
categories].category.members,
measures.[reseller sales amount], 3) ON 1,
measures.[reseller sales amount] ON 0
FROM   [Adventure Works]
WHERE [Date].[Calendar].[Month].&[2008]&[5]
```

This query uses NONEMPTYCROSSJOIN to work on three sets: promotions, resellers, and products. Note that this function does not require nesting when working with more than two sets. Furthermore, the function accepts the reseller sales amount measure to determine which tuples will be empty and therefore discarded from the result set. The last parameter (in this case 3) advises NONEMPTYCROSSJOIN how many sets are needed to be cross joined on the axis.

Sorting the query output

To make the output easier to decipher, you could use the ORDER function to sort the returned dimension members based on some criteria. In addition, many reports require limiting the results only to the best- or worst-performing hierarchy members. You can exploit the TOPCOUNT and BOTTOMCOUNT functions to meet such requirements.

How to do it...

Let's get started with sorting the query output.

1. The ORDER function accepts a set as the parameter and allows sorting in an ascending or descending manner, depending on the sorting expression. For example, the following query returns those cities in which the reseller sales amount for components exceeded $200000, ordering results based on the reseller sales amount:

```
SELECT ORDER (
    FILTER([Geography].[City].members, [Measures].[Reseller Sales
Amount] > 200000
```

```
AND [Geography].[City].CurrentMember.Name<> 'All Geographies'),
    [Measures].[Reseller Sales Amount], DESC)ON 0,
[Measures].[Reseller Sales Amount] ON 1
FROM [Adventure Works]
WHERE [Product].[Product Categories].[Category].[Components]
```

2. Another frequent requirement is to sort the output based on the city's name, rather than the amount of sales. The following query sorts cities based on their name in the ascending order, once again exploiting the `CurrentMember` function:

```
SELECT ORDER(
    FILTER([Geography].[City].members, [Measures].[Reseller Sales
Amount] > 200000
    AND [Geography].[City].CurrentMember.Name<> 'All Geographies'),
    [Geography].[City].CurrentMember.Name, ASC)
ON 0,
[Measures].[Reseller Sales Amount] ON 1
FROM [Adventure Works]
WHERE [Product].[Product Categories].[Category].[Components]
```

3. To find the top three cities in terms of their reseller sales amount, we could use the `TOPCOUNT` function. This function accepts a set as the first parameter, the number of members to return as the second parameter, and the criteria for finding the top members as the final parameter, as follows:

```
SELECT [measures].[reseller sales amount] ON 0,
TOPCOUNT([Geography].[City].[All Geographies].children, 3,
measures.[reseller sales amount]   ) ON 1
FROM [Adventure Works]
```

Note the usage of the `Children` function to obtain members at the leaf level of the `[Geography].[City]` attribute.

4. The `BOTTOMCOUNT` function does the opposite of `TOPCOUNT`; it finds the cities at the other end of the spectrum where reseller sales are minimal. In some cases we must further restrict the result set to find the bottom *N* members of the hierarchy that still have some activity. The following query finds the cities with the least reseller sales, that still have some sales which are greater than 0:

```
SELECT BOTTOMCOUNT(
FILTER (
   [Geography].[City].[All Geographies].children, [measures].
[reseller sales amount]>0),
   3, measures.[reseller sales amount]   )
ON 0,
[Measures].[Reseller Sales Amount] ON 1
FROM [Adventure Works]
WHERE [Product].[Product Categories].[Category].[Components]
```

Defining query level calculations and named sets

In addition to listing the existing dimension hierarchy members, MDX queries often include calculations. If your application repeatedly references the same calculation, you should define such calculations in the MDX script. However, ad hoc queries will often necessitate calculations that are not defined within the cube. Query-level calculations are defined using the WITH MEMBER clause. Calculations included within the Measures dimension are often called calculated measures, whereas within other dimensions they're referred to as calculated members. A named set allows grouping of one or more dimension members to perform additional calculations specific to the group or to more elegantly reference the collection. Use the WITH SET keywords to define the named set. Each query must specify the WITH keyword only once; if a query defines a calculated measure using the WITH MEMBER construct, you don't need to repeat WITH for the named set. In this case your query will have a notation similar to the following:

```
WITH MEMBER measures.my_calculated_measure AS "calculation
definition"
  SET my_named_set AS "set definition"
```

This section will also teach you how to use named sets for two common requirements: defining a date range and aggregating data for several dimension members.

How to do it...

Let's get started with defining query level calculations and named sets.

1. To define a calculated measure for deriving the average unit price, let's use the [reseller unit price] and [reseller transaction count] measures. The average unit price will be the unit price divided by the transaction count. We will also include the FORMAT_STRING="Currency" option to limit the number of digits to the right of the decimal points:

   ```
   WITH MEMBER [measures].[average unit price] AS

   [measures].[reseller unit price] / measures.[reseller transaction
   count], FORMAT_STRING="Currency"
   ```

2. At first glance this calculation looks good, but it includes a division operation, which will result in an error if the transaction count is 0. We will wrap the calculation in the IIF function and display N/A for "Not Available" in case the transaction count is indeed zero.

   ```
   WITH MEMBER [measures].[average unit price] AS IIF (measures.
   [reseller transaction count]=0, "N/A",
   ```

```
[measures].[reseller unit price] / measures.[reseller transaction
count]), FORMAT_STRING="Currency"
```

3. Lastly, you can specify a performance hint using the NON_EMPTY_BEHAVIOR
   property, which advises Analysis Services to consider the calculated measure empty
   if the underlying measure is empty. As discussed earlier, large cubes can have many
   empty cells. Traversing the huge cube space and applying the division to each cell
   individually can be slow; the NON_EMPTY_BEHAVIOR property helps SSAS eliminate
   empty cells from consideration. The final calculation along with the full query will look
   like this:

```
WITH MEMBER [measures].[average unit price] AS IIF (measures.
[reseller transaction count]=0, "N/A",
[measures].[reseller unit price] / measures.[reseller transaction
count]), FORMAT_STRING="Currency", NON_EMPTY_BEHAVIOR=measures.
[reseller unit price]

SELECT [Geography].[Country].[All Geographies].Children ON 0,
[Measures].[average unit price] ON 1
FROM [Adventure Works]
WHERE [Product].[Product Categories].[Category].[Components]
```

> For better performance it is recommended to use FORMAT_STRING
> to specify a value to return if a specific condition is met. For example,
> the previous query could be rewritten to return NULL if the reseller
> transaction count is zero. Next we would use FORMAT_STRING to
> cleverly substitute N/A for NULL values as follows:
>
> ```
> WITHMEMBER [measures].[average unit price] AS
> IIF (measures.[reseller transaction count]=0, NULL,
> [measures].[reseller unit price] / measures.[reseller
> transaction count]),
> FORMAT_STRING="$#,##0;;;\N\/\A"
> SELECT [Geography].[Country].[All Geographies].
> ChildrenON 0,
> [Measures].[average unit price] ON 1
> FROM [Adventure Works]
> WHERE [Product].[Product Categories].[Category].
> [Components]
> ```
>
> For more information on this topic please refer to http://technet.
> microsoft.com/en-us/library/ms146084.aspx.

4. Now suppose that you'd like to limit the result set only to those countries in which the reseller sales amount for the components category exceeded $300000. You could use the FILTER function to check the reseller sales amount in each country. To verify the output, let's include the reseller sales amount along with the average unit price on the rows axis:

```
WITH MEMBER [measures].[average unit price] AS IIF (measures.
[reseller transaction count]=0, "N/A",
[measures].[reseller unit price] / measures.[reseller transaction
count]), FORMAT_STRING="Currency"
SET [Successful Reseller Countries] AS
FILTER([Geography].[Country].[All Geographies].Children,
[measures].[reseller sales amount]>300000)
SELECT [Successful Reseller Countries] ON 0,
{[Measures].[average unit price], measures.[reseller sales
amount]} ON 1
FROM [Adventure Works]
WHERE [Product].[Product Categories].[Category].[Components]
```

5. The query in the previous step shows the output for each successful (in terms of reseller sales) country. Let's take it one step further to show the total number of reseller sales as well as the average unit price for all the successful countries combined. Use the AGGREGATE function to derive measure values for the Successful Reseller Countries named set as follows:

```
WITH MEMBER [measures].[average unit price] AS IIF (measures.
[reseller transaction count]=0, "N/A",
[measures].[reseller unit price] / measures.[reseller transaction
count]), FORMAT_STRING="Currency"
SET [Successful Reseller Countries] AS
FILTER([Geography].[Country].[All Geographies].Children,
[measures].[reseller sales amount]>300000)
MEMBER [Geography].[Country].[All Successful Countries] AS
AGGREGATE([successful Reseller Countries])
SELECT {[Successful Reseller Countries], [Geography].[Country].
[All Successful Countries]} ON 0,
{[Measures].[average unit price], measures.[reseller sales
amount]} ON 1
FROM [Adventure Works]
WHERE [Product].[Product Categories].[Category].[Components]
```

> Note that the AGGREGATE function uses the aggregation method applicable to each measure. In the previous example, AGGREGATE returns the average of all the unit prices and sum of all the reseller sales amounts.

6. The final requirement of this section is to display the average unit price and total reseller sales amount for successful countries during each month between January 2007 and June 2008. You can define a range of hierarchy members by using a colon (:) operator. The following query cross joins the requested date range (defined in the my_range named set) and successful countries on rows:

```
WITH MEMBER [measures].[average unit price] AS IIF (measures.
[reseller transaction count]=0, "N/A",
[measures].[reseller unit price] / measures.[reseller transaction
count]), FORMAT_STRING="Currency"
SET [Successful Reseller Countries] AS
FILTER([Geography].[Country].[All Geographies].Children,
[measures].[reseller sales amount]>300000)
MEMBER [Geography].[Country].[All Successful Countries] AS
AGGREGATE([successful Reseller Countries])
SET my_range AS {[date].[calendar].[month].&[2007]&[1]: [date].
[calendar].[month].&[2008]&[6]}
SELECT CROSSJOIN (my_range, {[Successful Reseller Countries],
[Geography].[Country].[All Successful Countries]}) ON 1,
{[Measures].[average unit price], measures.[reseller sales
amount]} ON 0
FROM [Adventure Works]
WHERE [Product].[Product Categories].[Category].[Components]
```

Navigating dimension hierarchies

Earlier in this chapter you learned how to use the CurrentMember function to retrieve the name of the current hierarchy member. MDX allows browsing hierarchies easily using similar functions, PrevMember and NextMember, which are extremely useful for trend analysis. Additionally, you can obtain hierarchy members using relative functions, such as children, ancestors, descendants, and parent, to build sets based on the members of interest. This section will list examples where these functions are particularly beneficial.

How to do it...

Let's get started with navigating dimension hierarchies.

1. To implement the `[Year-over-Year Growth in Reseller Sales Amount]` calculated measure, open the sample **Adventure Works 2012** database in **SQL Server Data Tools** (**SSDT**), navigate to **Adventure Works** cube's **Calculations** tab, and enter the expression that will follow. Note that we have two nested IIF functions. The first IIF function uses an ordinal function to determine whether we are at the `[Calendar Year]` level of the `[Date].[Calendar]` hierarchy and applies the calculation only at that level. The second IIF function uses the `PrevMember` function to ensure the previous calendar year member exists and has a non-zero value for the `Reseller Sales Amount` measure:

```
CREATE MEMBER CURRENTCUBE.[Measures].[Year-To-Year Reseller Sales
Growth]
 AS IIF([Date].[Calendar].CurrentMember.Level.Ordinal = 1,
IIF (
([Date].[Calendar].CurrentMember.PrevMember, measures.[Reseller
Sales Amount])=0
OR ISEMPTY([Date].[Calendar].CurrentMember.PrevMember),
 "N/A",
(([Date].[Calendar].CurrentMember, measures.[Reseller Sales
Amount]) -
([Date].[Calendar].CurrentMember.PrevMember, measures.[Reseller
Sales Amount]) )/
([Date].[Calendar].CurrentMember.PrevMember, measures.[Reseller
Sales Amount])
) , "N/A"
),
FORMAT_STRING = "Percent",
NON_EMPTY_BEHAVIOR = { [Reseller Sales Amount] },
VISIBLE = 1 ,  ASSOCIATED_MEASURE_GROUP = 'Reseller Sales'  ;
```

2. Save the database solution; Analysis Services objects won't have to be reprocessed, but the MDX script will be executed to apply the calculation you just added.

3. Open Excel and create a PivotTable based on the Adventure Works 2012 database. Include the `Reseller Sales Amount` and `Year-To-Year Reseller Sales Growth` measures on columns and the `[Date].[Calendar]` hierarchy on rows. As shown in the following output, SSAS applied the calculation to determine that reseller sales grew by 121.50 percent in 2007 and shrank by 49.93 percent in 2008, compared to prior years respectively. For all other years, Excel displayed **N/A** because year-over-year calculation of growth was not applicable. You could use the `NextMember` function in a similar way to compare the current values with those of the next calendar year:

CY 2005		N/A
CY 2006	$3,713,626.10	N/A
CY 2007	$8,225,508.77	121.50%
CY 2008	$4,118,716.85	-49.93%
CY 2009		-100.00%
CY 2010		N/A
Grand Total	**$16,057,851.72**	**N/A**

> To apply the same calculation across all the levels within the `[Date].[Calendar]` hierarchy, simply remove the outer IIF statement.

4. The next query finds the products that account for at least 10 percent of the total reseller sales amount for the respective category within May of 2008. To do so we first find the product's category using the ANCESTOR function and find the total reseller sales amount for that category. The ANCESTOR function accepts a dimension member as the first parameter and the level at which we need to find the ancestor. Next we compare the reseller sales amount for the current product with the total amount for the category, multiplied by 0.1:

```
WITH MEMBER measures.[sum for category] AS
SUM(ANCESTOR(product.[product categories].currentmember, product.
[product categories].[category])
, measures.[reseller sales amount])
MEMBER measures.[category] AS
ANCESTOR(product.[product categories].currentmember, product.
[product categories].[category]).name
SELECT {measures.category, measures.[reseller sales amount],
measures.[sum for category]} ON 0,
FILTER([Product].[Product Categories].product.members,
measures.[reseller sales amount] >= (measures.[sum for category] *
0.1)) ON 1
FROM [Adventure Works]
WHERE [Date].[Calendar].[Month].&[2008]&[5]
```

Products	Category	Reseller Sales Amount	Sum for Category
Hitch Rack - 4-Bike	Accessories	$6,400.32	$12,272.04
Sport-100 Helmet, Blue	Accessories	$1,343.59	$12,272.04
Hydration Pack - 70 oz.	Accessories	$1,861.54	$12,272.04
Short-Sleeve Classic Jersey, XL	Clothing	$3,055.57	$23,549.22

Products	Category	Reseller Sales Amount	Sum for Category
Women's Mountain Shorts, L	Clothing	$3,121.39	$23,549.22
Women's Mountain Shorts, S	Clothing	$3,262.23	$23,549.22
Classic Vest, S	Clothing	$3,703.37	$23,549.22

5. The next query finds the top-selling product for each category. To do so it uses the DESCENDANTS function to generate a set of all the products within the category first, then uses the TOPCOUNT function to identify the product with the higher reseller sales amount. Recall that TOPCOUNT returns a set—in this case a set of only one cell. You must use the ITEM function twice; first we use ITEM(0) to extract the first tuple from the set and then we use ITEM(0) to extract a single cell / dimension member. The last calculated member within this query obtains the reseller sales amount for the top-selling product:

```
WITH MEMBER measures.[top selling product for category] AS
TOPCOUNT (
DESCENDANTS([Product].[Product Categories].CurrentMember, 3),
1, measures.[reseller sales amount]).item(0).item(0).name
MEMBER measures.[product's reseller sales amount] AS
SUM(TOPCOUNT (
DESCENDANTS([Product].[Product Categories].CurrentMember, 3),
1, measures.[reseller sales amount]), measures.[reseller sales
amount])
SELECT [Product].[Product Categories].category.members ON 0,
{measures.[reseller sales amount], measures.[top selling product
for category],
measures.[product's reseller sales amount]
} ON 1
FROM [Adventure Works]
WHERE [Date].[Calendar].[Month].&[2008]&[5]
```

The result is as follows:

	Accessories	Bikes	Clothing	Components
Reseller Sales Amount	$12,272.04	$837,984.79	$23,549.22	$156,572.02
top selling product for category	Hitch Rack - 4-Bike	Mountain-200 Black, 38	Classic Vest, S	HL Touring Frame - Yellow, 54
product's reseller sales amount	$6,400.32	$57,741.95	$3,703.37	$13,853.96

Working with the Time dimensions

In the previous section you learned how to navigate dimension hierarchies. Date- and time-related dimensions are somewhat special because they are a part of nearly all business intelligence implementations, and much of the analysis focuses on examining the trends over time. MDX offers a number of functions for working specifically with date dimensions. In this section I will provide a couple of examples of the most frequently exploited time intelligence functions.

How to do it...

A very common reporting requirement is to display the running total of values for each timespan. Yet another frequent requirement is to compare the current values with that of an equivalent value during the previous week, month, quarter, or year. The following recipe shows the steps to display quarter-to-date and year-to-date running totals, in addition to reporting internet sales' values for each month. You will also learn how to compare the current measure's values with the corresponding values from a previous timespan:

1. Use the `PeriodsToDate` function to get a year-to-date value. This function accepts the attribute (or level) at which you wish to aggregate the measure as well as the member to which the values should be aggregated. The calculation will once again refer to the `CurrentMember` function to advise SSAS to aggregate year-to-date values to the current member of the `calendar` hierarchy:

```
WITH MEMBER [Measures].[YTD] AS SUM(PERIODSTODATE([Date].
[Calendar].[Calendar Year], [Date].[Calendar].CurrentMember),
[Measures].[Internet Sales Amount])
```

2. `PeriodsToDate` can work at any level of the time dimension. MDX also provides special cases of `PeriodsToDate` that work on specific levels: `MTD` function is for month-to-date, `QTD` for quarter-to-date, and `YTD` for year-to-date. Let's use `QTD` to also report the subtotals for each calendar quarter. Since `QTD` only works at the quarter level, you do not have to explicitly specify the attribute on which data needs to be summed:

```
MEMBER [Measures].[QTD] AS SUM(QTD([Date].[Calendar].
CurrentMember), [Measures].[Internet Sales Amount])
```

3. Next you specify the measures you wish to retrieve on columns and the month level of the calendar hierarchy on rows to define the whole query. Let's limit the output to the 2007 calendar year:

```
WITH MEMBER [Measures].[YTD] AS SUM(PERIODSTODATE([Date].
[Calendar].[Calendar Year], [Date].[Calendar].CurrentMember),
[Measures].[Internet Sales Amount])
```

```
MEMBER [Measures].[QTD] AS SUM(QTD([Date].[Calendar].
CurrentMember), [Measures].[Internet Sales Amount])
SELECT {[Measures].[Internet Sales Amount], [Measures].[YTD],
measures.[QTD]} ON 0,
[Date].calendar.[Month].members ON 1
FROM [Adventure Works]
WHERE [date].[calendar year].[cy 2007]
```

The query output should be similar to the following table. Note how quarter-to-date values are reset for each quarter whereas year-to-date values continue to grow throughout the year:

	Internet Sales Amount	YTD	QTD
Jan-07	$438,865.17	$438,865.17	$438,865.17
Feb-07	$489,090.34	$927,955.51	$927,955.51
Mar-07	$485,574.79	$1,413,530.30	$1,413,530.30
Apr-07	$506,399.27	$1,919,929.57	$506,399.27
May-07	$562,772.56	$2,482,702.13	$1,069,171.83
Jun-07	$554,799.23	$3,037,501.36	$1,623,971.06
Jul-07	$886,668.84	$3,924,170.20	$886,668.84
Aug-07	$847,413.51	$4,771,583.71	$1,734,082.35
Sep-07	$1,010,258.13	$5,781,841.84	$2,744,340.48
Oct-07	$1,080,449.58	$6,862,291.42	$1,080,449.58
Nov-07	$1,196,981.11	$8,059,272.53	$2,277,430.69
Dec-07	$1,731,787.77	$9,791,060.30	$4,009,218.46

4. You could use the `ParallelPeriod` function to instruct SSAS to march a specified number of timespans up the time hierarchy to obtain the needed value. This function accepts the attribute (level) that Analysis Services should examine and a number of periods to skip. The positive value of the second parameter will check for prior periods, whereas the negative value will check for periods that follow. For example, the following expression will get the internet sales amount for the month that is two months ahead of the current calendar month:

```
(ParallelPeriod([Date].[Calendar].Month, 2,  [Date].[Calendar].
CurrentMember),[Measures].[Internet Sales Amount] )
```

5. Next use the expression defined in the previous step to subtract the sales realized two months ago from the current sales for each month within the 2007 calendar year:

```
WITH MEMBER [Measures].[Compared To Two Months Ago] AS
[Measures].[Internet Sales Amount] -
(ParallelPeriod([Date].[Calendar].Month, 2,  [Date].[Calendar].
```

```
CurrentMember), [Measures].[Internet Sales Amount] )
SELECT { [Measures].[Internet Sales Amount], [Measures].[Compared
To Two Months Ago] } ON 0,
[Date].[Calendar].[Month].members ON 1
FROM [Adventure Works]
WHERE [date].[calendar year].[cy 2007]
```

The result is as follows:

	Internet Sales Amount	Compared to Two Months Ago
Jan-07	$438,865.17	$103,770.08
Feb-07	$489,090.34	($88,223.66)
Mar-07	$485,574.79	$46,709.62
Apr-07	$506,399.27	$17,308.93
May-07	$562,772.56	$77,197.77
Jun-07	$554,799.23	$48,399.96
Jul-07	$886,668.84	$323,896.28
Aug-07	$847,413.51	$292,614.28
Sep-07	$1,010,258.13	$123,589.29
Oct-07	$1,080,449.58	$233,036.07
Nov-07	$1,196,981.11	$186,722.98
Dec-07	$1,731,787.77	$651,338.19

MDX script's functionality

You already saw a couple of examples for defining calculated measures in the MDX script found on the **Calculations** tab within SSDT. Some MDX functionality applies only within the MDX script and not in queries. For example, you could define the calculation scope so that it only applies to certain hierarchy members. You can also use the ROOT function to refer to the topmost level of the hierarchy. The ROOT function isn't specific to the MDX script, but it is most commonly used in cube-level calculations.

The MDX script is evaluated when you first deploy the solution and anytime you change calculations; it doesn't require processing any objects (dimensions or partitions), but it could overwrite the existing cube values. Full discussion on how MDX scripts work is beyond the scope of this book. The examples in this section demonstrate how MDX-script-specific functions change the calculated values of the cube.

How to do it...

Let's get started with MDX script's functionality.

1. Scope assignment is used to overwrite an existing data value (or format). The assignment always includes the SCOPE and END SCOPE keywords. In this example, you will overwrite the existing reseller sales amount value for the [Hitch Rack -4 – Bike] product and set it to 75 percent of the total reseller sales amount for the accessories category. To note the difference prior to the assignment, run the following query:

   ```
   SELECT [product].[product categories].[product].[Hitch Rack -
   4-Bike] ON 0, [measures].[reseller sales amount] ON 1
   FROM [Adventure Works]
   WHERE [Date].[Calendar].[Month].&[2008]&[5]
   ```

   The result will be $6400.32.

2. Open **Script View** from the **Calculations** tab of the **Adventure Works** cube (hover your mouse pointer over the ribbon on the **Calculations** tab; the **Script View** button is right next to the **Form View** button that resembles a form), navigate all the way to the end of the MDX script, and add the following calculation:

   ```
   Scope
     (
         [Date].[Calendar].[Month].&[2008]&[5],
         [product].[product categories].[product].[Hitch Rack -
   4-Bike],
         [Measures].[reseller sales amount]
     );

       This =
               (
                   [Date].[calendar].&[2008]&[5],
                   [product].[product categories].[accessories]
               ) * 0.75;
   ```

3. Save the database. If you are making changes to the offline mode, you'll need to deploy the database to the server.

4. Rerun the query specified in step 1. This time the result is $9,204.03, which is 75 percent of the total [reseller sales amount], prior to applying the scope assignment.

5. While still on the **Calculations** tab, find the [Internet Ratio to All Products] calculation—you can hold down the *CTRL* key and press the letter *F* to open the **Find and Replace** dialog. Note how the calculation compares the [Internet Sales Amount] measure of the current member to the topmost member of the dimension using the ROOT function:

```
CREATE MEMBER CurrentCube.[measures].[Internet Ratio to All
Products] AS
Measures.[Internet Sales Amount] /
(
   ROOT( [product] ),
   Measures.[Internet Sales Amount]
),
Format_String = "Percent",
Associated_Measure_Group = "Internet Sales",
Non_Empty_Behavior = [Internet Sales Amount]
```

6. Switch to SSMS and execute the following query to see the calculated measure in action. The result will be a list of each product's subcategory that had sales ordered by the internet sales amount, along with the percentage of contribution to the total internet sales amount:

```
SELECT {measures.[Internet Ratio to All Products], measures.
[internet sales amount]} ON 0,
ORDER (FILTER (product.[product categories].[subcategory].members,
NOT ISEMPTY(measures.[Internet Sales Amount])),
Measures.[Internet Sales Amount], DESC) ON 1
FROM [Adventure Works]
```

Monitoring and tuning MDX queries

The best monitoring tool for MDX queries is **SQL Server Profiler,** which you could launch by navigating to **Start | All Programs | SQL Server 2012 | Performance Tools | SQL Server Profiler.** Profiler records various phases of the query execution, including the retrieval of data from partitions or dimensions, querying aggregations or memory cache as well as displaying the results to the application. Based on the Profiler output, we can surmise whether SSAS spends most of its execution time retrieving data from the storage engine or in the formula engine, meaning deriving calculated values after the data retrieval is complete.

How to do it...

Follow these steps for monitoring and tuning MDX queries.

1. Once the Profiler is open, go to **File | New Trace** and connect to your Analysis Services instance. Profiler allows choosing numerous events and columns that you could include in your trace. Ensure that the **Show all Events** checkbox is checked, then choose the following events:

   - **Progress Report Begin**
   - **Progress Report Current**
   - **Progress Report End**
   - **Query Begin**
   - **Query End**
   - **Calculate Non Empty End**
   - **Get Data From Aggregation**
   - **Get Data From Cache**
   - **Query Dimension**
   - **Query Subcube**
   - **Query Subcube Verbose**

2. Check the following columns to be included in the trace before clicking on the **Run Trace** button:

   - **Event Subclass**
   - **TextData**
   - **NTUserName**
   - **StartTime**
   - **Current Time**
   - **Duration**
   - **SPID**
   - **CPUTime**

   [Note that not all columns are available for each event.]

3. Switch to SSMS and run the following statement to clear the storage engine cache so that your execution results are not skewed:

```
<Batch xmlns="http://schemas.microsoft.com/analysisservices/2003/
engine">
  <ClearCache>
    <Object>
      <DatabaseID>Adventure Works DW</DatabaseID>
    </Object>
  </ClearCache>
</Batch>
```

4. Run a few MDX queries included in this chapter.

5. Stop the Profiler trace collection and examine the results. Pay particular attention to the duration column of the `Query End` event, as well as each `Progress Report End` event.

Full discussion of query tuning is beyond the scope of this book. However, normally, a query bottleneck is either in the storage or calculation engine. Storage engine queries are relatively straightforward to tune. You will need to pay attention to which partitions are taking longest to query. You might be able to add aggregations to this partition, or split the partition if only a small portion of it needs to be checked by each query. Refer to *Chapter 3, Creating Analysis Services Cubes*, for more information on designing useful aggregations and partitioning strategies. The calculation engine queries are much more complicated to tune and involve ensuring that your MDX uses the most efficient set of functions in the correct order.

You should also download and refer to Microsoft's white paper `http://www.microsoft.com/en-us/download/details.aspx?id=661` for troubleshooting MDX query bottlenecks.

There's more...

Writing MDX queries and calculations is a complex science and certainly warrants its own book. This chapter merely covered the basic concepts and most commonly encountered MDX constructs. To learn MDX in greater detail please refer to *MDX Solutions* or another book dedicated to this language.

7
Analysis Services Security

In this chapter, we will cover:

- ► Managing instance-level administrative security
- ► Managing database-level security
- ► Managing cube-level security
- ► Managing dimension hierarchy-level security
- ► Implementing dynamic security
- ► Implementing cell-level security

Introduction

This chapter teaches how to secure Analysis Services starting at the instance level and working all the way down to the individual cube cells. Analysis Services administrators have unrestricted access to all items within the server—they can restart the service, read and process data in every database, dimension, and cube, alter configuration settings, collect traces, and so on. This level of access is best reserved for database administrators. SSAS developers need full access to the database they're working with but not necessarily to the entire instance; each instance could host multiple databases constructed by multiple development teams. Individual users may need access to all or some of the cube and dimension data depending on their job requirements. In addition to explicitly defining the list of dimension members, you can also dynamically configure the security if your cube is queried by many users, each requiring access to a specific dataset.

Unlike the SQL Server relational engine, Analysis Services has no concept of its own security logins; it completely relies on the security of the Windows operating system. However, you can define very granular security settings for each Windows user or group.

Analysis Services builds a bitmap of the dimension members or cells that are available for reading or writing whenever the user connects to the instance. So, defining security adds some overhead to the application. Generally, if you don't have too many roles (several hundred) or if you use effective MDX functions for implementing dynamic security, such overhead is negligible.

Managing instance-level administrative security

Each Analysis Services instance has one server role reserved for administrators. All members of this role have unrestricted access to all objects on the instance. Membership in the administrator role is mandatory to perform the following operations:

- Create and drop databases
- Collect traces against multiple databases on the same instance in a single trace
- Stop/restart the instance
- Backup/restore databases
- Modify server configuration settings
- Grant server-level administrator permissions
- Detach/attach databases
- Synchronize databases (requires administrative permissions to both source and target instances)

How to do it...

To add members to the server administrator role, perform the following steps:

1. Connect to the SSAS instance to which you have administrative access using SSMS, right-click on the instance, and choose **Properties**.

2. Navigate to the **Security** tab of the resulting **Analysis Services Properties** dialog box. Click on **Add**, enter the domain and login name (for example, MyCorp\User), and click on **OK**.

3. By default, you can add individual users and security principles to the server role. If you need to add Windows groups, you must click on the **object types** button and check the **groups** box that is unchecked by default.

4. If you examine the script that SSAS runs behind the scenes using **SQL Server Profiler**, you'll find the two XMLA `Alter` commands, as shown in the following code snippet:

```
<Batch Transaction='true'>
<Alter AllowCreate="true"
ObjectExpansion="ObjectProperties">
<Object />
<ObjectDefinition>
<Server>
<ID>ComputerName\InstanceName</ID>
<Name> ComputerName\InstanceName </Name>
</Server>
</ObjectDefinition>
</Alter>
<Alter AllowCreate="true"
ObjectExpansion="ObjectProperties">
<Object>
<RoleID>Administrators</RoleID>
</Object>
<ObjectDefinition>
<Role>
<ID>Administrators</ID>
<Name>Administrators</Name>
<Members>
<Member>
<Name>DomainName\WindowsUserName</Name>
</Member>
</Members>
</Role>
</ObjectDefinition>
</Alter>
</Batch>
```

5. On the filesystem, the server administrator role's contents are found in the `Administrators.file_version_number.role.xml` file under the instance's data directory.

6. Users who are part of the host-level local administrator's group by default also have administrative permissions to SSAS. The `<BuiltinAdminsAreServerAdmins>` property controls this behavior. If you do not want local host administrators to administer Analysis Services, set this property to the value of `0` in the `msmdsrv.ini` configuration file found in the `config` folder under the Analysis Services installation directory.

7. The account that runs SSAS service by default has administrative permissions to the instance. This is controlled by the `<ServiceAccountIsServerAdmin>` configuration property.

Managing database-level security

Each SSAS instance could be shared for multiple projects. As long as databases can fit on the data drive and SSAS can handle processing and querying requests efficiently, there is no reason why you couldn't have many databases on a single instance. This is particularly true in development and quality assurance environments. Since each instance could be shared by multiple developers, it's generally best to provide each developer with the necessary permissions for the database that he/she is responsible for instead of granting unlimited server-wide permissions.

Database-level security is implemented through roles within each SSAS database. Each database can have many roles, normally one role per group of users that needs a specific level of access. Keep in mind that SSAS permissions are additive; if a user belongs to multiple groups, he/she will have all permissions available to each of the groups that he/she is a part of.

How to do it...

To define database-level permissions, perform the following steps:

1. Use SSMS to connect to the `AdventureWorksDW2012` database on your SSAS instance, right-click on the `Roles` folder within the database, and choose **New Role**. This activates the **Create Role** dialog.

2. Specify a descriptive role name on the **General** tab of the dialog. Optionally, you can also specify the role's description.

3. The **General** tab allows you to specify three levels of database access:

   - **Full control (Administrator)**: This level includes unrestricted access to create, alter, process, and drop objects within the database but not on other databases within the same instance. If you check this option, the other two options are automatically selected because they represent subsets of full database-wide permissions. This option also allows members to trace the Analysis Services activity within the current database.

   - **Process database**: This self-explanatory option allows us to process each object within the database. If you grant this option without the ability to read definition, the user will not be able to see the objects using any tool including SSMS but can still run XMLA commands for processing. This might be a good option for a junior DBA / developer who need not see that data but is responsible for ensuring that cube data stays up-to-date.

   - **Read definition**: This level allows us to browse metadata but does not permit us to create, modify, process, or drop objects. The opposite of previous options, the **Read definition** access, is often granted to cube users who need to see metadata without requiring the ability to update the objects' data through processing.

4. Switch to the **Membership** tab to add individual Windows users or groups. The process of adding/removing users is identical to the one described in the _Managing instance-level administrative security_ section.

> The **Data Sources** tab is used for data mining, which is beyond the scope of this book.

Managing cube-level security

You already learned how to define SSAS instance administrators and how to grant the necessary permission to cube developers. Now, it's time to secure the solution at the cube level so that each user is permitted to see only the data that they require to perform their job functions.

Each database could have multiple cubes. Cube-level data is also secured using roles, and (not surprisingly) cube-level security is defined on the **Cubes** tab.

How to do it...

Let's get started by performing the following steps:

1. Open the role that you created in the previous recipe, navigate to the **Cubes** tab, and note the **Access**, **Local Cube/Drillthrough Access** and **Process** settings.

2. Cube users could have three levels of access:

    ❑   None: They cannot read any data from the cube

    ❑   Read: They can read cube data

    ❑   Read/Write: They can read cube data and write-back values only if write-back is enabled

3. The DRILLTHROUGH permission allows role members to execute drillthrough actions and the DRILLTHROUGH MDX command against the specific cube. You could have some users who need access to detailed data whereas others could only require high-level summarized values.

4. **Local Cube** is an interesting option that allows cube users to download some or all of the cube data to their local desktop/laptop for offline analysis. Clearly, Local Cube is not a good option for saving an entire enterprise-level cube to a laptop, but it could be useful if an executive needs to run a few reports during his/her airplane trip to a remote office. If drillthrough / Local Cube access isn't granted, users will receive errors when attempting to create a local copy of the cube or drillthrough to detailed data.

> You can define a local cube by navigating to the **OLAP Tools | Offline OLAP** option in Excel's **Analyze** tab. Choosing this option activates the **Offline OLAP Setting** dialog that has a **Create offline data file...** button. It activates the **Create Cube File** wizard. The wizard allows you to choose the dimensions, dimension members, and measures that you would like to include in the local file and specify the full path and name of the file with the `.cub` extension.

5. The **Process** option allows role members to process measure groups within a particular cube. Generally, cube users do not need this permission on production instances. The majority of SSAS implementations only grant access to read cube data.

Managing dimension hierarchy-level security

So far so good; you've allowed cube-level access to users, but this might only be a part of the battle. Cube-level access does not restrict any dimensions or attributes. This means that each employee could see not only those sales that he/she is directly responsible for, but also the sales of his/her peers and managers. Furthermore, not all employees need to see highly sensitive data such as salaries and commission rates.

You can manage access to dimensions using the **Dimension Data** tab within the **Role Properties** dialog. The same dialog also has the **Dimensions** tab that is used less frequently and allows you to specify write access if the dimension write-back is configured; otherwise, all dimensions are available for read-only access. The **Dimension Data** tab, on the other hand, is for securing individual dimension attribute hierarchy members.

You will begin by implementing a simple requirement of only allowing the role to see bikes and accessories product categories in the sample database. The section that follows will examine a somewhat more complex requirement of dynamic security.

How to do it...

To restrict a role to see sales only for bikes and accessories, perform the following steps:

1. Create a new role within `Adventure Works DW2012` sample database and add a member, as shown earlier in this chapter.

2. Grant access to **Read definition** on the **General** page.

3. Grant the `Read` access to the `Adventure Works` cube on the **Cubes** page.

4. Navigate to the **Dimension Data** page. Take a moment to notice that this dropdown lists database dimensions as well as cube dimensions. Recall that each database dimension may or may not be included in each cube. Cube dimension's properties do not necessarily have to match the properties of the database dimension. If you define security at the database dimension level, the same security configuration will be applied to the corresponding cube dimensions as well.

5. Select the `Product` database dimension from the **Dimension** drop-down list.

6. Choose the **Deselect all members** option and then check the **Bikes** and **Accessories** categories as shown in the following screenshot:

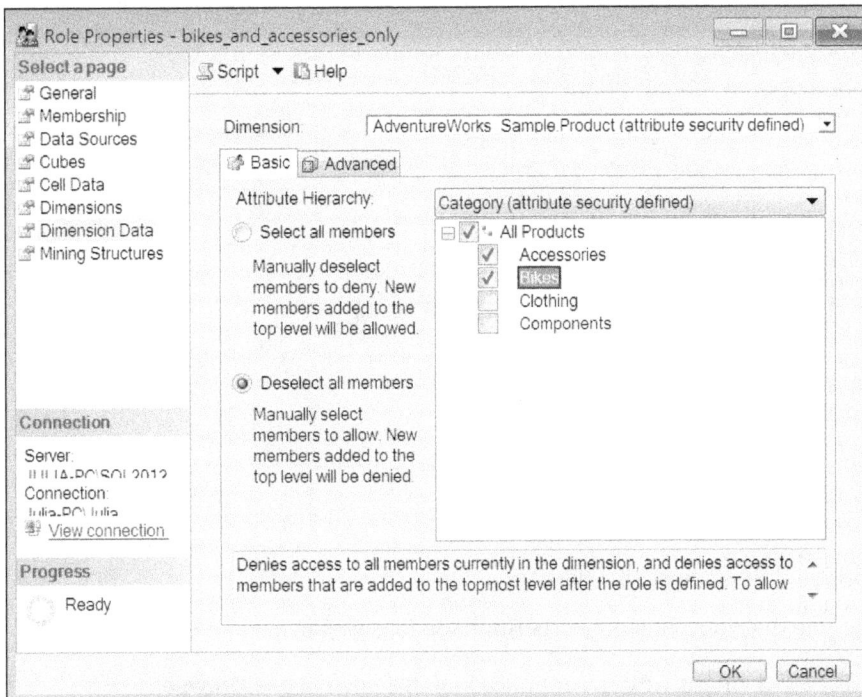

7. Switch to the **Advanced** tab and review the **Allowed member set**, **Denied member set**, and **Default member** boxes as well as the **Enable Visual Totals** checkbox as shown in the following screenshot. Clicking on the **Edit MDX** button next to the **Allowed member set**, **Denied member set** and **Default member** boxes, opens **MDXBuilder** to help you with defining the corresponding sets or default member:

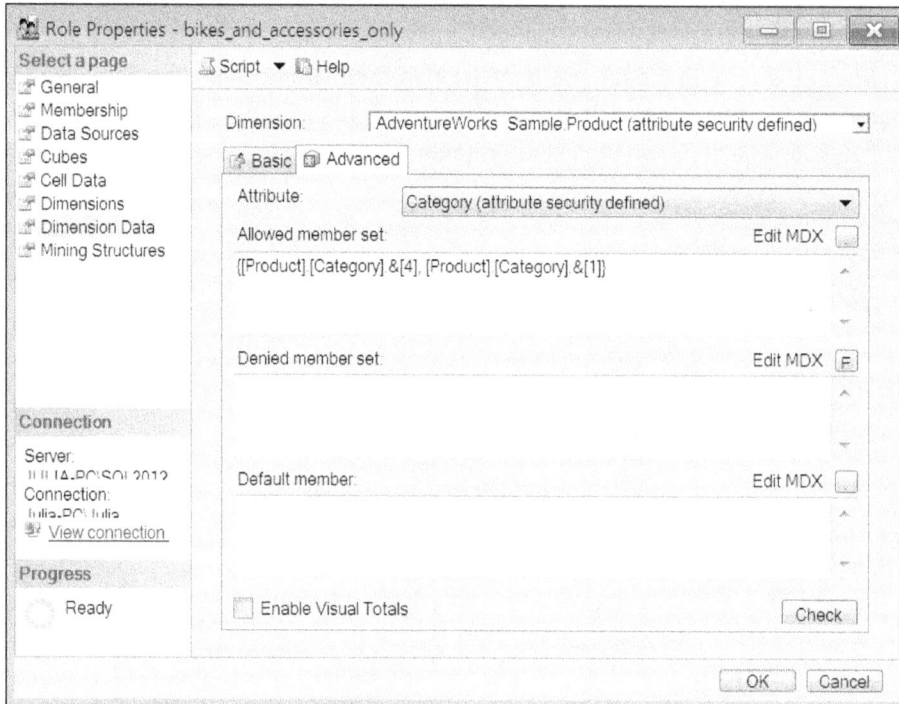

8. Click on **OK** to save the changes.

To test the role that you just created, perform the following steps:

1. Right-click on the `Adventure Works` cube and choose **Browse**.

2. Once the cube browser opens, click on the **Change User** button in the top-left corner, as shown in the following screenshot:

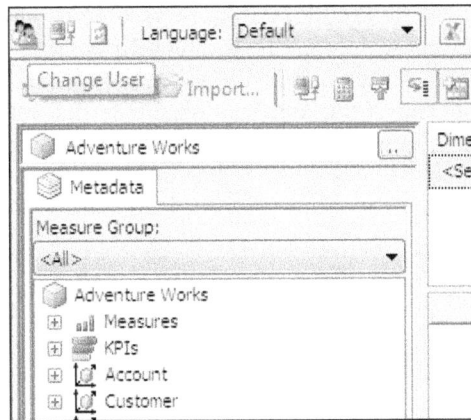

3. The previous step activates the **Security Context** dialog. By default, you'll browse the cube data using your own security context. You also have an option to specify a user name that belongs to the role you're testing (this must be in the domain_name\ user_name format) or the role itself. For this exercise, I'll use the bikes_and_ accessories_only role and click on **OK**, as shown in the following screenshot:

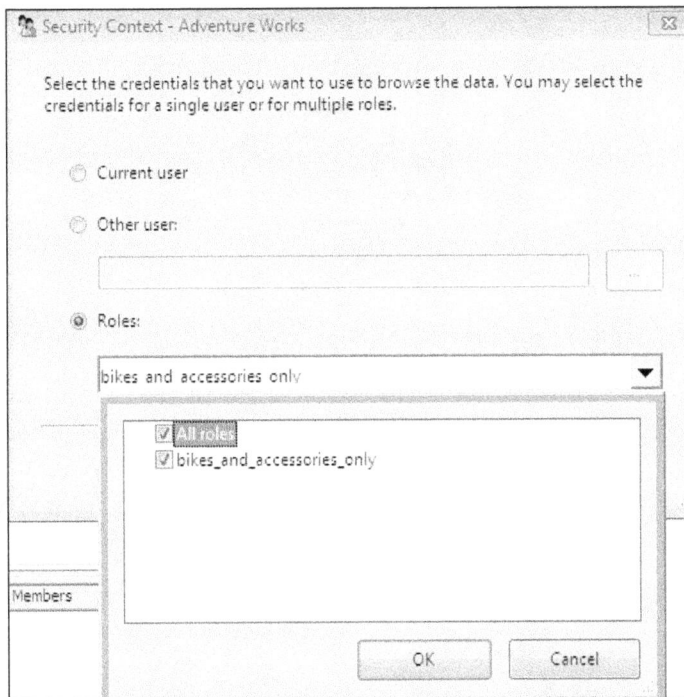

4. At this point, browsing the **Product Categories** hierarchy will be limited only to **Bikes** and **Accessories**. If we drop the **Product Categories** hierarchy on rows axis, SSMS will immediately flatten out the hierarchy to display all products and product subcategories under **Bikes** and **Accessories**. Similarly, if you try to filter the **Product Categories** hierarchy, you will only see subcategories and products under the restricted list of categories, as shown in the following screenshot:

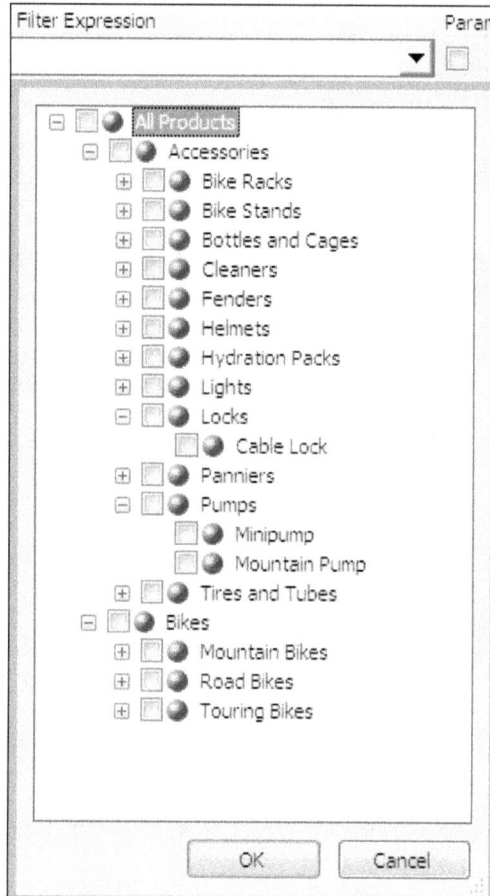

How it works...

At this point, you should have some questions regarding the various options that you saw while configuring a simplistic security role. You noticed that you could have chosen **Select all members** or **Deselect all members** prior to choosing which product categories to make available for the role. It's only natural to wonder what the difference between these two options is. If you choose **Deselect all members** first and check only the needed members, the checked members will be included in the allowed member set on the **Advanced** tab. Had you instead chosen **Select all members** and subsequently unchecked the members you did not want to expose, the unchecked member list would be shown in the denied member set. This does not make a big difference for the sample database, but consider what happens if we add a new product category to the dimension. If we specify the allowed members for the role, the new category will not be visible to the role members; on the other hand, if we include an explicit list of denied members with the role, the new category will be visible because it won't be part of the denied member set.

Keep in mind that we could define both allowed and denied member sets on the **Advanced** tab. In this case, SSAS will allow us to browse data for all members included in the allowed member set except those in the denied member set. To completely deny access to a hierarchy, include an empty set specified by the `{ }` notation in the allowed member set.

The default member box that you saw while configuring the role can be used to define the product category that will implicitly be used by any query that does not include a reference to the category hierarchy. For example, you could set the default member to `[Product].[Category].&[1]` so that the role members will see the measures specifically for the **Bikes** category unless their queries explicitly specify other categories. You normally define the default member for the role if the allowed member set does not include the hierarchy's default member (visible to roles with full access to the dimension). For example, if the default member is **All Categories** but you only want to expose **Bikes** and **Accessories** to a particular role, you could set the role's default category to **Bikes**.

Now, if you query the cube as a role member and choose **All Products** as the product category, you will see a different number than what you would see as the total of **Bikes** and **Accessories**. Although you have accomplished the goal of hiding the **Clothing** and **Components** categories, the role members can become suspicious and perhaps even doubt the validity of cube data because the sum of the categories they see does not add up to the total for all categories. Fortunately, the visual totals feature is here to help; once you check the **Enable Visual Totals** box on the **Advanced** tab, SSAS will calculate the aggregate value (in this case, the aggregate will be the sum of **Bikes** and **Accessories**) during query execution instead of displaying the aggregate value available in the cube that includes all product categories. Since the value must be calculated during query execution, the visual totals feature does add a slight performance overhead.

> Although we explicitly secured only the **Product Categories**
> hierarchy, the list of subcategories will also be restricted
> based on the available categories. If you browse the `Product`
> dimension as the `bikes_and_accessories_only` role,
> you will not see any subcategories for **Clothing** or **Components**.
>
> You could define different allowed/denied member sets from
> each dimension hierarchy depending on the cube. For example,
> users might want to see only the current and future years in the
> `Forecast` cube, but they will need to see the previous years'
> data in the `Actual Values` cube. Hence, the option to secure
> dimension data at database-dimension or cube-dimension level
> is available.

You can define allowed/denied members on multiple hierarchies of the same dimension.
For example, you could enter an empty set { } in the allowed member set for the `date`
attribute of the `Date` dimension to ensure that users cannot browse data for individual
dates. Additionally, you could also specify a set consisting of `[May 2005]` and `[June 2005]`
within the denied member set under the `Month Name` attribute to restrict users from viewing
data for these months.

You can secure the measures as you can for any cube dimension; look for **measures
dimension** under each cube within the **Dimension** drop-down box. Unfortunately, we don't
have an easy way of hiding calculated measures. If you prefer not to expose a calculation
for browsing, you can remove it from a particular perspective. However, keep in mind that
perspectives are not a security mechanism and, hence, a savvy user could still access the
calculation by referencing it explicitly in MDX queries.

> Yet another alternative is to define a regular measure with its value always
> set to `NULL` or `zero` and then use a `SCOPE` statement to overwrite the
> measure with a calculation. This way you will have a calculation exposed
> as a regular measure that could be secured.

Implementing dynamic dimension security

In the previous section, you learned how to restrict a role's access to certain dimension
hierarchy members. This worked well for a dimension with few categories and a single role.
As long as you can group users into a few roles depending on their job function, this approach
will suffice. However, when the number of roles grows to hundreds, you'll find that managing
security can become very cumbersome and tedious. Clearly, creating a new role to expose a
specific data set to each retail customer is unacceptable. Fortunately, you can work around
this limitation using a security measure group.

Although it takes several steps to implement, the security measure group utilizes relatively straightforward concepts. You need to identify the attribute to secure, perhaps the sales territory that each cube user should be able to browse. Next, you create a measure group defining the mapping between the user and sales territory. The security role will then use the `UserName` function within an MDX expression to determine the set of sales territories that the user is permitted to browse. This way, you can have a single role that manages security dynamically based on values found in the security measure group.

How to do it...

Let's get started by performing the following steps:

1. Create a user dimension table in the `AdventureWorksDW2012` sample relational database using the following code:

```
CREATE TABLE [dbo].[dimUser] (
[user_key] [int] IDENTITY(1,1) NOT NULL,
[user_login] [varchar](50) NULL,
 CONSTRAINT [pk_user_key] PRIMARY KEY CLUSTERED
(
[user_key] ASC
)WITH (PAD_INDEX = OFF, STATISTICS_NORECOMPUTE = OFF, IGNORE_
DUP_KEY = OFF, ALLOW_ROW_LOCKS = ON, ALLOW_PAGE_LOCKS = ON) ON
[PRIMARY]
) ON [PRIMARY]
```

2. Create the `FactUserTerritory` table by mapping users to sales territories as follows:

```
CREATE TABLE FactUserTerritory (
user_key INT,
sales_territory_key INT,
is_allowed BIT)
```

3. Populate the `dimUser` dimension table with a domain account that does not have administrative access to your SSAS instance. For example:

```
INSERT dimUser (user_login)
SELECT 'domain_name\JaneDoe'
```

4. Define mappings between the login and sales territory keys as follows:

```
INSERT FactUserTerritory
SELECT
(SELECT user_key
FROM dimUser
WHERE user_login='domain_name\JaneDoe'),
(SELECT SalesTerritoryKey
FROM DimSalesTerritory
WHERE SalesTerritoryCountry = 'Germany'),
1
```

5. Create a new Analysis Services project named `Security` in SSDT with the `Date`, `Promotion`, `SalesTerritory`, and `Reseller` dimensions. Please refer to *Chapter 2, Defining Analysis Services Dimensions*, for dimension recipes.

6. Add the `dimUser` and `FactUserTerritory` tables to your data source view.

7. Create a user dimension with a single attribute named `user` with `user_key` as the key column and `user_login` as the name column.

8. Add a cube named `AdventureWorks` to the `Security` project based on the `FactResellerSales`, `Date`, `Promotion`, `SalesTerritory`, `Reseller`, and `User` dimensions. Please refer to *Chapter 3, Creating Analysis Services Cubes*, for cube recipes. You do not have to set up a relationship between the `User` dimension and the `ResellerSales` measure group.

9. Add a second measure group to the `AdventureWorks` cube based on `FactUserTerritory`. Expose `UserTerritoryCount` (row count) as the only measure from the`FactUserTerritory` measure group. Ensure that `User` and `SalesTerritory` have regular relationships with `FactUserTerritory`.

10. Create a role named `Dynamic` within the `Security` project. Grant membership in this role to the domain user that you included in the `dimUser` table.

11. Grant the `Dynamic` role `Read` access to the `AdventureWorks` cube.

12. Navigate to the **Dimension Data** page, choose the `SalesTerritory` dimension, go to the **Advanced** tab, and choose the `Sales Territory Region` attribute.

13. Enter the following MDX expression in the **Allowed member set** box:

```
NONEMPTY([Sales Territory].[Sales Territory Region].members,
StrToMember("[user].[user].[" + UserName() + "]"),
measures.UserTerritoryCount))
```

14. Check the **Enable Visual Totals** box. The **Dimension Data** page should look as shown in the following screenshot:

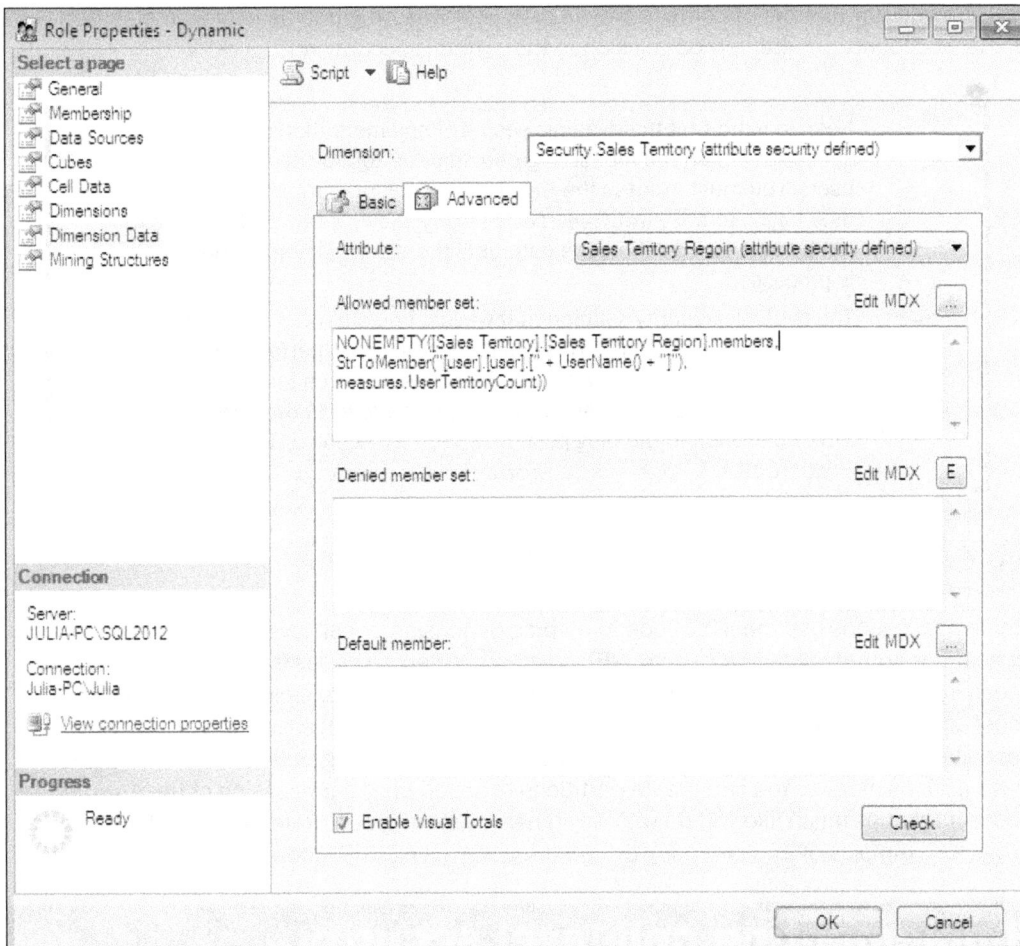

15. Save and deploy the project to your SSAS instance and process the database.

16. To test the role, open the cube browser and click on the **Change User** button to impersonate the domain user that you added to the `Dynamic` role. The user will only see the data for `sales territory region` = `"Germany"` and the corresponding visual total.

17. After you have confirmed that the dynamic security role works as expected, set the `User` dimension's and the `UserTerritoryCount` measure's visible property to `False`. These do not add any value to cube consumers; they are simply used for implementing security.

You can add any number of users to the `Security` measure group as long as the same domain accounts are granted permission to the dynamic security role.

> Keep in mind that the dynamic security implementation discussed in this section relies on the measure group. In order to provide access to new users, you must process the `Security` measure group after adding user logins to the `FactUserTerritory` table. Newly added users will not be able to read the cube data until the `Security` measure group is processed.
>
> The dynamic security solution that we just implemented uses the `StrToMember` function. This could result in some performance overhead when working with large data sets. For an alternative syntax for implementing a dynamic security role, please refer to the *A role security MDX tip* section in the blog post: `http://nickbarclay.blogspot.com/2008/01/pps-data-connection-security-with.html`.

There's more...

Some applications use the .NET code to enforce dimension or cell-level security within cubes. The primary reason for using .NET programs to secure cubes is that the `Security` measure group grows too large and processing it is often not a feasible option. However, most applications serve hundreds or thousands of users and processing the `Security` measure group is much quicker than processing other measure groups that are likely to have millions of rows. You can create partitions to speed up the processing of the `Security` measure groups much like you do with any other measure group. Refer to online forums and blogs for examples of implementing dynamic security using .NET code.

Implementing cell-level security

Restricting access to specific dimension members is normally sufficient even for very granular security schemes. However, in rare cases, you might have a need to secure individual cells in addition to specifying allowed and denied dimension member sets. Although I discuss cell-level security here, be warned that securing at the cell level can cause severe performance issues, particularly, for large cube implementations.

You can grant read-only, read-write, and read-contingent permissions at cell level. Read-write permissions only apply if the cube write-back is enabled. Read-contingent permissions define SSAS behavior for cells that are defined from other cells that are known as calculated members. If you grant read-contingent permission on a calculated member, you must ensure that the same role also has access to the members included in the calculated member's definition.

In addition to imposing performance overhead, cell-level security also introduces an issue with cube usability. Any cell that the role member isn't allowed to see will still be visible but will display the #N/A value instead of the actual cell value. You have some flexibility as far as overwriting #N/A in the client application is concerned. Nevertheless, the users will know that the cell exists, but they're not permitted to see its value. A cleaner solution would have hidden the cell completely so that the user would not be aware that the secured cell exists.

How to do it...

To restrict a role to see only the [internet order count] measure, perform the following steps:

1. Create a test role within the Adventure Works DW2012 sample database using SSMS and grant membership to a valid domain account.

2. Grant the Readaccess to the Adventure Works cube as discussed earlier in this chapter.

3. Navigate to the **Cell Data** tab of the role editor, check the **Enable read permissions** box, and enter the following MDX expression:

    ```
    Measures.CurrentMember IS measures.[internet order count]
    ```

4. Save the role and try browsing the cube as the domain account to which you granted membership in the role. All measures except [internet order count] will show up as #N/A (in SSMS, they will be displayed as NULL).

5. To grant read-contingent permissions, you can use the following expression:

    ```
    measures.CurrentMember IS measures.[sales amount]
        OR
    measures.CurrentMember IS measures.[average sales amount]
    ```

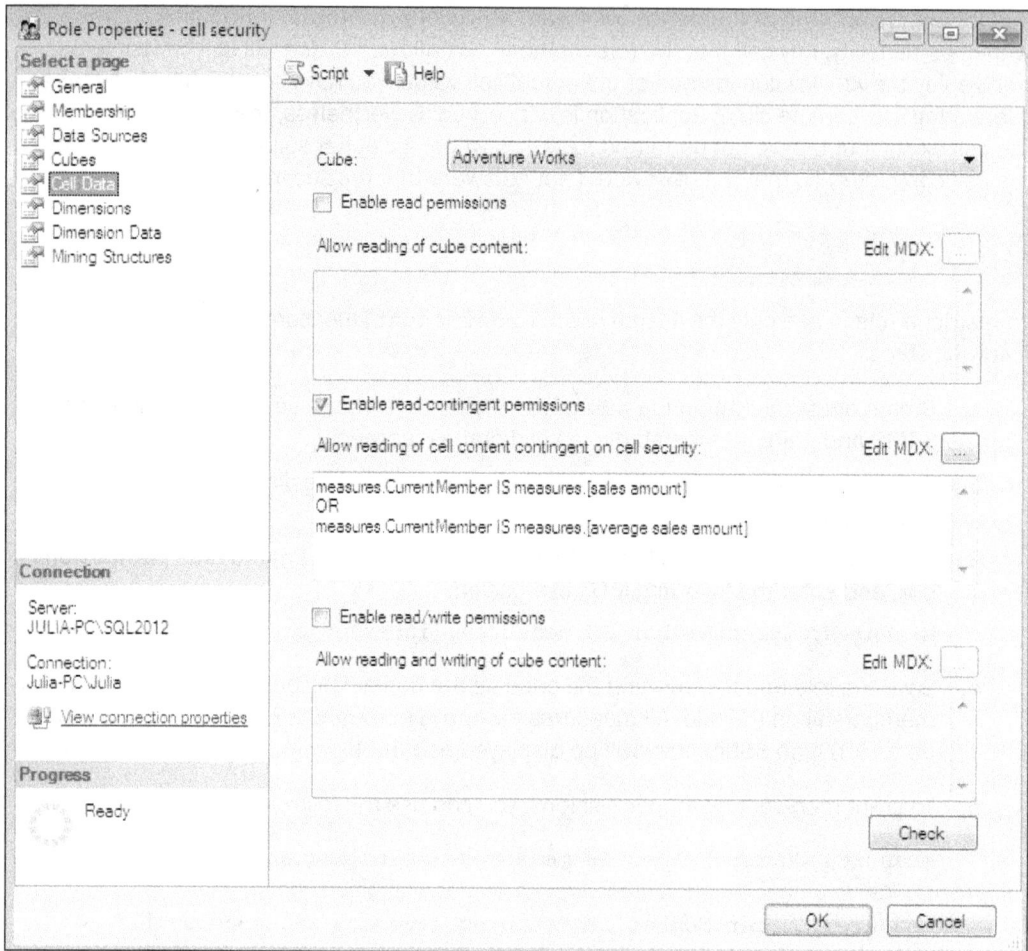

If you use the preceding expression to define read-contingent permission (as shown in the preceding screenshot), the role members will see #N/A for the calculated measure Average Sales Amount because you did not grant them the permission to see the Order Count measure that is necessary for calculating the average. On the other hand, if you enter the same expression under the **Enable read permissions** checkbox, role members will see the calculated measure even though they won't see the Order Count measure.

There's more...

In some cases, when you must use multiple fact tables, you have a choice of creating multiple cubes or a single cube with multiple measure groups. If you use a `Security` measure group, you should create a single cube with multiple measure groups because you would only have to process the `Security` measure group once. This is presuming that the same `Security` measure group can be used for securing dimension data for all other measure groups which may or may not always be the case.

8
Administering and Monitoring Analysis Services

In this chapter, we will cover:

- ▸ SSAS instance configuration options
- ▸ Creating and dropping databases
- ▸ Monitoring SSAS instance using Activity Viewer
- ▸ Monitoring SSAS instance using DMVs
- ▸ Cancelling a session
- ▸ Checking whether cubes are accessible
- ▸ Checking SSAS object sizes programmatically
- ▸ Backup and restore
- ▸ Synchronization
- ▸ Detaching and attaching databases

Introduction

As you have learned throughout the various chapters of this book, **SQL Server Analysis Services** (**SSAS**) is a data container in its own right, separate and apart from the SQL Server relational database engine. As such, SSAS has numerous configuration options, many of which alter its behavior. You can use dynamic management views, SQL Server Profiler, Performance Monitor, and other tools to monitor and troubleshoot SSAS activity.

If your environment has only one or a handful of SSAS instances, they can be managed by the same database administrators managing SQL Server and other database platforms. In large enterprises, there could be hundreds of SSAS instances managed by dedicated SSAS administrators. Regardless of the environment, you should become familiar with the configuration options as well as troubleshooting methodologies. In large enterprises, you might also be required to automate these tasks using the **Analysis Management Objects** (**AMO**) code.

Analysis Services is a great tool for building business intelligence solutions. However, much like any other software, it does have its fair share of challenges and limitations.

Most frequently encountered enterprise business intelligence system goals include quick provision of relevant data to the business users and assuring excellent query performance. If your cubes serve a large, global community of users, you will quickly learn that SSAS is optimized to run a single query as fast as possible. Once users send a multitude of heavy queries in parallel, you can expect to see memory, CPU, and disk-related performance counters quickly rise, with a corresponding increase in query execution duration which, in turn, worsens user experience. Although you could build aggregations to improve query performance, doing so will lengthen cube processing time, and, thereby, delay the delivery of essential data to decision makers. It might also be tempting to consider using ROLAP storage mode in lieu of MOLAP so that processing times are shorter, but MOLAP queries usually outperform ROLAP due to heavy compression rates. Hence, figuring out the right storage mode and appropriate level of aggregations is a great balancing act. If you cannot afford to use ROLAP, and query performance is paramount to successful cube implementation, you should consider scaling your solution. You have two options for scaling, given as follows:

- **Scaling up**: This option means purchasing servers with more memory, more CPU cores, and faster disk drives
- **Scaling out**: This option means purchasing several servers of approximately the same capacity and distributing the querying workload across multiple servers using a load balancing tool

SSAS lends itself best to the second option—scaling out. Later in this chapter you will learn how to separate processing and querying activities and how to ensure that all servers in the querying pool have the same data.

SSAS instance configuration options

All Analysis Services configuration options are available in the `msmdsrv.ini` file found in the `config` folder under the SSAS installation directory. Instance administrators can also modify some, but not all configuration properties, using **SQL Server Management Studio** (**SSMS**).

SSAS has a multitude of properties that are undocumented—this normally means that such properties haven't undergone thorough testing, even by the software's developers. Hence, if you don't know exactly what the configuration setting does, it's best to leave the setting at default value. Even if you want to test various properties on a *sandbox* server, make a copy of the configuration file prior to applying any changes.

How to do it...

To modify the SSAS instance settings using the configuration file, perform the following steps:

1. Navigate to the `config` folder within your Analysis Services installation directory. By default, this will be `C:\Program Files\Microsoft SQL Server\MSAS11.instance_name\OLAP\Config`.

2. Open the `msmdsrv.ini` file using Notepad or another text editor of your choice. The file is in the XML format, so every property is enclosed in opening and closing tags.

3. Search for the property of interest, modify its value as desired, and save the changes.

4. For example, in order to change the upper limit of the processing worker threads, you would look for the `<ThreadPool><Process><MaxThreads>` tag sequence and set the values as shown in the following excerpt from the configuration file:

```
<Process>
        <MinThreads>0</MinThreads>
        <MaxThreads>250</MaxThreads>
        <PriorityRatio>2</PriorityRatio>
        <Concurrency>2</Concurrency>
        <StackSizeKB>0</StackSizeKB>
        <GroupAffinity/>
    </Process>
```

To change the configuration using SSMS, perform the following steps:

1. Connect to the SSAS instance using the instance administrator account and choose **Properties**. If your account does not have sufficient permissions, you will get an error that only administrators can edit server properties.

2. Change the desired properties by altering the **Value** column on the **General** page of the resulting dialog, as shown in the following screenshot:

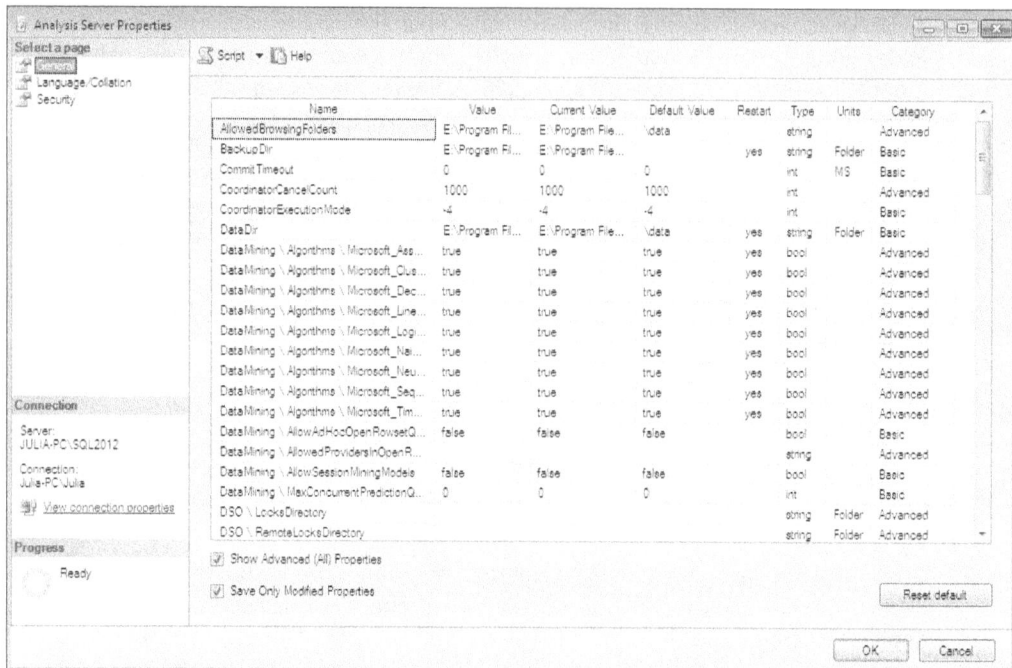

3. Advanced properties are hidden by default. You must check the **Show Advanced (All) Properties** box to see advanced properties. You will not see all the properties in SSMS even after checking this box. The only way to edit some properties is by editing `msmdsrv.ini` as previously discussed.

4. Make a note of the **Reset Default** button in the bottom-right corner. This button comes in handy if you've forgotten what the configuration values were before you changed them and want to revert to the default settings. The default values are shown in the dialog box, which can provide guidance as to which properties have been altered.

5. Some configuration settings require restarting the SSAS instance prior to being executed. If this is the case, the **Restart** column will have a value of **Yes**.

6. Once you're happy with your changes, click on **OK** and restart the instance if necessary. You can restart SSAS using the `Services.msc` applet from the command line using the `NET STOP` / `NET START` commands, or directly in SSMS by choosing the **Restart** option after right-clicking on the instance.

How it works...

Discussing every SSAS property would make this chapter extremely lengthy; doing so is well beyond the scope of the book. Instead, in this section, I will summarize the most frequently used properties.

Often, synchronization has to copy large partition datafiles and aggregation files. If the timeout value is exceeded, synchronization fails. Increase the value of the `<Network><Listene` `r><ServerSendTimeout>` and `<Network><Listener><ServerReceiveTimeout>` properties to allow a longer time span for copying each file.

By default, SSAS can use a *lazy* thread to rebuild missing indexes and aggregations after you process partition data. If the `<OLAP><LazyProcessing><Enabled>` property is set to 0, the lazy thread is not used for building missing indexes—you must use an explicit processing command instead. The `<OLAP><LazyProcessing><MaxCPUUsage>` property throttles the maximum CPU that could be used by the lazy thread. If efficient data delivery is your topmost priority, you can exploit the `ProcessData` option instead of `ProcessFull`. To build aggregations after the data is loaded, you must set the partition's `ProcessingMode` property to `LazyAggregations`. The SSAS formula engine is single threaded, so queries that perform heavy calculations will only use one CPU core, even on a multiCPU computer. The storage engine is multithreaded; hence, queries that read many partitions will require many CPU cycles. If you expect storage engine heavy queries, you should lower the CPU usage threshold for `LazyAggregations`.

By default, Analysis Services records subcubes requested for every 10th query in the query log table. If you'd like to design aggregations based on query logs, you should change the `<Log><QueryLog><QueryLogSampling>` property value to 1 so that the SSAS logs subcube requests for every query.

SSAS can use its own memory manager or the Windows memory manager. If your SSAS instance consistently becomes unresponsive, you could try using the Windows memory manager. Set `<Memory><MemoryHeapType>` to 2 and `<Memory><HeapTypeForObjects>` to 0. The Analysis Services memory manager values are 1 for both the properties. You must restart the SSAS service for the changes to these properties to take effect.

The `<Memory><PreAllocate>` property specifies the percentage of total memory to be reserved at SSAS startup. SSAS normally allocates memory dynamically as it is required by queries and processing jobs. In some cases, you can achieve performance improvement by allocating a portion of the memory when the SSAS service starts.

> Setting this value will increase the time required to start the service. The memory will not be released back to the operating system until you stop the SSAS service. You must restart the SSAS service for changes to this property to take effect.

The `<Log><FlightRecorder><FileSizeMB>`and `<Log><FlightRecorder><LogDu rationSec>` properties control the size and age of the `FlightRecorder` trace file before it is recycled. You can supply your own trace definition file to include the trace events and columns you wish to monitor using the `<Log><FlightRecorder><TraceDefinition File>` property. If `FlightRecorder` collects useful trace events, it can be an invaluable troubleshooting tool. By default, the file is only allowed to grow to 10 MB or 60 minutes. Long processing jobs can take up much more space, and their duration could be much longer than 60 minutes. Hence, you should adjust the settings as necessary for your monitoring needs. You should also adjust the trace events and columns to be captured by `FlightRecorder`. You should consider adjusting the duration to cover three days (in case the issue you are researching happens over a weekend).

The `<Memory><LowMemoryLimit>` property controls the point—amount of memory used by SSAS—at which the *cleaner* thread becomes actively engaged in reclaiming memory from existing jobs. Each SSAS command (query, processing, backup, synchronization, and so on) is associated with jobs that run on threads and use system resources. We can lower the value of this setting to run more jobs in parallel (though the performance of each job could suffer). Two properties control the maximum amount of memory that a SSAS instance could use. Once memory usage reaches the value specified by `<Memory><TotalMemoryLimit>`, the cleaner thread becomes particularly aggressive at reclaiming memory.

The `<Memory><HardMemoryLimit>` property specifies the absolute memory limit—SSAS will not use memory above this limit. These properties are useful if you have SSAS and other applications installed on the same server computer. You should reserve some memory for other applications and the operating system as well. When `HardMemoryLimit` is reached, SSAS will disconnect the active sessions, advising that the operation was cancelled due to memory pressure.

> All memory settings are expressed in percentages if the values are less than or equal to 100. Values above 100 are interpreted as kilobytes. All memory configuration changes require restart of the SSAS service to take effect.

In the prior releases of Analysis Services, you could only specify the minimum and maximum number of threads used for queries and processing jobs. With SSAS 2012, you can also specify the limits for the input/output job threads using the `<ThreadPool><IOProcess>` properties.

The `<Process><IndexBuildThreshold>` property governs the minimum number of rows within a partition for which SSAS will build indexes. The default value is `4096`. SSAS decides which partitions it needs to scan for each query based on the partition index files. If the partition does not have indexes, it will be scanned for all the queries. Normally, SSAS can read small partitions without greatly affecting query performance. But if you have many small partitions, you should lower the threshold to ensure each partition has indexes.

The `<Process><BufferRecordLimit>` and `<Process><BufferMemoryLimit>` properties specify the number of records for each memory buffer and the maximum percentage of memory that can be used by a memory buffer. Lower the value of these properties to process more partitions in parallel. You should monitor processing using the SQL Profiler to see if some partitions included in the processing batch are being processed while the others are waiting.

The `<ExternalConnectionTimeout>` and `<ExternalCommandTimeout>` properties control how long an SSAS command should wait for connecting to a relational database and how long SSAS should wait to execute the relational query before reporting timeout. Depending on the relational source, it might take longer than 60 seconds (that is, the default value) to connect. If you encounter processing errors without being able to connect to the relational source, you should increase the `ExternalConnectionTimeout` value. It could also take a long time to execute a query; by default, the processing query will timeout after one hour. Adjust the value as needed to prevent processing failures.

The contents of the `<AllowedBrowsingFolders>` property define the drives and directories that are visible when creating databases, collecting backups, and so on. You can specify multiple items separated using the pipe (|) character.

The `<ForceCommitTimeout>` property defines how long a processing job's commit operation should wait prior to cancelling any queries/jobs which may interfere with processing or synchronization. A long running query can block synchronization or processing from committing its transaction. You can adjust the value of this property from its default value of `30` seconds to ensure that processing and queries don't step on each other.

The `<Port>` property specifies the port number for the SSAS instance. You can use the hostname followed by a colon (`:`) and a port number for connecting to the SSAS instance in lieu of the instance name. Be careful not to supply the port number used by another application; if you do so, the SSAS service won't start.

The `<ServerTimeout>` property specifies the number of milliseconds after which a query will timeout. The default value is `1` hour, which could be too long for analytical queries. If the query runs for an hour, using up system resources, it could render the instance unusable by any other connection. You can also define a query timeout value in the client application's connection strings. Client setting overrides the server-level property.

There's more...

There are many other properties you can set to alter SSAS instance behavior. For additional information on configuration properties, please refer to product documentation at `http://technet.microsoft.com/en-us/library/ms174556.aspx`.

Creating and dropping databases

As discussed in *Chapter 7, Analysis Services Security*, only SSAS instance administrators are permitted to create, drop, restore, detach, attach, and synchronize databases. This recipe teaches administrators how to create and drop databases.

Getting ready

Launch SSMS and connect to your Analysis Services instance as an administrator. If you're not certain that you have administrative properties to the instance, right-click on the SSAS instance and choose **Properties**. If you can view the instance's properties, you are an administrator; otherwise, you will get an error indicating that only instance administrators can view and alter properties.

How to do it...

To create a database, perform the following steps:

1. Right-click on the `Databases` folder and choose **New Database**. Doing so launches the **New Database** dialog shown in the following screenshot.

2. Specify a descriptive name for the database, for example, `Analysis_Services_Administration Chapter`. Note that the database name can contain spaces. As you learned in the previous chapters, each object has a name as well as an identifier. The identifier value is set to the object's original name and cannot be changed without dropping and recreating the object; hence, it is important to come up with a descriptive name from the very beginning. You cannot create more than one database with the same name on any SSAS instance.

3. Specify the storage location for the database. By default, the database will be stored under the `\OLAP\DATA` folder of your SSAS installation directory. The only compelling reason to change the default is if your data drive is running out of disk space and cannot support the new database's storage requirements.

> I recommend procuring additional disk space rather than placing the database in a nondefault data folder. Not only does using a nondefault data folder make troubleshooting more difficult, but also it could cause issues during database synchronization.

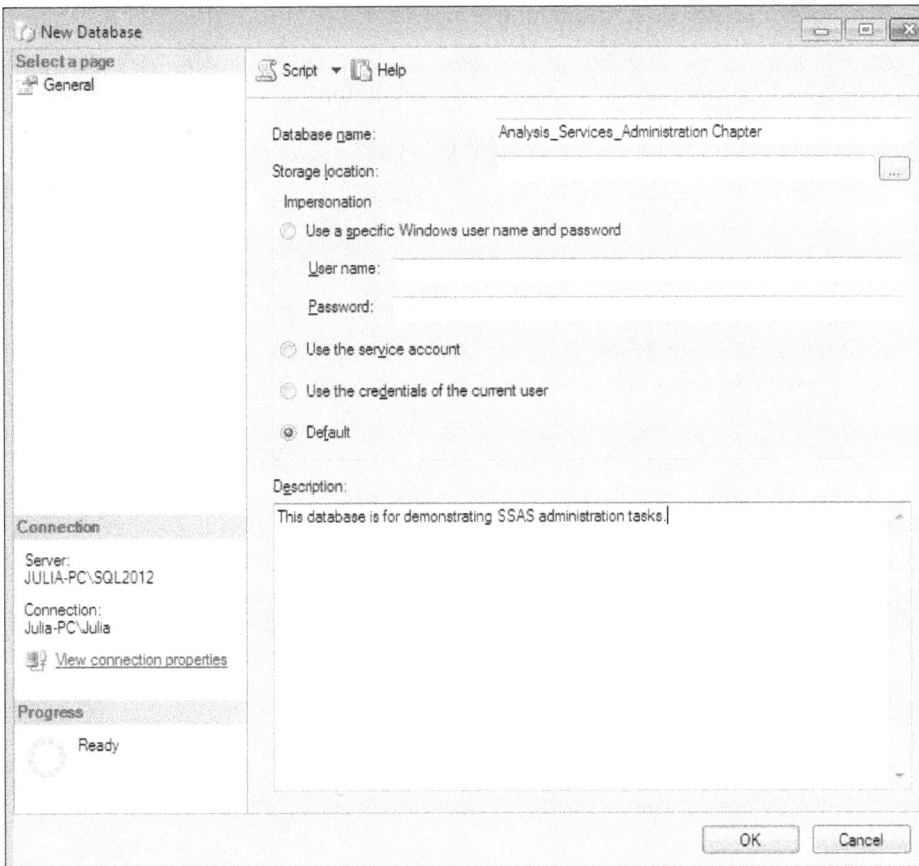

4. Specify the impersonation setting for the database. Remember from *Chapter 2, Defining Analysis Services Dimensions*, you could also specify the impersonation property for each data source. Alternatively, each data source can inherit the `DataSourceImpersonationInfo` property from the database-level setting. You have four choices as follows:

   □ **Specific user name (must be a domain user) and password**: This is the most secure option but requires updating the password if the user changes the password

   □ **Analysis Services service account**

   □ **Credentials of the current user**: This option is specifically for data mining

   □ **Default**: This option is the same as using the service account option

5. Specify an optional description for the database.

6. As with the majority of other SSMS dialogs, you can script the XMLA command you are about to execute by clicking on the **Script** button.

To drop an existing database, perform the following steps:

1. Expand the `Databases` folder on the SSAS instance, right-click on the database, and choose **Delete**.

2. The **Delete objects** dialog allows you to ignore errors; however, it is not applicable to databases. You can script the XMLA command if you wish to review it first.

3. An alternative way of scripting the `DELETE` command is to right-click on the database and navigate to **Script database as | Delete To | New query window**.

A good practice is to ensure that you have a database backup before deleting any database, just in case the wrong database is deleted or you need to get the database back online due to some unforeseen circumstance.

Unlike other database platforms, the Analysis Services database grows automatically. This could be a blessing or a curse depending on circumstances. SSAS shields the administrator from the mundane tasks of allocating additional space to the database or shrinking database files to save space. However, beware, since the SSAS instance will crash if it runs out of disk space during processing or synchronization. Also, SSAS does not check whether any users are logged on to the database when the `DELETE` command is executed; it is the database administrator's job to ensure that the database is no longer used before it is deleted.

Monitoring SSAS instance using Activity Viewer

Unlike other database systems, Analysis Services has no system databases. However, administrators still need to check the activity on the server, ensure that cubes are available and can be queried, and there is no blocking. You can exploit a tool named Analysis Services Activity Viewer 2008 to monitor SSAS Versions 2008 and later, including SSAS 2012. This tool is owned and maintained by the SSAS community and can be downloaded from `www.codeplex.com`.

To use Activity Viewer, you need to install Analysis Services OLE DB Provider for Microsoft SQL Server 2008, which you can obtain as a part of the SQL Server 2008 feature pack from Microsoft's website.

Activity Viewer allows viewing active and dormant sessions, current XMLA and MDX queries, locks, as well as CPU and I/O usage by each connection. Additionally, you can define rules to raise alerts when a particular condition is met.

How to do it...

To monitor an SSAS instance using Activity Viewer, perform the following steps:

1. Launch the application by double-clicking on `ActivityViewer.exe`.

2. Click on the **Add New Connection** button on the **Overview** tab. Specify the hostname and instance name or the hostname and port number for the SSAS instance and then click on **OK**.

3. For each SSAS instance you connect to, Activity Viewer adds a new tab. Click on the tab for your SSAS instance. Here, you will see several pages as shown in the following screenshot:

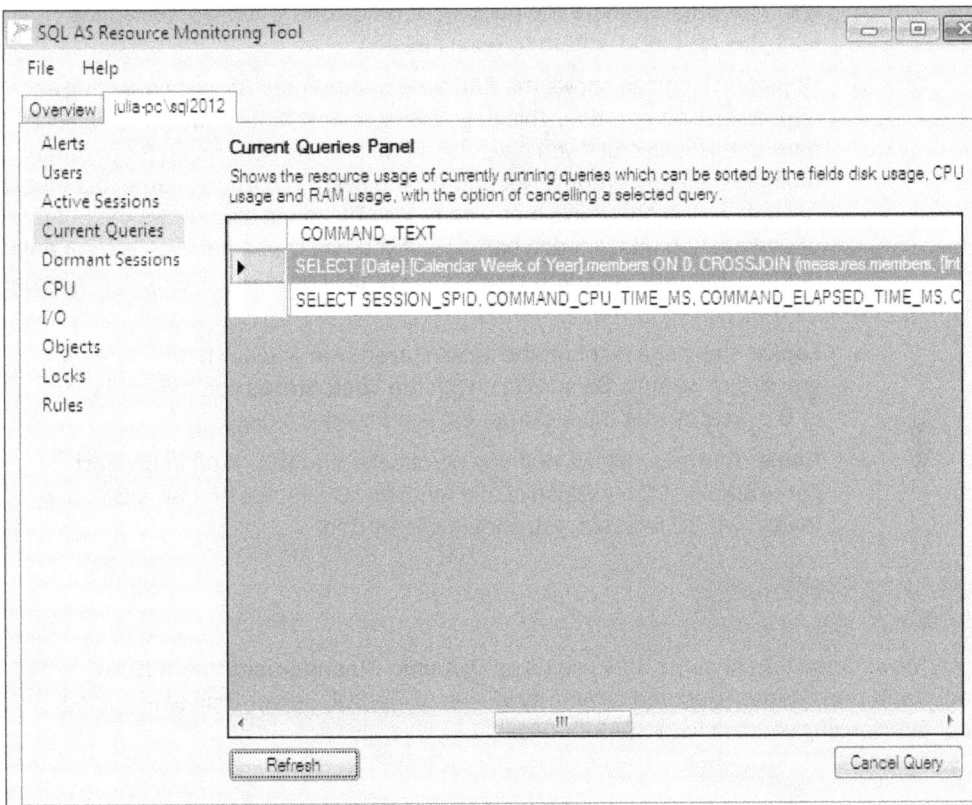

- **Alerts**: This page shows any sessions that met the condition found in the **Rules** page.

- **Users**: This page displays one row for each user as well as the number of sessions, total memory, CPU, and I/O usage.

- **Active Sessions**: This page displays each session that is actively running an MDX, **Data Mining Extensions** (**DMX**), or XMLA query. This page allows you to cancel a specific session by clicking on the **Cancel Session** button.

- **Current Queries**: This page displays the actual command's text, number of kilobytes read and written by the command, and the amount of CPU time used by the command. This page allows you to cancel a specific query by clicking on the **Cancel Query** button.

- **Dormant Sessions**: This page displays sessions that have a connection to the SSAS instance but are not currently running any queries. You can also disconnect a dormant session by clicking on the **Cancel Session** button.

- **CPU**: This page allows you to review the CPU time used by the session as well as the last command executed on the session.

- **I/O**: This page displays the number of reads and writes as well as the kilobytes read and written by each session.

- **Objects**: This page shows the CPU time and number of reads affecting each dimension and partition. This page also shows the full path to the object's parent; this is useful if you have the same naming convention for partitions in multiple measure groups. Not only do you see the partition name, but also the full path to the partition's measure group. This page also shows the number of aggregation hits for each partition. If you find that a partition is frequently queried and requires many reads, you should consider building aggregations for it.

- **Locks**: This page displays the locks currently in place, whether already granted or waiting. Be sure to check the **Lock Status** column—the value of **0** indicates that the lock request is currently blocked.

- **Rules**: This page allows defining conditions that will result in an alert. For example, if the session is idle for over 30 minutes or if an MDX query takes over 30 minutes, you should get alerted.

How it works...

Activity Viewer monitors Analysis Services using **Dynamic Management Views** (**DMV**). In fact, capturing queries executed by Activity Viewer using SQL Server Profiler is a good way of familiarizing yourself with SSAS DMV's.

For example, the **Current Queries** page checks the `$system.DISCOVER_COMMANDS` DMV for any actively executing commands by running the following query:

```
SELECT SESSION_SPID,COMMAND_CPU_TIME_MS,COMMAND_ELAPSED_TIME_MS,
   COMMAND_READ_KB,COMMAND_WRITE_KB, COMMAND_TEXT
FROM $system.DISCOVER_COMMANDS
WHERE COMMAND_ELAPSED_TIME_MS > 0
ORDER BY COMMAND_CPU_TIME_MS DESC
```

The **Active Sessions** page checks the `$system.DISCOVER_SESSIONS` DMV with the session status set to 1 using the following query:

```
SELECT SESSION_SPID,SESSION_USER_NAME, SESSION_START_TIME,
   SESSION_ELAPSED_TIME_MS,SESSION_CPU_TIME_MS, SESSION_ID
FROM $SYSTEM.DISCOVER_SESSIONS
WHERE SESSION_STATUS = 1
ORDER BY SESSION_USER_NAME DESC
```

The **Dormant sessions** page runs a very similar query to that of the **Active Sessions** page, except it checks for sessions with `SESSION_STATUS=0`—sessions that are currently not running any queries. The result set is also limited to the top 10 sessions, based on idle time measured in milliseconds.

The **Locks** page examines all the columns of the `$system.DISCOVER_LOCKS` DMV to find all requested locks as well as lock creation time, lock type, and lock status. As you have already learned, the lock status of 0 indicates that the request is blocked, whereas the lock status of 1 means that the request has been granted. Analysis Services blocking can be caused by conflicting operations that attempt to query and modify objects. For example, a long running query can block a processing or synchronization job from completion because processing will change the data values. Similarly, a command altering the database structure will block queries. The database administrator or instance administrator can explicitly issue the LOCK XMLA command as well as the BEGIN TRANSACTION command. Other operations request locks implicitly.

The following table documents the most frequently encountered Analysis Services lock types:

Lock type identifier	Description	Acquired for
2	Read lock	Processing to read metadata.
4	Write lock	Processing to write data after it is read from relational sources.
8	Commit shared	During the processing, restore or synchronization commands.
16	Commit exclusive	Committing the processing, restore, or synchronization transaction when existing files are replaced by new files.

Monitoring SSAS instance using DMVs

In the previous section you learned about a few DMVs referenced by Activity Viewer. Analysis Services supports many other DMVs not used by Activity Viewer. You can query DMVs directly using the SSMS or ASCMD command-line utility.

How to do it...

You can query DMVs by executing simple SELECT statements in the MDX query window within SSMS by performing the following steps:

1. Navigate to **FILE | New | Analysis Services MDX Query**.
2. Connect to your SSAS instance as an administrator.
3. Paste the DMV queries you captured using SQL Server Profiler (see the previous section, *Monitoring SSAS instance using Activity Viewer*). The SELECT statements that you can use for querying DMVs are somewhat limited:

    ❑ You can only query one DMV at a time and cannot join multiple DMVs.

    ❑ You can extract a subset of all the rows by specifying the TOP keyword and the ORDER BY clause.

    ❑ You can extract a subset of all the columns by explicitly listing column names or get all the columns using the star (*) operator.

    ❑ You cannot use the GROUP BY clause to aggregate data. You can set up a linked server from the SQL Server to Analysis Services and import DMV data into a relational table first if you wish to use GROUP BY or any other syntax elements not supported by SSAS DMVs.

How it works...

In this section I will discuss a few DMVs that are particularly useful for monitoring and troubleshooting Analysis Services, along with the SELECT statements used to query them.

To get a list of all the cubes and dimensions within the current database, you can query $system.MDSCHEMA_CUBES. Dimensions will be returned in the result set because you can query each dimension as though it were a cube using the $Dimension_Name notation. To obtain additional dimension specific metadata, such as the dimension's default hierarchy, dimension type, and whether the dimension is visible, check the $system.MDSCHEMA_DIMENSIONS DMV. Additional metadata for dimension hierarchies is available in $system.MDSCHEMA_HIERARCHIES. You can query all the MDSCHEMA_* DMVs as well as most other DMVs by simply running the SELECT * FROM DMV_NAME query.

To get a list of traces that currently monitor your SSAS instance, check `$system.DISCOVER_TRACES` as follows:

```
SELECT * FROM $system.DISCOVER_TRACES
```

You can find additional trace related metadata in `DISCOVER_TRACE_COLUMNS` and `DISCOVER_TRACE_EVENT_CATEGORIES`. To list the transactions running on the current instance, check `DISCOVER_TRANSACTIONS`.

You can use `$system.DISCOVER_DIMENSION_STAT` to get the member counts for each attribute. You must specify the database name and dimension name when querying this DMV. For example, the following query gets attribute member counts for the `Promotion` dimension in the `AdventureWorks_Sample` database:

```
SELECT * FROM SYSTEMRESTRICTSCHEMA (
    $SYSTEM.DISCOVER_DIMENSION_STAT, DIMENSION_NAME = 'promotion'
, DATABASE_NAME='AdventureWorks_Sample')
  ORDER BY Attribute_Count DESC
```

The following table shows the results:

DATABASE_NAME	DIMENSION_NAME	ATTRIBUTE_NAME	ATTRIBUTE_COUNT
AdventureWorks_Sample	Promotion	Discount Percent	11
AdventureWorks_Sample	Promotion	End Date	11
AdventureWorks_Sample	Promotion	Start Date	9
AdventureWorks_Sample	Promotion	Promotion Type	7
AdventureWorks_Sample	Promotion	Min Quantity	7
AdventureWorks_Sample	Promotion	Max Quantity	6
AdventureWorks_Sample	Promotion	Promotion Category	4

You can query $system.DISCOVER_PARTITION_STAT much the same way as DISCOVER_DIMENTION_STAT, except you must provide the cube name as well as measure group name and partition name, as shown in the following code snippet. The result will be the aggregation name and aggregation size.

```
SELECT * FROM SYSTEMRESTRICTSCHEMA (
    $SYSTEM.DISCOVER_PARTITION_STAT, PARTITION_NAME =
      'Internet_Sales_2005', CUBE_NAME = 'Adventure Works',
        MEASURE_GROUP_NAME = 'Internet Sales',
          DATABASE_NAME='AdventureWorks_Sample')
```

You can query $system.DISCOVER_PERFORMANCE_COUNTERS to obtain the current value of a specific performance counter, for example:

```
SELECT * FROM SYSTEMRESTRICTSCHEMA (
    $SYSTEM.DISCOVER_PERFORMANCE_COUNTERS, PERF_COUNTER_NAME =
      '\MSOLAP$SQL2012:Threads\Processing Pool Busy I/O job
        Threads')
```

There's more...

As you learned in this section, DMVs contain a lot of useful information about SSAS metadata and internals even though the product does not have any system databases. Please reference product documentation for the full list of DMVs at http://msdn.microsoft.com/en-us/library/hh230820.aspx.

Cancelling a session

If you have managed SQL Server or other relational database systems, you should be familiar with the unambiguous KILL command that disconnects the offending session and terminates the query executed on that session. Analysis Services has a similar statement, though it uses a somewhat milder term, CANCEL, perhaps more appropriate for the type of operation it performs. After all, the impact of terminating the session isn't always immediate, even in relational systems. If a user is running a large transaction affecting thousands or millions of records, it could take a long time to roll such transactions back. The CANCEL command is also different from KILL in a sense that it doesn't immediately terminate the session or query. Rather it tags the session to be terminated. SSAS periodically checks sessions and takes action on those sessions that have been tagged.

How to do it...

You can terminate a session using SSMS or ASCMD by performing the following steps:

1. Query `$system.DISCOVER_SESSIONS`, as shown earlier in this chapter, to find the **server process identifier** (**SPID**) of the session you wish to cancel.

2. Execute the XMLA command, similar to the following, to tag the session to be cancelled (substitute the correct `SPID` value):

```
<Cancel xmlns = "http://
   schemas.microsoft.com/analysisservices/2003/engine">
   <SPID>2790</SPID>
</Cancel>
```

> Cancelling a large processing or synchronization operation can take a long time because SSAS has to rollback the work it has done up to the second when the `CANCEL` command was issued.

Checking whether cubes are accessible

Microsoft does not provide any **database consistency checker** (**DBCC**) command for SSAS. However, this does not imply that Analysis Services objects could never get corrupted. In order to assure whether your cubes can be queried, you can set up a job that periodically runs very lightweight queries against each cube within your SSAS plant.

How to do it...

1. To check whether your cubes are available for querying, you could use the ASCMD utility to run a query similar to the following:

```
WITH member measures.is_accessible AS "1"
SELECT measures.is_accessible ON 0 FROM [adventure works]
```

Checking SSAS object sizes programmatically

Most SSAS databases contain data for a finite time span instead of perpetually accumulating data. After a while, data becomes stale and irrelevant for frequent analysis and should be either purged or migrated to a historical database. Since the volumes of the data we work with tend to grow quickly, we need to have a way of quickly checking the available disk space as well as the size of each object.

How to do it...

Microsoft supplies a couple of handy commands you could execute directly from the SSMS MDX query window to obtain the free disk space amount on the data drive.

1. You can execute `SYSTEMGETLOGICALDrives` within SSMS or from the ASCMD utility. The command doesn't take any parameters, as shown in the following code snippet:

    ```
    SYSTEMGETLOGICALDRIVES
    ```

    The following table shows the result:

Drive	Free Space
E:	5309

    The output of the `SYSTEMGETLOGICALDRIVES` command depends on the `AllowedBrowsingFolders` property value. Had I included `C:\` in the `AllowedBrowsingFolders` property value, the output would include both C and E drives.

2. You could use the `SYSTEMGETSUBDIRS` command to get subdirectories of a folder included in the `AllowedBrowsingFolders` property. For example, the following command retrieves folders for each database found under the SSAS data folder:

    ```
    SYSTEMGETSUBDIRS 'E:\Program Files\Microsoft SQL Server\MSAS11.
    SQL2012\OLAP\Data'
    ```

There's more...

As you can tell, the commands discussed in this section are very useful but somewhat limited because they don't provide the size of each data folder or each partition. SSMS allows obtaining the estimated size for one partition at a time (simply right-click on the partition and choose **Properties**); going through hundreds or thousands of partitions to collect the size of each is unacceptable. Fortunately, we can obtain the necessary information with a little effort, as shown in the following PowerShell script:

```
# script to obtain partition and measure group sizes
#load the Analysis Services assembly first so we can instantiate
Analysis Services object:
[Reflection.Assembly]::LoadFrom("E:\Program Files\Microsoft SQL
Server\110\SDK\Assemblies\Microsoft.AnalysisServices.dll")|out-null
$instance="Julia-PC\SQL2012"
$amoServer= new-object Microsoft.AnalysisServices.Server
#connect to the instance
```

```
$amoServer.Connect($instance)
#connect to the db and cube:
$db=$amoServer.databases.GetByName("AdventureWorks_Sample")
$cube = $db.cubes.GetByName("Adventure Works")
#loop over measure group partitions:
foreach ($mg in $cube.MeasureGroups)
    {
    $mg_size = 0
    $mg_name = $mg.name
    write-host "checking partitions in $mg_name measure group: "
    foreach ($partition in $mg.partitions)
        {
        $size = $partition.EstimatedSize;
        $size = $size / 1024 / 1024
        $size = [math]::round($size, 3)
        $partition_name = $partition.name;
        write-host "partition $partition_name is $size MB"
        $mg_size = $mg_size + $size
        }
        write-host "measure group $mg_name is $mg_size MB"
    }
#disconnect from the server
$amoServer.disconnect()
```

The output from this code will look similar to the following:

```
checking partitions in Internet Sales measure group:
partition Internet_Sales_2005 is 0.029 MB
partition Internet_Sales_2006 is 0.08 MB
partition Internet_Sales_2007 is 0 MB
measure group Internet Sales is 3.145 MB
checking partitions in Internet Orders measure group:
partition Internet_Orders_2005 is 0.739 MB
partition Internet_Orders_2006 is 0.569 MB
partition Internet_Orders_2007 is 0.501 MB
measure group Internet Orders is 2.243 MB
```

Scaling out SSAS solutions

As you learned in the introductory section of this chapter, Analysis Services is tuned for running a single query as fast as possible. This means that a single large query can use much of the available system resources and force other queries to wait. As a cube developer or database administrator, you need to take time to educate users on how to best use SSAS's power without bringing the production server to its knees. However, even fine-tuned cube design and queries leave room for scalability issues—a single server computer can only have a finite amount of system resources and, hence, can only serve a limited number of user requests. Additionally, you will often find that processing and querying activities conflict with each other; much like in any other database system, data readers can block writers and vice versa.

You have several methods at your disposal for scaling out Analysis Services solutions, given as follows:

▶ Backup databases on the processing instance and restore the databases to the querying instances

▶ Synchronize databases from the processing instances to querying instances

▶ Detach databases from the processing instance and attach them to querying instances in the read-only mode

Let's learn how to implement these scale out methods while considering the benefits and drawbacks of each.

Backup and restore

Assuring data availability is the primary responsibility of each database administrator, so collecting and validating SSAS database backups is essential for your job security. You can only collect full database backups—Analysis Services does not support backups at individual cube, measure group, or dimension level, nor does it support incremental or differential backups. Hence, when building SSAS databases, it is imperative to consider which data sets need to be backed up together. For example, if 80 percent of user queries examine current data and only 20 percent check historical data, you could implement two databases—one for historical and the other for recent data. If historical data changes rarely, you may only need to backup the historical database once a month, whereas the database with daily changes should be backed up more frequently. Much like other database platforms, when thinking about your SSAS backup strategy, you should consider how much data loss is acceptable. Some organizations consider Analysis Services backups optional because the underlying relational data source can be used to rebuild the MOLAP database. Although this is a valid statement, rebuilding SSAS database structure and reprocessing all objects could take considerably longer than restoring it from a valid backup. In addition to being one of the methods for assuring continuous data availability, backup and restore could also be used for scaling out SSAS implementations.

How to do it...

To collect Analysis Services database backup, perform the following steps:

1. Connect to the instance using SSMS, expand the `Databases` folder, right-click on the database of interest, and choose **Back Up**. Doing so activates the **Backup Database - AdventureWorks_Sample** dialog shown in the following screenshot.

2. Supply the full path and name of the backup file. The file extension must be `.abf`. If you do not explicitly specify the path, the backup file will be stored in the backup directory as defined in the `msmdsrv.ini` configuration file.

3. Specify whether the backup should be compressed. Analysis Services initially reserves more space than it actually requires for storing the backup and subsequently compresses the file (if the **Apply compression** box is checked).

4. Specify whether the backup should be encrypted with a password. Use this option judiciously; if you forget or misplace the password, the backup file is useless because you won't be able to restore the database from it. However, if you don't encrypt your backups, you need to store them securely, or someone could restore your backup and access all your organization's data.

5. Specify if the existing backup file should be overwritten and whether any remote partitions should be backed up. Remote partitions are seldom used.

6. Take a note of the advice included at the bottom of the **Remote partition backup location** dialog regarding the ROLAP, HOLAP, and MOLAP storage modes and corresponding backup actions. You can script the XMLA backup command or execute directly by clicking on the **OK** button.

> I recommend appending the backup collection date and time to the backup file's name so that each backup has a unique name. You could write a simple script to check the backup folder and only keep a certain number of backup files for each database after the current backup command is complete.

After you collect the backup, you can restore it to another server for scaling out or to the same server in case the database becomes corrupted. Perform the following steps to restore the database:

1. Connect to the instance where you wish to restore the database, expand the `Databases` folder, right-click on the `Databases` folder, and choose **Restore**. This activates the **Restore Database** dialog shown in the following screenshot.

2. Specify the full path and name of the backup file. You can click on the **Browse...** button to find the file (this will only allow you to browse the folders specified in the SSAS instance properties); alternatively, you can type the entire string into the textbox.

3. Specify the name of the database you wish to restore. You could restore over an existing database, in which case you must check the **Allow database overwrite** box or you can restore by creating a new database.

4. Specify the security settings for the restore operation; you can either copy all security roles or skip security. This option only applies to existing databases. For example, if you are restoring the production database backup to a test SSAS instance, the security settings in the two environments might be different. In this case, you can skip security during restore.

5. If the backup file was encrypted, you must specify the password.

6. The **Storage location** textbox allows specifying an optional alternate/nondefault location for database files. By default, files will be copied to the `\OLAP\data` folder of the SSAS installation directory specified in the SSAS instance properties.

7. The **Partitions** page of the dialog allows restoring remote partitions as well as specifying alternate locations for individual partitions. Use this flexibility with care; placing datafiles in a nondefault location makes debugging difficult.

> You can restore a database using a different name than the name of the database you backed up.

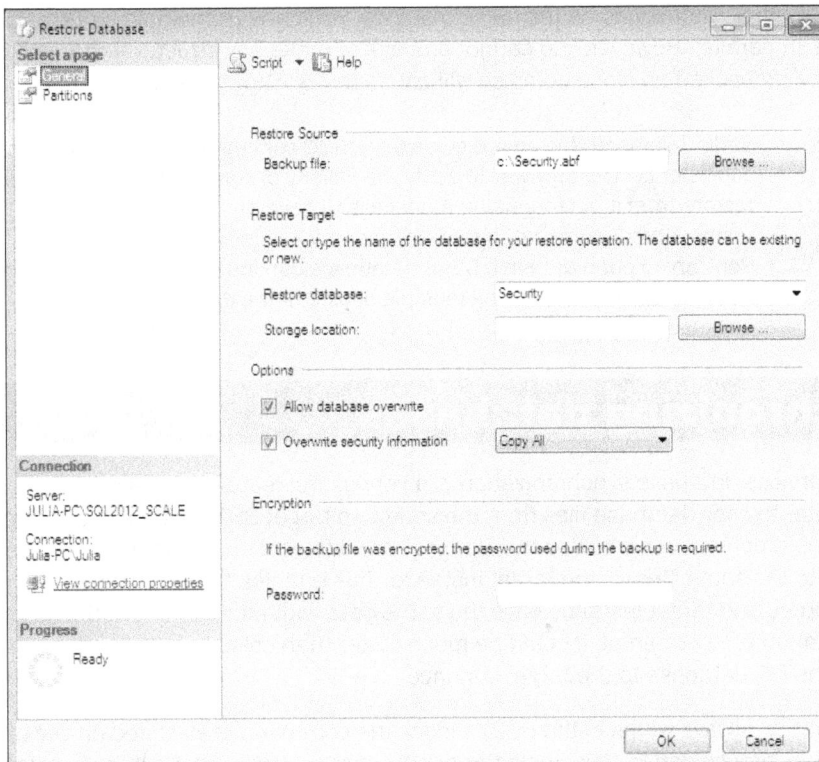

How it works...

Analysis Services creates a temporary folder—the folder name is **globally unique identifier** (**GUID**)—for the database being restored and extracts all datafiles into this folder. After all the files have been copied, the existing database folder is deleted, and the temporary folder is renamed from GUID to the actual database name.

Keep in mind that if you're restoring an existing database it will continue to remain online—available for queries—while the `restore` command is running. Therefore, you will need sufficient disk space to hold both the existing and new copy of the database until the `restore` command copies all files to the temporary data folder. So, if you are restoring a 100 GB database, you will need at least 200 GB to continue using the existing database while it is being restored.

If you host multiple databases on the same instance, you can run multiple `backup/restore` commands in parallel. However, you cannot process or make any structural changes to the database being backed up since doing so will cause the `backup` command to fail.

> Sadly, Microsoft does not provide any DBCC commands to check backup consistency. The only way to verify the validity of your backup is to actually restore from it. A reasonable practice is to have an automated job that restores production database backups to a test (standby) instance. Contrary to popular belief, SSAS databases can indeed get corrupted for various reasons. So, having multiple copies of the database and valid backups is highly prudent.

Synchronizing databases

Analysis Services database synchronization is a very useful feature that allows the database administrator to copy database files from the source to target SSAS instance. Synchronization is always incremental; it only copies the files that are different on the source instance as compared to the same files on the target instance. This enables the administrator to ensure that the source and target instance have the same data with minimal effort. Because synchronization is incremental, it could be much faster than collecting the backup and restoring the full database to the target instance.

Synchronization always works in the `pull` mode—the command is executed on the target instance. Synchronization is also single threaded, which means that it only copies one file at a time and there is no way to force copying multiple files in parallel. This normally isn't an issue for dimension files because these tend to be relatively small. However, partition data and aggregation files can get quite large and copying only one file at a time could be prohibitively slow. You can synchronize an existing database or synchronize to an instance that currently does not have the database; in this case, SSAS will have to copy every file to the target.

How to do it...

To synchronize a database, perform the following steps:

1. Connect to the target instance using SSMS, right-click on the `Databases` folder, and choose **Synchronize**. Skip the **Welcome** screen.

2. Specify the source SSAS instance and the database you wish to copy. The same screen allows you to choose the destination (target) data folder. Unless your data drive is out of disk space and you must choose an alternate location, use the default values and click on **Next**.

3. Review the list of partitions on the next screen to get an idea of how much data will need to be copied.

4. The screen that follows allows you to choose whether data should be compressed during synchronization; this is the default and recommended option. Additionally, you can choose to copy all security settings, ignore security, or transfer only the security roles without including the role members. Much like the case when restoring the database, security options are useful when transferring data from production to QA or test environments.

5. The **Synchronization** wizard allows you to execute synchronization right away or save the command to a file. You do not have the option of scripting the command to the query window or clipboard. The `Synchronize` XMLA command will look like the following:

```
<Synchronize xmlns:xsi = "http://www.w3.org/2001/XMLSchema-
    instance" xmlns:xsd = "http://www.w3.org/2001/XMLSchema"
      xmlns = "http://schemas.microsoft.com/analysisservices/
        2003/engine">
    <Source>
      <ConnectionString>Provider = MSOLAP.5;Data Source =
        julia-pc\sql2012;Integrated Security = SSPI;Initial
          Catalog = AdventureWorks_Sample</ConnectionString>
      <Object>
        <DatabaseID>AdventureWorks_Sample</DatabaseID>
      </Object>
    </Source>
    <SynchronizeSecurity>CopyAll</SynchronizeSecurity>
    <ApplyCompression>true</ApplyCompression>
</Synchronize>
```

How it works...

As you already know, the `Synchronize` command runs on the target instance. However, you cannot process or make changes to the source database while it is being synchronized. This is implemented through an explicit `BEGIN TRANSACTION` command on the source instance. Once all the files are copied over to the target instance data folder and synchronization is ready to commit its work on the target instance, SSAS issues an explicit `ROLLBACK TRANSACTION` command on the source instance to release locks and allow resuming processing.

The `Synchronize` command generates an in-memory list of all database files on both the source and target instances (presuming, of course, that the target instance already has the database you're about to sync). Synchronization next compares the metadata on two instances and comes up with the list of files that have a different version number, name, or size on the two instances. The files that are different are copied to a temporary folder on the target instance. The temporary folder uses a GUID as the name. Once all new files are copied, the existing files (identical on the source and target) are copied from the target instance's existing database folder to the temporary data folder. Once the GUID folder has all the files, SSAS deletes the existing database folder and renames the GUID folder to have the same name as the database. Synchronization also increments the data folder version number.

Much like the `restore` function, synchronization keeps the existing database online while new files are being copied. Therefore, if you're copying the large majority of database files, you will need free space to support two copies of the same database at the same time.

As you already learned, synchronization compares file version numbers, in addition to file sizes and creation dates. If you want to avoid having to transfer all files, it is best not to process any items on the target instance because doing so will change the file version numbers even if the file contents do not change.

Due to its incremental design, synchronization can be considerably faster than `backup` and `restore`. On the other hand, synchronization failure (perhaps due to a network outage) can often lead to target database corruption. If the target database is corrupted, we must either restore it from a backup or drop the corrupted version and run a full synchronization from another instance. Yet another disadvantage of synchronization is that it does not create a copy of the database as the `backup` command does. If the source database has incorrect data (or even a corruption issue), synchronization quietly transfers the problem to the target instance.

Detaching and attaching databases

You are now familiar with `backup` and `restore` as well as synchronization methods for scaling out SSAS solutions. However, as you learned in the previous section, synchronization is single threaded and must transfer only one file at a time. Fortunately, you can use the `Detach` and `Attach` features along with the `Robocopy` command for copying files to ensure the faster delivery of files from the source to target instance.

When you detach a database, SSAS leaves the data folder in its current location and creates a detach logfile. You can copy the entire data folder to another host or another instance's data folder and reattach the database. Keep in mind, however, that unlike synchronization, the `Detach` and `Attach` methods do not copy the data for you; you must come up with your own routine (script) for copying data. Additionally, you can attach a previously detached database in the read/write mode to only one instance. For all other instances, you must attach the database in the read-only mode. For most environments, this is acceptable because large databases rarely use write-back, and data must be processed on only one instance.

The `Detach` and `Attach` operations simply update the server metadata; they don't have to copy files or change security. Hence, both are very fast.

How to do it...

To detach a database, perform the following steps:

1. Connect to the SSAS database of interest using SSMS, right-click on the database, and choose **Detach**. This activates the **Detach Database** dialog.

2. You can specify the password that will be used for encrypting the detached database. As with the `backup` command, document the password in a secure location if you intend to encrypt the database. You can script the `Detach` command—it will look similar to the following code snippet:

```
<Detach xmlns = "http://schemas.microsoft.com/
  analysisservices/2003/engine">
  <Object>
    <DatabaseID>ssas_cookbook_chapter3</DatabaseID>
  </Object>
</Detach>
```

3. After you run the command, you will find a file named `ssas_cookbook_chapter3.detach_log` in the `Database` folder.

To attach a previously detached database, perform the following steps:

1. Connect to the target SSAS instance (or the same instance from which you previously detached the database) and choose **Attach**.

2. If you encrypted the database prior to detaching, you must provide the password.

3. Specify the full path to the folder with the detached database. You have an option to attach the database from its current location (without copying any files) or from a different location after you copy the database files to that location.

4. If you script the `Attach` command, it will look similar to the following code snippet:

```
<Attach xmlns = "http://schemas.microsoft.com/
  analysisservices/2003/engine">
  <Folder>E:\Program Files\Microsoft SQL Server\
    MSAS11.SQL2012\OLAP\Data\ssas_cookbook_chapter3.0.db
      </Folder>
  <ReadWriteMode xmlns = "http://schemas.microsoft.com/
    analysisservices/2008/engine/100">ReadOnly
      </ReadWriteMode>
</Attach>
```

5. If you prefer to attach in the read-write mode, simply replace `Readonly` with `ReadWrite` within the command previously shown.

If you do not copy files and attach the database to multiple SSAS instances from the same location in the read-only format, you'll be able to use CPU and memory resources on multiple hosts when sharing the same disk resource. Although this option might sound attractive, test your queries thoroughly to ensure that storage-intensive queries still perform to your expectations.

How it works...

As you learned, the Detach and Attach operations are nearly instantaneous because they only modify the SSAS instance metadata and do not have to copy any files. In order to make the same files available on different hosts, you must copy the files yourself, either manually or through code. Robocopy (**Robust File Copy**) is a command-line tool, which you could use to copy files. It is available as part of the Windows Resource Kit. Robocopy is multithreaded, out of the box on Windows 2008. If you use prior versions of the Windows operating system, you cannot take advantage of multithreading but you can be creative and launch multiple instances of Robocopy in parallel, each copying one set of data. One approach is to copy all the files with a certain extension in the same Robocopy session; this approach is not particularly effective because it copies dimension files very quickly but larger partition files still have to wait. A better approach is to launch a separate Robocopy session for each partition. Reference the Robocopy documentation for necessary switches and syntax examples.

The Detach/Robocopy/Attach method could be the fastest way of ensuring that multiple SSAS instances have the same data. However, unlike synchronization, this method does not provide an automated way of copying files. Additionally, this method does not make a copy of the database (unlike the backup command); hence, it could quietly transfer incorrect data or corruption issues from source to target. Remember too that we can only have one copy of the database attached in the read-write mode—all other copies must be read-only. Once a database is in the read-only mode, you cannot process any objects or write data back to any object. Furthermore, you can no longer drop the database. If you need to drop the read-only database, you must detach it first and then manually delete its files from the data folder.

Each of the scale-out methods requires a third-party solution for balancing the querying load across multiple SSAS instances. The common implementation of load balancing distributes queries using the Round-robin approach; however, this approach could lead to one instance being heavily loaded, while others are virtually idle due to the lightweight queries. A better approach is to check CPU and/or memory usage on each host and send each query to the host with least resource utilization. Please refer to the SQLCAT team blog for more information regarding query load balancing and scaling out SSAS solutions at http://www.sqlcat.com.

9
Using Tabular Models

In this chapter, we will cover:

- ▶ Creating a Tabular Model
- ▶ Working with data sources and loading data
- ▶ Modeling the data
- ▶ Creating a hierarchy
- ▶ Creating a calculated measure
- ▶ Creating a calculated column
- ▶ Creating a KPI
- ▶ Analyzing your model in Excel
- ▶ Deploying Tabular Models
- ▶ Scripting Tabular Models using XMLA
- ▶ Processing Tabular Models
- ▶ Partitioning Tabular Models
- ▶ Implementing perspectives
- ▶ Implementing security in Tabular Models
- ▶ Automating Tabular Model processing

Introduction

This chapter covers the concepts of creating **SQL Server Analysis Services** (**SSAS**) Tabular Models that are included in SQL Server 2012. Tabular Models are the enterprise implementation of the xVelocity In-Memory Analytics Engine models that were introduced with Power Pivot and SQL Server 2008 R2. Often, Tabular Models are the result of working with Power Pivot models. The Power Pivot and Tabular Models are built on the same technology. However, there are some features which are not included in Power Pivot but are available in Tabular such as DirectQuery, partitions, and higher-level security. In this chapter, we will focus on building Tabular Models in SSAS using Visual Studio.

We will be using **SQL Server Data Tools** (**SSDT**) in this chapter to create our model. Much of the work that we do in the initial creation of the model can also be done using Microsoft Excel 2010 or Microsoft Excel 2013 with the Power Pivot add-in. The design interface is very similar, so you will be able to use much of what you learn here to create Power Pivot models as well. As a result, I will be calling out those features that are exclusively the domain of SSAS so that you are able to understand the expanded capabilities of the Tabular Model.

In this chapter, we will be using the SQL Server sample database, `AdventureWorksDW2012`, which can be downloaded from `www.codeplex.com`. The sample work in this chapter will focus on the Internet Sales fact table (`factInternetSales`) and its related dimension tables.

Creating a Tabular Model

In this recipe, we will walk through creating a Tabular Model database project using SSDT. As you begin working with Tabular Models, you will see that some of the complexities in setting up a good multidimensional model do not apply. While working with multidimensional models, you typically need all of the data organized and ready for consumption by Analysis Services. However, Tabular Models are much more forgiving. The key design requirement to take into consideration is: What data does the business need? As a result, we will create a model database here and work through model modifications in the following recipes.

Getting ready

Before you create your first Tabular Model database, you must have an installation of Analysis Services with a Tabular Model instance available to you. This can be a local installation or a network installation. This is required because a Tabular Model database is developed in *real time* using the xVelocity In-Memory Analytics Engine and RAM to store the database while you are working with it.

How to do it...

Let's get started on our Tabular Model by performing the following steps:

1. Using SSDT, choose to create a new project. This will bring up the **New Project** dialog. From this dialog, there are three methods to create a new Tabular project. Two of them are import options: **Import from PowerPivot** and **Import from Server (Tabular)**. Although they are not the subject of this recipe, I do want to call these options out. The **Import from Power Pivot** option is particularly effective while upgrading a Power Pivot model to take advantage of the Tabular Model features in Analysis Services. This usually includes expanded requirements such as security, processing, and partitioning. You can create a Tabular Model that serves as a template that can be modified to meet any business needs. This makes the **Import from Server (Tabular)** option compelling for scenarios that can use baseline models for targeted analysis.

2. We are going to pursue the first option in the list that allows us to build a Tabular Model using Visual Studio. Select **Analysis Services Tabular Project**, give the new project a name, and set a location that will work for you.

3. Once you have set these details, click on **OK** to create the project. This will create a new solution, a new project, and a development database on your tabular instance.

> If you have a local Tabular Model instance of SSAS, the project will point to that. However, if the project cannot discover the tabular instance, you will be prompted to select the instance to be used for the project.

4. In the project's solution explorer, you will see your project and a `Model.bim` file. This file is the container for your Tabular Model. However, as I mentioned before, the actual development requires a tabular instance.

> Only one BIM file will exist in the project. Tabular database projects only support one model.

5. If you open up SQL Server Management Studio and connect to your tabular instance, you will see a new tabular database, which has the name of the project, the name of the user, and GUID to make up the name.

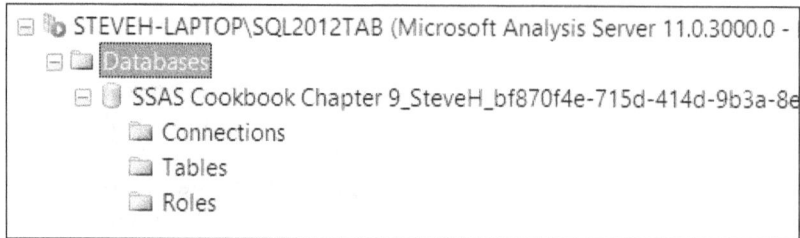

```
STEVEH-LAPTOP\SQL2012TAB (Microsoft Analysis Server 11.0.3000.0 -
  Databases
    SSAS Cookbook Chapter 9_SteveH_bf870f4e-715d-414d-9b3a-8e
      Connections
      Tables
      Roles
```

There's more...

If you need to change the target server for your tabular development, you can do that by modifying the settings for the model. Right-click on `Model.bim` and select **Properties**. From this **Properties** page, you can change **Workspace Server** and set **Workspace Retention**. The server just needs to have an Analysis Services tabular instance on it.

The **Workspace Retention** property is used to set how the tabular instance manages your model when the project is closed. **Workspace Retention** is set to **Unload from Memory** by default. This has the following three options: **Keep in Memory**, **Unload from Memory**, and **Delete Workspace**. **Keep in Memory** will keep the workspace database in memory even after you have closed the project. **Unload from Memory** will remove the database from the memory. **Delete Workspace** will remove the database from the server once you have closed the project. The **Delete Workspace** and **Unload from Memory** options force you to reload the data whenever you want to work on your project. You should choose the best option based on the resources you have available on your workspace server.

Working with data sources and loading data

In the previous recipe, you created the project; now it is time to load data into the model. Unlike other data modeling or data projects you have worked with, the Tabular Model loads the data into the model as soon as you define the data source and specify the data to load. This is a step beyond **What You See Is What You Get** (**WYSIWYG**). In this case, you see the data and the effects of all changes you make to it in real time.

The other thing is that you can load all types and sources of data into the model and relate the data after the data has been loaded. Data from a relational database, a text file, a data feed, or even a Power Pivot model can all be loaded into the same Tabular Model for analysis.

In multidimensional models, you will create a data source and then a data source view. The next step is to finish designing the dimensions and measure groups. Once you have completed the design, you will load data. In a Tabular Model, creating the data source and loading the data are done simultaneously.

In our example, we will be loading tables from the `AdventureWorksDW2012` database. We will be using the project that was created in the previous recipe as the target for our recipe.

How to do it...

In your project, you will notice that there is no concept of creating a data source:

1. Open the model by double-clicking on `Model.bim` or choose **Open** from the context menu. Once the model is open, you will be looking at a blank tab in the Visual Studio IDE.

2. From the **MODEL** menu at the top of the IDE, choose **Import from Data Source**. As you can see, there is no **create data source** option. Instead, once you select your data, it will be loaded into memory on the target Tabular Model instance.

   It is very important to understand the size of the data you are planning to work with in your Tabular Model. If you have a lot of rows, very wide rows, or a combination thereof, you may need to start with a sample set or a filtered set of data to keep the loading time shorter and to manage memory consumption better during the development process.

3. Once you click on **Import from Data Source**, you will open the **Connect to a Data Source** dialog. In our example, we will be using **Microsoft SQL Server** to connect to our `AdventureWorksDW2012` database. However, many different data sources are supported by Tabular Models, and while the process may vary from source to source, the result is the same—data is imported into your model.

4. Once you have selected your data source, click on **Next**, and you will be prompted to fill out the connection information.

5. As you complete the connection information, Microsoft will create a name based on the properties you have specified, such as `SqlServer ServerNameSQL2012DB AdventureWorksDW2012` in our case. As you can see, it concatenated the data source, server name, and database name. While being informative, something like `Adventure Works DW` would also be easier to understand and work with. This also solves an issue where you need to change the server name at a later time, but you want to keep the same connection name.

6. On the next dialog, you will be prompted for the impersonation information. The purpose of this information is to set a user or a set of credentials that can be used by the tabular instance to refresh the data. You can specify a user account or use the service account if your instance's service account has access to the data source.

7. Our next step allows us to choose the data. There are two ways to get data from a relational data source: you can choose from a list of tables and views, or you can write a query. In most cases, you will find that selecting from tables and views will be a quicker solution.

8. The **Select Tables and Views** dialog has a number of important features including the ability to find related tables and filter the data. In our example, we will select the `FactInternetSales` table and then click on **Select Related Tables**. The selected six additional tables are listed in the information area below the list, as shown in the following screenshot:

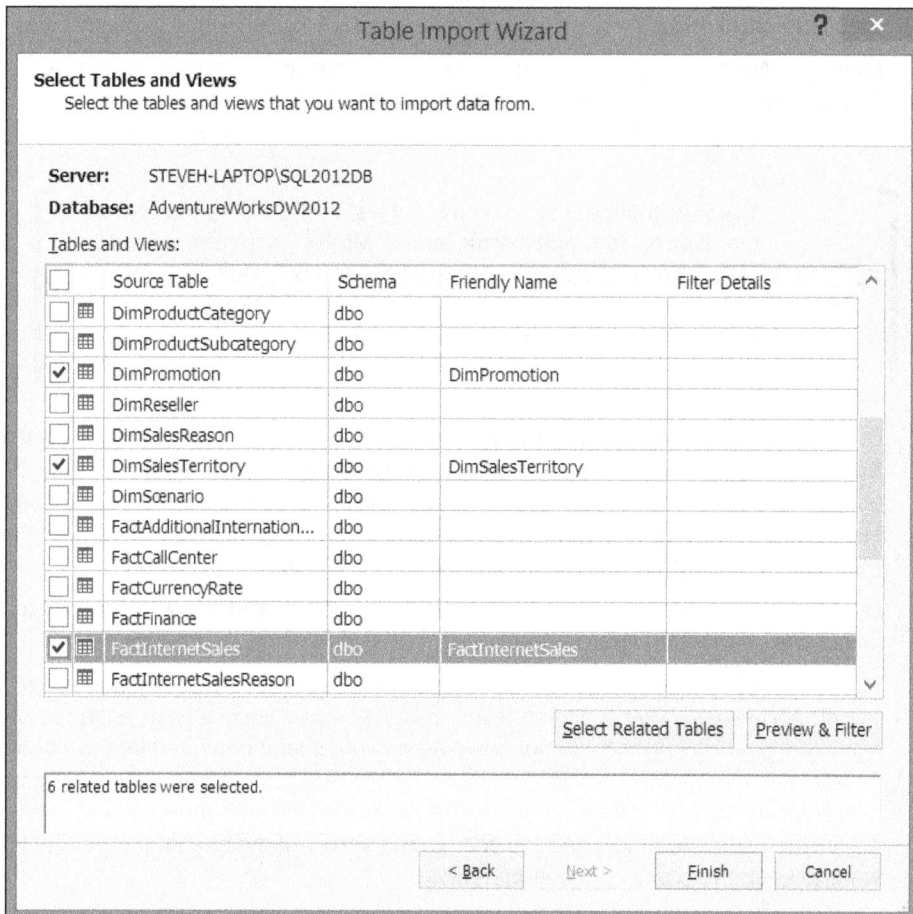

	Source Table	Schema	Friendly Name	Filter Details
	DimProductCategory	dbo		
	DimProductSubcategory	dbo		
✔	DimPromotion	dbo	DimPromotion	
	DimReseller	dbo		
	DimSalesReason	dbo		
✔	DimSalesTerritory	dbo	DimSalesTerritory	
	DimScenario	dbo		
	FactAdditionalInternation...	dbo		
	FactCallCenter	dbo		
	FactCurrencyRate	dbo		
	FactFinance	dbo		
✔	FactInternetSales	dbo	FactInternetSales	
	FactInternetSalesReason	dbo		

6 related tables were selected.

9. We still have a couple of steps to complete before we are done. The next task to do on this screen is to set a friendly name for each of the tables. In our example, this is fairly straightforward. We will remove the prefix and add spaces where needed. For example, `DimPromotion` will become `Promotion`.

10. You can also preview and filter the data here. From the preview dialog, you are able to filter, sort, and reduce the width of your table. You can filter the table by clicking on the down arrow on the right-hand side of the column header. This will open a drop-down list of distinct values from the column you are working with. You can select one to many of the options, and the table will be filtered appropriately, as shown in the following screenshot:

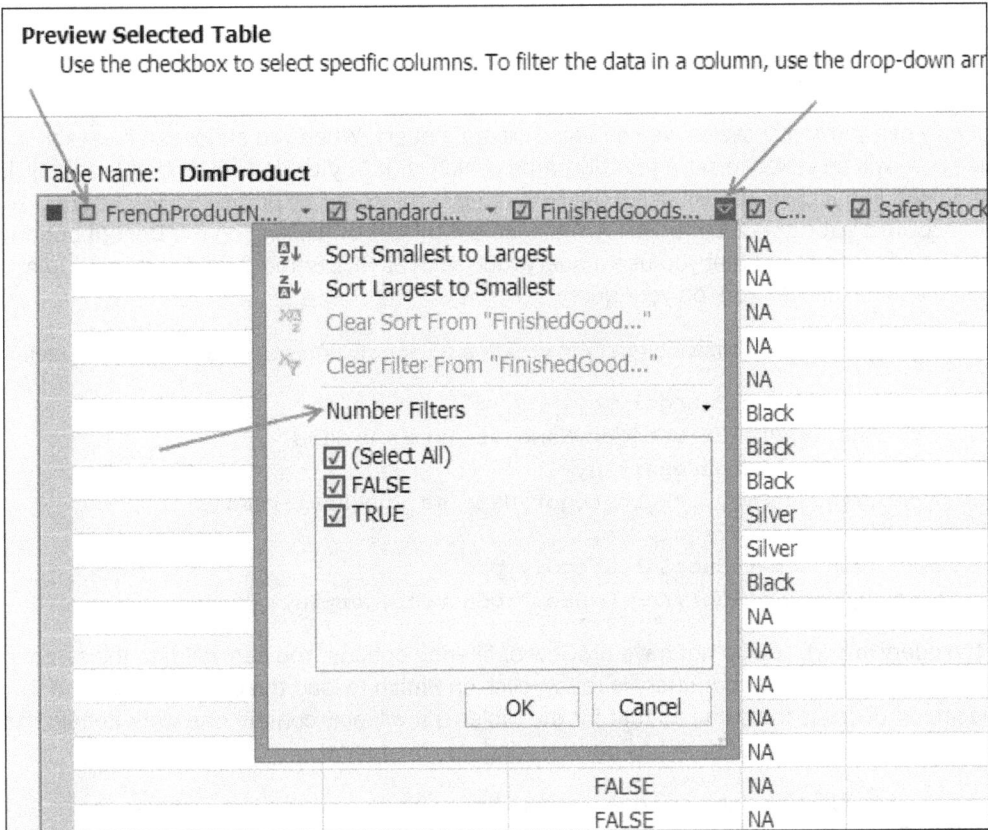

11. There are also sensitive filters for different data types that handle ranges and more complex filtering options. You can sort the data from the same drop down. You can reduce the width of your table by unselecting the columns using the checkbox to the left of the column header. The preceding screenshot shows where all of these options are.

12. Once the data has been selected and filtered, click on **Finish**. The data will start importing, showing the current table being imported and the number of rows transferred to the model.

> Reducing columns at the data source will help improve performance during the design process and ultimately in the final model.

13. After the data has been successfully loaded, you will see an *Excel-like* display of the imported data. At this point, you should save the model so that you do not lose your work.

There's more...

Not only can you select tables, you can also create a query. When you choose to create a query, you will be asked to set a friendly name (which is `Query` by default) and enter the SQL statement. In our case, we will use a query to bring in the contents of the `ProductCategory` and `ProductSubCategory` tables. A designer is available by clicking on the **Design** button, but I would recommend that you use a query tool, such as SQL Server Management Studio, to do the initial design work on your query.

We are going to use the following query to create a `ProductCategory` table in our model:

```
select pc.ProductCategoryKey
    ,pc.EnglishProductCategoryName as CategoryName
    ,psc.ProductSubcategoryKey
    ,psc.EnglishProductSubcategoryName as SubcategoryName
from DimProductCategory pc
inner join DimProductSubcategory psc
on pc.ProductCategoryKey = psc.ProductCategoryKey
```

In the query import, you do not have preview or filtering options. You can validate the syntax from here though. Once your query is ready, click on **Finish** to load the data into the model. The import dialog is the same as that for the tables but will only contain one work item in this case. Once it is done, your data has been loaded into the model.

If you need to add more tables or queries from the same data source, you can use the **Existing Connections** button on the toolbar or the **MODEL** menu. This will open up a dialog with the data sources you have already created. By naming your connections in a meaningful way, this dialog will allow you to add data easily from the existing connections in your model.

Modeling the data

Now that the data has been loaded, there are a few modeling techniques that should be applied to the model. Due to the mash up nature of the Tabular Models, you will likely need to do the following common clean up operations:

- ▸ Update column names
- ▸ Fix data types and formats
- ▸ Add relationships

You will learn how to do each of these in this recipe.

Getting ready

Before you can model data, you will need data in your model. If you have not loaded data yet, refer to the previous recipe on loading data.

How to do it...

You will be working in SSDT to make the changes.

1. Our first change is to update the column names. The column names should be user-friendly and easy to understand.

2. You can rename the column by right-clicking on the column and selecting **Rename Column** from the shortcut menu. In some complex scenarios, you may be required to rename all of the columns. In particular, this will likely be required for text loads that may be loaded with column names; for example, Column1, Column2, and so on.

> As a best practice, you should update column names when the data is loaded and before you begin updating the model. This will prevent issues with calculations that are added to the model later and are dependent on the column names.

3. It is also important to verify and fix any data types that were not properly identified during the load. While loading from relational data sources is usually not a problem, it is a common issue from file-based or feed-based sources.

4. You can change the data type in the **Properties** page of the selected column. In the **Basic** section, you will see the **Data Type** property, which has a drop-down list of the supported types.

> Tabular Models only support a few basic data types: text, whole number, decimal number, currency, date, and TRUE/FALSE. The default type is text and will often be the only type used for text file loads.

5. You can also change the data format in the **Properties** page of the selected column. In the **Basic** section, you will see the **Data Format** property, which uses a drop-down list to let you select the correct format and type for the column.

> Always fix the data type before working with the format. Once you have corrected the data type, the data format drop-down list will display the valid options for the type.

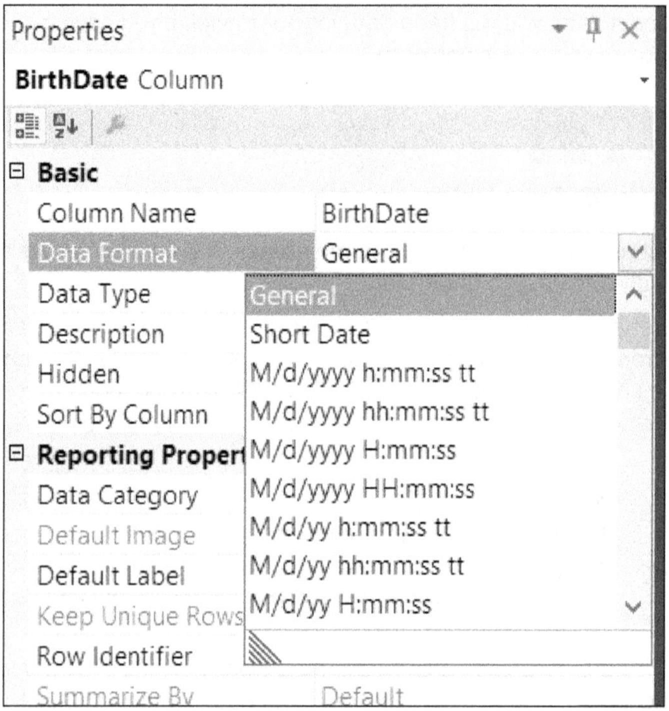
Properties
BirthDate Column
Basic
Column Name
BirthDate
Data Format
General
Data Type
Description
Hidden
Sort By Column
Reporting Propert
Data Category
Default Image
Default Label
Keep Unique Rows
Row Identifier
Summarize By
Default
General
Short Date
M/d/yyyy h:mm:ss tt
M/d/yyyy hh:mm:ss tt
M/d/yyyy H:mm:ss
M/d/yyyy HH:mm:ss
M/d/yy h:mm:ss tt
M/d/yy hh:mm:ss tt
M/d/yy H:mm:ss

6. The third model modification is adding relationships. Relationship building is likely the most important part of the modeling process as it allows the user to interact with the data in interesting ways. However, you should fix columns and data types prior to working with the relationships.

7. In SSDT, you should look for the diagram view. This is the easiest way to visualize the data relationships. You can get to the relationship view either by accessing the main menu or a small button on the design surface. Navigate to the menu option via **MODEL | Model View | Diagram View**. The button on the design surface is at the lower right-hand corner on your Model.bim tab. Refer to the following screenshot to see what to look for:

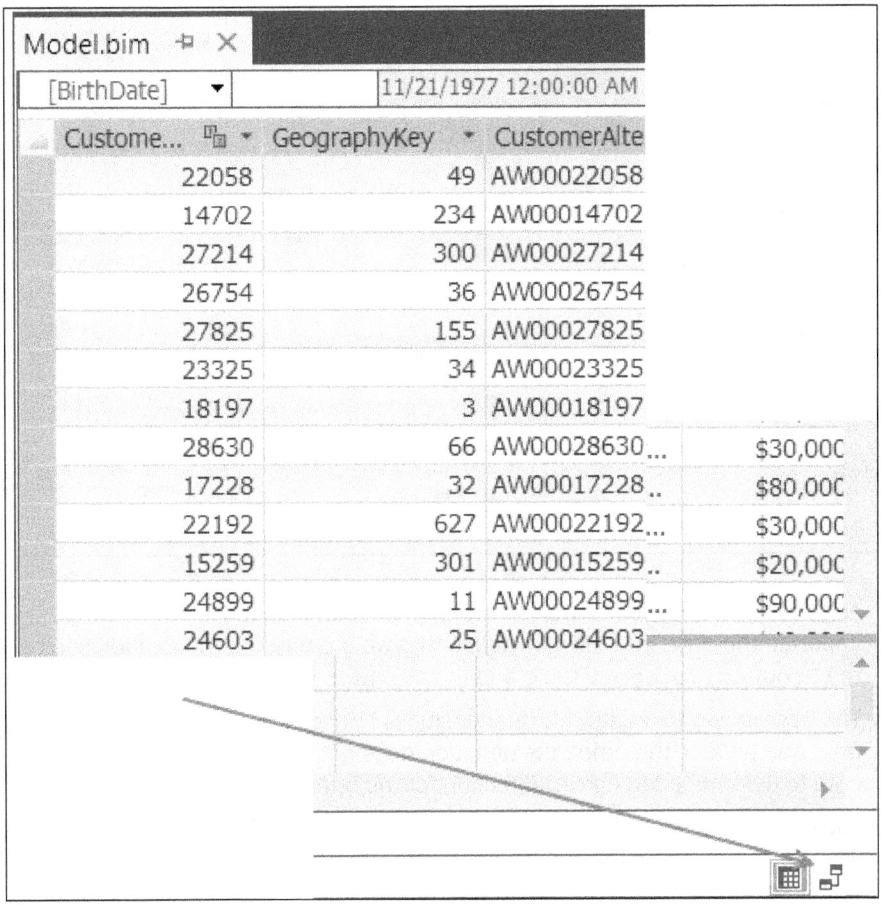

8. Once you open the diagram view, you will see how the relationships are mapped in your model, as shown in the following screenshot:

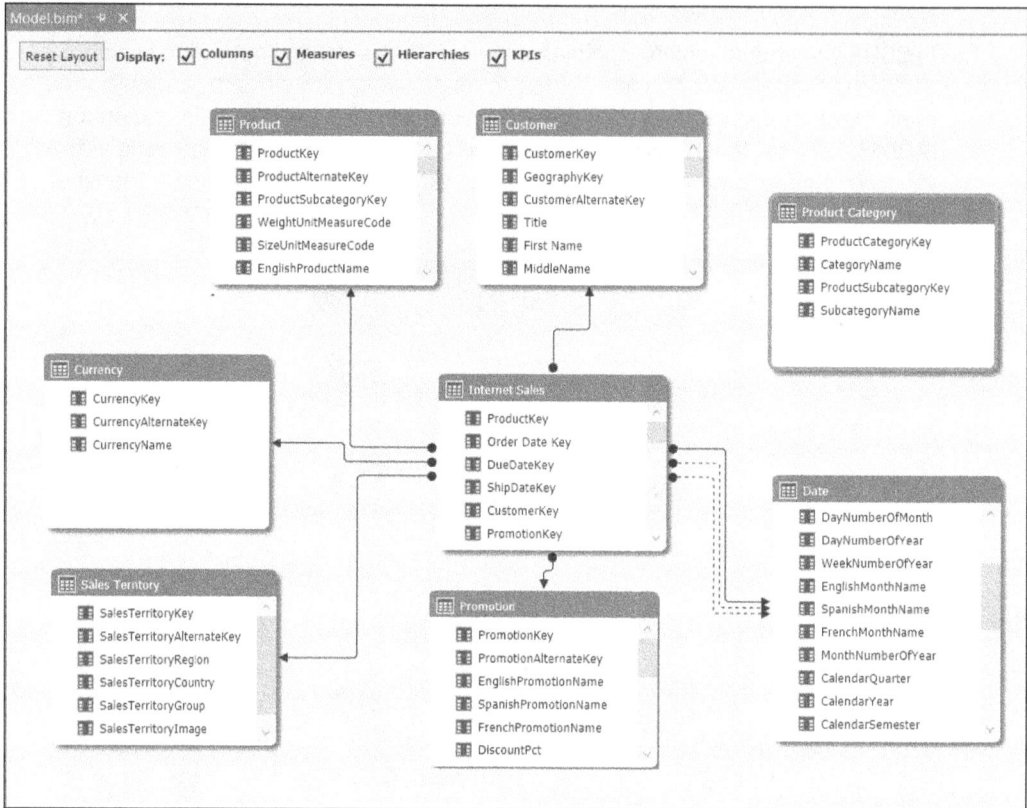

9. As you can see, SSAS was able to identify the relationships in our model when we imported the data. You will also notice that we are missing the relationship between the `Product Category` table and the `Product` table.

10. The easiest way to create this relationship is to drag `ProductSubCategoryKey` from one table to the other; the direction does not matter as SSAS will evaluate the data to determine the correct direction for the relationship.

11. You can also create the relationship by right-clicking on the column name in either view and by selecting **Create Relationship...**. This will open up a dialog that allows you to select the tables and fields in the relationship.

12. You need to be aware of a couple of restrictions around relationship building. The Tabular Model does not support a multifield relationship. Tabular Models also do not support role-playing dimensions. If you look at the preceding screenshot, you can see that the relationships between the `Date` table and the `Internet Sales` tables include dotted lines. These represent nonactive relationships in the model. Only active relationships can be used in major parts of the data analysis natively.

> Inactive relationships can still be used through DAX. Refer to *Chapter 10, DAX Calculations and Queries*, to see how DAX can be used to extend the model.

How it works...

While loading the data, SSAS evaluates the data and sets the settings (previously discussed) based on what it can learn from the data source. For instance, if foreign keys are discovered in the incoming data, and the related tables are also imported at the same time, relationships will be added to the model during the initial load. (Subsequent loads with new tables will not include the relationships.) The model will also evaluate data types during this initial load and set them in the model. These features work well with metadata-rich data sources such as relational databases. However, some sources provide little to no information during the load process, such as text files, and need to be reconciled as previously mentioned.

There's more...

Actually, there are many other options you can use to refine your model. The following are just a few additional options you should consider while you are finishing your model:

- Specifying the date table
- Setting the default columns
- Hiding the columns from client tools
- Hiding the tables from client tools

> You should note that the sorting and filtering of data within the design surface of SSDT does not affect the data presented to the user. These features help you as a designer to view relevant data during the modeling process.

Once the date table is specified, time intelligence can be applied to the data. You can specify a table as a date table by navigating to **TABLE | Date | Mark As Date Table** when the table is selected. In our example, select the `Date` table and then set it as the `Date` table for the model. Usually, this will detect and set the date column of this table as well, but it is always good to verify that the correct column was identified.

You can also designate certain columns as part of the **Default Field Set** property. This can be done from the **Properties** page for a column or a table. In the **Reporting Properties** section, click on the ellipse button to the right of the **Default Field Set** property. This will allow you to select the fields and the order of those fields that represent the *default* view of the table. This can be used by some client tools that enable you to select a table instead of individual fields while creating visualizations.

Often, there are fields included in the model that do not need to be seen or used by the users. You can hide these by using the Context menu on a column and selecting the **Hide from Client Tools** option, or by changing the value of the **Hidden** property on the **Properties** page. The same options work for tables; you just need to select the table instead of the column.

See also

> ▶ If you need to use a multifield relationship between tables within the model, checkout the *Creating a calculated column* recipe. Calculated columns can reshape the data to make relationships work.

Creating a hierarchy

As with multidimensional models, hierarchies can be helpful while defining the relationship between the fields in a table. The Tabular Model allows you to add hierarchies that can be used by client tools.

How to do it...

You will need to open the diagram view (**MODEL | Model View | Diagram View**) in order to work with hierarchies. In this recipe, we will be using the `Date` table and creating a calendar and fiscal hierarchy, which are used pretty commonly, by performing the following steps:

1. In the diagram view, you need to click on the **Create Hierarchy** button on the `Date` table. This will add a hierarchy section to the bottom of the table. You will assign a name to the hierarchy here and then drag fields to add to the hierarchy.

2. Our hierarchy will be fairly simple. Drag the columns down to the hierarchy. You need to drag the first column directly on to the hierarchy name.

3. Each column thereafter, you will drag and place in the preferred order of the hierarchy. I would recommend that you drag the columns by always adding new columns to the bottom of the field list; for example, `CalendarYear`, `CalendarQuarter`, `EnglishMonthName`, `FullDateAlternateKey`.

4. Now that you have the fields, you can rename them in the hierarchy in the **Properties** page or from the context menu. This can be helpful if you plan to re-use columns in other hierarchies. In our example, we will be reusing `EnglishMonthName` and `FullDateAlternateKey`, and we will rename them to `Calendar Month` and `Calendar Day`, respectively.

5. Now, let's add the `Fiscal` hierarchy. To create this hierarchy, right-click on the `FiscalYear` column, and select **Create Hierarchy**. This will add `FiscalYear` as your first level in a new hierarchy, which you can name `Fiscal`. Next, you drag the fields you want in this hierarchy. Once you have completed these activities, your `Date` table should look like the following screenshot:

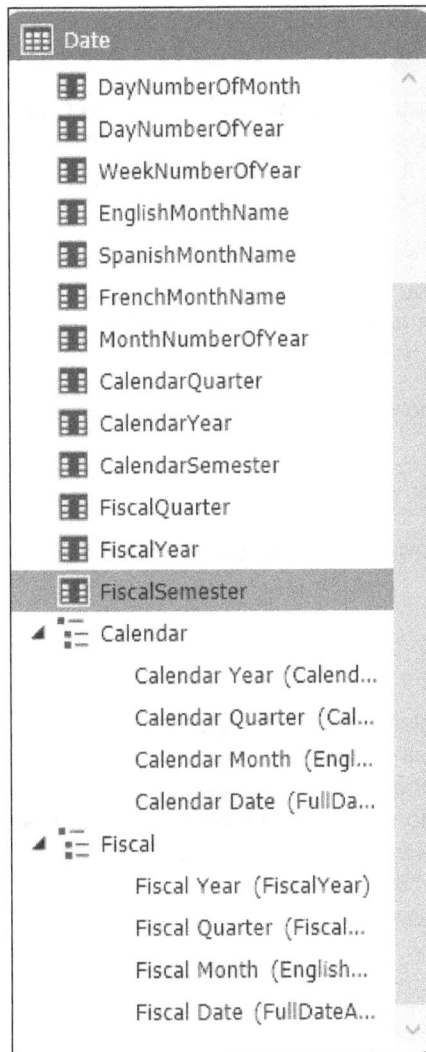

There's more...

You can modify the hierarchies later as needed. From the Context menu on the hierarchy, you can change the order of the fields in the hierarchy or remove fields that no longer fit in your hierarchy. For example, if you wanted to add the semester levels to the hierarchies, you can drop those anywhere into the hierarchy and move them to the proper location.

Creating a calculated measure

One of the great strengths in a model is the ability to create calculated measures and calculated columns. This recipe will cover calculated measures, and the next recipe will discuss calculated columns. However, this is a good place to differentiate between the two.

A good example of a calculated measure would be the sum of sales in our sample model. In this case, we will want to slice the sum by many different values within the model, such as date, customer, and product. A calculated measure will use these values to create a slice of references that are used to get the sum of sales.

One example of a calculated member is a formatted customer name such as Last name, first name. In this case, you need to use the context of the row in the table as part of the calculation because each row will use its values in the calculation. More on calculated columns can be found in the next recipe.

In this recipe, you will learn how to create calculated measures within the model.

Getting ready

You need to have the data view of the model open. Open the Internet Sales table and we will begin.

How to do it...

In the Internet Sales table, select the SalesAmount column. The quickest way to add a calculated measure is by using the Aggregation button on the toolbar, which also looks like a sum symbol. Because the most common aggregation used in analytic models is sum, it is therefore the default option. However, the drop down will create averages, counts, distinct counts, max, and min aggregations for the selected column as well.

1. Select the `Sales Amount` column, and then click on the sum symbol. This will create a new calculated measure in the measure grid below the column. If you click on the cell in the measure grid, you will see the DAX formula used to create the calculation. It should be similar to the following formula:

    ```
    Sum of SalesAmount:=SUM([SalesAmount])
    ```

2. If you want to change the name, you can change it in the formula bar or in the **Properties** page using the **Measure Name** property. The name precedes the colon and equal sign. The expression would look like the following, when the name is changed to `Total Sales`:

    ```
    Total Sales:=SUM([SalesAmount])
    ```

    > One of the key differences between the Tabular Model and the multidimensional model is its support for distinct counts. Distinct counts require additional work in multidimensional models, whereas this is not required in the Tabular Models.

3. You can also add calculations based on multiple columns. In our next example, we will calculate the effective tax rate by dividing the tax amount by the sales amount. As a calculated measure, we want this to still be a sliceable value. To create this calculation, we will add a formula anywhere in the measure grid at the bottom of the design surface. The formula we will add is as follows:

    ```
    =SUM('Internet Sales'[TaxAmt])/ SUM('Internet Sales'[SalesAmount])
    ```

4. When you add this formula in the measure grid, it is assigned a generic name such as `Measure 1`. As previously mentioned, you can and should change the name. You can also change the formatting in the **Properties** page. This measure should be in the percent format.

See also

▶ For a more detailed discussion on DAX, refer to *Chapter 10, DAX Calculations and Queries*, where more complex DAX calculations will be discussed.

Creating a calculated column

Unlike calculated measures, calculated columns use row context with the formula. Calculated columns also are helpful for nonaggregated calculations such as concatenated text values like formatted full names (Last Name, First Name).

How to do it...

Using the data grid design view, there are a couple of ways to add the column. You can right-click on a column header, and use the **Insert Column** option to add a column to the left of the selected column. The other option is to go to the far right of the data grid, and you will see an undefined column with **Add Column** in the header:

1. Let's create a full name column in the `Customer` table for reporting. Click on the **Add Column** header at the end of the grid.

2. In the formula bar at the top of the grid, add an equal sign. To add the last name to the formula, scroll over to the left and select any value in the `LastName` column. This will add `[LastName]` to the formula.

> While not applicable here, you can also change tables and select columns from other tables to add to the formula. This works best with related tables.

3. After adding the last name, add the following characters `& ", " &` and then type `" [F"`, and you should see `[FirstName]` in the intellisense list. Click on `[FirstName]` and hit *Enter*. This will add the column at the end of the data grid. The completed formula is `[LastName] & ", " & [FirstName]`.

> Be aware that hitting *Enter* while the item is highlighted in the intellisense list will complete the entry and build the column. If you are not done creating the formula, you may find this frustrating. Use the *Tab* key instead while writing formulas to avoid this issue.

4. Once you have completed the formula, you should rename the column to `Full Name`.

There's more...

In the *Modeling the data* recipe, I mentioned that data can be related using calculated columns. This is important while working with data from different sources where the data may not be naturally related. You can resolve this issue by using calculated columns which will support relationships. A quick example would be bringing in an external ZIP code reference table named `ZipCode`. If your `Address` table had the ZIP+4 format, (55778-4224) and the new `ZipCode` table only had ZIP codes without the "+4" (55778), you could create a calculated column on the `Address` table to strip those extra five characters off (`=Right([Address].[ZipCode],5)`). Now, a relationship is possible between the new column in `Address` and the existing column in `ZipCode`.

See also

▶ Check out more options for creating calculated columns in *Chapter 10, DAX Calculations and Queries*, in the section on DAX formulas.

Creating a KPI

Key Performance Indicators (**KPI**s) are used to visualize specific metrics that represent the overall health of what is being measured, such as sales or growth. The Tabular Model supports the creation of KPIs that can be used in various client tools.

Getting ready

You need to first create a calculated measure. We will use two new calculations for this KPI in the `Internet Sales` table. In Measure Grid, create a new measure in the `Total Product Cost` column, named `Total Cost`. You can do this by simply clicking on a cell in the column in Measure Grid in the `Total Product Cost` column. Next, use the aggregation shortcut on the toolbar to create a SUM measure and rename the column `Total Cost`.

Once you have `Total Cost` created, you will use `Total Cost` and `Total Sales` created in the previous recipe to create a new measure named `Cost Percent`. In Measure Grid, click on a cell and add the following expression to the formula bar:

```
Cost Percent:=[Total Cost] / [Total Sales]
```

All that is left is to set the format for this new calculation to percentage with two decimal places. This will help with the presentation of the new calculation.

> As mentioned previously, it is very important that you use good names and formatting as you create measures. Consider this as a best practice, and make it a habit when designing Tabular Models.

How to do it...

Now that we have the supporting measures created, we can add the KPI by performing the following steps:

1. You can add a KPI by right-clicking on the calculated measure or using the Create KPI icon on the ribbon. This will open the following screenshot:

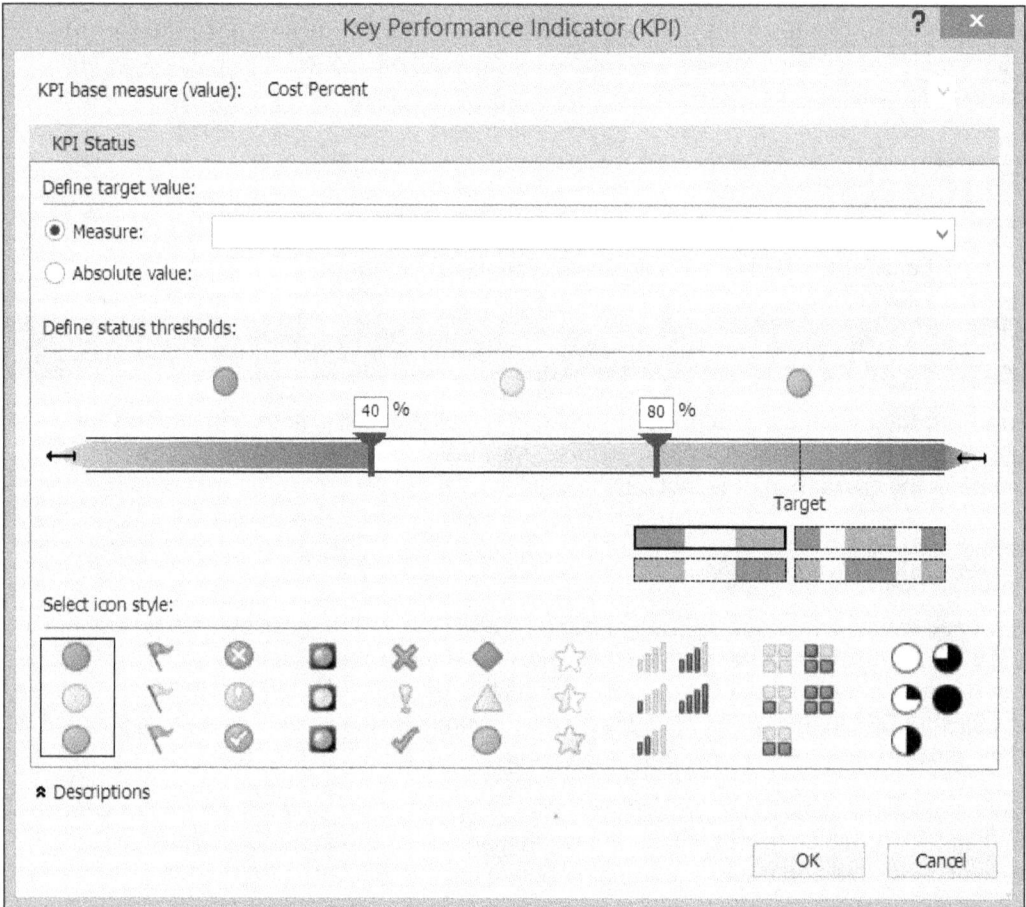

If you look at the preceding screenshot, you will notice the four key elements that make up a KPI: KPI base measure, target value, status thresholds, and icon style. Let's work through each element.

2. When you create the KPI, you select a calculated measure in the measure grid. This becomes the base measure. The role of the base measure is the value which will be measured against the target value. In our example, **Cost Percent** is our KPI base measure.

3. The target value can be sourced from one of two areas. The first option is to use another calculated measure. You would use that option when you can use calculation for targets. For instance, if you created a calculation to represent the previous year's sales, you could use that as the target. In our example, we are using a percentage value, which lends itself well to using the other option, an absolute value. Let's say that you set a target of 50 percent of the total cost for all sales. Then you would select the **Absolute value** option and put 0.5 into the textbox.

4. Next, you need to define the status thresholds. There are four sample color grids in the lower right-hand side of the threshold definition. These represent your options to create your thresholds. They represent how to display the KPI based on the distance from the target. The threshold options will change based on the icon set selected.

5. Select the first icon set, which has the red, yellow, and green circles.

6. Next, you need to select the threshold style in the lower left-hand corner, which has three colors in the order green, yellow, and red. This lets us represent lower cost percentages as good and higher percentages as bad. At this point, you would notice a dotted line on the threshold bar named **Target**. This bar represents the target value.

7. Our next decision is to split the threshold among our three options. Drag the left-most marker to the **Target** bar. It should now have **0.5** as the value above it. This means that we are marking our target or lower as "good" or green.

8. Next, we need to determine what the range for "concerned" or yellow should be. You can set this at **0.6**. Even if you do not see that much room on the right-hand side of the threshold bar, keep moving the marker as it will expand as you need it to. You can also enter values directly into the white boxes above the markers.

9. Your finished dialog should look like the following screenshot:

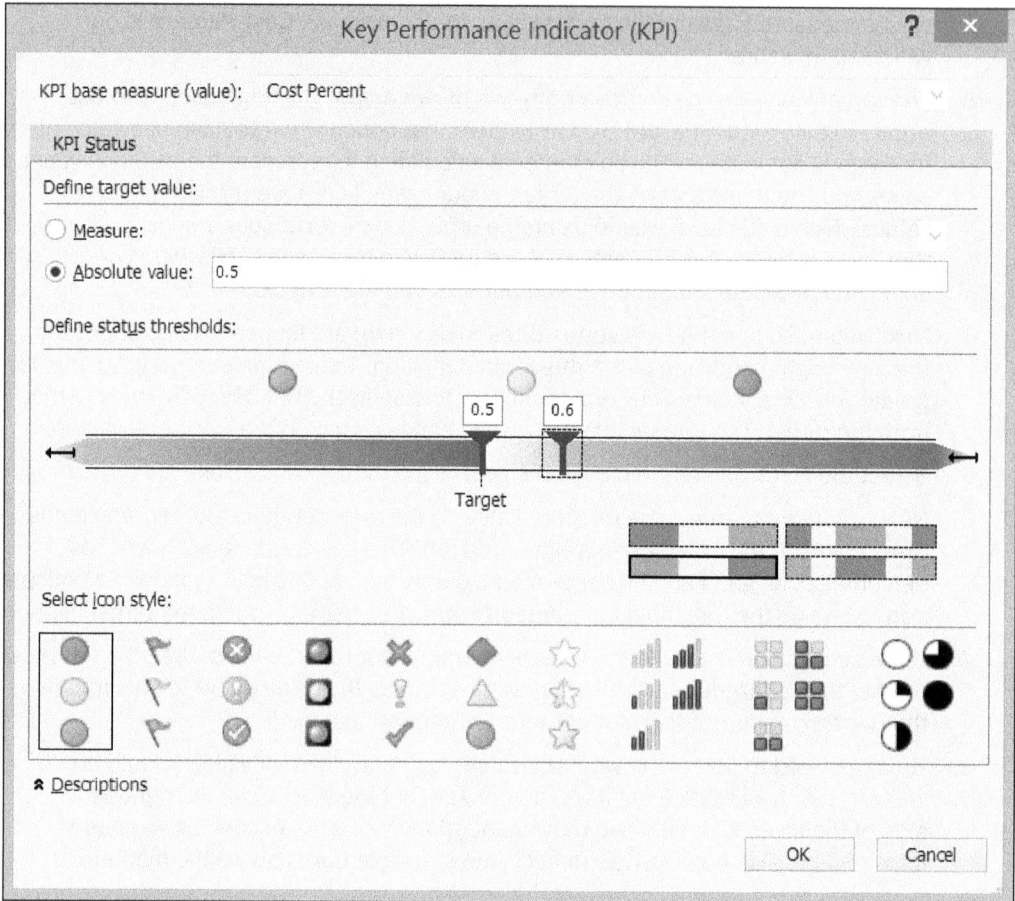

10. In Measure Grid, you will see a change to your measure. It now has a small Chart icon in the cell, as shown in the following screenshot:

There's more...

KPIs can use a different set of thresholds based on some of the other icon sets. Right-click on your `Cost Percent` measure, and choose **Edit KPI settings...**. With the dialog open, let's experiment with some of the options available to us. Let's choose the circle icon set. This changes our options as shown in the following screenshot:

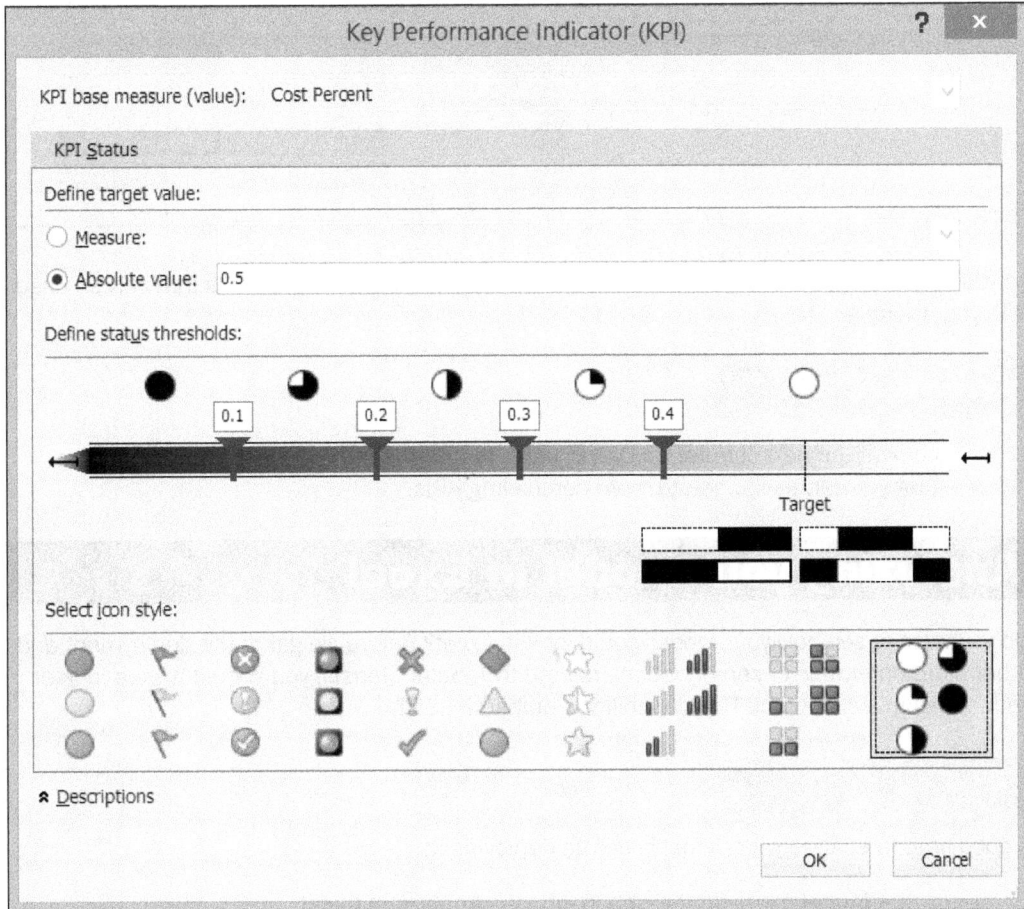

As you can see, you now have five markers. While our data does not present itself well in this scenario, it does demonstrate the fact that more than three icons can be used with the KPIs.

The last scenario uses one of the tricolor options with five segments. Select the threshold set that is red, yellow, green, yellow, red. This option allows you to set a KPI where "close to target" is good. This will create four markers, but they actually still only have three states: good, concerned, and bad.

Define status thresholds:

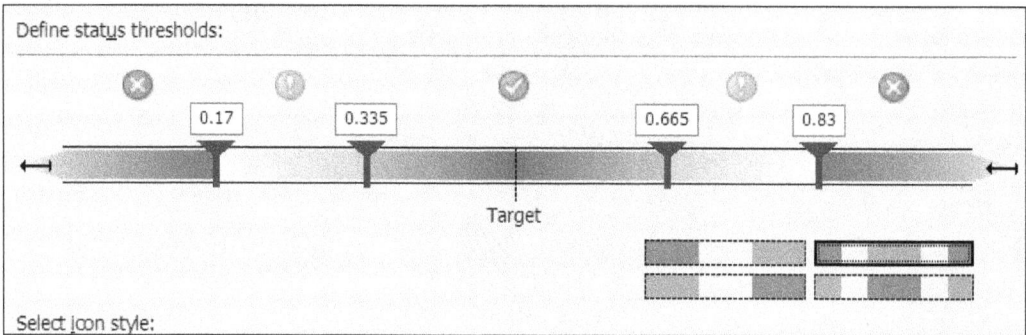

As you can see from these examples, you are able to create a variety of KPIs that can be used with your models.

See also

▶ Look at the next chapter on DAX in order to understand more complex calculations that you can use to create more compelling KPIs.

Analyzing your model in Excel

Do you want to see how your model would look in Excel? Before we get to the deployment and other more enterprise or server options related to Tabular Models, you should have a look at your model in a client tool. This capability is built into SSDT.

How to do it...

A good time to analyze your model is before deploying it:

1. In the **Model** menu on the ribbon, choose **Analyze in Excel**.
2. You will be prompted to choose a few options that we will discuss later. Leave the defaults and click on **OK**.

In Excel, you can use the Pivot Table to check measures, hierarchies, and KPIs that you have created so far. This is a nice, quick check on how your data will look to an end user.

There's more...

When you first choose to analyze the data in Excel, you are presented with multiple options about how you want to view the data. As you can see, you have the option to choose different users, roles, and perspectives when analyzing the data. This will allow you to verify security settings (users and roles) as well as perspectives when you analyze the data.

See also

▸ For more information on security, see the *Implementing security in Tabular Models* recipe. You can also check out perspectives in the *Implementing perspectives* recipe.

Deploying Tabular Models

Next up is deploying your model. There are a number of clickable methods to deploy your model.

Getting ready

Before you start deploying your model, it is important to set your deployment settings. This allows you to set the target server for deployment. You will find the deployment configuration in the project's properties. You can change the **Deployment Server** settings here. You are also able to set up multiple deployment configurations, such as test, development, and even production using the **Configuration** dropdown.

How to do it...

The following steps will describe how to deploy your model using SSDT, the deployment wizard, and the deployment utility:

1. You can deploy to a server using SSDT by right-clicking on the project and choosing **Deploy**. This will deploy the project to the targeted, actively configured deployment server.

2. As you can see from the dialog, metadata is deployed first, and then each table is loaded.

3. Open up **Microsoft SQL Server Management Studio** to see the deployed database. You will see that the connection and table folders have content.

> According to Microsoft documentation, you should not use the SSDT option for production deployment. Some properties will be overwritten in this scenario. See `http://technet.microsoft.com/en-us/library/gg492138.aspx` for more details.

4. The quickest way to get to the deployment wizard is to use Search in Windows 7 or Windows 8. Click on the **Deployment Wizard** result to open up **Analysis Services Deployment Wizard**.

5. On the next dialog, you will be asked to select a database to deploy. This database can be found in the `bin` folder in your `SSAS Cookbook Chapter 9` project folder, if you have built your project.

6. If you did not change the `Model.bim` file, your database will be named `Model.asdatabase`. Click on **OK** and then on **Next**.

7. This opens up the dialog for the installation target. In this dialog box, you need to specify the server and the database you plan to deploy. If your active configuration has the correct target, you should be able to click on **Next** and move the **Specify Options for Partitions and Roles** dialog. Leave the default settings at this point and click on **Next**.

8. In the **Specify Configuration Properties** dialog, you can change the connection information as well as the impersonation information for the configuration. These are currently based on the settings you set up before. In our case, you can select the first two checkboxes, which will retain your deployment settings.

> This allows you to change these properties prior to a production deployment. It will allow your DBAs or similar roles to set credentials upon the deployment, which helps meet a number of compliance considerations in various industries.

9. The next dialog, **Select Processing Options**, we will also leave it with its default settings.

10. Finally, in the next dialog, you have one last chance to back out as you will overwrite the existing database with the same name. Once you click on **Next** here, you will deploy the database. After it is complete, you have one more dialog box, which will close the dialog.

11. The `Deployment` utility is a command-line deployment option. This option uses the ASDATABASE file as well. So let's open command prompt and deploy the database using this option. You will find the executable here:

```
C:\ProgramFiles(x86)\MicrosoftSQLServer\110\Tools\Binn\
ManagementStudio
```

> If you only have one installation of SSAS on your server, you can just use the executable directly as follows:
> ```
> C:\>AnalysisServices.Deployment.exe
> ```
> If you just run the executable file, it will open up an instance of the Deployment Wizard UI.

How it works...

When the project is deployed for the first time, the database is created and will be loaded into memory. As part of your planning, you will need to make sure you have enough memory on the server to support all of the models you are deploying and developing.

Subsequent deployments will update the schema of the database and fully reload the data in the database on the server.

When the server is shut down, all of the Tabular Model databases are written to a disk so that they are not lost. Once the server is restarted, the models are loaded back from the disk, but not refreshed. When deploying the models to the server, you need to plan for the space needed to hold the models as well as the time required to write and read the models during the service start-up and shut-down cycles.

There's more...

One key advantage of using the `Deployment` utility is that it gives you the ability to deploy in silent mode, which suppresses the dialogs during deployment.

You will need to use the `s` switch. You have the option of adding a location to write a log file out as well. Here is the full command line to use when deploying in silent mode with a log file:

```
C:\>"C:\Program Files (x86)\Microsoft SQL Server\110\Tools\Binn\
ManagementStudio\Microsoft.AnalysisServices.Deployment.exe" "C:\Source\
SSAS Cookbook\SSAS Cookbook Chapter 9\SSAS Cookbook Chapter 9\bin\Model.
asdatabase" /s:"C:\Source\Logs\SSAS Cookbook Chapter 9.log"
```

This will deploy and fully reprocess the database and send the log information to the file as specified.

See also

▸ You can also use XMLA, AMO, synchronization, and backup-restore to deploy models. For more information on these options check out the Tabular Model Solution Deployment at `http://technet.microsoft.com/en-us/library/gg492138.aspx`.

▸ Check out the next recipe to learn more about using XMLA with Tabular Models.

Scripting Tabular Models using XMLA

In this recipe, you will learn how to create XMLA files that can be used for a variety of purposes including deploying and processing.

Getting ready

Unlike most of our work to this point, we will now be working primarily out of SQL Server Management Studio. We will also be working with a deployed Tabular Model database. If you have not deployed your database yet, refer to the previous recipe for deployment options.

How to do it...

While XMLA can definitely look daunting, generating XMLA scripts is quite easy, as shown in the following steps:

1. Open up **Microsoft SQL Server Management Studio**, and connect to the tabular instance you are using for development.

2. Right-click on the database and navigate to the following sequence of options: **Script | Script Database as | CREATE To | New Query Editor Window**. This will generate the XMLA script to create the database in the query window. If you want to create a new database on a different server, you can use this script.

3. The same technique can be used to generate multiple XMLA scripts for use in other tools. For instance, right-click on the database and select **Process** from the menu. This will open a dialog box for processing the database (reloading the data). You can set the properties you would like, and then instead of clicking on **OK**, use the **Script** button at the top of the dialog box to generate XMLA to process the database using the selected options.

   Any script created here can be executed in SQL Server Management Studio or any other tool that can execute XMLA.

There's more...

You can also use the `Deployment` utility to generate XMLA for deployment. You need to use the d and o switches. The o switch is used to generate output files, which is exactly what we need in this case. The d switch tells the utility not to connect to the specified targets to create the script that is needed to generate the create database script. Here is the command line:

```
C:\>"C:\Program Files (x86)\Microsoft SQL Server\110\Tools\Binn\
ManagementStudio\Microsoft.AnalysisServices.Deployment.exe" "C:\Source\
SSAS Cookbook\SSAS Cookbook Chapter 9\SSAS Cookbook Chapter 9\bin\Model.
asdatabase" /d /o:"C:\Source\SSAS Cookbook\SSAS Cookbook Chapter 9\SSAS
Cookbook Chapter 9\bin\Model.xmla"
```

Processing Tabular Models

Once a Tabular Model has been loaded initially, you may need to reload the data to pick up new data or handle data source refinements. Unlike a multidimensional model, which does not need data to work, the Tabular Model starts out in a processed state.

How to do it...

The Processing primarily occurs during development, while using **Microsoft SQL Server Management Studio**:

1. In order to process the database, individual tables, or partitions, you merely need to right-click on the object and select the **Process** option. This will open the **Process** dialog box.

2. From here you will pick your processing option and click on **OK** to process the selected object.

How it works...

Processing the model refreshes the data or the metadata depending on the processing option chosen.

As you can see **Process Default** is available to all objects. This will process any table or partition that is currently unprocessed and update the internal structures including calculations and hierarchies. **Process Full** replaces all components, data, and internal structures. **Process Clear** does the opposite and removes all data in the database, table, or partition. **Process Data** will reload the data in the selected table or partition. After either a **Process Clear** or **Process Data** option is run, you should run a **Process Recalc** option, which will rebuild all of the calculations, relationships, and other structures used in the model.

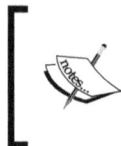

> If you process a partition fully or incrementally, you may get an error which refers to duplicate keys. This will happen when the data you add causes a duplicate key to appear in tables or relationships that require unique values within the model.

Process Defrag optimizes the table structures within the model. This is essentially a clean-up operation that should be run occasionally to keep the solution running smoothly.

Finally, the **Process Add** option only applies to the **Process Partition** option. This option allows you to add only new data. SSAS does not check the existing data, so you are responsible for making sure the partition can accept new rows and not run into duplicates.

> In order to get to the **Process Partition(s)** dialog, you need to right-click on the table and select the **Partition** option. This will open the partitions dialog box. Click on the **Processing** button (three green arrows in a circle) to open the dialog.

There's more...

Table-based processing means you can choose volatile tables to process more frequently. Because of the nature of how relationships are built; "bad" data will not prevent the processing of data where related data is missing. This happens because the data in a Tabular Model is essentially outer-joined.

See also

- There is no incremental or partial process supported outside of partitions. You can learn how to create partitions in the next recipe.

- In the previous recipe on XMLA, you learned how to generate XMLA for processing at any level.

Partitioning Tabular Models

Partitions in Tabular Models are one of the key features you would use Tabular Models to support. This is the best way to support incremental processing of data in Tabular Models.

> Power Pivot models do not support partitions.

Getting ready

In order to implement partitions, you need to have an existing table. You also need to have a partitioning plan. Most often, partitioning makes the most sense when working with data that resembles a fact table with a high row count and lots of measures. We only have one data table in our model, `Internet Sales`. `Order Date`, that looks like the best candidate for partitioning. It is unlikely that we will get orders out of sequence that will cause us to reprocess a large number of partitions. Next, we need to determine the scheme we will use. We will focus on a historic partition, a previous six months partition, and a current partition.

How to do it...

Creating partitions in a Tabular Model is fairly straightforward. You will need to bring focus to the table you want to partition, the `Internet Sales` table, by performing the following steps:

1. There are two easy ways to get the partition dialog box. You can select the **TABLE | Partitions...** option on the menu or use the **Partitions** button on the toolbar. Both options are available when a table is selected and shown in the following screenshot. This will open the **Partition Manager** dialog as shown in the following screenshot:

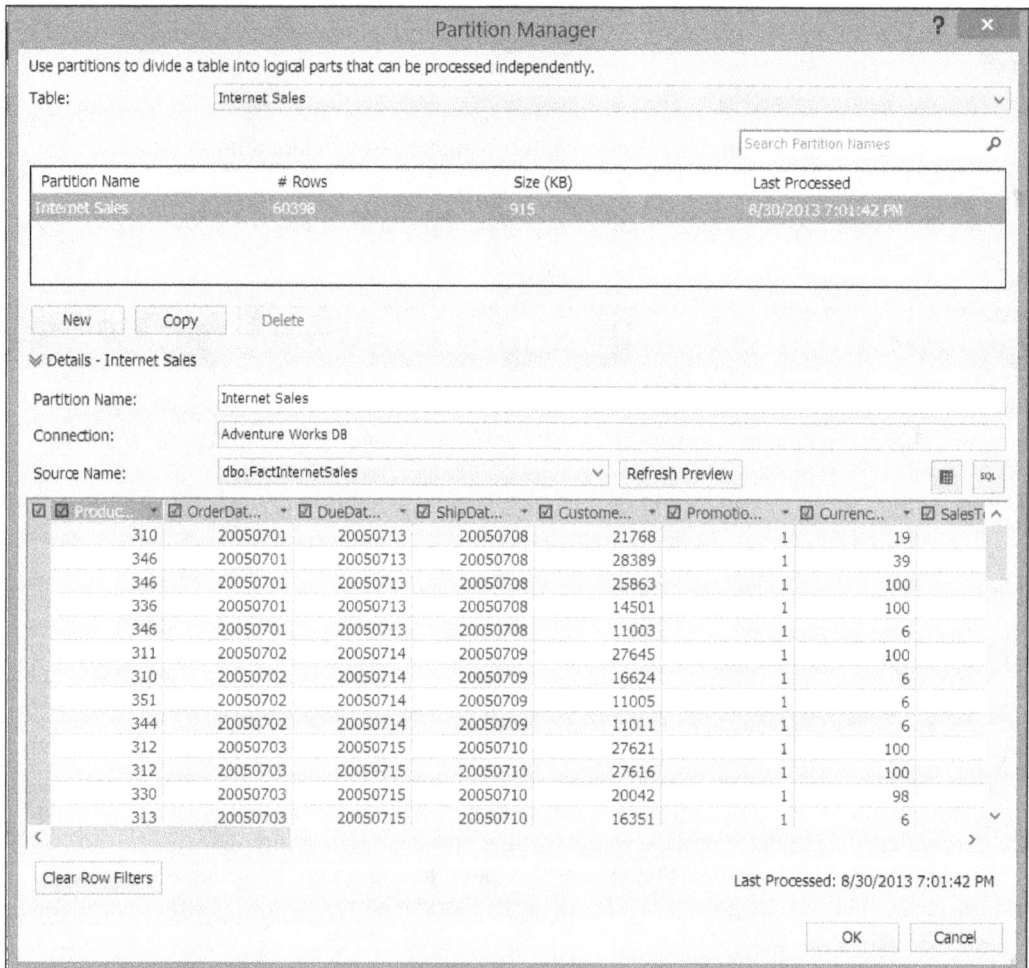

Partition Manager

Use partitions to divide a table into logical parts that can be processed independently.

Table: Internet Sales

Search Partition Names

Partition Name	# Rows	Size (KB)	Last Processed
Internet Sales	60398	915	8/30/2013 7:01:42 PM

New   Copy   Delete

Details - Internet Sales

Partition Name: Internet Sales

Connection: Adventure Works DB

Source Name: dbo.FactInternetSales   Refresh Preview

☑ ☑ Produc... ▾	☑ OrderDat... ▾	☑ DueDat... ▾	☑ ShipDat... ▾	☑ Custome... ▾	☑ Promotio... ▾	☑ Currenc... ▾	☑ SalesT...
310	20050701	20050713	20050708	21768	1	19	
346	20050701	20050713	20050708	28389	1	39	
346	20050701	20050713	20050708	25863	1	100	
336	20050701	20050713	20050708	14501	1	100	
346	20050701	20050713	20050708	11003	1	6	
311	20050702	20050714	20050709	27645	1	100	
310	20050702	20050714	20050709	16624	1	6	
351	20050702	20050714	20050709	11005	1	6	
344	20050702	20050714	20050709	11011	1	6	
312	20050703	20050715	20050710	27621	1	100	
312	20050703	20050715	20050710	27616	1	100	
330	20050703	20050715	20050710	20042	1	98	
313	20050703	20050715	20050710	16351	1	6	

Clear Row Filters   Last Processed: 8/30/2013 7:01:42 PM

OK   Cancel

2. As you can see, here every table exists as a single partition that contains all of the data. Our next step is to create a new partition by clicking on the **New** button. You will now see that a new partition has been added named `Internet Sales`. It is currently exactly the same as the initial partition.

> If we stop here, it will duplicate the data in our table. There is nothing here that will magically prevent the duplication of the data. This is the responsibility of the modeler.

3. Your next step is to change the definition of the partition. Before we go any further, delete the partition you just created. Highlight the `Internet Sales` partition, and click on the **SQL** button above the table in the **Partition Manager** dialog as shown in the following screenshot:

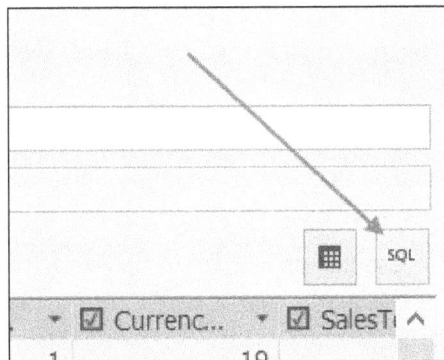

You should now see a window with the following SQL statement:

```
SELECT [dbo].[FactInternetSales].* FROM [dbo].[FactInternetSales]
```

4. We will use this as our starting point. Our first partition will be the historical partition. It will be for all orders that were placed prior to 2008. Our SQL statement will now look like the following:

```
SELECT [dbo].[FactInternetSales].* FROM [dbo].[FactInternetSales]
where OrderDateKey < 20080101
```

> The data in our `Internet Sales` fact table only includes data from July 1, 2005 through July 31, 2008. Orders from 2008 will be used to build the additional partitions.

5. Next, we want to rename this partition `Internet Sales - History`. Click on **OK**, and the partition definition will be applied to the table.

6. You will notice that the data has not been refreshed. Navigate to **MODEL | Process Table ...** to reprocess the data. The rows processed have been decreased to around 30,000 and only include orders prior to 2008.

7. You will now add the next two partitions: `Internet Sales - 6 Months` and `Internet Sales - Current`. Open the **Partition Manager** dialog again. Now, we will copy the partition using the **Copy** button. Click on that twice and two new partitions will be created: `Internet Sales - History Copy` and `Internet Sales - History Copy - Copy`.

8. Click on either one, and we will modify it to become our six-month partition by renaming it to `Internet Sales - 6 Months` and changing the `Where` clause in the SQL Statement to the following:

   `Where OrderDate between 20080101 and 20080630`

   This will create a partition to cover the first six months of 2008.

9. Click on the unmodified copy and change its name to `Internet Sales - Current`, and set its `Where` clause to:

   `Where OrderDate > 20080630`

   This will create the final partition for you, and you will now have three partitions you can use to manage processing or data reloads.

10. Click on **OK** and reprocess the table.

> The last-processed information does not come from your development model; it comes from the deployed model. To see accurate processing information from your development model, you will need to use **Microsoft SQL Server Management Studio**. Right-click on the `Internet Sales` table and select **Partitions**. This will open the **Partitions** dialog from the selected model. Remember that your development model has a GUID as part of its name.

There's more...

Partition management is a key part of your model design. What if you wanted to move the data from the six-month partition into your historical partition? Partitioning supports merging partitions. To do this, open up **Microsoft SQL Server Management Studio** and right-click on the table. Select the **Partitions** option from the context menu, and it will open a dialog that is shown in the following screenshot.

Select the two partitions you want to merge. Once you have them selected, the Merge icon, which has two arrows pointing at each other, will become activated. Click on the Merge icon, and the **Merge Partition** dialog will open. Once it is open, you can see that **Target Partition** is our `Internet Sales - History` partition, and the selected **Source Partition** option is the `Internet Sales - 6 Months` partition. At this point, if we want to merge more partitions at the same time, we can do so by selecting the other partitions to merge.

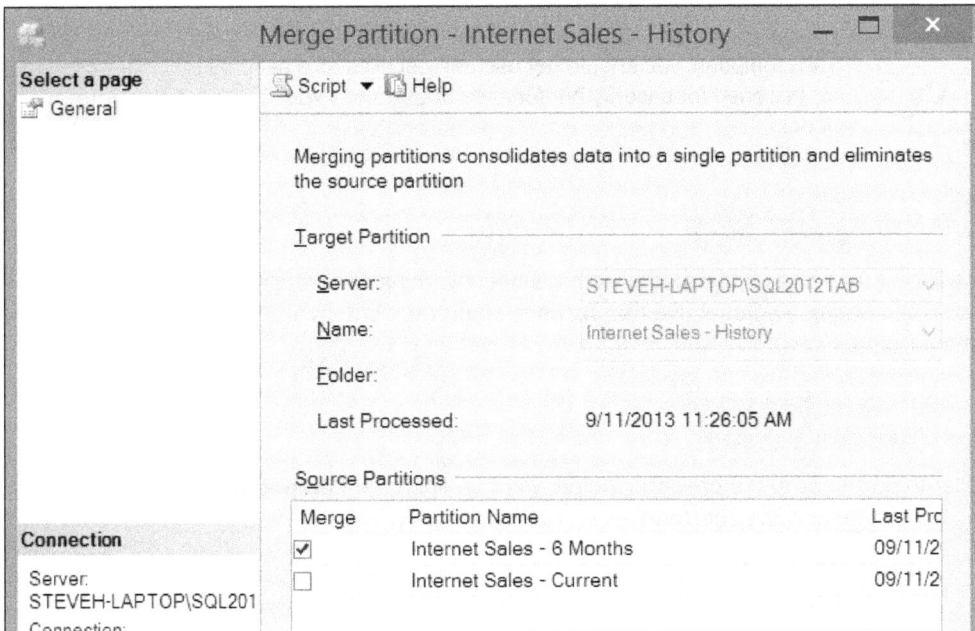

Click on **OK**, and the partitions will be merged. The **Partitions** dialog will now only show two partitions. From here, you can also process the new partition to complete the process.

> If you deploy the model to the server using SSDT and have not merged the partitions in the same way, the partition design in SSDT will overwrite any changes made in **Microsoft SQL Server Management Studio**.

See also

▶ Partitions can be created using XMLA and PowerShell as well. The recipe on XMLA discusses how to script processes using SSMS. Refer to the recipe on creating multidimensional partitions for more details on using PowerShell to create partitions with XMLA.

Implementing perspectives

Perspectives are similar to views in relational databases. Perspectives allow you to create views of the model that may serve a specific function or help a specific user group. For instance, you could create perspectives that only show finance measures and dimensions. You can reduce the number of visible tables and the fields for users to make the user experience better.

> While tempting, you should not use perspectives as a security tool. They are not designed for security but for ease of use and visual organization of the model.

Getting ready

You will be expanding on the model we have been working on throughout this chapter. We will be creating a perspective that focuses on product orders and hides most of the customer data.

How to do it...

Similar to partitions in the previous recipe, you can open the **Perspectives** dialog from the toolbar or menu and then perform the following steps:

1. In the **Perspectives** dialog, click on the **New Perspective** button. You can name this perspective `Product Order`. There is a series of checkboxes in the new column next to the table and the field definition on the right.

2. Because this perspective focuses on products, select the `Product` and `Product Category` tables. If you expand the `Product` table, you will see that all fields have been selected. Next, expand the `Internet Sales` table, and select some fields that you feel are relevant to this perspective, such as `Order Date`, `Order Quantity`, `Sales Amount`, `Average Sales`, `Total Cost`, and `Total Sales`.

As you can see, calculated measures and members are included in the list of fields to select.

The following screenshot shows a partial view of what your perspective selection may look like:

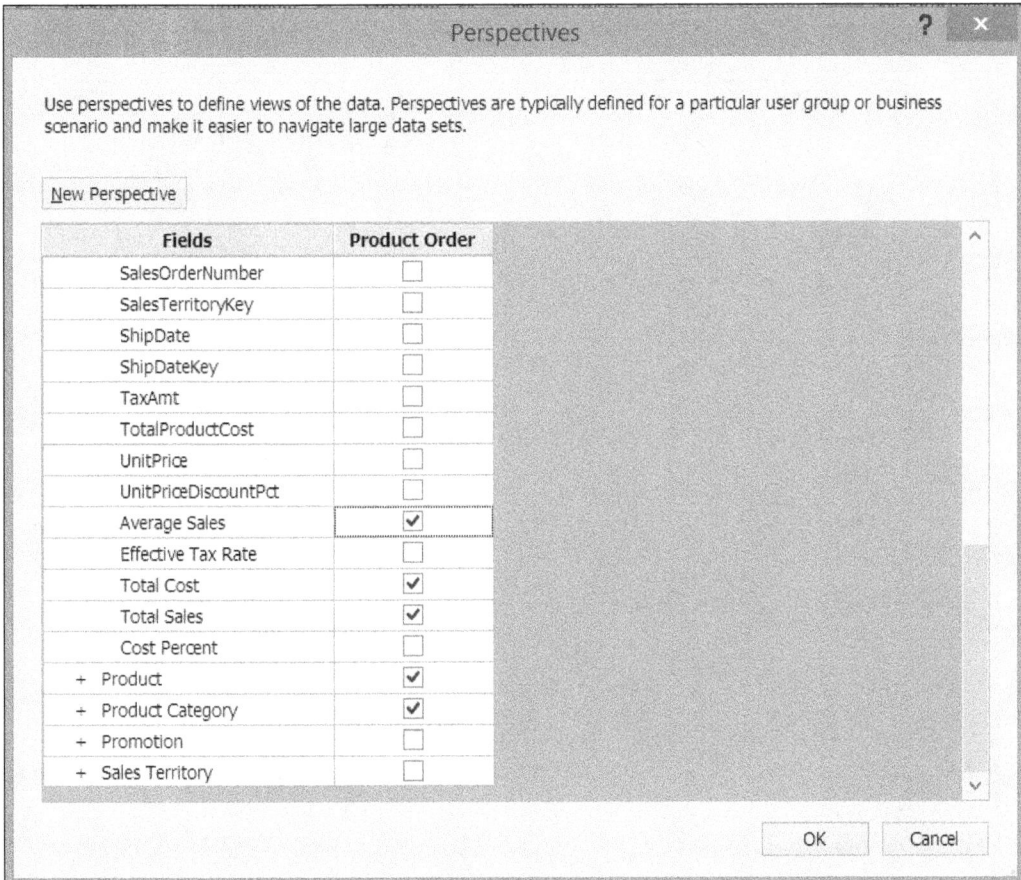

3. Click on **OK**, and you have successfully created a new perspective.

There's more...

SSDT allows you to see the impact of your perspective. You can change the perspective in SSDT by using the **Select Perspective** dropdown on the toolbar or by selecting it from the **MODEL | Perspectives | Select** menu. This will filter the view in the designer, as shown in the following screenshot:

OrderQuantity	UnitPrice	UnitPriceDiscountPct	SalesAmount	OrderDate
1	$4.99	0	$4.99	8/4/2007 12...
1	$4.99	0	$4.99	8/4/2007 12...
1	$4.99	0	$4.99	8/5/2007 12...
1	$4.99	0	$4.99	8/7/2007 12...
1	$4.99	0	$4.99	8/7/2007 12...
1	$4.99	0	$4.99	8/8/2007 12...
1	$4.99	0	$4.99	8/8/2007 12...
1	$4.99	0	$4.99	8/8/2007 12...
1	$4.99	0	$4.99	8/9/2007 12...
1	$4.99	0	$4.99	8/9/2007 12...
1	$4.99	0	$4.99	8/10/2007 1...
1	$4.99	0	$4.99	8/11/2007 1...
1	$4.99	0	$4.99	8/13/2007 1...
1	$4.99	0	$4.99	8/13/2007 1...
1	$4.99	0	$4.99	8/14/2007 1...
1	$4.99	0	$4.99	8/15/2007 1...
1	$4.99	0	$4.99	8/16/2007 1...
1	$4.99	0	$4.99	8/16/2007 1...
1	$4.99	0	$4.99	8/17/2007 1...
1	$4.99	0	$4.99	8/18/2007 1...
1	$4.99	0	$4.99	8/20/2007 1...
1	$4.99	0	$4.99	8/21/2007 1...
1	$4.99	0	$4.99	8/22/2007 1...
1	$4.99	0	$4.99	8/24/2007 1...
1	$4.99	0	$4.99	8/25/2007 1...
1	$4.99	0	$4.99	8/26/2007 1...
1	$4.99	0	$4.99	8/27/2007 1...
1	$4.99	0	$4.99	8/29/2007 1...
1	$4.99	0	$4.99	8/31/2007 1...
1	$4.99	0	$4.99	9/6/2007 12...

Total Sales: $2...
Average Sales: ...
Total Cost: $1...
Cost Percent: ...

Product | **Internet Sales** | Product Category

Record: 32 of 60,398

See also

▶ Check the effect of your perspectives from your user's viewpoint using the **Analyze in Excel** feature mentioned in the previous recipe.

Implementing security in Tabular Models

One of the key differentiators or reasons to move Power Pivot models into SQL Server Analysis Services is security. Tabular Models support a much more robust security model than what is available in Power Pivot in Excel or SharePoint.

Getting ready

In order to work with security, you will need some users that you can assign to the roles. In my solution, I have added `SteveReader` and `SteveFiltered` to my local computer. Normally, you would be using Active Directory users and groups to manage your security. If you have a test or development environment with users at your disposal, use them. In either case, you will need users to complete this next recipe.

How to do it...

You can open the **Role Manager** dialog by clicking on the **Roles** button on the toolbar or the **Roles** option in the **MODEL** menu item. This will open the **Role Manager** dialog. You will be creating a read-only role, which will prevent a user from reloading data or making changes to the model:

1. This can be done by clicking on the **New** button, which will add a new role. Rename the role `Read Only` and select the **Read** permissions from the dialog.

2. Next, click on the **Members** tab in the lower half of the dialog, and add the user or group to which you want to give **Read Only** permissions to your model. Now the dialog should show your changes.

> As you likely would have noticed, there are other permissions available. Here is a brief breakdown of these permissions and what they allow:
>
> **None:** No permissions assigned
>
> **Read:** Read data
>
> **Read and Process:** Read data and reload data
>
> **Process:** Reload data, but no ability to read
>
> **Administrator:** Full access

3. We also made no changes in the **Row Filters** tab when we created the `Read Only` user. As a result, the permissions that were assigned apply to the entire model. By assigning a group to our `Read Only` role, that group would be able to use our entire model in their analysis.

4. Let's add a filtered role that only allows the role to see data related to a specific sales territory, that is, Central. This territory is defined in the `Sales Territory` table. Once again, you open the **Role Manager** dialog. Add a new role named `Central Sales`. Assign the **Read** permission to the new role, and add your filtered user to the **Members** area.

5. Now, you double-click on the **DAX Filter** cell by Sales Territory. You get no help at all. So, you will need to create the filter by hand. Add the following filter to the dialog:

```
=[SalesTerritoryRegion]="Central"
```

You need a DAX formula that will return a `Boolean` value . In this case, the formula tests the name of the region and sets the result to `TRUE` or `FALSE`.

> In order to create this formula, I created it as a calculated member in the model. This allowed me to verify the results and the syntax. Once I was done, I removed the column.

Now you have a role that will only show data that is available based on that filter in related tables. In this case, your `Sales` table will be filtered. If you want to have this filter apply to other lists, you could create a lookup table that associates data such as customers directly with the sales territories, which would result in a filtered customer list as well.

How it works...

Role-based security in the Tabular Model is very similar to role-based security in multidimensional models. Permissions within the model are additive, which means user permissions are accumulative across all the roles they belong to. For instance, this means that administrators cannot be limited in their ability to see the data even if that user has read-only permissions on a table.

There's more...

You want to verify that your roles and users have the expected permissions. You can do this using the **Analyze with Excel** feature. When you open the **Analyze with Excel** dialog, you can see that you have the option to select users, roles, and even perspectives. If you use the `Central Sales` role you created and click on **OK**, you will see the effect of the role using Excel. This helps administrators test security during development and helps verify the results, which are what you need to support the role you created.

Automating Tabular Model processing

Power Pivot models in Excel are manually processed only, and Power Pivot models in SharePoint can be scheduled at the data source level. Tabular Models take this one step further by allowing you to process partitions in your model. This allows you to use partitions to keep processing windows short and your model impact low.

Getting ready

In order to work with automation, you should have a deployed version of your Tabular Model to work with. To see how to deploy your model, see the previous recipe on the subject. You should also have a scheduling tool, preferably SQL Server Agent, available to create the job.

How to do it...

1. In **Microsoft SQL Server Management Studio**, open the tabular instance of SQL Server Analysis Services. Right-click on the database you would like to process, and click on the **Process Database** option on the shortcut menu. In the **Process Database** dialog, choose the processing mode you would like to use. (I will be using **Default** for the examples.) Then click on the **Script** button at the top. This will open a new query window with XMLA in it.

    ```
    <Process xmlns = "http://schemas.microsoft.com/
      analysisservices/2003/engine">
      <Type>ProcessDefault</Type>
      <Object>
        <DatabaseID>SSAS Cookbook Chapter 9</DatabaseID>
      </Object>
    </Process>
    ```

2. Next, we need to create the job in SQL Server Agent. Open up a new job in SQL Server Agent. Give the job a name such as `Process SSAS Cookbook Model`.

3. Next, select the **Steps** page and click on **New** to create a new step. In this step, set the following properties:

    - **Step Name**: `Process Model`
    - **Type**: `SQL Server Analysis Services Query`
    - **Run As**: Choose a **Run As** account with permissions to the database
    - **Server**: Server name
    - **Database**: `SSAS Cookbook Chapter 9`
    - **Command**: Use the preceding code

4. Click on **OK**, and this will save the step. You can then set the schedule as needed to process the database.

There's more...

You can also follow the same steps and process individual tables and partitions. This allows you the flexibility to only process those objects which have changes in them.

> My preference is to use the **Full processing** mode when processing SSAS objects. This requires the least amount of overall maintenance. I only move away from this when processing times interfere with usage.

See also

▸ There are a couple of projects on CodePlex that describe other automation techniques using AMO and PowerShell. Check these out if using SQL Server Agent is not a possibility:

   ❑ Tabular Database PowerShell Cmdlets at `http://tabularcmdlets.codeplex.com/`

   ❑ Tabular AMO 2012 at `http://tabularamo2012.codeplex.com/`

10

DAX Calculations and Queries

This chapter will expand on concepts introduced in *Chapter 9, Using Tabular Models*, and cover these topics in greater depth:

- ▶ Combining tables using calculated columns
- ▶ Adding a calculated column
- ▶ Creating measures
- ▶ Testing a Tabular Model in Excel
- ▶ Using the CALCULATE Function
- ▶ Querying a Tabular Model

Introduction

DAX (**Data Analysis Expressions**) is actually a combination of two languages. It is fundamentally a simple expression language, consisting of functions that work very much like Excel functions, which return either values or objects that can be used by other functions. Additionally, DAX is also a query language that can be used to execute requests for a Tabular semantic model and return an entire result set for use by a reporting tool or application to display data. DAX is an evolution of previous expression languages and those familiar with MDX and Excel functions will recognize its heritage.

Our journey down the DAX path will begin with an introduction to the fundamental components of DAX expressions. You will learn to use several useful functions that can be applied to business logic and get answers to business-related questions. Expanding on the topics introduced in the previous chapter, we will use calculated columns to combine data from two source tables and then design calculated measures from numeric columns in the `Internet Sales` fact table.

Combining tables using calculated columns

To begin working with calculated columns, we'll make a modification to the Tabular Model design created in the previous chapter. In a business intelligence solution, we often combine data from multiple source tables to simplify the structure and make it easier for users to navigate and report on information. Previously, we used a T-SQL query to join the `Product Subcategory` and `Product Category` table information to populate a single table in the semantic model. To gain experience with a different table design technique and develop new skills, we will change the approach.

Getting ready

You're going to make a design modification to the Tabular Model you created in *Chapter 9, Using Tabular Models*. If you would like to keep that project in its current state for reference, you can make a copy of the project folder for backup purposes. Otherwise, we'll just pick up from where we left off and continue to work in the same Tabular Model.

How to do it...

You'll start with the work you did in the previous chapter:

1. Open the **SQL Server Data Tools** (**SSDT**) project you created in the previous chapter.

2. Using the **Solution Explorer**, double-click on the `Model.bim` file to open it in the model designer. You should be looking at the tables in the grid view.

3. Click on the `Product Category` tab at the bottom to view the rows and columns in this table.

4. On the `Table` menu, find and select the `Table Properties` item. This opens the **Edit Table Properties** dialog.

5. Take a quick look at the query script that uses a join operator to combine the columns of two tables. The steps following this screenshot will have you replace it with similar functionality in the model.

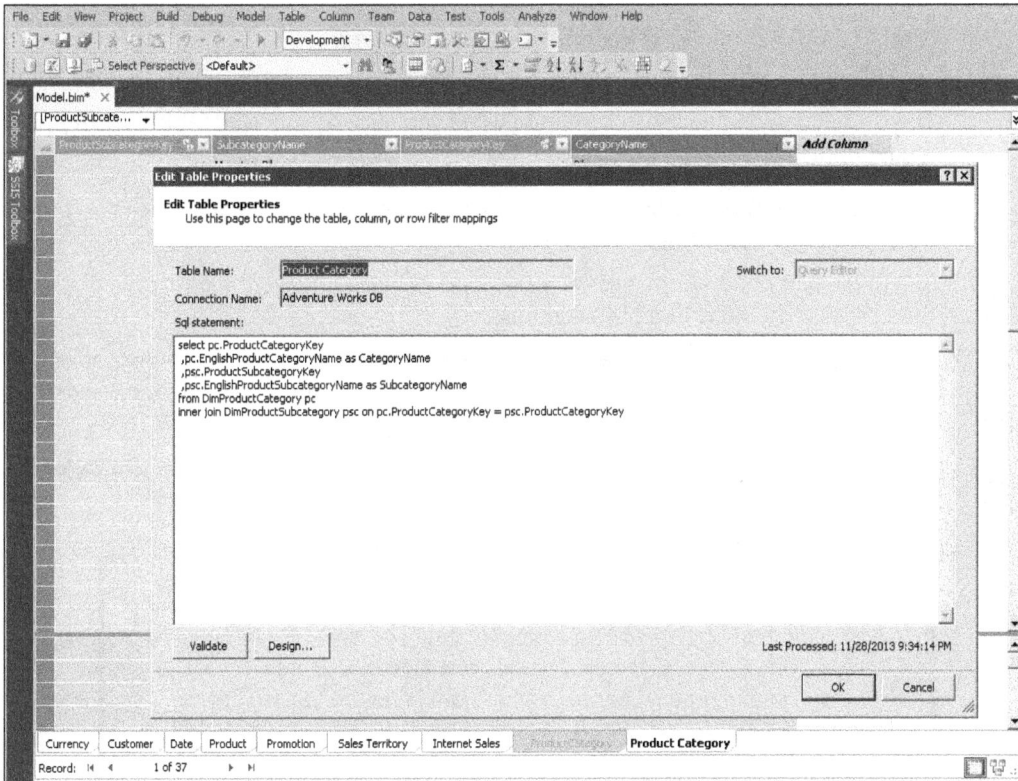

6. Close this window.

7. Right-click on the `Product Category` tab and delete it from the model.

8. Now, import the **Product Category** and **Subcategory** tables separately and then use a calculated column to serve the same purpose as the table you just deleted.

9. On the **Analysis Services** toolbar, the third icon is **Existing Connections**. Click on this icon to open the **Existing Connections** dialog.

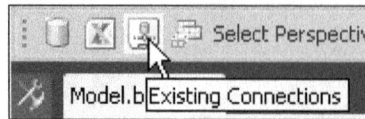

The connection on this list was created when you initially imported tables into the model from SQL Server.

10. On the **Existing Connections** dialog window, click on **Open** to select more tables and data to import. The **Table Import Wizard** opens.

11. Select the first option from a list of tables and views to choose the data to import and then click on the **Next** button to continue.

12. The next page, titled **Select Tables and Views**, allows you to select multiple objects to import. For each, you can include or omit different columns, rename the imported table, and filter unwanted records.

13. Click on the checkboxes to place a check mark in front of the **DimProductCategory** and **DimProductSubcategory** tables.

> The next step may not seem perfectly intuitive until I explain the purpose. Oftentimes in the semantic model, we need to import objects used for internal purposes. We also need to give visible objects the best names and hide those that will only be used internally. You will rename two imported tables with the first table used only for internal purposes. After you're done with the final design, the new Product Category table will contain both product category and subcategory information.

14. In the `Friendly Name` column for the **DimProductCategory** table, rename the table to `_ProductCategory`.

15. Rename the **DimProductSubcategory** table to `Product Category`.

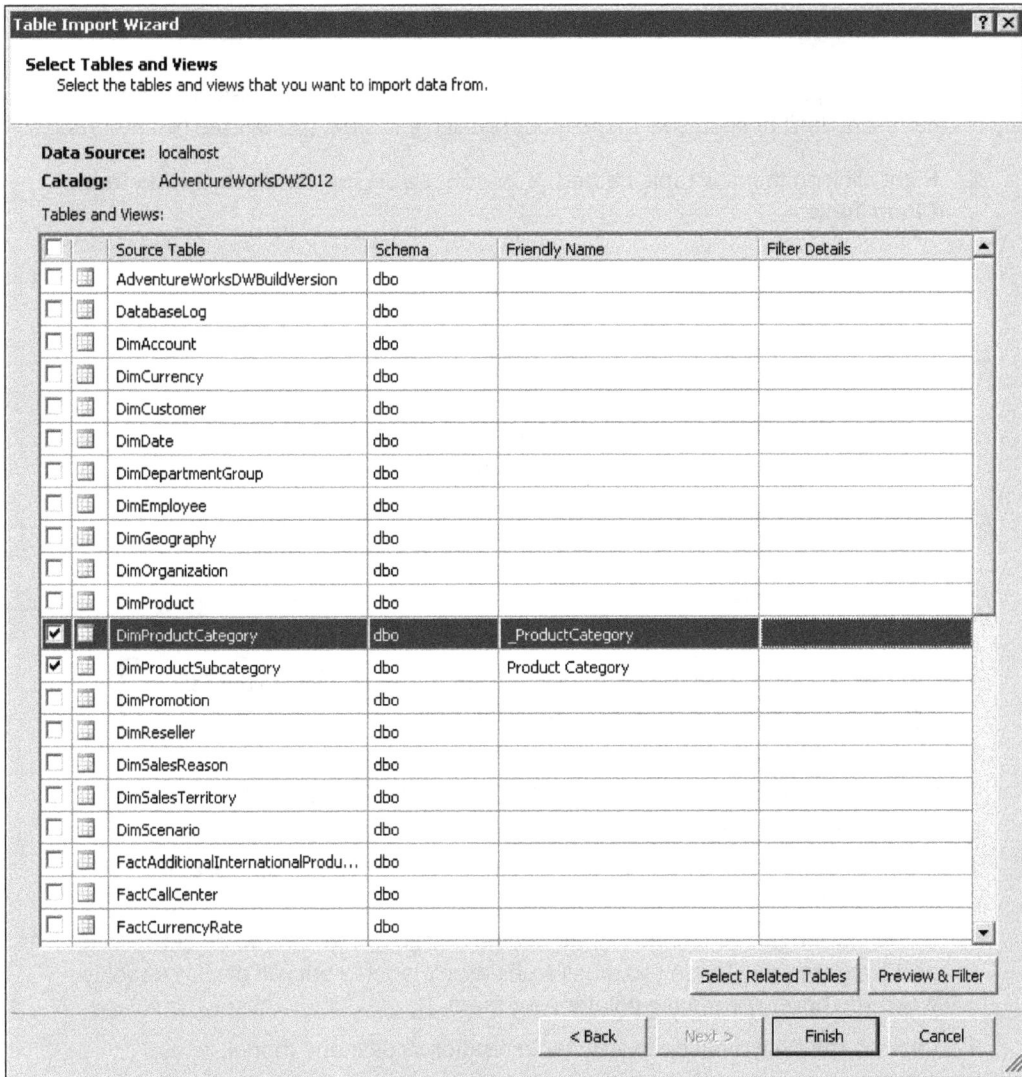

16. With the row for the **DimProductCategory** table highlighted, click on the **Preview & Filter** button to open a window showing the columns for the table.

17. Uncheck the boxes for all the columns except for **ProductCategoryKey** and **EnglishProductCategoryName**; click on **OK** to close this window.

18. Repeat the same steps for the **DimProductSubcategory** table. Uncheck all columns except for **ProductSubcategoryKey**, **EnglishProductSubcategoryName**, and **ProductCategoryKey**; click on **OK** to close the window and return to the list of all the tables in the **Table Import Wizard**.

19. Click on **Finish** to import both the tables and then click on **Close** to close the wizard.

There's more...

Now to tidy things up... With the goal of keeping the model as simple as possible, hide the objects that users don't need to see. In the model design grid view, you will see two new tables:

1. Right-click on the new table named `_ProductCategory` and select **Hide from Client Tools**.

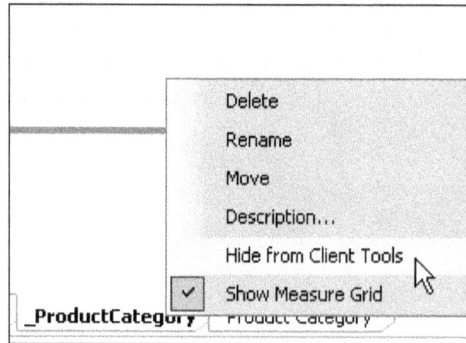

> In model design, it's common to rename objects to provide simple and friendly names for users.

2. Click on the tab for the `Product Category` table and then right-click on the `EnglishProductSubcategory` column header.

3. From the menu, select the option to rename the column and change the name to `SubcategoryName`.

4. In the lower right-hand corner of the model designer, you can switch between grid and diagram view. These two small icons aren't labeled but will display a tooltip when you hover the mouse pointer over them.

5. Click on the Diagram icon to view table relationships in the model.

6. Add a relationship between the `Product` and `Product Category` tables by dragging the `ProductSubcategoryKey` column in the `Product` table to the `ProductSubcategoryKey` column in the `Product Category` table.

7. Add a relationship between the `Product Category` table and the hidden `_ProductCategory` table by dragging the `ProductCategoryKey` column in the `Product Category` table to the `ProductCategoryKey` column in the `_ProductCategory` table.

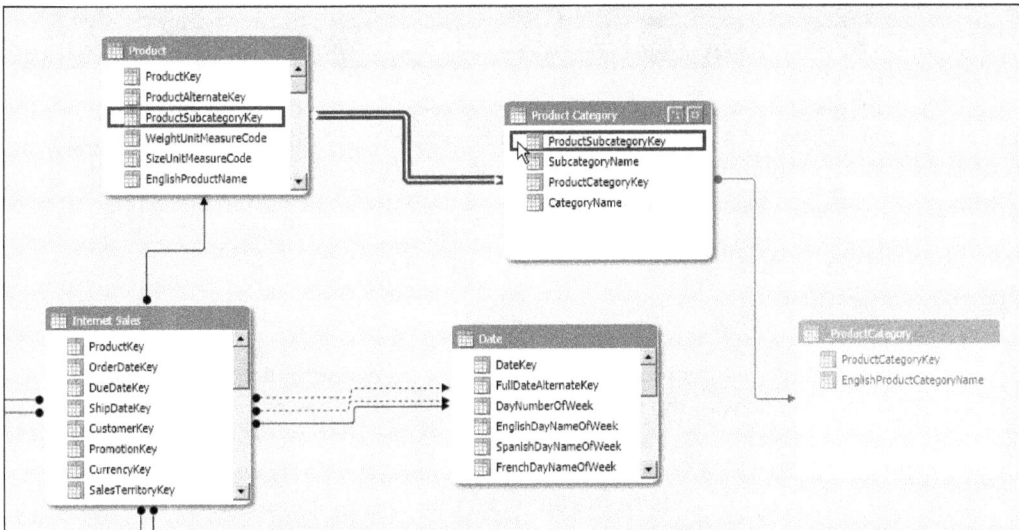

8. Right-click on the `Product Category` table and hide the two key columns.

9. To return to the grid view and work with a single table, you can right-click on the header of the `Product Category` table and click on **Go To**.

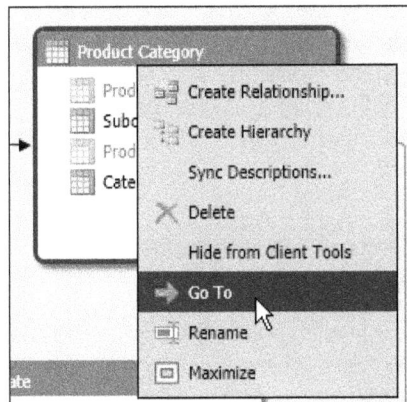

Now, we're ready to add a calculated column to the table.

Adding a calculated column

Calculated columns serve many purposes but are usually used to combine values from multiple columns or derive a new value from another column. We don't normally aggregate values or perform complex business logic in the same way that we would in a measure. The key concept is that calculated column logic is applied to each row in a table. Keep in mind that this can also add storage and memory overhead.

Getting ready

If you're working through the instructions in this chapter from start to finish, you should be in the right place to continue with the next step. Get in the habit of saving your work often. If you have the project open and you're looking at the model designer, just click on the Save All icon on the toolbar that looks like a stack of floppy disks. (I haven't saved anything to a floppy disk for a while, but somehow this remains the universal icon to save your work.)

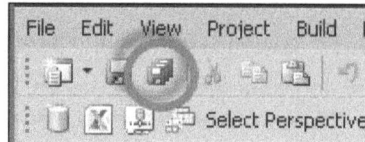

If your project isn't already open, then open the project in SSDT and use **Solution Explorer** to open the `Model.bim` file. When the model designer window opens in the grid view, click on the tab at the bottom of the model designer to edit the `Product Category` table.

How to do it...

You can add a new column at any position in the table. For convenience, the right-most column is a placeholder for a new calculated column:

1. Either right-click or double-click on the heading of the column labeled `Add Column`, rename it to `CategoryName`, and then press the *Enter* key. It's a subtle thing but get used to pressing the *Enter* key to save your changes to expressions.

2. Place the cursor in any cell in this new column. Start typing an expression with an equal to sign, then type the letter `R`. Notice that a drop-down list below the formula box displays functions and objects that match the text you type. Type or select the word `RELATED`. When you have the object or function name selected in the drop-down list, press the *Tab* key to select it.

> The `RELATED` function accepts one argument, which is the table and column reference for any table related to the current table through a direct or indirect relationship.

3. You can complete the expression by selecting items in the drop-down list as you type.

> You should learn to work with this feature as it can help avoid mistyped object names and spelling errors. There are caveats to the autocompletion feature that can lead to syntax errors unless you learn to work within its capabilities and outside of its limitations. I suspect that as the product matures in future versions, we will see some fine-tuning and optimization. Personally, I find this feature helpful most of the time but I have learned to anticipate certain patterns of behavior. In particular, if an object name (such as a table or column name) has already been entered into an expression and you use autocompletion to select a different object, the tool will replace the object reference but add redundant quote marks or bracket characters. These can be hard to spot at a glance and will result in a syntax error. Another rather unfortunate feature of the tool is that when a syntax error is introduced to an expression, especially when the expression is long and complex, after reporting an error, it will revert to a previous state and you will lose changes. While making changes, I've learned to copy the entire expression to the clipboard before pressing the *Enter* key. This way, I can paste the expression, make corrections, and then save changes (of course, after recopying the new expression to the clipboard).

4. After typing the open parenthesis after the RELATED function name, type the underscore character to show objects in the hidden _ProductCategory table.

5. Click on the EnglishProductCategoryName column, type the close parenthesis, and press *Enter* to save the expression.

   That's it! By creating a relationship between these two tables, hiding one and then using the RELATED function to reference a related column in the hidden table, we have essentially joined the subcategory and category information into a single table.

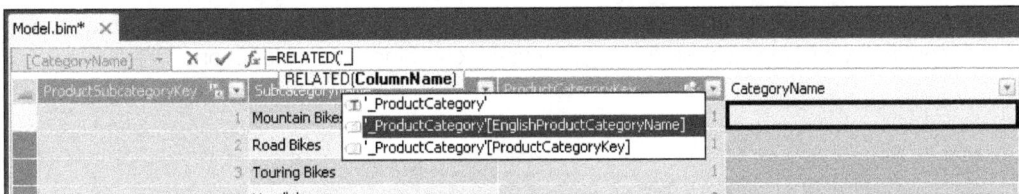

6. Switch to the Date table in the grid view.

7. Right-click on the FullDateAlternateKey column header and rename the column to FullDate.

8. Change the **Format** property to **Short Date**. This was covered in *Chapter 9, Using Tabular Models*.

9. On the **Table** menu, navigate to **Date | Mark As Date Table** and use the `FullDateAlternateKey` as the date identifier.

    You will use this table in calculations a little later. This is a critical step as the date lookup table is required for time-intelligence functions to work correctly.

Creating measures

A calculated measure performs aggregation in the model efficiently by processing calculations on the server during query time. Measures can be defined using simple aggregate functions, or they can include complex business logic by using combinations of functions.

Getting ready

In a Tabular Model, a table can play two roles either as a container for measures (often referred to as a measure group or fact table) or a lookup table (often referred to as a dimension table in multidimensional models). When a model is processed, the Tabular processing engine determines the role of tables and applies the appropriate metadata to them in the final model. If a table has non-summarized or non-numeric columns, it shows up in the client application as a lookup table and these columns become attributes. If a table has numeric columns that can be summarized or it contains defined measures, it may be presented by the client tool as a measure group. If a table contains the attribute columns and summary numeric columns and/or measures, it can actually play both the roles and will show up in most client tools as two separate tables having the same name. Remove or hide all of the columns and leave only the measures in a table containing the measure base columns. Column and measure names must be unique in a table, so it's a good idea to plan ahead when naming columns and make it a point to use different names for measures and the numeric columns in your measure table. The following exercise will make this clear.

How to do it...

Creating measures can be done in two ways:

- ▶ Creating AutoSum measures
- ▶ Creating calculated measures

Creating AutoSum measures

Simple measures may be added to a model that aggregate a column of numeric values. The **AutoSum** feature creates a measure using a selected aggregate function (such as SUM, AVERAGE, DISTINCTCOUNT, COUNT, MIN, or MAX) and automatically gives the measure a name such as Sum of Sales Amount. This is a good way to get started with creating measures, but you may not want to have every measure in your model begin with the text Sum of.

Working with a measure table that contains numeric columns, you will hide the base columns, create calculated measures, and apply formatting properties:

1. Select the Internet Sales table in grid view.

2. Select all of the key columns (the first eight columns whose names end with the word Key) and hide them. You can use the *Shift* key to click on and select a range of columns.

3. Right-click on the selected range and then click on **Hide from Client Tools**.

4. I'll show you a trick that will save time when using the AutoSum feature to create measures. Select each of the following columns and use the Properties window to set the `Format` property as indicated in the following table:

Column Name	Format Property
OrderQuantity	Data Format: Whole Number
	Show Thousand Separator: True
UnitPrice	Currency
ExtendedAmount	Currency
UnitPriceDiscountPct	Currency
DiscountAmount	Currency
ProductStandardCost	Currency
TotalProductCost	Currency
SalesAmount	Currency
TaxAmt	Currency
Freight	Currency

5. Select the range of numeric columns listed in the table and click on the **Hide from Client Tools** menu option.

6. With the range still selected, click on the AutoSum icon on the toolbar designated with the Σ (Sigma) icon. This creates a measure for each column in the Calculation Pane below.

7. The lazy model designer might leave the default measure names as `Sum of...` but we will rename our measures.

Number		RevisionNumber		OrderQuantity		UnitPrice		ExtendedAmount		UnitPriceDisco
1		1		1		$4.99		$4.99		
1		1		1		$4.99		$4.99		
1		1		1		$4.99		$4.99		
1		1		1		$4.99		$4.99		
1		1		1		$4.99		$4.99		
1		1		1		$4.99		$4.99		
1		1		1		$4.99		$4.99		
1		1		1		$4.99		$4.99		
1		1		1		$4.99		$4.99		
1		1		1		$4.99		$4.99		
1		1		1		$4.99		$4.99		
1		1		1		$4.99		$4.99		
1		1		1		$4.99		$4.99		
1		1		1		$4.99		$4.99		
1		1		1		$4.99		$4.99		

This is a convenient way to define a measure for a numeric column. When you use the AutoSum feature, this actually creates a new measure in the Calculation Pane just as you would define a measure manually. The measure also inherits the formatting properties of the base column if they have been set.

> The Calculation Pane is displayed at the bottom on the grid view designer.
> Measures can be defined in any cell. Also, the name of the new measure
> is the original column name prefixed with the text Sum of.

8. Select each measure cell and then change the name in the formula box using the expressions listed in the following step.

   A convenient convention for renaming the measure is to add a space between the two words in each column name.

9. Change the name of each measure using this convention. For the **Freight** measure, change the name to Freight Cost.

```
Order Quantity:=SUM([OrderQuantity])
Unit Price:=SUM([UnitPrice])
Extended Amount:=SUM([ExtendedAmount])
Unit Price Discount Pct:=SUM([UnitPriceDiscountPct])
Discount Amount:=SUM([Discount Amount])
Product Standard Cost:=SUM([ProductStandardCost])
```

```
Total Product Cost:=SUM([TotalProductCost])
Sales Amount:=SUM([SalesAmount])
Tax Amt:=SUM([TaxAmt])
Freight Cost:=SUM([Freight])
```

10. Take a look at the columns in the table. We have key columns, which you have hidden, and we have the base columns for measures, which you have hidden. The remaining visible columns are not needed, so you will delete them.

11. Delete each remaining column that is not hidden. Make sure that you don't delete the key columns and numeric measure base columns that you hid earlier. You can delete a column by selecting it and then pressing the *Delete* key or by right-clicking on the column and choosing **Delete Column** from the menu.

> As a rule, if you don't need a column from the source data, delete it. It's easier to add a column later if you decide you need it than to have unnecessary data in the model, which can impact performance and memory.

12. To inspect measures, select the cell in the Calculation Pane below the table grid.

13. The properties for each selected measure are displayed in the **Properties** window on the right-hand side of the designer. You can verify the name of the selected measure or any other object with the drop-down list displayed at the top of this window.

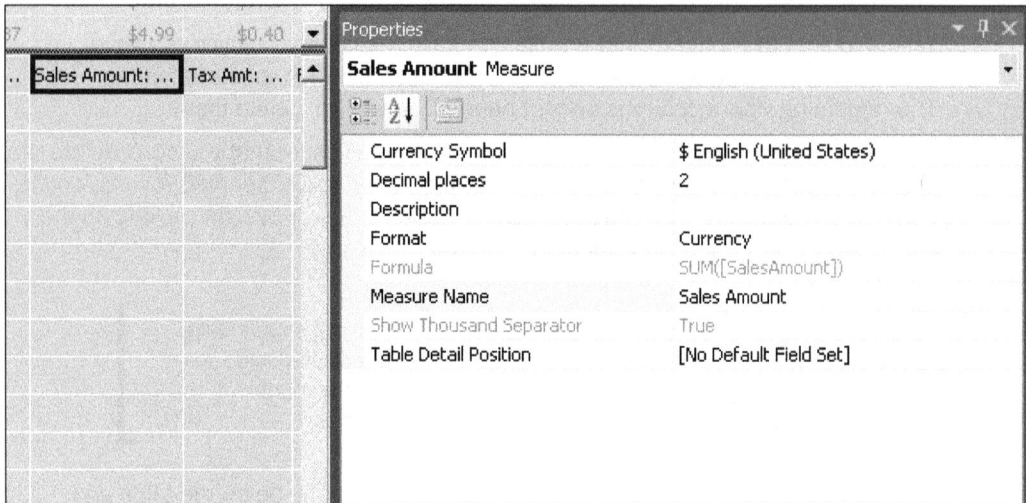

14. Check the **Format** property for the new measures using the **Properties** window on the right-hand side of the model designer. Since the base column properties were set correctly, you should see the same **Format** property setting in the measure. If not, you can change it in this window.

Creating calculated measures

It's great that we can define measures to add up a column of numbers, but we can provide more business value with more specific calculations. We'll start with a few simple calculations and then introduce DAX functions to add logic and business rules.

The Calculation Pane, located below the table grid, was designed to emulate an Excel worksheet. The placement of the current set of measures in the columns below the base numeric columns is actually just for convenience, and measures can really be placed in any cell:

1. Select a cell below the `Total Product Cost` measure and enter the following calculation script. When you get to each measure reference, you can click on a measure cell or type the open square bracket and then select the measure name from the list of objects.

   ```
   Net Cost:=[Total Product Cost] + [Tax Amt] + [Freight Cost]
   ```

2. Press *Enter* to validate the expression and save the changes.

3. With the new measure cell selected, use the **Properties** window to set the **Format** property to `Currency`.

4. Select the cell to the right, and enter this expression to define a calculation named `Net Profit`. You will also format this measure as `Currency`.

    `Net Profit:=[Sales Amount] - [Net Cost]`

5. In the next cell, define a calculated measure named `Net Margin`.

    `Net Margin:=[Net Profit] / [Sales Amount]`

    This expression produces a ratio value that we want to format as a percentage.

6. After writing the expression, set the **Format** property to **Percent** and the **Number of Decimal Places** field to the value `2`.

Testing a Tabular Model in Excel

Excel is a convenient tool to browse and query a Tabular Model so that you can validate your design. Rather than opening Excel and connecting to the deployed model on the Tabular server, you can open Excel directly from the model designer and connect it to the workspace database.

How to do it...

You will use Excel to browse the Tabular Model using the data in the active workspace database on the development machine. Before you continue, make sure you have Excel 2010 or Excel 2013 installed on the development computer:

1. On the left-hand side of the toolbar in the model designer, click on the Analyze in Excel icon. Again, this icon is not labeled but has a tooltip when you hover over it.

    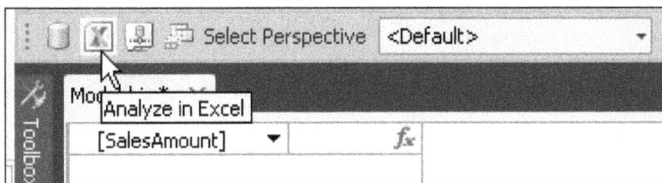

    This action will open an instance of Excel, create a connection to the model workspace, and open a PivotTable. A small dialog opens titled Analyze in Excel.

2. Click on the **OK** button to accept the default settings. Excel may open in the background. If it doesn't appear to open right away, watch for the Excel icon in your Windows task bar and then click on it to bring Excel to the foreground.

Understanding Row Context

When you define a calculated column that references values from different columns in a table, that expression is applied, individually, to each row in the table. In *Chapter 9, Using Tabular Models*, you created a `FullName` calculated column that concatenates the `FirstName` and `LastName` column values on each row. Earlier in this chapter, you used the `RELATED` function to look up the product category for every product subcategory row. In these examples, it's easy to think about how these expressions are applied within the context of each row. When working with measures, we extend the same concept of filter context to calculate values that aggregate or apply functional logic to the values of all filtered rows. We'll look at some examples to examine this behavior:

1. With any cell in the `PivotTable` selected, use the **PivotTable Fields** list to check the **CategoryName** option in the `Product Category` table. This adds a row to the `PivotTable` for each category. In the `Internet Sales` table measure group/table, check the `Sales Amount`, `Net Profit`, and `Net Margin` measures.

PivotTable queries the model and displays one category per row, and for each row, the measures are calculated in the context of that row. The first row is for the `ProductCategory` name: `Accessories`. For every row in the `Product Category` table with that value, the model navigates through the relationship to the `Product` table to get a filtered set of rows. It then navigates to the `Internet Sales` table and gets all the related rows for those products; for this set of rows, it applies the calculations. The model adds up all the `Sales Amount` values and then performs the `Net Profit` and `Net Margin` calculations within the context of rows related to `Accessories`. Does this make sense?

2. Leave Excel open so we can keep using it.

Understanding Filter Context

Now that you have the concept of Row Context, you shouldn't have any trouble understanding its cousin, Filter Context. To get started, I'll introduce an important DAX function called CALCULATE.

Using the CALCULATE function

The purpose of the CALCULATE function is to apply a measure or calculation expression to a filtered set of rows, usually by calling another function that returns a table object. We will use the FILTER function to explicitly filter rows in the `Internet Sales` table where related rows from the `Sales Territory` table have a `SalesTerritoryCountry` column value equal to `United States`. Using these functions, we will define the filter context.

How to do it...

Follow the given steps to use the CALCULATE function:

1. Return to the `Internet Sales` table in grid view and select a new cell in the Calculation Pane. Write a new calculated measure named US Sales as follows:

```
US Sales:=CALCULATE( [Sales Amount],   'Internet Sales',
   'Sales Territory'[SalesTerritoryCountry] =
   "United States" )
```

2. Move on to another cell and write a similar measure named Non-US Sales. The only difference from the previous example is that the value is not equal to `United States`. It should look similar to the following code:

```
Non-US Sales:=CALCULATE( [Sales Amount], 'Internet Sales',
   'Sales Territory'[SalesTerritoryCountry] <>
   "United States" )
```

Test the Measures in Excel

1. Switch back over to Excel, and on the **Data** ribbon, click on **Refresh All**. With the `PivotTable` selected, you should see the `US Sales` and `Non-US Sales` measures added to the `Internet Sales` fact table.

2. Check both of these measures to add them to the `PivotTable` columns. Alongside the total sales for each product category, for all the sales territories, we see the contribution in the US along with the Non-US Sales.

Working with Time Intelligence

Now let's have some fun with dates. Several DAX functions contain built-in date logic that simplifies the otherwise complex logic for comparing and accumulating values across dates and time. We'll start with a function called TOTALMTD. This function accepts a single date value and returns a table object filled with all the dates from the beginning of the month up to that date. By using this in the second argument for the CALCULATE function, we can calculate the month-to-date accumulation for any measure value:

1. Create a new measure in the `Internet Sales` table by entering the following text in an open cell in the Calculation Pane:

   ```
   Sales MTD:= TOTALMTD ( [Sales Amount], 'Date'[FullDate] )
   ```

2. Move to an open cell and enter the following expression. This measure will calculate the sales amount for a period of time exactly one year earlier than the current period.

```
Sales Prior Year:=CALCULATE([Sales Amount]
          , SAMEPERIODLASTYEAR( 'Date'[FullDate] )
          )
```

You can experiment with Excel and visualize the model in different ways. In the following example, after opening Excel, I added a PivotChart, chose a line chart, and added the `FullDate` field from the `Date` table to the chart axis. I added the `Sales Amount` and `Sales Prior Year` measures from the `Internet Sales` fact table. Via the **PivotChart Tools | Design** ribbon, I inserted a timeline based on the `FullDate` field in the `Date` table.

You can see that by comparing the `Sales Amount` values side-by-side with the previous year in the `Sales Prior Year` measure, we can see that sales have increased significantly; using the timeline, we can compare sales with the prior year for a more specific period of time.

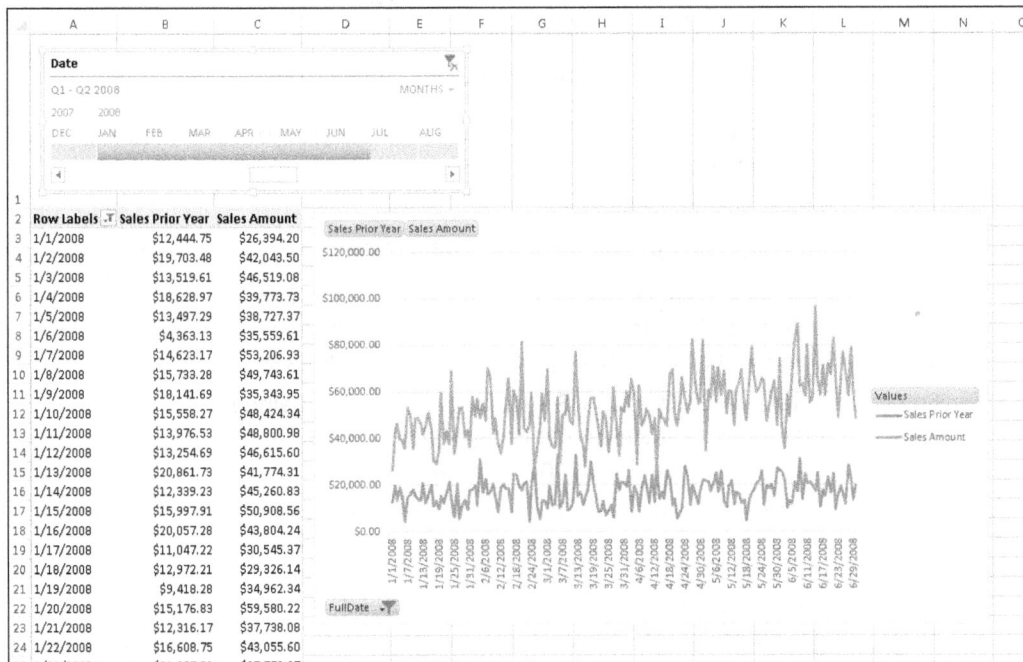

Querying a Tabular Model

Two query languages are used with the Tabular implementation of SSAS Tabular. Any client tool that generates MDX can connect to and browse a model because Tabular exposes the same interface and metadata as a multidimensional SSAS database. This is how Excel currently interfaces with a Tabular Model from a PivotTable or PivotChart.

With handwritten queries, you also have the option to use the DAX query syntax. In this section, I'll give you a brief tour of the fundamental constructs of a DAX query and the most essential commands used to get results and navigate a model.

Getting ready

In the *Deploying Tabular Models* recipe in *Chapter 9*, *Using Tabular Models*, using Data tools, the deployment wizard, and the deployment utility, you configured the SSDT project to create a database named SSAS Cookbook Chapter 9.

To start with this recipe, please follow the given steps:

1. Follow the instructions in that recipe to return to the **Project Property Pages** dialog and change the name of the database to SSAS Cookbook Chapter 10.

2. Deploy and process that database.

3. We will use the **SQL Server Management Studio** (**SSMS**) to query the new database.

4. If SSMS is still open from the last time you used it, use the **Connect** drop-down button above **Object Explorer** on the left-hand side of the window. If not, open SSMS and in the **Connect to Server** dialog, choose **Analysis Services**.

5. Enter the server name (if your SSAS Tabular server uses a named instance, enter the server and the instance name separated by a backslash such as LocalHost\TABULAR), and click on the **Connect** button.

   You will see the server and the instance name in the **Object Explorer** with a blue SSAS Tabular icon, similar to what is shown in the following screenshot:

   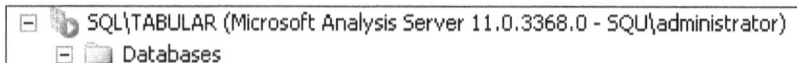

6. Expand the **Databases** node and right-click on the SSAS Cookbook Chapter 10 database. Go to **New Query...** | **MDX**.

How to do it...

Hold on a second! We just told the SQL Server Management Studio that we are going to run MDX queries against a Tabular database. Can this be right? It is because SSMS doesn't actually know the difference between MDX and DAX but the Analysis Services data provider does. We can actually run both MDX and DAX queries in the query window. Let's get started.

DAX queries can be quite simple. One of the core missions of SSAS Tabular and Power Pivot was to keep things just as simple as possible. In MDX, users had to learn a lot of new concepts such as measure groups, dimensions, hierarchies, levels, sets, and tuples. In the Tabular world, we use simple concepts such as tables, measures, and columns. Adhering to that goal, let us execute the following steps:

1. We introduce the EVALUATE statement that really means "show me a table." In the query window, type the following query:

    ```
    EVALUATE Customer
    ```

2. Click on the **Execute** button on the toolbar, and you will see the entire content of the **Customer** table displayed in the results grid.

    A lot of information is returned by the query. We can return a subset of columns by using the SUMMARIZE function. This function takes the table name followed by any number of column names.

3. Enter the following query script, select the text, and click on **Execute**.

    ```
    EVALUATE SUMMARIZE(Customer, [FirstName], [LastName])
    ```

    When executed, the query only returns two columns:

Customer[FirstNa...	Customer[LastNa...
Erika	Navarro
Nancy	Sai
Katie	Holt
Shannon	Sanz
Sydney	Jones
Dawn	Pal
Zachary	Hayes
Alexandra	Campbell
Samantha	Perry
David	Miller
Thomas	Jai
Felicia	Townsend

4. Now we can add a measure by providing an alias name followed by the table and column reference. The SUMMARIZE function, like other functions of the same type, accepts an unlimited number of columns or alias and measure pairs as parameters.

5. Let's add the Sales Amount measure from the Internet Sales table.

6. Make the following addition to the query and run it in the query window:

```
EVALUATE SUMMARIZE(Customer, [FirstName], [LastName]
                , "Sales Amt", 'Internet Sales'[Sales Amount])
```

The results include the new Sales Amt measure defined in the query as shown in the following screenshot:

Customer[FirstName]	Customer[LastName]	[Sales Amt]
Erika	Navarro	53.99
Nancy	Sai	33.98
Katie	Holt	1143.46
Shannon	Sanz	4.99
Sydney	Jones	30.97
Dawn	Pal	1164.47
Zachary	Hayes	64.47
Alexandra	Campbell	2361.95
Samantha	Perry	91.58
David	Miller	39.98
Thomas	Jai	5915.53
Felicia	Townsend	2309.97

There's more...

DAX supports a lot of the same essential constructs of the T-SQL language such as the ability to filter and order results. A basic element of a DAX query is that the relationship between tables has already been established in the model and therefore there is no need to join tables in the query as you would in SQL. This isn't to suggest that we can't use more complex techniques to join non-related tables or combine data in unique ways. DAX affords a lot of advanced functionality when it's needed.

If we change the SUMMARIZE function to begin with the Internet Sales table, we can add table and column references for any table that is related either directly or indirectly. Ordering the results is similar to SQL using the ORDER BY clause followed by a series of table and column references. Let us execute the following step to query the Model:

1. Write a new query using the following text and then execute it:

```
EVALUATE SUMMARIZE('Internet Sales', Customer[FirstName]
    , Customer[LastName], 'Product Category'[CategoryName]
    , "Sales Amt", 'Internet Sales'[Sales Amount])
ORDER BY Customer[LastName], Customer[FirstName]
    , 'Product Category'[CategoryName]
```

The results are shown in the following screenshot, which shows us the total of sales for each product category purchased by each customer:

Customer[FirstName]	Customer[LastName]	Product Category[CategoryName]	[Sales Amt]
Aaron	Adams	Accessories	63.97
Aaron	Adams	Clothing	53.99
Adam	Adams	Accessories	141.98
Alex	Adams	Accessories	34.99
Alex	Adams	Bikes	1700.99
Alexandra	Adams	Bikes	3578.27
Allison	Adams	Bikes	1552.48
Allison	Adams	Clothing	49.99
Amanda	Adams	Accessories	109.97
Amanda	Adams	Clothing	24.49
Amber	Adams	Accessories	34.99
Amber	Adams	Bikes	1303.48

2. To filter results you can use, you guessed it, the FILTER function, which wraps a table expression and operates on the columns and values it contains. You can do it by entering the query, selecting the text, and executing it as follows:

```
EVALUATE
FILTER(
    SUMMARIZE('Internet Sales', 'Date'[CalendarYear]
        , Customer[FirstName], Customer[LastName]
        , 'Product Category'[CategoryName]
        , "Sales Amt", 'Internet Sales'[Sales Amount])
        , 'Date'[CalendarYear] = 2008)

ORDER BY Customer[LastName], Customer[FirstName]
    , 'Product Category'[CategoryName]
```

The query returns only the sales figure for 2008, grouped by Customer and Category.

See also

The DAX expression and the query language consists of about 180 functions with more being added as the language evolves. You're not going to need to know how to use all of these commands and functions, but having a good reference is helpful. The DAX Function Reference pages on the TechNet site are a good place to begin. These can be found at `http://technet.microsoft.com/en-us/library/ee634396.aspx`.

One of the coolest tricks I have learned about DAX was something *Darren Gosbell*, a SQL Server MVP from the UK, showed me not long ago. I was commenting that not all of the latest DAX functions were included in Microsoft's online official documentation at the time. Darren showed me that when a new feature is added to the language, the documentation actually gets added to the language metadata that you can view by running a **dynamic management view** (**DMV**). Check this out; run the following query in any MDX query window:

```
SELECT * FROM $System.MDSchema_Functions
```

This returns the complete online help and contextual metadata for both DAX and MDX. If you want MDX only, use this expression in the WHERE clause: `origin = 1`. For DAX only, the WHERE expression would be WHERE `origin = 3` OR `origin = 4` (the DMV query syntax doesn't support extended SQL commands such as the IN function). Putting it all together, we can use the following query to return complete documentation for the DAX language:

```
SELECT
    INTERFACE_NAME
  , FUNCTION_NAME
  , [DESCRIPTION]
  , PARAMETERINFO
FROM $System.MDSchema_functions
WHERE origin = 3 or origin = 4
```

We've covered the basics in this chapter to get you started and to lay a foundation that you can build upon. With this basic understanding of DAX expressions, calculated columns, measures, and DAX queries, you can use additional functions that provide specific capabilities and features.

A dedicated DAX query tool, called DAX Studio, can be downloaded from `http://daxstudio.codeplex.com`. This Excel add-in is an excellent resource developed by members of the SQL Server MVP community for writing and editing DAX queries.

11

Performance Tuning and Troubleshooting Tabular Models

This chapter will address the following topics:

- ▸ Understanding usability limits
- ▸ Optimizing and managing a model's design
- ▸ Diagnosing performance issues
- ▸ Using performance tools
- ▸ Investigating query performance with SQL Server Profiler

Introduction

This chapter will help you understand how to optimize a data model for performance and to utilize memory and other system resources effectively. The topic of performance tuning and troubleshooting is a little different than most of the other chapters you've read so far. So troubleshooting isn't a purely prescriptive exercise where you follow a set of steps with a predictable outcome. It is both an art and a science that often requires investigation and an iterative approach to eliminate possible issues.

Understanding usability limits

A man goes to see his doctor and says, "Doctor, it hurts when I do this," and the doctor says, "Don't do that." Performance tuning can only go so far as to remedy a problem that might simply be a usability issue. Tabular technology can do impressive things with data, but every technology has its practical limits, and the best solution might be to change the approach or to educate users in ways to have a better experience. We will begin with an example to demonstrate this principle.

Getting ready

Using Excel to browse the Tabular Model created in *Chapter 10, DAX Calculations and Queries*, you will play the role of a business user. Your objective is to first get the total of year-to-date sales daily and then the customers and the products they purchased. We will typically look at the report at the end of each month, so we'll need to filter the data by year and month.

How to do it...

Use the following steps to create a sales report in Excel:

1. Open Excel 2013 and place the cursor in any blank worksheet.

2. On the **DATA** tab of the ribbon, choose **From Other Sources** and then choose **From Analysis Services**.

3. In the **Data Connection Wizard**, enter your Tabular instance name and click on the **Next** button.

4. Select the database you deployed in *Chapter 10, DAX Calculations and Queries*, and then click on the **Next** button.

5. Click on the **Finish** button and save the connection if prompted.

6. On the **Import Data** dialog box, click on **OK** to insert a PivotTable at the current position in the sheet.

7. Use the field list to the right to add the `FullDate` field from the `Date` table to **ROWS**, and add the `Sales YTD` field measured from the `Internet Sales` table to **VALUES**.

> Take a look at what we have done so far. You've asked the query engine to perform the `Sales YTD` calculation 1,280 times, adding the daily values to the previous values on each day of the same year. For December 31 of each year, it would add at least 365 values to calculate the value in that cell, but it does all of this very quickly.

8. Add the `LastName` field from the `Customer` table to **ROWS** and notice how long it takes.

9. Add the `EnglishProductName` field from the `Product` table. Go get a coffee or take a break because this is going to take a while.

   After a few minutes, Excel will display the message: **The PivotTable report will not fit on the sheet. Do you want to display as much as possible?** Excel is indicating that the **PivotTable** size exceeds its limit.

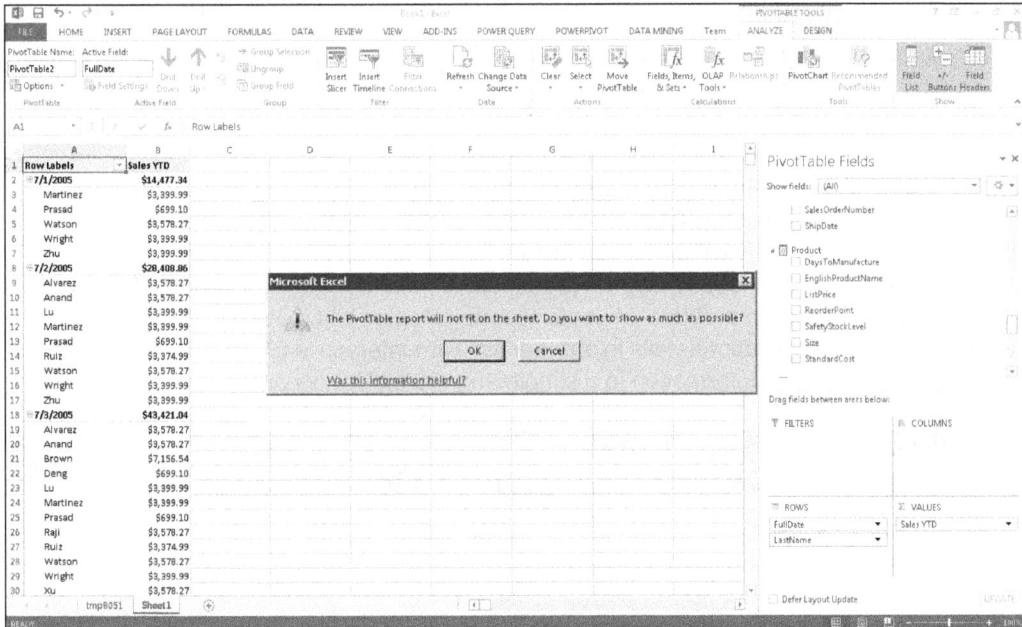

10. Click on **OK** and scroll down to the bottom row.

    You have added over one million rows to the sheet, but you only have room for about two-thirds of the available data.

11. In the field list, expand the **Calendar** hierarchy in the `Date` table, right-click on the **CalendarYear** field, and add this field as a slicer.

Let's stop here because this was not a good user experience, and we haven't achieved our objective. Many users would be frustrated and either call the help desk or just give up at this point.

There's more...

The solution to this problem is actually quite simple but requires that users are educated about the practicality of consuming any significant volume of data.

If the same level of detailed reporting is a requirement, filters should be applied before selecting the fields that would result in cross-joining values on the rows. In our case, we can filter by year and month to reduce the result size and improve performance. Repeat the previous exercise, but prior to step 7 of the previous section, perform the following additional steps:

1. Add **CalendarYear** and **MonthNumberOfYear** as filters.
2. Select a value from each of these cells before adding other fields to the rows or columns of the PivotTable report.

Another approach is to help users understand the value of summarizing and slicing data, rather than drilling down to raw details in a single report. If slicers or filters were applied on dimensional members such as product category, product, and customer, we could have displayed daily details without adding the product and customer to the details of the report and creating the cross-join problem. Multiple reports can also be created to get customer details in one list and product details in another list, with interactive filters and slicers that can bring us to the same information in a simple and more effective presentation.

Optimizing and managing a model's design

As the designer of a Tabular Model, your experience is affected by different factors than those of the consumers of the solution you deploy.

Managing memory usage

A common issue that users encounter with the Power Pivot add-in for Excel occurs when a large volume of data is imported that uses all the available memory resources on the local computer. This is especially true when running a 32-bit operating system or Office edition with restricted memory resources. The logical path for many of these solutions is to migrate the desktop Power Pivot model to a Tabular Model that runs on a well-equipped server.

The **xVelocity In-Memory Analytics Engine** is designed to utilize memory, rather than disk I/O, to provide improved performance when compared to more conventional technologies. Since models reside entirely in memory, the way we think about providing and managing resources must be fundamentally different than it would be for managing relational databases or even multidimensional semantic models. The simple reality is that when a Tabular database server doesn't have enough memory to hold all of the data in the model, it simply will not work. In many ways, the xVelocity In-Memory Analytics Engine is less complicated and can be easier to troubleshoot. Many problems can be avoided by simply providing extra memory to hold data, process objects, and execute queries.

Many database administrators and virtual server administrators aren't accustomed to thinking about server management in this way. In fact, the objective when configuring a virtual server is to restrict memory and CPU resources as much as possible so they can be allocated to other virtual machines on the same physical hardware. Make sure that when you specify the memory requirements for a Tabular Analysis Services server, you should not only consider the size of each model that will be loaded into memory but also the additional headroom needed for growth, object processing, and other contingencies.

Specific issues will require investigation and systematic troubleshooting steps, but consider these general guidelines that may help to prevent or resolve many common issues:

- ▶ If the Tabular server is used to run other services such as the SQL Server relational engine, restrict the memory allocated to those services so the Tabular instance doesn't have to compete for the required memory.

- ▶ Monitor the rate of compression for each table and database. Investigate and optimize objects that are not being compressed effectively by eliminating unused columns, and use conservative data types, especially for columns that contain sparse and redundant values.

- ▶ After estimating the size of each Tabular database on the server, once the data is compressed, allow at least 20 percent of more memory as a contingency buffer.

- ▶ Allow additional memory to facilitate object processing. The total memory that is required will largely depend on the processing strategy. For databases that use the **Process Full** option, allow twice the amount of memory that is required when the database is at rest, while the database is being processed.

- ▶ Use a partitioning strategy to reduce the memory overhead on the server and control the use of memory on development machines. If you can process a single partition containing added rows or process partitions for groups of rows one at a time, this will reduce the overall use of memory during the processing time.

Diagnosing performance issues

The practice of performance tuning can range from being simple to being very complex, but most issues are easy to resolve through effective design and by applying simple troubleshooting steps and techniques. Sometimes problems are obvious and can be resolved easily. In more challenging cases, we must consider the possible causes and then eliminate possibilities to discover the remaining options. Fortunately, in most models, performance issues can be addressed without extensive experimentation. If your models have large volumes of data, many tables, complex relationships, or layers of complex calculation logic, you have a higher likelihood of running into performance problems that you'll need to sort out.

Processing and query-related performance

The xVelocity In-Memory Analytics Engine consists of a storage engine and a query engine that work in tandem to return query results and perform calculations. A fundamental understanding of these components is helpful, much like a basic understanding of automotive principles is helpful to diagnose problems with a car. Some problems are discovered and corrected by reading the instrument panel or engine code displayed by a diagnostic computer. Some problems can be discovered and resolved by listening to the engine to find a pulley, bearing, or belt making noise. A few more elusive problems require the expertise of a certified mechanic and can't be fixed easily by tinkering and experimenting. Troubleshooting the Tabular storage and query engine is similar.

Using performance tools

Your design and management tool belt will contain several tools that will help you with troubleshooting, optimization, and performance tuning. These may consist of:

> ▸ SQL Server Management Studio
> ▸ DAX Studio add-in for Excel
> ▸ Windows Task Manager and Resource Monitor
> ▸ SQL Server Profiler

Task Manager and Resource Monitor

The most convenient method to check system resources and activity is that of using performance tools in the Windows Task Manager. You can access the Task Manager in any version of Windows using *Ctrl + Alt + Delete* or by right-clicking on the Windows task bar. Use the **Performance** tab to view a summary of CPU and memory usage on the computer. Memory use is typically the most important factor to consider first. This will tell you how much RAM is available on the system and how much is currently in use by the Tabular engine and other processes. Use the **Processes** tab to see whether any other services or applications are competing for memory. You should typically be concerned when memory use is consistently over 80 percent or spiking over 90 percent, but there are many other factors to consider. On a production server, you should maintain a memory reserve to cover for multiple models being loaded into the memory and have enough additional memory for database processing.

The CPU usage is also an important factor in performance. If all the CPU cores are running high consistently when queries run, this could be an indication of inefficiencies in the model design or the calculation of formulas. Disk I/O and network performance are usually less important in monitoring Tabular's query performance but can be important considerations when processing the database, tables, or partitions. Depending on your version of Windows, you can get a more extensive view of these resources and processes using the button on this dialog to open **Resource Monitor**.

Dynamic Management Views

Several **Dynamic Management Views** (**DMVs**) were added to the SQL Server to support Tabular Model's design and optimization. These views are queried using OLE DB for Analysis Services data provider, which is also used to run DAX and MDX queries against Analysis Services.

A complete list of DMVs is available in the MSDN Library under the topic **Use Dynamic Management Views (DMVs) to Monitor Analysis Services**, which is located at: http://msdn.microsoft.com/en-us/library/hh230820.aspx.

There are 59 DVMs related to SQL Server Analysis Services in SQL Server 2012. Most, but not all, of these views apply to both multidimensional and Tabular SSAS databases since both platforms expose objects through XML/A interfaces.

To query a DMV, open an MDX query window in the SQL Server Management Studio with a connection to your Tabular instance. Even though you are using the same query interface to write MDX and DAX queries, the query syntax for DMVs is very similar to T-SQL. Because of the lack of support for advanced query operators for DMVs, it's often easiest to copy the results of a query into Excel or a SQL Server table and then use other methods to filter and examine the results. For example, to get the memory use of all the tables in a database, you would first need to use the following query to return information for all the objects on the server:

```
select
    ObjectParentPath,
    ObjectID,
    MemoryUsed
from $system.DISCOVER_MEMORYUSAGE
```

The `ObjectParentPath` column contains a complete reference to each object in the form of `<Server\Instance>.Databases.<Database Name>.<Object Name>`. This string can be parsed to filter and discriminate the objects of interest.

One of the most convenient ways to discover and query SSAS Dynamic Management Views is to use the DAX Studio tool. This is an installable add-in for Excel that you can download from the Microsoft CodePlex community code sharing site at http://daxstudio.codeplex.com/.

DAX Studio has many other useful features and is, in many ways, a superior query tool to SSMS, with features such as code completion, syntax checking, and query keyword color coding.

BISM server memory report

One very good example and useful application of this DMV is in an Excel workbook created by *Kasper de Jonge* from the Analysis Services product team at Microsoft. This workbook contains a Power Pivot model that runs a simple query, similar to the previous example, to populate a table with calculations used to analyze the memory usage of various database objects in comparison to other objects. The results are displayed in Excel PivotTables with conditional formatting to proportionally highlight larger objects as shown in the following screenshot:

You can get more information and download the from Kasper's blog at `http://www.Power Pivotblog.nl/what-is-using-all-that-memory-on-my-analysis-server-instance`. Keep in mind that this is a simple application and just one of the many useful DMVs; this DMV returns approximated values that can be affected by different factors, but it does provide useful information for quick and easy problem solving.

Now we'll do some serious performance testing. To set this up, we need a calculation added to the model that demands more resources. Depending on how a query is constructed, the following calculation might take several seconds to run. Keep in mind that our Tabular database is quite small, but if this measure is used with several million rows of data loaded into the model, it could take several minutes to run:

1. Add the following measure to a cell in the measures grid of the `Internet Sales` table. Don't enter any carriage returns; the text wraps to fit on the printed page of the book.

    ```
    Qty Ratio Over Reorder Point:=DIVIDE([Order Quantity],
      sum(Product[ReorderPoint]))
    ```

2. Press *Enter* to validate and create the measure. Now, move on to another cell and enter the following calculation all on one line:

    ```
    Last Order Qty Ratio Over Reorder
      Point:=sumx(values('Internet Sales'[ProductKey]),
      CALCULATE([Qty Ratio Over Reorder Point],
      LASTNONBLANK('Internet Sales'[OrderDate],
      [Qty Ratio Over Reorder Point]))))
    ```

3. Again, press *Enter* to validate and save the measure.

4. Deploy the database to the SSAS Tabular instance like you did in *Chapter 10, DAX Calculations and Queries*.

5. Now we're ready to query the model and use the new measure. Open Excel to create a new workbook.

6. On the **DATA** tab, select the **From Other Sources** icon in the **Get External Data** group.

7. Select **From Analysis Services**. Enter the server and instance name and click on the **Next** button. Select the database name. Click on **Next** and then click on **Finish** to complete the connection.

8. When prompted, add a PivotTable report.

9. Right-click on **CalendarYear** and select **Add as Slicer**.

10. In the slicer, click on select **2005**.

11. From the `Date` table, expand **More Fields**.

12. Select the `FullDate` field to add it to **ROWS**.

13. From the `Product` table, select the `EnglishProductName` field to be added to **ROWS** under the `FullDate` field.

14. From the `Internet Sales` measure table at the top of the fields list, select the following measures:

    ❏ `Order Quantity`

    ❏ `Qty Ratio Over Reorder Point`

    ❏ `Last Order Qty Ratio Over Reorder Point`

15. Use the slicer to select different years. Also, use the clear all icon at the top-right corner of the slicer to release the filter and include all the years. The time to run each query may vary from one to multiple seconds.

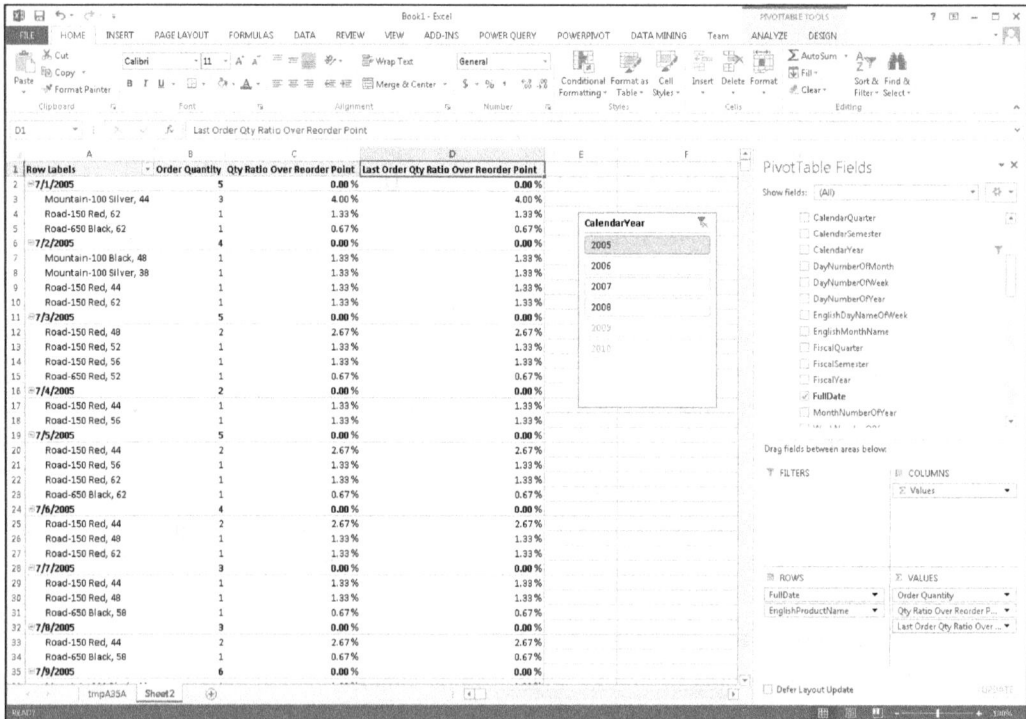

You will use this PivotTable to capture the query that Excel generates when you interact with slicers and other elements used to browse the Tabular Model.

Investigating query performance with SQL Server Profiler

The most important step in determining performance bottlenecks is to find the cause. You need to discover specific events that are taking too long to run or provide evidence of the issue. The most effective way to decompose a query and understand the individual tasks it performs is to run a trace using the SQL Server Profiler. Often times, this is simple but it can also be a tedious and time-consuming process, depending on the complexity of the issue.

How to do it...

Let's get started with running a Profiler trace:

1. You will open **SQL Server Profiler** and start a trace to capture events on the Analysis Services instance.

2. From the **Microsoft SQL Server 2012** program group, expand **Performance Tools** and click on **SQL Server Profiler**.

3. Click on the top-left button on the toolbar to start a **New Trace**.

4. When prompted, connect to the Tabular instance of Analysis Services.

5. On the **Trace Properties** dialog, switch to the **Events Selection** tab.

6. Check the box in the lower-right corner of the dialog labelled **Show all events**.

7. In the **Events** list, uncheck every box in the leftmost **Events** column. Scroll all the way to the bottom and make sure every event is deselected.

8. Scroll back to the top and check the leftmost box in the **Events** column to include the following events in the final set of objects:

   ❑ **Query Begin**

   ❑ **Query End**

   ❑ **DAX Query Plan**

   ❑ **Calculate Non Empty End**

❑ **VertiPaq SE Query End**

❑ **Serialize Results End**

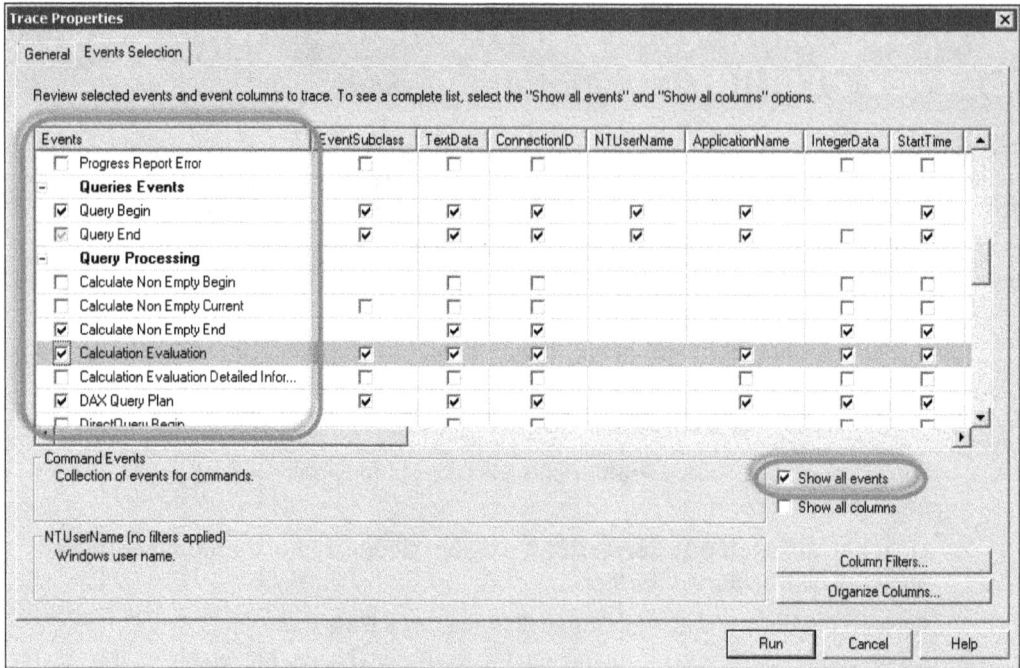

9. When you're ready, click on the **Run** button.

Keep in mind that when the query begins to fire and does what it is supposed to do, it will be capturing every interaction that Excel has with Analysis Services, which includes interactions with the field list, filters, slicers, and the PivotTable. We want to capture only the events that fire when you change the slicer.

We will make one simple interaction, capture the trace, and then stop the trace capture. Ready? Here we go:

1. Switch to Excel and use the slicer to click on **CalendarYear 2007**.

2. Switch back to the **SQL Server Profiler**. You will see the query activity being captured.

3. As soon as you see the **Query End** event added to the trace, click on the red stop button on the toolbar, labelled **Stop Selected Trace** in the tooltip. This stops the trace and continues to show the results in the grid.

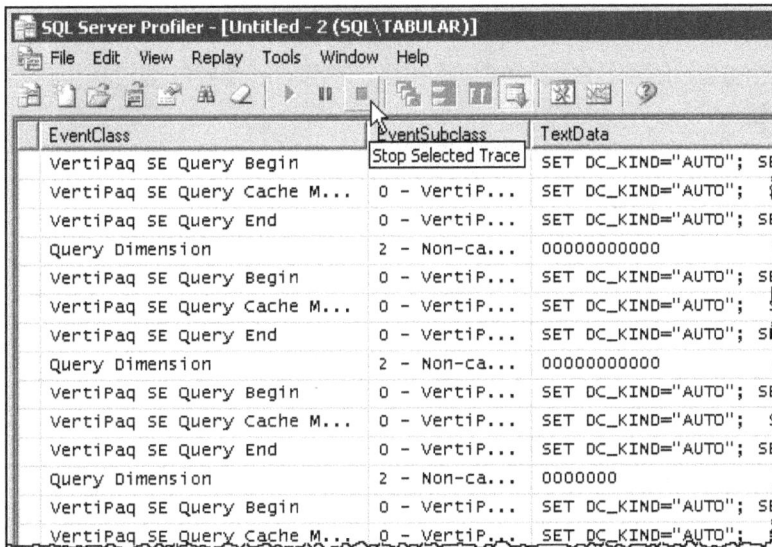

To perform another trace, you can click on the eraser icon on the toolbar to clear all the events and then click on the **Start** button to start a new trace.

4. Clear and restart the trace using the toolbar in the **SQL Server Profiler**. The **Clear Trace Window** button looks like an eraser and the **Start Selected Trace** button is a green play arrow.

5. Return to Excel and use the clear filter icon in the top-right corner of the **CalendarYear** slicer to release the filter and include all the years.

6. Return to the **SQL Server Profiler** and watch the query trace run.

7. When the **Query End** event is captured, stop the trace as shown in the following screenshot:

There's more...

Each entry in the table provides detailed information about different activities performed by Analysis Services. Click on each row to view the trace details in the pane under the grid. If you look at each row, it will essentially tell you the story of what went on, beginning with setting up the query, choosing the slicer value, choosing a filter value, preparing an execution plan, and then executing the query. Scroll to the right and note the **Duration** and **CPUTime** columns. These values tell you the number of milliseconds it took for those events.

You can use the SQL Server Profiler with the SQL Server Management Studio to reproduce a query for further analysis. You should first clear the SSAS query cache to avoid masking a query performance issue with cached results from a previous query execution by performing the following steps:

1. Switch to **SQL Server Management Studio**.

2. Add a few carriage returns to the end of the text in the open query window.

3. Add the following XML/A query, adding the name of the deployed database instead of the `--Database Name--` placeholder:

```
<ClearCache xmlns="http://schemas.microsoft.com/
   analysisservices/2003/engine">
```

```
<Object>
<DatabaseID> --Database Name-- </DatabaseID>
</Object>
</ClearCache>
```

4. Highlight only this text and execute the query.

> You should run this query to clear the execution cache each
> time, prior to running a test query, to measure performance.

5. Switch back to the **SQL Server Profiler**.

6. Select the last row for the **Query End** event.

7. Select and copy the entire row of text from the pane under the grid to the clipboard.

8. Switch back to SSMS and insert a few more carriage returns to the bottom of the query window.

9. Paste the query text from the clipboard.

10. Select only the new text and then execute the query.

There are other events you can add to a trace to get useful information. For example, the **Calculation Evaluation** event returns detailed information about the execution options the query engine uses for each stage of the query, but this information is very verbose and can be time consuming to analyze.

Now you have a way to capture a query created by Excel or any other client tool and then rerun the query in Management Studio. You can make changes to the calculation logic to test performance and results and then easily rerun the query. This can be an invaluable technique to investigate how different tools are interacting with a Tabular Model and generating a query script.

Following a few simple guidelines, designing and using Tabular Models for optimal performance is fairly uncomplicated. After all, an SSAS Tabular Model is simple and performs very well as long as the application remains true to the design principles of the technology. Larger and more complicated models are more prone to experience issues with performance and errors, as is the nature of technology in general.

See also

The Microsoft white paper titled *Performance Tuning of Tabular Models in SQL Server 2012 Analysis Services* contains extensive guidance to analyze performance and optimize design at a deeper level. This document can be downloaded from `http://msdn.microsoft.com/en-us/library/dn393915.aspx`.

Miscellaneous Analysis Services Topics

This appendix will cover:

- ▶ Considerations when building a SSAS solution against nonSQL Server data sources
- ▶ Common yet confusing SSAS errors
- ▶ Dimension properties
- ▶ Performance considerations for many-to-many dimension relationships
- ▶ DirectQuery with Tabular Models

Working with non-SQL Server data sources

As discussed throughout the book you normally build cubes based on the SQL Server relational database. SQL Server DBA's and cube developers don't always share responsibilities, although some responsibilities may overlap. Generally, cube developers have database owner permissions to the relational source, which allows them to define necessary data structures for dimensions and partitions. However, in the real world the aforementioned assumptions do not always hold. Analysis Services solution can be developed on top of any relational data source to which you could connect to using .NET or OLEDB providers. The data warehouse might be owned by a different team than the one responsible for developing Analysis Services objects. Database administrators might only be willing to provide read access to the tables and no permission to create additional objects.

In the easiest scenario, you can exploit **SQL Server Integration Services** (**SSIS**) to import data from a nonSQL Server relational source into a SQL Server database and use it as the staging data repository. Once data is in the SQL Server you can use either stored procedures or SSIS to load data into fact and dimension tables as needed.

In a more complicated scenario, the company might not allow you to use the SQL Server even for a relational data warehouse or a staging area. The reasons for this could vary but aren't really relevant to this discussion—the bottom line is that you must create a SSAS solution using Oracle, db2, Sybase, Teradata, or another relational platform. This complicates development because you must learn at least the basics of SQL flavor, used by the relational data source, to define named queries and calculations. Additionally, you must also become familiar with errors that the relational data source might raise during processing (and queries, in case you use a ROLAP storage). The transaction isolation levels supported by each RDBMS can also be different, and the various classes of objects can be implemented using a different nomenclature. For example, the SQL Server implements ROLAP aggregations as indexed views, but db2 does not support indexed views—similar objects in db2 are called **Materialized Query Tables** (**MQT**). Lastly, not every database vendor allows looking under the hood as Microsoft does using Profiler, and majority of the vendors offer support for textual (not graphical) query execution plans.

In this section, I will cover a few "gotchas" in case you find yourself developing SSAS solutions against nonSQL Server data sources.

SSAS data structures

Most SSAS solutions are built using fact and dimension tables. If you must develop against a database using the third normal form, you may have to define the necessary objects in your data source views as named queries and/or named calculations. This is relatively straightforward as long as you have the necessary permissions to the underlying objects (tables or views) and you are comfortable using the SQL syntax of a given RDBMS. Additionally, you'll need the parameters for connecting to the relational data source using a .NET or OLEDB provider supplied either by Microsoft or another vendor. Keep in mind that Microsoft will not support third-party providers. If you have any issues during processing or ROLAP queries, you'll have to work directly with the vendor who supplied the driver.

Transaction isolation levels

By default, Analysis Services uses a read-committed transaction isolation level. With this level enforced, you should never experience data consistency issues. You could improve processing performance by using a read-uncommitted transaction isolation level, because the relational database wouldn't have the locking overhead while reading the fact and dimension table data. To ensure that each processing command reads uncommitted data, you can edit the cartridge corresponding to the relational data source. For example, you can reference a knowledge-based article: `http://support.microsoft.com/kb/959026` for instructions to read the uncommitted data in db2 data sources. Please note that if you alter the cartridge, every statement will read uncommitted data—you won't be able to control it for individual statements. Furthermore, you cannot add query hints to SQL statements used in the named queries or partition definitions. This is because Analysis Services uses such SQL statements as subqueries and writes an outer query prior to sending the statement to the relational source—using query hints in subqueries is not permitted.

Processing performance issues

Analysis Services' processing performance largely depends on how fast you can execute queries against the relational data source. If you're limited to read-only access, you need to speak with the DBAs and see if they could review the query execution plans and come up with necessary indexes. Bear in mind that SSAS does not offer much flexibility in how the processing queries are written—you need to capture the progress report begin and progress report end events in SQL Profiler during processing to obtain the SQL statements. As discussed in the previous chapters, you can adjust the `ProcessingGroup` dimension property and use the `ByTable` option instead of the default `ByAttribute` option to run only one query while processing the dimension; by default, SSAS will run one query per attribute. You can also adjust queries defining each partition as necessary. To maximize processing performance, you should try processing as many partitions in parallel as possible. From the performance perspective, it is always preferable to build a true Star schema model instead of using a normalized database model.

You may also run into processing performance issues if you have a very large number of dimensions and measures in your fact table. In some Star schema models, each new attribute is celebrated with a separate dimension. This approach is simple to implement results in very wide fact tables. In fact with such a data model each row read during processing might require more than one buffer. If this is the case, you should try splitting measures into different measure groups. Better yet, try to combine some of the dimensions, build necessary attribute relationships, and use role-playing dimensions whenever appropriate.

Common yet confusing SSAS errors

Although documenting every SSAS error you could encounter is well beyond the scope of this book, there are common errors you may encounter that are particularly obscure and might leave you scratching your head for days. Hopefully, the explanations and troubleshooting steps included here will help alleviate some of your headaches.

Binding is too small

The term "binding" in the Analysis Services context indicates mapping of a relational database column to a dimension attribute. You can expect binding errors if you change the column data type without adjusting your data source view or attribute properties. SSAS doesn't update properties automatically; any time you make changes to the relational schema, you should also apply corresponding changes in the SSAS project.

You can encounter another set of binding errors when data contains invalid XML characters. Ensure your attributes are configured to account for such characters.

Attribute key cannot be found

Although quite benign and easy to troubleshoot when encountered during partition processing, the missing attribute key error can also pop up when running Process Update against dimensions. The key to understanding the reason for error lies in how Analysis Services processes attributes. The query for processing a specific attribute also includes any related attributes. For example, if we're processing the date dimension, the query sent to the relational database for the month name attribute will be the following code:

```
SELECT
  DISTINCT
    [dbo_DimTime].[dbo_DimTimeCalendarYear0_0] AS
      [dbo_DimTimeCalendarYear0_0],
    [dbo_DimTime].[dbo_DimTimeMonthNumberOfYear0_1] AS
      [dbo_DimTimeMonthNumberOfYear0_1],
    [dbo_DimTime].[dbo_DimTimeMonthName0_2] AS
      [dbo_DimTimeMonthName0_2],
    [dbo_DimTime].[dbo_DimTimeMonthNameValue0_3] AS
      [dbo_DimTimeMonthNameValue0_3],
    [dbo_DimTime].[dbo_DimTimeCalendarQuarter0_4] AS
      [dbo_DimTimeCalendarQuarter0_4]
  FROM
    (
      SELECT [CalendarYear] AS [dbo_DimTimeCalendarYear0_0],
      [MonthNumberOfYear] AS [dbo_DimTimeMonthNumberOfYear0_1],
      EnglishMonthName+' '+ CONVERT(CHAR (4), CalendarYear)
      AS [dbo_DimTimeMonthName0_2],
      CAST(CONVERT( CHAR(2), MonthNumberOfYear) + '/ ' +
      '1/'+CONVERT(CHAR(4), CalendarYear)
      AS DATE ) AS [dbo_DimTimeMonthNameValue0_3],
      [CalendarQuarter] AS [dbo_DimTimeCalendarQuarter0_4]
      FROM [dbo].[DimDate]
    )
  AS [dbo_DimTime]
```

Analysis Services retrieves calendar quarter and calendar year, along with month number and month name columns. While calendar year and month number are the key columns for the month name attribute, Analysis Services retrieves the calendar quarter column because the month name attribute is directly related to the calendar quarter attribute (you can confirm that through the attribute relationships' tab in SSDT). If, due to data consistency issues, the query retrieving calendar quarter attribute members get a key not retrieved by the month name attribute's processing query, the dimension processing job will fail and report the missing attribute key error. The best way to troubleshoot such errors is to grab the `SELECT` statements executed by Analysis Services and execute them against your relational data source. More than likely you have a problem in the data extraction, transformation, and loading layer.

Undefined column name

You might encounter this error while processing SSAS objects after altering a data source view to add a column to a named query, or after adding a column to an existing table or view. General troubleshooting steps include checking the data source to ensure that the column name is spelled correctly and that the login account reading data from the relational source has the necessary permissions. However, this error could simply be due to memory corruption. If so, restarting Analysis Services will resolve the issue.

DSV does not contain definition for an xyz column

Though it seems obvious, this error isn't always caused by a misspelled column name. Keep in mind that XMLA is case sensitive. If you have a dimension definition that has the column name in uppercase, whereas the data source view has the same column in lowercase, you will get an error. The resolution is to fix either the data source view or the dimension definition so that the columns' case match.

Operation is cancelled

This error could have two root causes:

- ▶ The user became impatient with the processing or querying job and cancels it. Clearly such errors are benign. As a cube developer or DBA, you need to identify the operation details and take corrective actions to assure improved query performance.

- ▶ Analysis Services ran out of memory. You can check the Windows error log or the `msmdsrv.log` file for additional error messages indicating out of memory condition. If you consistently experience out of memory condition, you should migrate the application to 64-bit Analysis Services and/or add memory to the host.

File is corrupted

Perhaps one of the most dreaded errors, this message indicates exactly what it says. The bottom line is that you need to reprocess the affected object. If corruption affects dimension index or partition aggregation files, you only need to run the `ProcessIndexes` command. If the fact file is corrupted, you need to fully reprocess the entire partition. Fortunately, Microsoft has made great strides towards fixing potential corruption issues over the years, so you shouldn't see many occurrences of such errors with the latest builds of the software.

Keep in mind that synchronization doesn't check for file corruption—it simply copies files from a source to target instance. Hence, if you use synchronization you could replicate the problem before it is detected. One practice that could help you detect dimension file corruption is to run the `ProcessIndexes` command against dimensions—if any files are corrupted the command will fail. Clearly, your code needs to be smart enough to trap the errors and take the corrective action.

Error encountered in the transport layer

This error could be encountered during querying or synchronization and normally indicates a transient network connectivity issue. If you repeatedly encounter such errors during synchronization, consider the increasing server send timeout and server receive timeout properties on both source and target instances.

Internal error or unexpected exception

This indicates an issue with MSFT code—you should open a case with support and look for memory dumps generated around to the time of the error. Fortunately, MSFT consistently tries to fix bugs in the latest releases of the software; be sure to check for a list of fixes included in each service pack and cumulative update.

Deadlock

Deadlocks have a somewhat different meaning in SSAS compared to relational database systems. Deadlock error advises that processing or metadata operation attempted to but could not acquire necessary locks due to a conflicting operation. I have most commonly observed this error when the user attempts creating a session-level cube, using Excel's grouping functionality. Creating session-level cubes against large databases can be a very time-consuming operation, during which attempts to create or delete partitions could fail with the deadlock error. If your users commonly create session-level cubes to group dimension members, you should try to define named sets, which contain the desired dimension member groups.

Dimension properties

The following table summarizes most frequently used dimension properties:

Dimension property name	Explanation
AttributeAllMemberName	Specifies the name of the top level of each attribute hierarchy. For example, if you set this property for promotion's dimension to `All Adventure Works Promotions`, each attribute hierarchy will show `All Adventure Works Promotions` as its top level. The default value is `All`.
	This property does not apply to user-defined hierarchies. You can set the `ALLMemberName` property for each user-defined hierarchy to override its default.

Dimension property name	Explanation
StorageMode	The default value is MOLAP (Multi-dimensional OLAP), which stores dimension data in Microsoft's proprietary multidimensional storage format. The other option is ROLAP, which leaves data in the relational data source. If the storage option is ROLAP, MDX queries are resolved by sending the necessary SELECT statements to the relational source and retrieving data at query time. With previous releases of the software, very large dimensions had to use the ROLAP mode because of the string store data limit—see the StringStoresCompatibilityLevel property. The MOLAP mode generally outperforms ROLAP and is hence preferred. If you find that dimension processing time is exceedingly long and delivering data to users is more important than query performance, you could try using ROLAP.
	Note: SSDT shows an InMemory option in a drop-down box for this property; however, the InMemory option is only available for the Tabular Model, discussed in this book.
ErrorConfiguration	It defines how Analysis Services should handle processing errors. Refer to *Chapter 5, Optimizing Dimension and Cube Processing*, for more information.
ProcessingGroup	The default value is ByAttribute, which sends a separate SELECT statement to the relational source for each attribute during dimension processing. Additionally, ByAttribute includes a DISTINCT keyword to ensure that we only return unique attribute values. The ByTable option sends a single SELECT statement for the entire dimension without using the DISTINCT keyword. Refer to *Chapter 5, Optimizing Dimension and Cube Processing*, for more information.
ProcessingMode	The default value is regular. The other option is lazy aggregations, which allows building indexes using the background thread, thereby shortening dimension-processing time. Refer to *Chapter 5, Optimizing Dimension and Cube Processing*, for more information.

Dimension property name	Explanation
`StringStoresCompatibilityLevel`	In Analysis Services versions prior to 2012, dimension string store files were limited to 4 GB. If your MOLAP dimension string store file exceeded the 4 GB limit, processing would immediately fail and report an error similar to: "File system error: A FileStore error from WriteFile Occurred. Physical file:`\\?\N:\Analysis Services\ Data\database name\...\2.string. data`. Logical File:.. Errors in the OLAP Storage Engine: An error occurred while processing an XYZ object". One of the most anticipated fixes in 2012 is the `StringStoresCompatibilityLevel` option, which removes the 4 GB limit if it is set to 1100. If you restore a database from a backup file collected using a previous Analysis Services version, this property defaults to 1050. If the database was created using the 2012 version, the compatibility level is set to 1100 by default.
`MDXMissingMemberMode`	It controls how Analysis Services handles queries, which reference members that do not exist in the dimension. Many reports based on MDX queries explicitly reference dimension members. Some dimension members that once existed could have been removed. By default, Analysis Services 2012 simply treats such data as null—so the report will return nothing for missing members. The other option is `Error`—if you use this value, Analysis Services will report an error any time the MDX query references a missing member.
`UnknownMember`	This property controls how Analysis Services behaves if it does not find the expected dimension member during processing. The record could be ignored, converted to an "unknown" member, or hidden. The available property values are `None` (default), `Visible`, `Hidden`, or `AutomaticNull`. An unknown member generally exposes an issue within your data source. If you prefer to not display such rows at all, set this property to `Hidden`. If you prefer to identify issues (perhaps during quality assurance testing), make `UnknownMember` visible. By default the unknown members show up as `unknown`, but you can change the `UnknownMemberName` dimension property if you prefer to display it as something different, for example, "unspecified" or "undetermined". The value of `None` indicates that an unknown member is not used.

See also

Discussing each dimension property is beyond the scope of this book—you can refer to product documentation for properties not mentioned in the preceding table.

Performance considerations for many-to-many dimension relationships

As you learned in *Chapter 3*, *Creating Analysis Services Cubes*, many-to-many dimension relationships allow modeling complex business requirements, but this design option should not be abused because it is associated with a performance penalty. When your query involves many-to-many dimension relationships, Analysis Services retrieves data from both measure groups (data measure group and intermediate measure group) as well as the intermediate dimension; subsequently SSAS joins the results of these queries in memory before deriving the result set returned to the requesting application. Since, we cannot materialize many-to-many relationships, we must try to minimize their usage and look for opportunities to tune performance using other methods. The best way to optimize many-to-many relationships is to minimize the size of the intermediary measure group, thereby reducing the footprint required for retrieving intermediary measure group's data into memory, as well as the time it takes to join results to the primary measure group's data. Additionally, you can build suitable partitions and aggregations on data and intermediate measure groups to further reduce the size of data sets that will be joined during the query execution time.

Microsoft has published a white paper documenting the recommended practices for tuning many-to-many query performance. You can download the white paper from `http://www. microsoft.com/en-us/download/details.aspx?id=137`.

DirectQuery with Tabular Models

DirectQuery is a deployment option available in Tabular Models, which allows the developer to use the relational data instead of the in-memory data in the model. This feature is still immature and needs to be understood to determine how this can be used.

Data sources

DirectQuery can only use SQL Server and SQL Server PDW databases as sources. No other relational or non-relational sources are supported including Oracle, SQL Server Analysis Services or files. In this case, using DirectQuery would be valuable if using a SQL Server data source and either real-time changes or large data volume are required in your solution.

Security

The role-based security in the Tabular Model is not supported with DirectQuery. The security within the data source, however, is supported.

Design limitations

Calculated columns are not supported in a table based on a DirectQuery source. While calculated measures and KPIs are supported, the DAX formula support is limited. It is possible to use derived columns in the source to overcome some of the calculation issues. Even these workarounds may not have the desired results as there are also cases where the calculations differ between the standard Tabular Model and DirectQuery model. This is caused because the SQL Server engine and the xVelocity engine can handle these calculations slightly differently.

Client restrictions

Only clients who work with DAX are able to interact with a model using DirectQuery. This eliminates many tools such as SQL Server Reporting Services and Excel Pivot Tables. They do work with Power View reports.

When choosing whether to use DirectQuery, you will need to evaluate the preceding limitations to determine if it is a good choice in your solution. In most cases, the limitations seem to outweigh the benefits.

Index

F

fact relationship 76
FILTER function 162, 289
Format property 280
FormatString property 65, 68
Form View button 170

G

globally unique identifier (GUID) 217

H

hierarchy
  creating 236, 237
Hybrid OLAP (HOLAP) 87

I

Inherit option 21
InMemory option 313
instance-level administrative security
  managing 176
  members, adding 176, 177
InvalidXMLCharacters property 69
IsAggregatable property 48
isolation property 22

K

Key Performance Indicators. *See* **KPI**
KPI
  about 114, 241
  creating 242-246
  defining 114-118

L

Local Cube 179

M

many-to-many dimension relationships
  performance considerations 315
many-to-many relationship 77
Materialized Query Tables (MQT) 308
MDX 10, 48, 151

MDXMissingMemberMode property 314
MDX queries
  monitoring 171, 173
  tuning 171, 173
MDX script's functionality
  about 169
  using 170, 171
MeasureExpression 68
measure expressions
  defining 122, 123
measure groups
  defining 58-64
  dimension usage 74-77
Measure Name property 239
measure properties
  aggregation function 67
  Aggregation function 68
  Data type 68
  DisplayFolder 68
  FormatString 68
  MeasureExpression 68
  setting 65-69
  Source 69
  Visible 69
measures
  AutoSum measures, creating 275-280
  calculated measures, creating 280, 281
  creating 274
  defining 58-61
  properties, measuring 65-69
Members tab 261
MembersWithData property 52
Memory><LowMemoryLimit> property 200
model design
  memory usage, managing 294
MultiDimensional eXpression. *See* **MDX**
Multidimensional models
  choosing 10
  requirements 11
Multi-Dimensional OLAP (MOLAP) 86

N

NameColumn property 42
named calculations
  creating 29-31

[PACKT] enterprise
PUBLISHING professional expertise distilled

Thank you for buying
SQL Server Analysis Services 2012 Cube
Development Cookbook

About Packt Publishing

Packt, pronounced 'packed', published its first book "*Mastering phpMyAdmin for Effective MySQL Management*" in April 2004 and subsequently continued to specialize in publishing highly focused books on specific technologies and solutions.

Our books and publications share the experiences of your fellow IT professionals in adapting and customizing today's systems, applications, and frameworks. Our solution-based books give you the knowledge and power to customize the software and technologies you're using to get the job done. Packt books are more specific and less general than the IT books you have seen in the past. Our unique business model allows us to bring you more focused information, giving you more of what you need to know, and less of what you don't.

Packt is a modern, yet unique publishing company, which focuses on producing quality, cutting-edge books for communities of developers, administrators, and newbies alike. For more information, please visit our website: www.PacktPub.com.

About Packt Enterprise

In 2010, Packt launched two new brands, Packt Enterprise and Packt Open Source, in order to continue its focus on specialization. This book is part of the Packt Enterprise brand, home to books published on enterprise software – software created by major vendors, including (but not limited to) IBM, Microsoft and Oracle, often for use in other corporations. Its titles will offer information relevant to a range of users of this software, including administrators, developers, architects, and end users.

Writing for Packt

We welcome all inquiries from people who are interested in authoring. Book proposals should be sent to author@packtpub.com. If your book idea is still at an early stage and you would like to discuss it first before writing a formal book proposal, contact us; one of our commissioning editors will get in touch with you.

We're not just looking for published authors; if you have strong technical skills but no writing experience, our experienced editors can help you develop a writing career, or simply get some additional reward for your expertise.

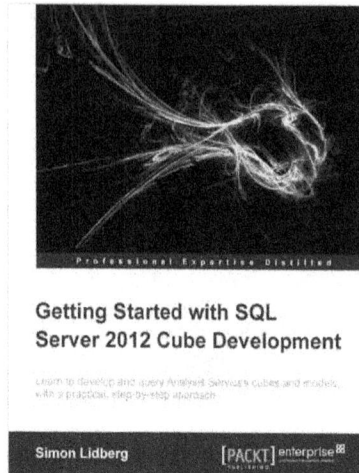

[PACKT] enterprise ✕
PUBLISHING   professional expertise distilled

Getting Started with SQL Server 2012 Cube Development

Learn to develop and query Analysis Services cubes and models, with a practical, step-by-step approach

Simon Lidberg   [PACKT] enterprise ✕

Getting Started with
SQL Server 2012 Cube
Development

ISBN: 978-1-84968-950-2   Paperback: 288 pages

Learn to develop and query Analysis Services cubes and modules, with a practical, step-by-step approach

1. Learn how to develop a complete business intelligence solution using SQL Server 2012

2. Understand the difference between tabular in-memory models and OLAP cubes, and which to use where and when

3. Add advanced features such as key performance indicators (KPIs) and calculated measures to your business intelligence model

---

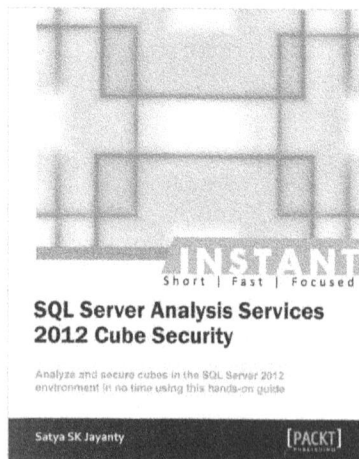

INSTANT
Short | Fast | Focused

SQL Server Analysis Services 2012 Cube Security

Analyze and secure cubes in the SQL Server 2012 environment in no time using this hands-on guide

Satya SK Jayanty   [PACKT]

Instant SQL Server Analysis
Services 2012 Cube Security

ISBN: 978-1-84968-870-3   Paperback: 68 pages

Analyze and secure cubes in the SQL Server 2012 environment in no time using this hands-on guide

1. Learn something new in an Instant! A short, fast, focused guide delivering immediate results

2. Get to know what's new in BI space

3. Learn about tools & tricks to secure the data layers

4. Implement best practices for Security administration

Please check **www.PacktPub.com** for information on our titles

[PACKT] enterprise
PUBLISHING
professional expertise distilled

MDX with Microsoft SQL Server 2008 R2 Analysis Services Cookbook

ISBN: 978-1-84968-130-8   Paperback: 480 pages

80 recipes for enriching your Business Intelligence solutions with high-performance MDX calculations and flexible MDX queries

1. Enrich your BI solutions by implementing best practice MDX calculations

2. Master a wide range of time-related, context-aware, and business-related calculations

3. Enhance your solutions by combining MDX with utility dimensions

MDX with Microsoft SQL Server 2008 R2 Analysis Services: Cookbook

80 recipes for enriching your Business Intelligence solutions with high-performance MDX calculations and flexible MDX queries

Tomislav Piasevoli   [PACKT] enterprise

Microsoft SQL Server 2012 Security Cookbook

ISBN: 978-1-84968-588-7   Paperback: 322 pages

Over 70 practical, focused recipes to bullet-proof your SQL Server database and protect it from hackers and security threats

1. Practical, focused recipes for securing your SQL Server database

2. Master the latest techniques for data and code encryption, user authentication and authorization, protection against brute force attacks, denial-of-service attacks, and SQL Injection, and more

3. A learn-by-example recipe-based approach that focuses on key concepts to provide the foundation to solve real world problems

Microsoft SQL Server 2012 Security Cookbook

Over 70 practical, focused recipes to bullet-proof your SQL Server database and protect it from hackers and security threats

Rudi Bruchez   [PACKT] enterprise

Please check **www.PacktPub.com** for information on our titles

www.ingramcontent.com/pod-product-compliance
Lightning Source LLC
Chambersburg PA
CBHW080918220326
41598CB00034B/5609

* 9 7 8 1 8 4 9 6 8 9 8 0 9 *